CW01314010

MAKE THE BEST OUT OF YOUR WORKING HOLIDAY VISA IN AUSTRALIA

LAND A JOB QUICKLY

DEAL WITH ALL THE PAPERWOROK

TRAVEL

HELPSTAGE
Internship offers

WWW.HELPSTAGE.NET

HELPSTAGE
Internship offers

Copyright © Marie Planchat
All rights reserved.

ISBN : 9798363369568
Marie Planchat
Fontenguillère
24560 Saint-Perdoux
France
Printed by Amazon
£16,00
Published in December 2022.

All rights of reproduction, adaptation and translation, in whole or in part, reserved for all countries. The author or publisher is the sole owner of the rights and responsible for the content of this book.

Contents

01
INTRODUCTION
PAGE 1

02
VISA APPLICATION
PAGE 3
Am I eligible?
The visa application explained step by step
How long does it take to get the visa?
Asking for a second visa

03
CHOOSE A CITY OF ARRIVAL | PAGE 17
Advantages and disadvantages of each city
Consider the cost of living
Leave in the right season
The competition upon arrival and the English level required
Getting your plane ticket

04
BEFORE DEPARTURE: 4 ADMINISTRATIVE STEPS
PAGE 36
The international driving licence
Choosing an insurance
My phone
My bank

05
WRITING A CV FOR THE AUSTRALIAN MARKET
PAGE 40
What to put on your resume
Template of a ready-made CV
Resume template
Photo or not?

06
ON ARRIVAL: THE PROCEDURES | PAGE 46
Open a bank account
Apply for TFN
Choose a phone operator
Buy a van

07

ADOPTING THE AUSTRALIAN LIFESTYLE | PAGE 58
The Australian mindset
Australian habits
Speaking Australian slang
Australian food

08

SYDNEY | PAGE 66
What to see/ what to do
Accommodation in Sydney
The job market and salary in Sydney
Landing a job quickly
Interview with David
The hospitality industry
The RSA in Sydney
Hotel and restaurant addresses
Going out and meeting people in Sydney

09

MELBOURNE | PAGE 109
What to see/ what to do
Accommodation in Melbourne
The job market and salary in Melbourne
Landing a job quickly
Interview with Clément
The hospitality industry
The RSA in Melbourne
Hotel and restaurant addresses
Going out & meeting people in Melbourne

10

BRISBANE | PAGE 144
What to see/ what to do
Accommodation in Brisbane
The job market and salary in Brisbane
Landing a job quickly
The hospitality industry
The RSA in Brisbane
Hotel and restaurant addresses
Going out and meeting people in Brisbane

11

CAIRNS | PAGE 168
What to see/ what to do
Accommodation in Cairns
The job market and salary in Cairns
Landing a job quickly
The hospitality industry
The RSA in Brisbane
Hotel and restaurant addresses
Going out and meeting people in Cairns

12

PERTH | PAGE 189
*What to see/ what to do
Accommodation in Perth
The job market and salary in Perth
Landing a job quickly
Interview with Mathieu
The hospitality industry
The RSA in Perth
Hotel and restaurant addresses
Going out and meeting people in Perth*

13

DARWIN | PAGE 213
*What to see/ what to do
Accommodation in Darwin
The job market and salary in Darwin
Landing a job quickly
The hospitality industry
The RSA in Darwin
Hotel and restaurant addresses
Going out and meeting people in Darwin*

14

ADELAIDE | PAGE 231
*What to see/ what to do
Accommodation in Adelaide
The job market and salary in Adelaide
Landing a job quickly
The hospitality industry
The RSA in Adelaide
Hotel and restaurant addresses
Going out and meeting people in Adelaide*

15

HOBART | PAGE 251
*What to see/ what to do
Accommodation in Hobart
The job market and salary in Hobart
Landing a job quickly
The hospitality industry
The RSA in Hobart
Hotel and restaurant addresses
Going out and meeting people in Hobart*

16

**WORK ON A SOLAR FARM
PAGE 271**
*The basics
Solar farms directory*

17

THE ROAD TRIP | PAGE 278

Renting or buying a vehicle?
Where to rent a van or a car?
The must-see road trips
🚐 *The great ocean road*
🚐 *From Sydney to Brisbane*
🚐 *From Brisbane to Cairns*
🚐 *From Perth to Esperance*

18

SUPPLEMENT: THE HARVEST GUIDE | FRUIT PICKING | PAGE 300

Working conditions and pay rates
Beware of scams: working hostels/contractors
Sign a contract!
How do I contact the farms?

Map + Where to go, depending on the season
Farm addresses and contacts
Where to Stay
New South Wales
Northern Territory
Queensland
South Australia
Tasmania
Victoria
Western Australia

It's far away from everywhere, it has perfect weather and it's doing well economically! Australia is luring more and more people who want to get away from their lives back home and experience something new.

Many young people and even recent graduates in Europe and America are finding it difficult to land jobs at home, so Australia seems like a very attractive destination to build a career, or even just to improve your English while working and travelling, thanks to the famous 'Working Holiday Visa'. Nevertheless, since the borders have reopened, fewer backpackers are coming to Australia. Before Covid, there were around 225,000, and this number dropped to less than 80,000 this year, mainly due to the cost of airfare.

The good news is that you will have less competition to land a job quickly when you arrive.

The 'Working Holiday Visa' just requires an online formality on the Australian Embassy website, so if you are between ages 18 and 30 (35 for Canadians, Danish, French, Irish and Italian) and you can pay the AUD $510 for the visa, you can go and work in Australia!

There is no quota and you will be able to work in Australia for one year (6 months maximum at the same company).

Australia has a strong economy thanks to its proximity to Asia and the fact that it's a new country.

The first fleet of ships with potential settlers arrived in Australia only 234 years ago in 1788! As it is a young country, '**optimism and dynamism**' are the name of the game in the big cities.

There is something magical about Australia, something that really grabs you and makes you want to stay. The year-round sunshine probably plays a major role in this pull, but that's not the whole story. Australians are amongst the most welcoming and positive people on earth. They don't like to talk about problems. They avoid speaking negatively, and you will rarely hear an Australian complaining about his or her life. 'Such is life' and 'No worries' are part of the vocabulary in Australia.

Australians don't take life too seriously.

INTRODUCTION

You will meet laid-back people who smile and who are positive and who would not leave their country for all the money in the world!

The people make the place, but Australia is not only about sun and people. It is also a huge country, full of contrasts and varying landscapes. Whereas Melbourne's climate is European, Darwin's is tropical. You can even sometimes experience all four seasons in one day in the same city.

In Australia, you can drive for hours without passing a single vehicle on the road. Driving on these endless roads is a truly unique experience that you will probably remember for the rest of your life.

70% of Australians live on the East Coast in the big cities close to the sea. The rest of the country is almost empty !

When you approach a recruiter in Australia, you need to be aware of the culture and adopt the positive attitude and courage of its people. They get up with the sun, do things for themselves before going to work like running, going to the gym or surfing; they live outdoors and have a great respect for nature.

Don't be surprised to see people on Bondi Beach at 6:00 in the morning, running or surfing. It is part of the culture, so you should get up early too!

This guide aims to facilitate all your steps and answer all the questions you may have before leaving, and also to anticipate those that arise once you are there. It will help you maximize your chances of success and make the most of this unique year, well prepared and with peace of mind.

If you are forthcoming, adventurous and open-minded, you will possibly not only find a job, but also have the most amazing year (or two) of your life.

You have been warned! If you go to Australia, you may never come back!

VISA APPLICATION

Am I eligible?

To be able to work in Australia, you must obtain a Working Holiday Visa. To do so, you must be between 18 and 30 years old (35 years old for Canadians, Danish, French, Irish and Italian - you can apply until the day before your 36th birthday - or until your 31st birthday if you are not Canadian, Danish, French, Irish or Italian), have AUD $5,000 in your account and have a passport from one of the following countries:

Belgium, France, Luxembourg, Switzerland, Canada, Republic of Cyprus, Denmark, Estonia, Finland, Germany, Hong Kong, Ireland, Italy, Japan, Republic of Korea, Malta, Netherlands, Norway, Sweden, Taiwan, The United Kingdom, Argentina, Austria, Brazil, Chile, China, Czech Republic, Ecuador, Greece, Hungary, Indonesia, Israel, Malaysia, Mongolia, Peru, Poland, Portugal, San Marino, Singapore, Slovak Republic, Slovenia, Spain, Thailand, Turkey, Uruguay, United States of America, or Vietnam.

WHY DO I NEED AUD $5,000 IN MY BANK ACCOUNT?

Australian immigration authorities want to ensure that all workers arriving in Australia have sufficient financial resources to support themselves for the first few weeks.

The visa application explained step by step

There are two types of Working Holiday Visas, the 417 and 462, depending on your nationality you will need to apply for one or the other. Check which one you have to ask on:
https://immi.homeaffairs.gov.au/visas/getting-a-visa/visa-listing/work-holiday-462 (for 462)
or
https://immi.homeaffairs.gov.au/visas/getting-a-visa/visa-listing/work-holiday-417

Here, I will explain the steps for the visa 417 but it is the same process for the visa 462.

# VISA APPLICATION

Working Holiday visa (subclass 417)

Features

This visa is for young people who want to holiday and work in Australia for up to a year.

Requirements

You might be able to get this visa if you:

- are at least 18 but not yet 31 years of age
- do not have a dependent child accompanying you at any time during your stay in Australia
- have a passport from an eligible country.

You might be able to apply online by clicking the 'Apply now' button below, if you have a passport from an eligible country. See 'How to Apply' for a list of eligible countries.

If you cannot apply online you can lodge a paper application form.

⇨ **Apply Now**

Download PDF Form

A window will open. Click on "create an ImmiAccount".

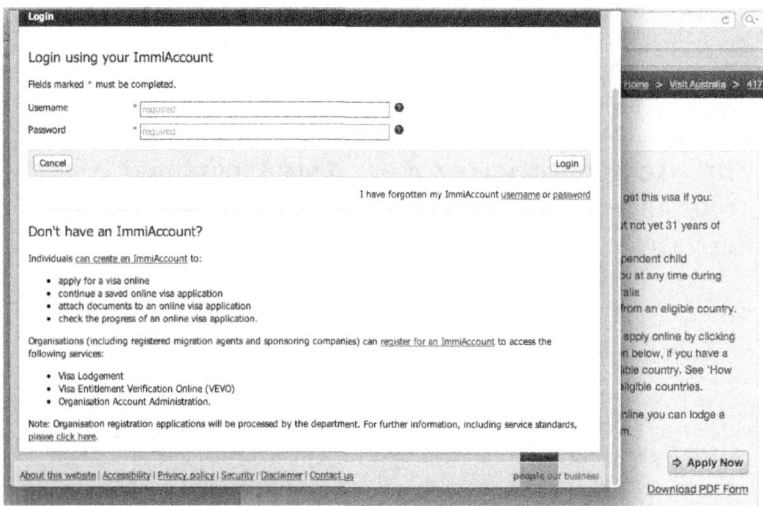

4

VISA APPLICATION

Fill in all the required information in the fields.

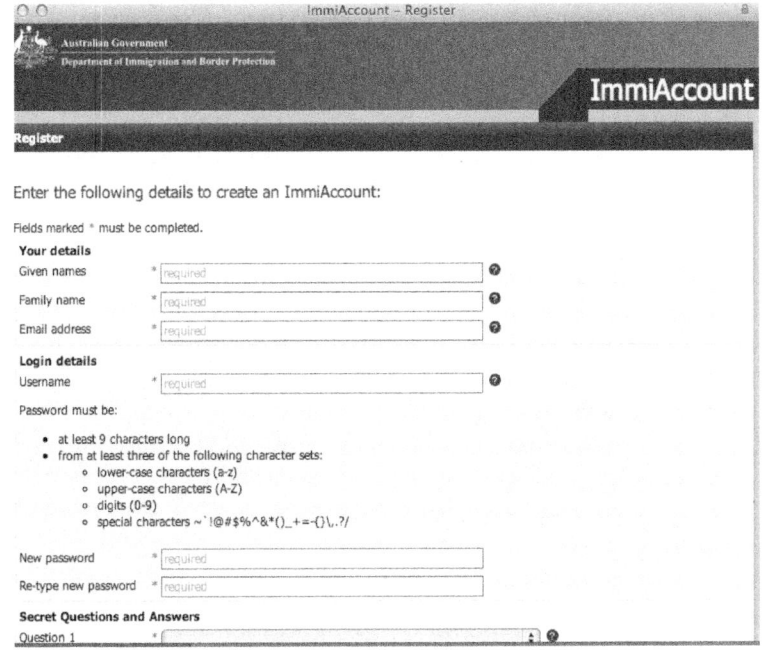

Once you have completed the online form, you will receive a confirmation email. You will then just have to click on the link you received to confirm your email.

A new window will open. Click on 'I have read and agree to the terms and conditions'.

HOW LONG WILL MY VISA BE VALID?

The visa allows you to work in Australia for one year, including 6 consecutive months with the same employer.

Important: You must apply from outside Australia.

VISA APPLICATION

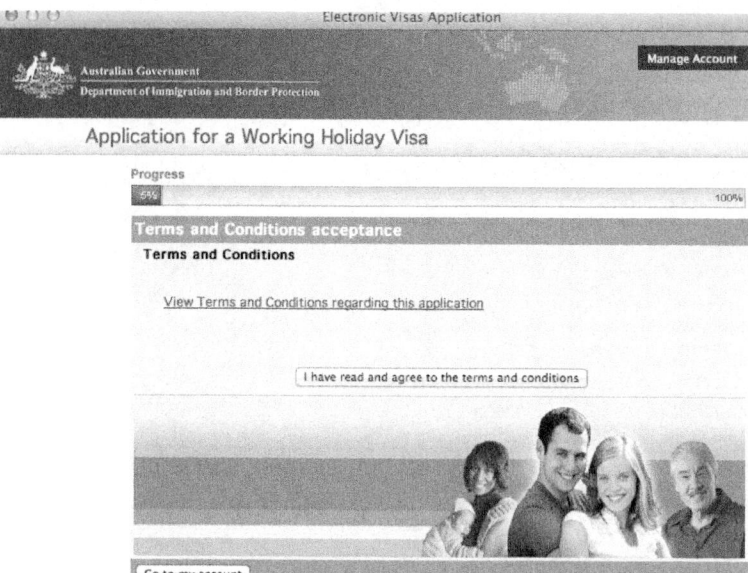

Click on "next".

VISA APPLICATION

Fill in your details and click on "Next" at the bottom.

Answer the 3 questions about your status and what you plan to do when you arrive in Australia. You can track your progress at the top of the page in green.

Click on "Next" when you have answered all the questions.

7

A transaction number will appear in a new window. You must then fill in all the fields and click on "Next".

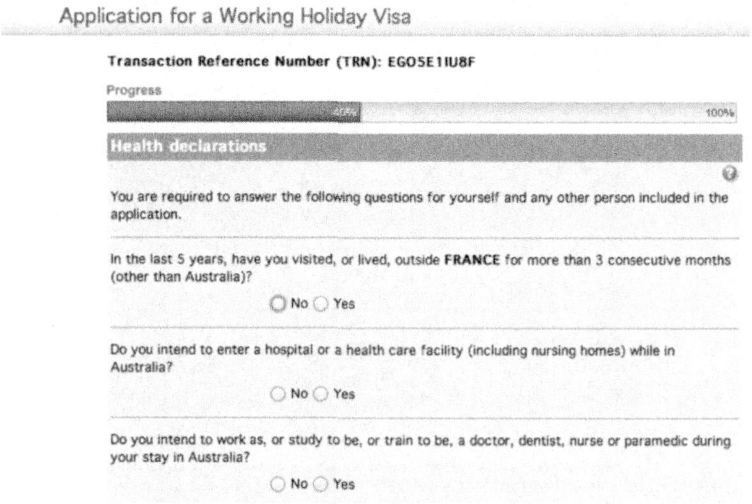

Ditto. Answer NO to the following questions.

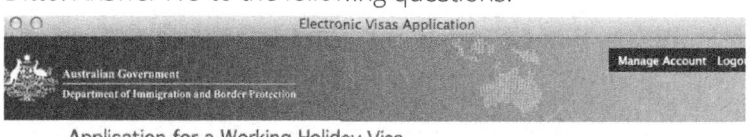

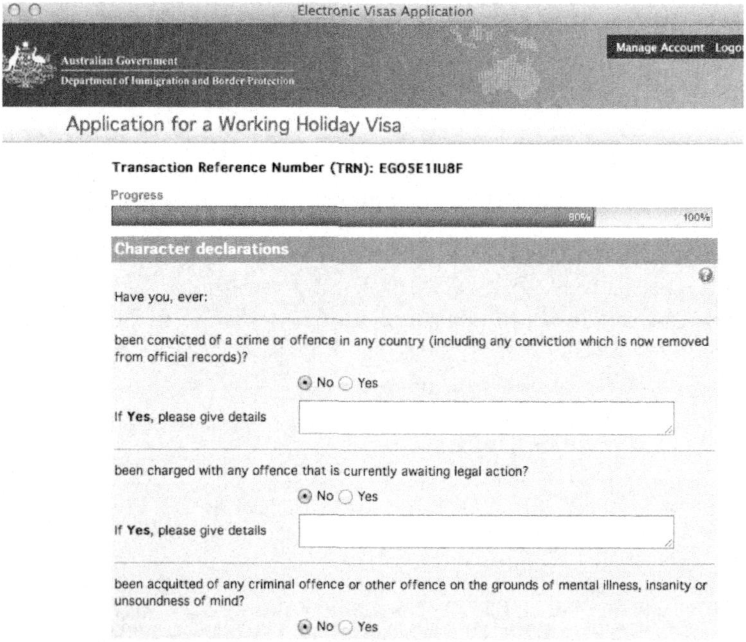

VISA APPLICATION

CAN I LEAVE AUSTRALIA AND RETURN DURING THE 12 MONTHS?

Yes, you can leave the country as many times as you want until your Working Holiday Visa expires.

You are now 95% of the way through. These are just questions to verify what you have just declared.
Answer YES to all questions.

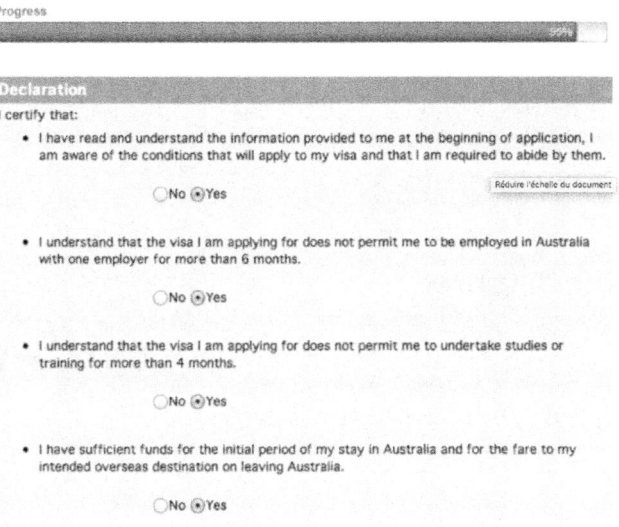

On the next page, check that all your information is correct.
A new window will open. Click on "Submit Now".

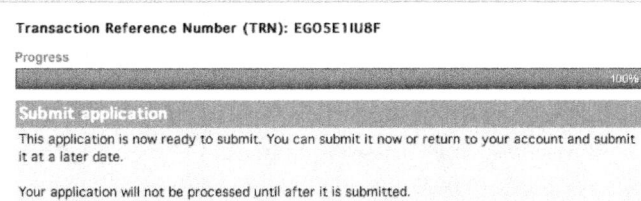

VISA APPLICATION

You will now arrive at the payment page where you need to pay the AUD $510; once this is done, you just have to wait to receive an email indicating: '**Visa granted**'.
It takes anywhere from a few hours to a month.
You can choose to make the payment later; come back to your account whenever you want and click on the 'Manage Payment' link.

You have to upload two documents: your passport and the bank statement proving the AUD $5,000 in your account. Sometimes, the upload doesn't work. In this case, you have to change the name of your documents and try again. If it still doesn't work, don't panic, there is probably a bug on the website.
This happens frequently so don't worry. Just come back later and try again.

Processing time

HOW LONG WILL IT TAKE TO RECEIVE MY VISA?
25% of applications: Less than 1 day
50% of applications: Less than 1 day
75% of applications: 8 days
90% of applications: 44 days

Some applicants receive their visas within hours of making their payment. While this may come as a surprise, yes, it is your visa as long as it says "Visa Granted" in the email.

The visa is a number received by email. Your visa is automatically activated for one year at Australian immigration.
Note that when you arrive in a major Australian city, everything is automated and you will simply have to scan your passport on a machine, without even having to talk to a border agent.

VISA APPLICATION

Please note that these deadlines may be extended if you have visited Asia in the last few months.
If this is the case, it is likely that Australian immigration will ask you for a lung x-ray to ensure that you do not have tuberculosis.
This will be requested on your visa application page. You will need to go to a radiologist to have these x-rays taken. The radiology office will be responsible for sending them to immigration.

It looks like this:

Examinations required

This person is required to complete health examinations for this visa application. Click on the link below to organise these health examinations.
Organise health examinations. ❓
Once this person's health examinations results have been assessed by the department this page will be updated to reflect this.
Note: If this person does not complete the required health examinations the visa application can be refused.

It is expensive (about US $150) and it is not reimbursed.
Is this a racket or a precautionary principle?
It's up to you to judge, but if you don't take the tests, your visa application may be rejected.

ASKING FOR A SECOND VISA

Applying for a second visa: working 88 days on a farm to stay in Australia for 2 years

WHAT JOBS QUALIFY FOR A SECOND VISA?
Plant cultivation/animal breeding
Fishing and pearl culture
Arboriculture and felling
Mining
Construction
Woofing (unpaid work) also works if it falls into the above categories

To obtain a **second Working Holiday Visa**, and therefore be able to stay in Australia for 2 years, you will have to do **88 days of farm work,** and double that if you want to stay for 3 years.

This is what many backpackers choose to do as soon as they arrive in Australia.

These 88 days take into account weekends if you work full time, for example if you work from Monday to Friday 8 hours a day.

In order to apply for this second visa, your employer will have to give you your payslips and fill out form 1263. You will have to sign this document.

Download your **1263 form** at the following link:
http://www.dtearth.com.au/wp-content/uploads/2015/06/Working-Holiday-Visa-Employment-Verification-Australian-Immigration-Form-1263.pdf

12

ASKING FOR A SECOND VISA

Australian Government
Department of Immigration and Citizenship

Working Holiday visa: Employment verification

Form
1263

THIS IS NOT AN APPLICATION FORM

About this form

Important – Please read this information carefully before you complete your Employment verification. Once you have completed your Employment verification we strongly advise that you keep a copy for your records.

Who should use this form?

This form is for people who are in Australia as holders of a Working Holiday visa and who wish to apply for a second Working Holiday visa.

This form is to record details of employment in a specified field or industry in regional Australia.

Other evidence of specified work may include original or certified copies of payslips, group certificates, payment summaries, tax returns and employer references. Providing this evidence with this form will enable your application to be assessed more quickly.

The completed form should be retained and may be requested by the Department of Immigration and Citizenship (the department) after you lodge your application electronically to verify your specified work. If lodging a paper application, please attach this form.

To be eligible for a second Working Holiday visa, the applicant must have undertaken work for a minimum of 3 months (88 days in total) in a **specified field or industry*** in a designated area of **regional Australia****.

Specified work is any type of work in the list below:

- **plant and animal cultivation:**
  - cultivating or propagating plants, fungi or their products or parts;
  - general maintenance crop work;
  - harvesting and/or packing fruit and vegetable crops;
  - immediate processing of animal products including shearing, butchery in an abattoir, packing and tanning;
    Note: Secondary processing of animal products, such as small goods processing and retail butchery is not eligible.
  - immediate processing of plant products;
  - maintaining animals for the purpose of selling them or their bodily produce, including natural increase;
  - manufacturing dairy produce from raw material;
  - pruning and trimming vines and trees.

Eligible regional Australia postcodes

Regional areas	Postcodes
New South Wales (most areas except the greater Sydney area, Newcastle, the Central Coast and Wollongong)	2311 to 2312 2328 to 2411 2420 to 2490 2536 to 2551 2575 to 2594 2618 to 2739 2787 to 2898
Northern Territory	Entire Territory
Queensland (most areas except the greater Brisbane area and the Gold Coast)	4124 to 4125 4133 4211 4270 to 4272 4275 4280 4285 4287 4307 to 4499 4510 4512 4515 to 4519 4522 to 4899
South Australia	Entire State
Tasmania	Entire State
Victoria (most areas except the greater Melbourne area)	3139 3211 to 3334 3340 to 3424 3430 to 3649 3658 to 3749 3753, 3756, 3758, 3762, 3764 3778 to 3781 3783, 3797, 3799 3810 to 3909 3921 to 3925 3945 to 3974 3979 3981 to 3996
Western Australia (most areas except Perth and surrounding areas)	6041 to 6044 6083 to 6084 6121 to 6126 6200 to 6799

(Information about harvest work opportunities in regional Australia can be found at the Harvest Trail website at www.jobsearch.gov.au/harvesttrail)

Some vacancies on the Harvest Trail website may not be in the above eligible postcodes.

---

* For further information please see *'Specified work'* **www.immi.gov.au/visitors/working-holiday/417/eligibility-second.htm**

** *'Regional Australia'* is restricted to areas within the postcodes listed in the opposite table.

© COMMONWEALTH OF AUSTRALIA 2009

ASKING FOR A SECOND VISA

- **fishing and pearling**:
  - conducting operations relating directly to taking or catching fish and other aquatic species;
  - conducting operations relating directly to taking or culturing pearls or pearl shell.
- **tree farming and felling**:
  - felling trees in a plantation or forest;
  - planting or tending trees in a plantation or forest that are intended to be felled;
  - transporting trees or parts of trees that were felled in a plantation or forest to the place where they are first to be milled or processed or from which they are to be transported to the place where they are to be milled or processed.
- **mining**:
  - coal mining;
  - construction material engineering
  - exploration;
  - metal ore mining;
  - mining support services;
  - oil and gas extraction;
  - other non-metallic mineral mining and quarrying.
- **construction**:
  - building completion services;
  - building installation services;
  - building structure services;
  - heavy and civil engineering construction;
  - land development and site preparation services;
  - non-residential building construction;
  - residential building construction;
  - other construction services.

Specified work:
- does not need to be paid work.
  Example: Work undertaken as a volunteer or through the Willing Workers on Organic Farms (WWOOF) scheme may also qualify if the work you undertook falls with the specified work definition above.
- does not need to be undertaken as a direct employee
  Example: Work in the list above as a contractor is eligible.
- must be listed above
  Example: Working as a nanny for a farmer would not be eligible.

14

ASKING FOR A SECOND VISA

Your personal details

1 Your full name as it appears on your passport

2 Other names you are known by, if any
(including aliases, previous married names, names other than on your passport)

3 Your date of birth — DAY MONTH YEAR

4 Your passport number

Your employment details

5 Details of employment in specified industries in regional Australia

You must keep a record of all dates worked. You will require this information when lodging your Working Holiday visa application electronically.

If you have worked for the same employer on more than one occasion, you should record each period of employment separately or attach a separate document containing these details.

If you have more employer details than will fit in the spaces below, attach a separate document containing these details.

You should attach evidence of your specified work (see page 1). This will allow your application to be assessed more quickly.

A *I confirm the following work has been undertaken*

- Employee's full name
- Type of work
- Actual number of days worked
- Start date (DAY MONTH YEAR)
- End date (DAY MONTH YEAR)
- Postcode where work was completed
- Business name and address
- Employer's telephone number
- Employer's full name
- Employer's ABN
- Signature of employer
- POSTCODE
- Name of contact for work verification (eg. payroll officer/direct supervisor)
- E-mail address (if available)
- Contact person's telephone number

B
- Employee's full name
- Type of work
- Actual number of days worked
- Start date (DAY MONTH YEAR)
- End date (DAY MONTH YEAR)
- Postcode where work was completed
- Business name and address
- Employer's telephone number
- Employer's full name
- Employer's ABN
- Signature of employer
- POSTCODE
- Name of contact for work verification (eg. payroll officer/direct supervisor)
- E-mail address (if available)
- Contact person's telephone number

C
- Employee's full name
- Type of work
- Actual number of days worked
- Start date (DAY MONTH YEAR)
- End date (DAY MONTH YEAR)
- Postcode where work was completed
- Business name and address
- Employer's telephone number
- Employer's full name
- Employer's ABN
- Signature of employer
- POSTCODE
- Name of contact for work verification (eg. payroll officer/direct supervisor)
- E-mail address (if available)
- Contact person's telephone number

© COMMONWEALTH OF AUSTRALIA, 2009

1263 (Design date 11/09) - Page

ASKING FOR A SECOND VISA

D Employee's full name | Type of work | Actual number of days worked

Start date DAY MONTH YEAR End date DAY MONTH YEAR Postcode where work was completed

Business name and address | Employer's telephone number ( ) | Employer's full name

POSTCODE | Employer's ABN | Signature of employer

Name of contact for work verification *(eg. payroll officer/direct supervisor)* | E-mail address *(if available)* @ | Contact person's telephone number ( )

E Employee's full name | Type of work | Actual number of days worked

Start date DAY MONTH YEAR End date DAY MONTH YEAR Postcode where work was completed

Business name and address | Employer's telephone number ( ) | Employer's full name

POSTCODE | Employer's ABN | Signature of employer

Name of contact for work verification *(eg. payroll officer/direct supervisor)* | E-mail address *(if available)* @ | Contact person's telephone number ( )

Your contact details

6 Your e-mail address

7 Current residential address
(If applying in Australia, please give your current address in Australia)
Note: A post office box address is not acceptable as a residential address. Failure to give a residential address will result in your application being invalid.

POSTCODE

8 Address for correspondence
(This may be required by the department to communicate with you about your application. If the same as your residential address, write 'AS ABOVE')

POSTCODE

9 Your telephone numbers
Mobile
COUNTRY CODE   AREA CODE   NUMBER
Office hours ( ) ( )
After hours ( ) ( )

Your declaration

WARNING: Giving false or misleading information is a serious offence.

10 *I declare that the information I have supplied on this form is complete, correct and up-to-date in every detail.*

Your signature

Date DAY MONTH YEAR

We strongly advise that you keep a copy of your Employment verification and all attachments for your records.

16

CHOOSING A CITY OF ARRIVAL

SYDNEY

Sydney is the number one destination for Working Holiday Visa holders. Why is it so?

Advantages

🔍⊕ The sun shines every day, and the people are beautiful, welcoming and warm!

🔍⊕ Like its cousin Melbourne, it's almost impossible not to know what to do in Sydney; there's always an event to attend.

🔍⊕ It's a beautiful city. Taking the ferry and passing the Opera House by boat could be your daily routine! The botanical gardens, the Harbour Bridge, the beaches, in short, you'll be amazed.

🔍⊕ Like Melbourne, Sydney is culturally diverse. It is very easy to meet people, be invited to a *barbie* (barbecue) or join a city tour.

🔍⊕ A big city means lots of job opportunities.

Disadvantages

🔍⊖ The cost of living can seem exorbitant when you are not prepared. Accommodation, transport and food are more expensive than in other Australian cities. So, if you don't find a job very quickly when you arrive (after recovering from the jetlag anyway!), don't stay too long, at the risk of seeing your savings melt like snow in the sun!
Many backpackers make this mistake when they arrive in Sydney.
If after three weeks of intensive searching you still don't have a job, don't insist on staying and just move to another city.

If Australian immigration asks you to have AUD $5,000 in your bank account, it is precisely to cope with those first few weeks of inactivity in a city where everything is expensive.

CHOOSING A CITY OF ARRIVAL

MELBOURNE

Most backpackers who arrive in Australia debate between Melbourne and Sydney.

Advantages

🔍⊕ If you are afraid of being too out of place when you arrive, Melbourne is the solution for you because its climate and atmosphere are similar to Europe or most parts of the US.
As Australia is a young country, it doesn't have much history, so while you might feel a certain lack of culture in most cities, this is not at all the case in Melbourne. The city has a great tourist office and offers a wide range of museums, theatres and events to keep you entertained.

🔍⊕ The number of cafes and restaurants is a good thing if you are looking for a job in the hospitality industry. You will have a better chance of finding a job quickly.

🔍⊕ The cost of living is more reasonable than in Sydney.

🔍⊕ Melbourne is a great city for going out because there are so many restaurants and cafes to choose from. There is a real coffee culture, unlike in Darwin or Perth, for example. Food and fashion are omnipresent.
In the 1850s, large gold nuggets were discovered in Victoria. The gold rush attracted people from all over the world to this part of Australia, which partly explains the mix of nationalities and the fact that Melbourne has the third largest Chinatown in the world (after San Francisco). So you will find incredible cuisine coming from all over the world: Italy, Japan, China, Greece, Spain, etc.

CHOOSING A CITY OF ARRIVAL

Disadvantages

🔍⊖ The abundance of things to do means that you will spend a lot of money on outings.

🔍⊖ Climate: There are often four seasons in one day.
If you are hoping for year-round warmth, Melbourne is not the destination to choose. If you land in July, you will be cold!

🔍⊖ The city is so cosmopolitan that you may feel like you are not really in Australia. If you are looking for a change of scenery, consider another city like Darwin or Brisbane.

 BRISBANE

The capital of Queensland, Brisbane comes in third place.

Advantages

🔍⊕ Brisbane (*Brisbie* to the locals) is situated in the middle of the East Coast and enjoys an exceptional climate. If you like warmth and tropical weather, this is your city.

🔍⊕ It is a city on a human scale, unlike Melbourne or Sydney. The inhabitants call it 'the small village'. To give you an idea, it has about half the population of Melbourne (Melbourne has almost 5 million inhabitants). This creates a feeling of familiarity and a really relaxed atmosphere. When someone says 'too easy', it just means yes!

🔍⊕ It is a very student-based city with a lot of young working people who meet to go out in Fortitude Valley. You will meet people easily in Brisbane.

CHOOSING A CITY OF ARRIVAL

🔍⊕ Brisbane is the gateway to Queensland, and therefore the gateway to exceptional natural sites such as Fraser Island, Airlie Beach, Magnetic Island and so on. You can start a road trip to the North or to the South.

🔍⊕ It is a strategic city if you want to do farm work. It is a paradise for those searching for fruit-picking work (there are many farms).

Disadvantages

🔍⊖ In terms of culture, you might get bored. There is not the effervescence that Sydney or Melbourne have.

🔍⊖ When it comes to food, there are plenty of Asian food choices but not many European or American options. If you are addicted to cheese or your brand of vegan bread, this will quickly run up your food and entertainment budget.

🔍 CAIRNS

Cairns is located in the extreme north of Queensland, about 1700 kms north of Brisbane. Its population is about 150,000.

Advantages

🔍⊕ Like Brisbane, Cairns enjoys sunshine all year round. However, it is much more humid in the summer season (November to May) with peaks of over 40 degrees (104 °F).

🔍⊕ Its proximity to the Great Barrier Reef makes it a favorite spot for diving and snorkeling enthusiasts. Many companies offer snorkeling or day trips in the pristine waters, the best way to see blue and yellow fish, rays or jellyfish!

20

CHOOSING A CITY OF ARRIVAL

🔍⊕ There are many job opportunities in the tourism industry, a sector that recruits and sustains the city. If you have experience as a dive instructor, guide, or in the hotel and restaurant industry, Cairns is a good choice.

🔍⊕ A lower cost of living, much more accessible than the rest of Australia. You can easily save money by working.

Disadvantages

🔍⊖ It is a small town. The downtown area is easily walkable in its entirety. Active people who are not interested in the underwater world might get bored.

🔍 DARWIN

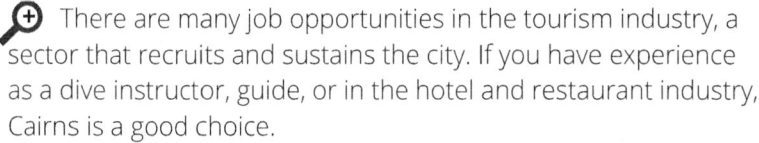

A little smaller than Cairns, Darwin is located in the Northern Territory.

Advantages

🔍⊕ Small downtown where you can walk to everything.

🔍⊕ It is about 30 degrees (86 °F) all year round. There are two seasons, the dry season and the wet season, but the temperature does not change.

🔍⊕ The wages are higher than the rest of Australia and more generally the place to be if you want to go straight to your 3- or 6-month farm job.
Jobs that are valid for your 2nd or 3rd visa are mostly found here.

🔍⊕ Probably the most relaxed and friendly people in Australia! Here, we greet each other without knowing each other and engage in conversation easily. You will never see that in Melbourne or Sydney.

🔍⊕ Darwin is the gateway to two major national parks: Litchfield and Kakadu.

CHOOSING A CITY OF ARRIVAL

Disadvantages

🔎 Apart from pubs and horse racing, the city does not offer many choices of activities.

PERTH

Perth is the capital of the state of Western Australia.
It is the most remote city in the world because it is surrounded by the endless ocean on one side and thousands of kilometers of desert on the other! This makes it a special place that you either love or hate.

Advantages

🔎 Perth is the capital of outdoor sports. The locals live outside, on their surfboards, skateboards or in their tents in a national park. Nature lovers will not be disappointed. The beaches are beautiful.

🔎 Perth is a city on a human scale. It is nevertheless the 4th largest city in Australia with nearly 2 million inhabitants.

🔎 Perth is the only major city on the West Coast, which means that the rest of the coast is almost empty. Sure, you'll have to drive a lot of kilometers or miles, but you've got some of the most beautiful places in the country, less crowded than the very popular East Coast. Head north to Broome and the Kimberley! Or head south to Esperance and its kangaroos on the beach.

🔎 Wages are high and because it is a much less popular city than the East Coast cities, there is less competition in the job market.

🔎 The atmosphere in Perth is relaxed and casual. It is not uncommon to see people walking barefoot on the streets, or others in swimsuits with their beach towels over their shoulders on the train.

CHOOSING A CITY OF ARRIVAL

Disadvantages

🔎 It is a bit cool in winter (between June and September).

🔎 Meeting people is not as easy as in other cities. Making local friends seems to be a little more difficult than elsewhere.

🔎 You will be a bit far from everything and you will have to travel several hundred kilometers to reach another big city.

 ADELAIDE

Smaller than Brisbane or Sydney, Adelaide is a sparkling and dynamic city that is worth knowing. Why is it so?

Advantages

🔎 The inhabitants are very welcoming and humour is their second nature.

🔎 In terms of gastronomy, it is at the top of the list with the largest market in the Southern Hemisphere. There is a real culture of good wine and good food. Festival-wise, it's not bad either as Adelaide hosts the "food and wine" festival in April and the famous Fringe Festival in March (Mad March)!

🔎 Less popular than Melbourne or Sydney, Adelaide offers more employment opportunities.

🔎 The most beautiful sunsets!

🔎 There are some cool day trips from the city: the famous Barossa Valley wine region. A three-hour drive from the city center takes you through the vineyards, with kangaroos hopping along the road! Adelaide is also the gateway to Kangaroo Island. Take the ferry and you are on an island still well preserved from mass tourism, with incredible Australian fauna and flora.

23

CHOOSING A CITY OF ARRIVAL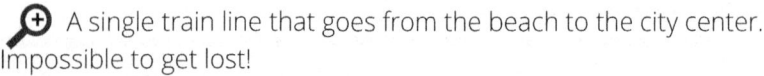

⊕ A single train line that goes from the beach to the city center. Impossible to get lost!

Disadvantages

⊖ Below-freezing temperatures in winter.

HOBART

We finish our tour with the capital of Tasmania, bigger than Darwin or Cairns with its 200,000 inhabitants.

Advantages

⊕ The starting point for those who want to pick fruit and vegetables, as the island is covered with fields and agricultural farms.

⊕ Little competition with other travelers looking for a job.

⊕ Tasmania is a paradise for nature lovers.
Hobart is a small town; in just a 30-minute drive, you are in the middle of the fields.

Disadvantages

⊖ As in Perth, it can be difficult to connect with the locals, certainly because these are the two cities most distant from the rest of the population.

⊖ It is very cold in winter! In summer, temperatures rarely exceed 30 degrees (86°F). For those who get cold, this is not a destination to choose.

CHOOSING A CITY OF ARRIVAL | COST OF LIVING

Consider the cost of living.

 **Sydney**

Let's start with the city of choice for Working Holiday Visa holders.

Shared accommodation

In the Sydney CBD, having your own room in a shared apartment or house will cost you a minimum of AUD $300-400/week, so a total of AUD $1200-1600/month. Below that, you share the room with one or more people. Prices per week can reach AUD $500 or more.

If you are going with two people and want to share a room, you can find a place from AUD $250/week. Below that, you'll have all kinds of options (like renting a couch!).

Sydney being an expensive city, some people don't hesitate to rent out their couch. For a decent and comfortable accommodation **downtown,** count AUD $800/month if you share and **AUD $1200-1400/month** if you want your own room. This is the average price. Of course, you can always find a bigger and better place and therefore more expensive.

In the northern and western suburbs (1h max. from downtown; Castle Hill, Parramatta, Chatswood, Burwood, etc), you will find a single room for a minimum of AUD $190-300/week, so AUD $760-1200/month, less if you share the room with another person. Again, this is an average price. If you are a surfing addict or simply love the beach atmosphere and want **to live at the beach**, you will need to have **almost the same budget as living in Sydney CBD, even more.**

Expect to pay AUD $350-450/week to live in Bondi Beach, Coogee Beach or Manly. Bondi is an upscale beachfront neighborhood, a bit overrated. For more tranquility, choose Coogee which is less popular. For a hippie-surfer atmosphere, choose Manly. To sum up, to live by the sea without going too far from Sydney, count on a minimum of AUD $1400-1800/month.

CHOOSING A CITY OF ARRIVAL | COST OF LIVING

The food budget

If you cook at home and shop at the big stores like Woolworths for example, count about AUD $100/week, or AUD $400/month.
If you buy take-out to eat at work (at Subway for example), count AUD $50/week minimum on top. You can eat a sandwich for about ten dollars in the center of Sydney. A simple menu in a restaurant costs about 20 dollars.
The total monthly cost for food is about **AUD $600.**
If you are a coffee addict, you should know that a coffee at Starbucks in Sydney costs AUD $5 minimum. I'll let you do the math for your monthly coffee budget!

Transportation

With the Opal card, it costs about **AUD $50/week** if you use the transport every day (AUD $3.61 per trip), so AUD $200/month.
You can use buses, trains and ferries.

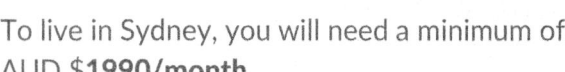

To live in Sydney, you will need a minimum of
AUD $**1990/month.**
This does not take into account outings and other activities.

 ## Melbourne

In second place, Melbourne has a lower cost of living than Sydney.

Shared accommodation

To live in the **Melbourne CBD** or in **the Southbank, Docklands or South Yarra areas**, having your own room in a shared apartment or house will cost you a minimum of AUD $170-250/week, so a total of AUD $600-1000/month. Below that, you would share the room with one or more people.
Of course, you can always find a bigger, better located, and therefore more expensive room.

CHOOSING A CITY OF ARRIVAL | COST OF LIVING

For the seaside (St Kilda), you will find a single room for a minimum of AUD$ 230-350/week (it can quickly go up to 400 depending on the season you arrive), so AUD $920-1400/month, less if you share the room with another person. This is an average price.

The food budget

If you cook at home and shop at the supermarket, count about AUD $100/week, or AUD $400/month. If you buy take-away food to eat at work (Subway, KFC, Starbucks, etc), it will cost you around AUD $50/week, which is AUD $200/month, which adds up to **AU$600/month for the monthly food budget.**

Same remark about coffee as for Sydney. Melbourne is the coffee capital of Australia. You will quickly spend AUD$5 here, AUD $5 there, which will quickly increase your budget!

Transportation

In Melbourne, you can take advantage of the free tramway, the Free City Circle (route 35), which goes around the city and stops at the main points of interest. Otherwise, you have the **Myki Pass** (or the mobile version on your phone). The Myki Pass costs about AUD $46/week, so **AUD $184/month**. With this card, you can use trains, tramways and buses.

To live in Melbourne, you will need a minimum of **AU$1784/month.**

This does not take into account outings and other activities.

Brisbane

Brisbane has a more reasonable cost of living than Sydney.

Shared accommodation

To live in **Brisbane City**, having your own room in a shared apartment or house will cost you a minimum of AUD $250-350/week, so a total of AUD $1000-1400/month.

Below that, you might share the room with one or more people.

CHOOSING A CITY OF ARRIVAL | COST OF LIVING

If you want to live in the lively **Fortitude Valley** area, expect to pay AUD $250-350/week for a private room (AUD $1,000-$1,400/month).

For the **South Brisbane** area, prices vary from the lowest (AUD $200/week) to much more expensive rents (AUD $400/week). You will find everything in this area, which seems to have increased its rents over the last three years.

The food budget

If you cook at home and shop at the supermarket, it costs about AUD $100/week, or AUD $400/month. If you buy take-out to eat at work (fast food style; Subway, KFC, Starbucks), count AUD$ 50/week, or AUD $200/month more. If the company where you work offers you lunch (if you work in a restaurant for example) or if a kitchen is at your disposal to heat up your meals, the food budget will obviously vary.
The total monthly cost is **AUD $600/month.**

Transportation

In Brisbane, you have the **Go Card**, which can be reloaded and makes the price of a trip AUD $3.45 (AUD $5 if you don't have the Go Card). If you take the train 5 times a week, it costs AUD $ 35/week, so **AUD $140/month.**
Note that the CityHopper bus is free, as is the ferry.

To live in Brisbane, you should therefore count on a minimum of **AU$1940/month**. This does not take into account outings and other activities.

28

CHOOSING A CITY OF ARRIVAL | COST OF LIVING

 **Cairns**

Shared accommodation

To live in Cairns, having your own room in a shared apartment or house will cost you a minimum of AUD $185-$300/week, so a total of AUD $740-$1,200/month. Of course, you can always find a bigger and more expensive room, but in general, a room for AUD $200/week will have its own en-suite bathroom.

The food budget

If you cook at home and shop at the supermarket, it costs about AUD $100/week, or AUD $400/month. If you buy take-away food to eat at work, it will cost you AUD $50/week, which is AUD $ 200/month more. This adds up to **AU$600/month.**
It is possible to spend less than that because depending on your taste, you can have sushi for less than AUD$ 10 - Asian food being quite popular and cheap in Queensland.

Transportation

Cairns being a small city, you will most likely be able to do everything on foot. However, there are buses that you can easily take. A bus ticket costs AUD $2.40. If you use the transport twice a day for five days, you should spend less than **AUD $100/month.**

• •

To live in Cairns, you should therefore count on a minimum of **AUD $1670/month**. This does not take into account outings and other activities. Knowing that in Cairns, there are many discount coupons and free drinks everywhere. It is not an expensive city to go out in.

29

CHOOSING A CITY OF ARRIVAL | COST OF LIVING

 Darwin

Shared accommodation

To live in Darwin, having your own room in a shared apartment or house will cost you a minimum of AUD $200-300/week, so a total of **AUD $800-1200/month.**

The food budget

If you cook at home and shop at the supermarket, count about AUD $100/week, or AUD $400/month. If you buy take-away food to eat at work, count AUD $50/week, that is AUD $200 per month more. The total monthly amount is **AUD $600/month**.
Like in Cairns, you have many Asian restaurants where you can eat for less than AUD $10.

Transportation

Darwin being a small city, you will most likely be able to do everything on foot. However, there are buses that you can easily take; a 7-day bus ticket costs AUD $20. So you should spend **AUD $ 80/month.**

· ·

To live in Darwin, you should therefore count on a minimum of AUD **$1680/month**. This does not take into account outings and other activities.

 Adelaide

Shared accommodation

To live in Adelaide, having your own room in a shared apartment or house will cost you a minimum of AUD $170-270/week, so a total of **AUD $680-1080/month.**

CHOOSING A CITY OF ARRIVAL | COST OF LIVING

The food budget

If you cook at home and shop at the supermarket, count about AUD $100/week, or AUD $440/month. If you buy take-away food to eat at work, count AUD $50/week, or AUD $200/month more. The total monthly amount is **AUD $600/month.**

Transportation

With the Metro Card, you will pay **AUD $107** for a 28-day pass. If you don't want to opt for the monthly pass, the trip will cost you AUD $5.90 each way.

To live in Adelaide, you should therefore count on a minimum of **AUD $1587/month**. This does not take into account outings and other activities.

Perth

Shared accommodation

There are not really any offers of flatshares in Perth city center. The offers will be more in the inner and outer suburbs.

For example, you can find a room in a shared apartment in East Victoria for less than AUD $200/month. Your budget will average a minimum of AUD $170-270/week to live in the Perth suburbs, so **AUD$ 680-1080/month.**

To live in Subiaco or Leederville (the closest suburbs), it will cost you a minimum of AUD $200-350/week, so a total of **AUD $800-1400/month.**

For those who want to live by the water (Fremantle, Cottesloe, Scarborough, etc), count on AUD $240-$325/week, so AUD **$960-$1,300/month**, but availability in this area is low.

CHOOSING A CITY OF ARRIVAL | COST OF LIVING

The food budget

If you cook at home and shop at the supermarket, count about AUD $100/week, or AUD $400/month. If you buy take-away food to eat at work, count AUD $50/week, that is AUD $200/month more. The total monthly amount is **AUD $600/month**.

Transportation

Transperth is a network of buses, trains and ferries in the city of Perth. You will pay between AUD $3.30 and AUD $5.00 each way depending on the area. Assuming you take the bus or train twice a day five days a week, you will spend an average of **AUD $132/month.**

To live in Perth, you should therefore count on a minimum of **AUD $1722/month**. This does not take into account outings and other activities.

Hobart

Shared accommodation

To live in Hobart, it will cost you a minimum of AUD $190-230/week, so a total of **AUD $760-920/month.**
However, you can find homestays for less than AUD $170/week.

The food budget

If you cook at home and shop at the supermarket, count about AUD $100/week, or AUD $400/month. If you buy take-away food to eat at work, count AUD $50/week, or AUD $200/month more. The total monthly amount is **AUD $600/month**.

32

CHOOSING A CITY OF ARRIVAL | COST OF LIVING

Transportation

Metro Tas is the local bus system, which also serves Burnie City and Launceston. For a trip into the city, you will pay between AUD $3.50 and AUD $4.80 one way depending on the area.
Assuming you take the bus or train twice a day five days a week, you will spend an average of **AUD $140/month.**

To live in Hobart, you should therefore count on a minimum of **AUD $1580/month**. This does not take into account outings and other activities.

Important :
For accommodations, these are the average prices found on the websites Gumtree and Flatmates. If you want to check where you are going and secure your reservation in advance, you can book on Airbnb. This will cost you more than the prices listed above, but with customer reviews, you know what you'll be getting.
Another advantage: Once you have the owner's contact info, you can negotiate a long-term monthly rate directly with him/her.

Here is the ranking of cities (minimum monthly budget from highest to lowest):
1- **Sydney** : AUD $1990
2- **Brisbane** : AUD $1940
3- **Melbourne** : AUD $1784
4- **Perth** : AUD $1722
5- **Darwin** : AUD $1680
6- **Cairns** : AUD $1670
7- **Adelaide** : AUD $1587
8- **Hobart :** AUD $1580

Darwin AUD $1680
Cairns AUD $1670
Brisbane AUD $1940
Perth AUD $1722
Adelaide AUD $1587
Sydney AUD $1990
Melbourne AUD $1784
Hobart AUD $1580

Minimum monthly budget in AUD$

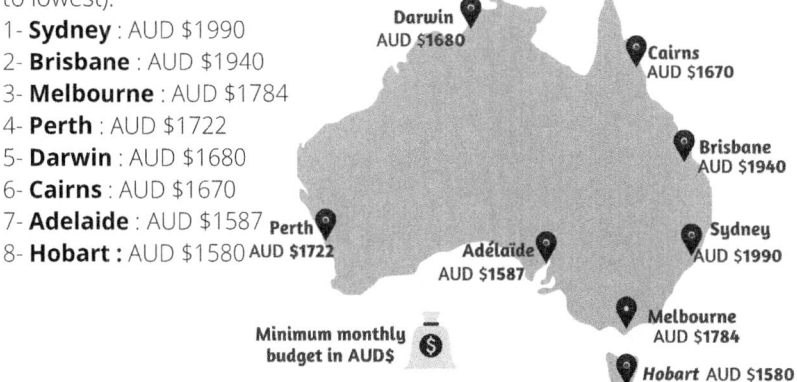

Adelaide and Hobart are the two cities to choose if you don't want to spend too much money when you arrive.

LEAVE IN THE RIGHT SEASON

Leave in the right season

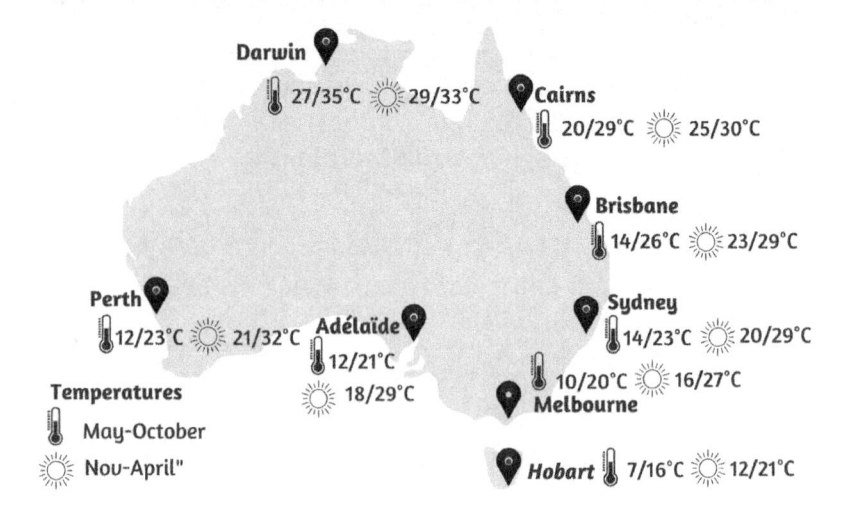

Darwin 27/35°C ☀ 29/33°C
Cairns 20/29°C ☀ 25/30°C
Brisbane 14/26°C ☀ 23/29°C
Perth 12/23°C ☀ 21/32°C
Adélaïde 12/21°C ☀ 18/29°C
Sydney 14/23°C ☀ 20/29°C
Melbourne 10/20°C ☀ 16/27°C
Hobart 7/16°C ☀ 12/21°C

Temperatures
🌡 May-October
☀ Nov-April"

For those interested in working in the hospitality industry, the best time to arrive in Melbourne, Perth, Adelaide, Hobart or Sydney is just before the January/February school vacations. Arriving before the Christmas holidays can be a good plan. The high season in Cairns or Darwin is between June and October, during the dry season. Brisbane is ideal all year round.

For those who wish to do farm work, you will simply have to avoid arriving in the winter period (except for lemons and grapes in the south of the country, for example).
If you were to arrive in Hobart in June, you would have trouble finding work in this area. It would be better to arrive during the summer season, from about September to April in the cities of South Australia, and between May and November in the North, for example, for melon or mango picking in Darwin.
In Western Australia, you can arrive in October to pick strawberries until the end of February. If you arrive in April/May, it will be tomatoes. In Queensland, it's bananas all year round!

CHOOSING A CITY OF ARRIVAL | COMPETITION

The competition on arrival and the level of English

Before choosing your arrival city, you should consider the possible competition. 80% of visa holders arrive in Sydney or Melbourne. Brisbane and Perth are second.

Imagine the number of possible competitors knowing that each year, there are approximately 200,000 candidates who arrive (1st and 2nd visas combined)!

It should be kept in mind that the majority of arrivals come from the United Kingdom (30,000/year), so if English is not your native language, be prepared to face some competition.

In addition to the British, there are also about 8,000 Irish arriving each year and the same number of Americans. You will therefore be competing in a job market flush with natives of an Anglo-Saxon country.

In short, if you have a very average level of English and you arrive in Melbourne or Sydney, the job search will not necessarily be as simple as if you go fruit picking directly in Darwin.

However, if you have experience in the restaurant industry, it will not be very difficult to learn the sector's basic vocabulary in a short period of time. You just need to be persistent and motivated.

Seeing that you're reading this book in English, it is very likely that there will be no language problems in Australia!

(source BR0110 Working Holiday Maker visa program report)

The plane ticket

There is a great comparison site called Google Flights (https://www.google.com/flights) which allows you to see the flight cost for a range of dates. This way, you'll know right away the minimum price you will pay.

The departure months to avoid are the end of December and the whole month of August.

A return ticket to Australia costs on average from USD $850 to USD $1,200 depending on the airline and the season.

BEFORE DEPARTURE: THE DRIVING LICENCE

To make it through your 20-hour flight, it is recommended to fly with an airline that offers a minimum of comfort like Emirates or Cathay Pacific. You will recover faster from jetlag because you will be better rested. If you can avoid flying on Air India, for example, do so. To get a good price, you should book in advance, ideally 3 months before departure, and even earlier if you can.

BEFORE LEAVING: 4 ADMINISTRATIVE STEPS

The international driving licence

If you drive in Australia and are stopped on the road, you will be asked to present an International Driving Licence in addition to your original licence.

The application for an international driver's license is a process that is done from your country of origin. The procedure varies from one country to another. Your license will be valid from 1 to 3 years.

In Great Britain or Northern Ireland, you just need to go to the post office and prove that you have a full UK driver licence from Great Britain or Northern Ireland. You will have to pay £5.50.
https://www.gov.uk/driving-abroad/get-an-idp

For US citizens, you need also to apply in person. You must complete this document online
https://www.aaa.com/vacation/docs/IDP_Application2a.pdf
print it out and bring it to your nearest AAA office, along with two passport photos and a photocopy of both sides of your driver's license.
The procedure costs US$20. More information on the website:
https://www.aaa.com/vacation/idpf.html

For Canadians, you need to go to a BCAA office with this document printed and filled out https://www.caa.ca/app/uploads/2021/02/IDP-en_Application-Form_February-2019.pdf, along with two passport-sized photos and CAN$25 in cash or by card.

BEFORE DEPARTURE: CHOOSING AN INSURANCE

Choosing an insurance policy

Before leaving for Australia, it is strongly advised to take out international insurance. Going to the doctor for a simple consultation or having an operation can be very expensive.
Some insurance companies offer special Working Holiday assistance. The most important thing to check with an insurance company is whether you will have to advance money and whether there is an excess. When there is an excess, your insurance company will charge you a maximum of 250€ (when the excess is that amount) on the total cost of your medical expenses and reimburse you the rest.

World Nomads

Founded in 2000, World Nomads is an international insurance company specializing in Working holiday visa holders. It's one of the most popular insurance providers for travelers on a Working Holiday Visa in Australia. Travelers from more than 150 countries, including the USA and UK, can get travel insurance from World Nomads.
WHV insurance offered by World Nomads is tailor-made to meet the specific coverage needs of travelers.
World Nomads offer two types of travel insurance plans: Standard and Explorer. The Standard plan is inexpensive but comes with lower coverage limits, while the explorer plan is more expensive but offers higher limits. The Explorer plan is a great choice for travelers looking for additional coverage that includes adventure sports.
Travelers who get WHV insurance from World Nomads can benefit from Trip Cancellation coverage that protects them if the trip is canceled due to unforeseen or unexpected reasons.
You can adjust your insurance policy if you decide to extend your trip.
You can also pause your insurance coverage if you need to pause your trip.

BEFORE DEPARTURE: CHOOSING AN INSURANCE

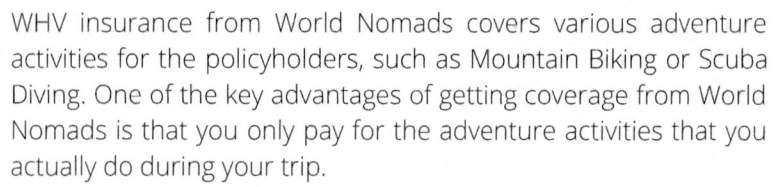

WHV insurance from World Nomads covers various adventure activities for the policyholders, such as Mountain Biking or Scuba Diving. One of the key advantages of getting coverage from World Nomads is that you only pay for the adventure activities that you actually do during your trip.

World Nomads provides 24/7 steadfast emergency phone assistance to its policyholders. The actual cost of travel insurance for travelers on a working holiday visa in Australia depends on a wide range of factors, such as age, trip length, and the countries you're planning to visit in addition to Australia.

Cost per Year: $701 (for the Standard Plan)

You can get a quote by visiting the official website of World Nomads: www.worldnomads.com.

Go Walkabout

Established in 1999, Go Walkabout is a UK-based company that provides affordable travel insurance to UK citizens travelling to Australia on the Working Holiday Visa.

The company's WHV insurance offers incredible flexibility to its policyholders. So, if you want to add additional coverage, an activity, or a destination to your insurance policy, you just need to email its customer service department, and a customer care official will reply to you with a quote and payment instructions.

Go Walkabout ensures the 24/7 availability of medical professionals to provide on-time medical care to its policyholders. Travel insurance from Go Walkabout covers more than 99 sports and adventure activities. It also covers leisure pursuits without requiring you to pay an extra cost.

Go Walkabout insurance is based on a specially designed WHV policy that covers a wide range of jobs that policyholders might be doing in the UK.

Your Go Walkabout insurance policy covers all common losses during your trip and stay in Australia, such as baggage, personal possessions and travel documents. You also get trip cancellation coverage if your trip is canceled due to covered reasons. Trip cancellation coverage reimburses you for the cost of your flight and accommodation.

BEFORE DEPARTURE: MY PHONE / MY BANK

The cost of travel insurance depends on factors like your age, length of stay in Australia, and any additional countries you want to visit during your trip.
Cost per Year: £172 (for Standard Plan) & £243 (for Plus Plan).
You can get a quick quote by visiting the official website of Go Walkabout: www.go-walkabout.co.uk

You will also find other insurance companies such as Allianz, April or Europ Assistance.
You do not need to subscribe months in advance. It can be done the week before your departure, knowing that on the online form, you will have to indicate a fixed departure date to be insured from then.

My Phone

Before you leave, you should check that your phone is unlocked so you can use an Australian SIM card in it when you arrive.
If you bought your phone separately from your plan, which is more often the case nowadays, it will already be unlocked. However, if you bought your phone at a good price because it was included in a plan, you will have to have it unlocked by your operator.
If you forget to do it before leaving, don't panic, you can have it unlocked either in a store in Australia or online via your operator's website.

My bank

Ideally, you should have your card de-capped. Why ?
So you don't end up in Alice Springs on a holiday with a blocked card! (This is a true story!).
Depending on your situation, you will need to pay for airfare, housing (probably with a deposit) and other living expenses. Check with your bank to see how much your credit card limit is to cover your expenses upon arrival, but also for possible large expenses along the way, such as the purchase of a van, for example, or the deposit for a camper van rental.
The ideal is to have two cards, stored in your belongings in different places, to face all eventualities.

WRITING A CV FOR THE AUSTRALIAN MARKET

What to put in your CV/resume?

You will save a lot of time if you prepare your resume before you arrive, but, in Australia, you have to adapt your resume to every job you apply for, so, 'one resume fits all' doesn't work out here. You will have to prepare a separate resume for each job you apply for.

Nevertheless, for jobs in the restaurant industry or fruit picking, you can afford to send the same CV to everyone.

Australians like long resumes, so they must be at least two pages in length. This doesn't mean though that you have to list your professional experiences in detail. You need to be precise and concise and, once again, remember to adapt your text to the offer you're applying for.

A CV in Australia looks like this:
Contact details / Visa (you must specify that you are on a Working Holiday and the dates)
Career objectives
Key Skills & Work Experience

The first lines of your resume have to describe what your professional perspectives are, carefully using words from the job advertisement you are applying for.

Print a few copies before you leave. This can always be useful if you plan to visit restaurants or recruitment agencies in the city. You can put your WhatsApp number on it before you have your Australian number.

Template of a ready-made CV

What are the best tools to create a resume quickly?
You can use the ready-made template from the Australian recruitment website Seek.
All you have to do is fill in the fields!
https://www.seek.com.au/career-advice/article/free-resume-template

WRITING A CV FOR THE AUSTRALIAN MARKET

Full Name
0000 000 000
emailaddress@domain.com   Suburb, State, Postcode

Key skills

- Skill one
- Skill two
- Skill three
- Skill four
- Skill five
- Skill six
- Skill seven
- Skill eight

Education

Course or qualification
from Institution Name
Graduated YYYY

Course or qualification
from Institution Name
Graduated YYYY

Summary

This is your elevator pitch where you have just a few lines of text to sell yourself to a potential employer. Try to keep it brief and to the point.

Career history

Role Title at Company Name
Month YYYY – Month YYYY
Overview of role in 1 to 2 lines
Key responsibilities
Insert 2 to 3 key responsibilities
Achievements
Insert 2 to 3 achievements

Role Title at Company Name
Month YYYY – Month YYYY
Overview of role in 1 to 2 lines
Key responsibilities
Insert 2 to 3 key responsibilities
Achievements
Insert 2 to 3 achievements

Interests

Insert 2 to 3 interests

References

Available upon request

WRITING A CV FOR THE AUSTRALIAN MARKET

Full Name

emailaddress@domain.com | 0000 000 000 | Suburb, State, Postcode

---

Summary This is your elevator pitch where you have just a few lines of text to sell yourself to a potential employer. Try to keep it brief and to the point.

Career history

Role Title at Company Name
Month YYYY – Month YYYY

Overview of role in 1 to 2 lines

Key responsibilities

Insert 2 to 3 key responsibilities

Achievements

Insert 2 to 3 key achievements

Role Title at Company Name
Month YYYY – Month YYYY

Overview of role in 1 to 2 lines

Key responsibilities

Insert 2 to 3 key responsibilities

Achievements

Insert 2 to 3 key achievements

Education

Course or qualification from Institution Name
Graduated YYYY

Course or qualification from Institution Name
Graduated YYYY

Key skills Skill one, Skill two, Skill three, Skill four, Skill five, Skill six, Skill seven, Skill eight, Skill nine, Skill ten

References Available upon request

WRITING A CV FOR THE AUSTRALIAN MARKET

Resume template

Here is an example of a resume.
Marie is applying for a job in Human Resources in Melbourne. She didn't put her photo on her resume. You can feel free to put one on or not.

MARIE BRAUD

• HR/Talent acquisition advisor • Working Holiday Visa •

PROFILE

International (France, Morocco, Finland) and Multidisciplinary academic degrees (bachelor in psychology, Master in Human Resources, MBA in intercultural management)
More than 4 years experience in Human Resources in Morocco and Canada and 3 years in marketing in France

HR expertise acquired
Staffing, coaching and follow-up candidate, customer relations, International HR politics, diversity management, career management, performance management, mobility management, succession planning, business analysis, intercultural management, training.

Soft skills
Open minded, active listening, pro-activity, challenge oriented, flexibility, interpersonal communication skills, sense of initiative, team-player, result oriented, intercultural management skills, stress management

IT skills
Microsoft office 2010 : excel, word, powerpoint, outlook. SPSS, SAP HR, Social network : twitter, linkedIn, viadeo, google+

Language
French (native), English (expert), German (intermediate), Chinese (basic), Arabic (basic)

EDUCATION

2012 - 2013 • Laurea, Helsinki, Finland
MBA in **service innovations**. Specialty: HRM/ development of cross cultural competences

2011 - 2012 • IAE Corse (Institute of Company Management), Corte, France
Master 2 **Human Resources**. Specialties: E-recruitment/ Management of Diversity (Admitted with good honors)

(04) 290 1092 2093 • +33 09 1092 2092 • mariebraud@email.com

WRITING A CV FOR THE AUSTRALIAN MARKET

2010 - 2011 • Laurea, Helsinki, Finland
Master 1 Management of **Human Resources and value competences**
University Mohammed 5, Rabat, Morocco (Admitted with good honors)

2009 - 2010 •University Rennes 2, Rennes, France
Bachelor in Psychology, Specialty : Social Psychology/ group dynamic

January 2014 • Training and courses:
CRHA, Montreal, Canada. Courses: **HR 2**

EXPERIENCE

March 2017 — Systematix, Montreal, Canada
August 2019 — **IT Talent acquisition advisor**
- Requirements analysis with the client
- Head hunting and networking
- Interviews
- Coaching and career management
- Mobility and diversity management
- Business development of new accounts
- 2.0 marketing HR project/ community management:
    - Strategy presentation
    - Analysis of gaps and issues
    - Creation of forums and Corporate pages
    - Animation of workshops
- Writing service offering on the International HR strategy
- Identification of issues, risks and impacts of change
- Design communication strategies and training plans
- Participation in operational meetings
- Participation in networking events: cocktail, team bulding, golf, ...

Achievements:
50 recruits in two years, development of the employer brand, development of new clients and business partners, editorial diversity policy and strategy of international talent acquisition.

February 2017 — IDL Expert conseil, Montreal Canada
Diversity management consultant
- Establishment of a service offer to provide a training about intercultural communication
- Definition of processes and tools to support best practices in diversity management
- Design of the training plan and change management.

(04) 290 1092 2093 • +33 09 1092 2092 • mariebraud@email.com

WRITING A CV FOR THE AUSTRALIAN MARKET

March 2014 Agence vitae conseil (CGI group), Casablanca, Morocco
October 2016 **RPO/HR business partner**
- Advisor role for managers :
    - Analysis of IT job market in Maghreb (competition, HR best practices of talent attraction compensation)
    - Recommendations of recruitment improvements
    - Support operational staff needs
    - Interviews
    - Management of expatriates candidates on-boarding process in collaboration with the client
- Coach/team leader role :
    - In charge of the reporting between client/agency with dash-boards
    - Team leader of 3 recruiters : coaching and training about IT jobs and HR role

Achievements:
100 hires in one year (4 person team), participation in the implementation of HR policies and practices.

Additional experiences abroad

2013 /1 month Humanitarian action, 1 month in Morocco, Mauritania and Senegal Project "La Caravane de l'amitié"

2012 /3 months French teacher in Istanbul, Turkey

2011 /3 months Humanitarian action, Luxor, Egypt (Association Key of Life)

2010 /3 months Linguistic exchange in Berlin, Germany

2010 /3 weeks Linguistic trip

References available on request

(04) 290 1092 2093 • +33 09 1092 2092 • mariebraud@email.com

ON ARRIVAL : THE PROCEDURES

Photo or not?

I would say it is a personal choice rather than a rule. Let's just say it's not mandatory to include one. If a recruiter doesn't want to hire you because of your piercing or haircut, it's likely that seeing you in person will give the same impression.

The choice is yours. If you choose to put a photo on, it might as well be a good one. Forget about party photos, vacation photos or even worse, photos with sunglasses on! (yes, I've seen this!).
Do we have to talk about photos with filters? Avoid!
If you don't think the photo is to your advantage, then don't put it on.

ON ARRIVAL: THE PROCEDURES

Open a bank account

Before you leave home, you can negotiate with your bank to minimize the costs of withdrawal; some banks even offer free withdrawals for the first month.
For obvious reasons there aren't many banks or ATMs in the outback, and Westpac is no exception, but it is still the most popular bank in Australia and particularly among backpackers.

St George Bank's cash machines are great for withdrawing money free of charge, but there aren't many of them around. Commonwealth Bank, ANZ and NAB are very present, and if you are planning to go to New Zealand after Australia, ANZ would be a good choice.

For withdrawals from ATMs (Cash Machines), you will be charged a fee if you don't use your own bank's ATMs. On average, each withdrawal from a different bank's ATM will cost you around AUD$2.

However, the choice of bank doesn't really matter because their conditions are pretty much the same. It's worth getting a bank account that's easy to open.

ON ARRIVAL : THE PROCEDURES

With a passport and an address (it can be a friend's), you can go to any branch and put AUD$20 into the account, wait for your international transfer to be made with the Swift code you're given and hey presto!
You will receive your debit card within 3-5 days. Easy!
I do not recommend getting a credit card because you could get into trouble if you miss a payment because the costs are huge!
If you want to open a savings account, the NAB offers attractive rates.
Hopefully Australia will be an Eldorado for your bank account!

nab
www.nab.com.au

Commonwealth Bank of Australia
www.commbank.com.au

westpac
www.westpac.com.au

ANZ
www.anz.com/personal

st.george
www.stgeorge.com.au

Apply for TFN : Tax File Number

A Tax File Number (TFN) is a unique nine-digit number issued by the Australian Taxation Office (ATO) to individuals and organisations. This number helps the ATO to administer tax and other Australian Government systems. You can only apply for your TFN once you're in Australia. You cannot do it from your home country. http://www.ato.gov.au/

If you are doing an internship in Australia and are given a cash allowance by your host company, you won't necessarily need a Tax File Number, but if you apply for a paid job, a TFN is not mandatory but you might have to pay more taxes if you don't have one. Any future employer will ask you for this number, and if you don't have one, you may not get paid, so make sure you get one!

ON ARRIVAL : APPLY FOR A TAX FILE NUMBER

How do I get my TFN?
Go to the Australian Taxation Office (ATO) website and fill out the form. Make sure you have your proof of identity handy because you'll need it. You can either post the original documents or, if you're afraid of losing your original documents in the post, you can send certified copies or take them to any ATO office.
By post:
Australian Taxation Office, PO Box 9942, Moonee Ponds VIC 3039
If you choose to go to an office in person, please refer to the list here: http://www.ato.gov.au/.
You will receive your TFN through the post up to 28 days after the date the ATO receives your completed application. So you need to have a postal address in Australia.
If you don't have one, you can ask a friend, your hostel or your employer if you can use theirs.

What does 'certified copies of my documents' mean?
This means that photocopies of your original documents must be stamped by an authorized person.
You can go to the nearest Australian Embassy in your home country and get your documents certified. You can also ask them to recommend an authorized translation service, because if your documents are not in English, you will need to have them translated.

What does 'proof of identity' mean?
You can use your passport, your birth certificate, your national identity card or your drivers licence.
You need to provide TWO identity documents. Be careful if you provide your drivers licence, as the address on this document must be the same as the address on your TFN application.
You will only receive one Tax File Number in your lifetime so keep it safe. I would advise you to email it to yourself so that you always have it to hand.

ON ARRIVAL : APPLY FOR A TAX FILE NUMBER

Tax Return & Superannuation

Income tax is deducted at source and appears on your payslip. Today, you no longer receive a refund when you leave the country permanently, which is counterbalanced by a reduced withholding tax rate of 15%.

With regard to pension contributions (superrenewal), since July 1, 2017, the amount refunded is taxed at 65%. At the end of the year, your return allows you to check the adequacy between the amount due and prepayments. Most often, this difference shows an overpayment, which is then refunded directly to your bank account within the usual 14 working days from the filing of the return.
This is your Tax Return.
In most cases, the amount recovered is between AUD $2,000 and AUD $3,000, and in the best cases AUD $5,000 to AUD $5,500.
To get this money back, you will need to log on to https://www.ato.gov.au/Individuals/Lodging-your-tax-return/

I suggest that you find a job before applying for a TFN, because you may not know where you'll be or how long you're likely to stay in one place.

See on the following page how to apply for your TFN, step by step.

49

ON ARRIVAL : APPLY FOR A TAX FILE NUMBER

Log on to the site:
www.ato.gov.au/Individuals/Tax-file-number/Apply-for-a-TFN/

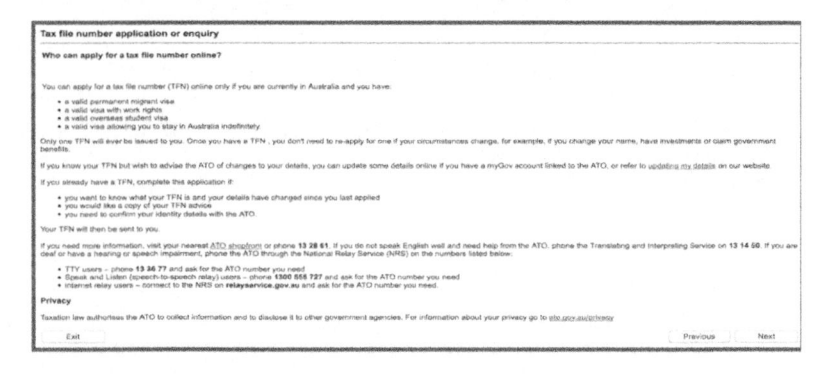

This part is easy! You just need to fill in your passport number, your country of origin and state if you have been to Australia before.

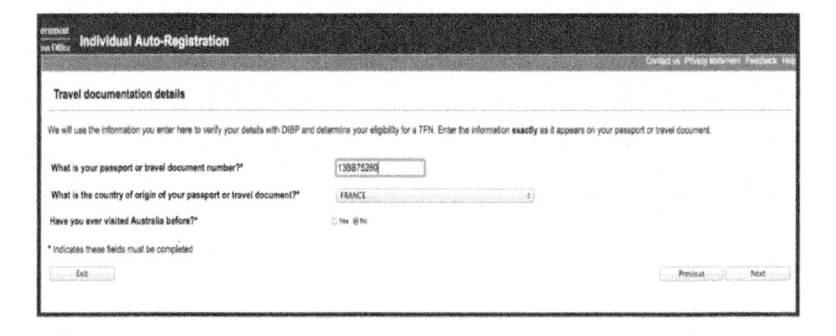

On the next page, you will simply need to fill in your contact information and specify whether you are married or not. Then click on "next".

ON ARRIVAL : APPLY FOR A TAX FILE NUMBER

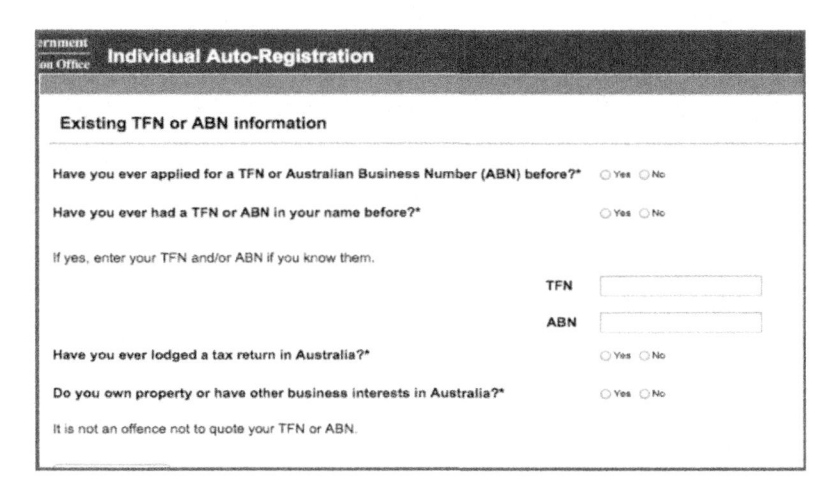

The following questions are intended to clarify whether you have ever been declared in Australia.

Simply answer "No" to all questions if you have never been to Australia.

ON ARRIVAL : APPLY FOR A TAX FILE NUMBER

In the next section, enter your address in Australia as well as in your home country. Please remember that the address you enter must match the address on both of your IDs. Then click on "Next".

Address details
What is your Australian postal address?
Your TFN advice will be sent to this address during the next 28 days. Your postal address can be a post office (PO) box or street address.
Address line 1: *
Address line 2:
Town or suburb: *
State or Territory: *
Postcode: *
What is your current home address?
Your home address cannot be a post office (PO) box number. If you are applying as a temporary visitor your residential address may be your home country address.
Is your current home address the same as your postal address (as above)? *   ○ Yes ● No
If 'No', enter your current home address:
Address line 1:
Address line 2:
Town or suburb:
State or Territory:
Postcode:
Country (If not Australia):
Exit

In the following section, enter your phone number so that Immigration can easily contact you if they have any questions. Click on "Next".

ON ARRIVAL : APPLY FOR A TAX FILE NUMBER

On the last page, you must click on "submit".
And that's it, your request has been submitted!

Choosing a phone operator

In Australia, there are three main telephone operators: Telstra, Optus and Vodafone.
All three charge roughly the same rates, although network coverage may differ from one operator to another.
If you are traveling in the outback, Telstra has better coverage in remote areas.
The pre-paid card costs a minimum of AUD$30.

If you didn't have your phone unlocked before landing in Australia, you can buy a basic Nokia type phone for AUD$39 (not practical if you use Facebook and internet!).
Finally, don't commit to a plan without making sure you can pay for it monthly.

ON ARRIVAL : CHOOSING A PHONE OPERATOR + BUYING A VAN

	Telstra	vodafone	OPTUS
Prepaid card	AU$30	AU$30	AU$30
Calls to same operator	Free from 6pm to 6am	Unlimited	up to AU$450
SMS in Australia	Free from 6pm to 6am	Unlimited	Unlimited
Datas	400 MB	500 MB	500 MB
Expiration	30 days	28 days	28 days
Standard cost SMS Australia	29 cents	29 cents	29 cents
Standard cost MMS Australia	50 cents	50 cents	50 cents
Standard cost SMS abroad	35 cents	36 cents	37 cents
Standard cost MMS abroad	75 cents	76 cents	77 cents
Standard cost call/minute	30 cents/call	89 cents/minute	90 cents/minute
SIM activation	directly on the website	directly on the website	directly on the website
	www.my.telstra.com.au	www.optus.com.au/activate	www.vodafone.com.au/personal
Recharge	www.my.telstra.com.au	www.optus.com.au/recharge	www.vodafone.com.au/personal

Buying a van

It is recommended to buy a van only if you plan to work outside the big cities or if you plan a road trip of more than three months.

There is no need to buy a van if you are looking for a job in Sydney or another major city, as public transportation is generally efficient.

The budget to buy a van can easily go up to AUD $10,000. For a medium sized van, you should expect to pay **AUD $4000-6000.**
If you don't have such a high budget, you can opt for a station wagon for less than AUD $3000 and convert the back of the car into a bed simply by adding a mattress. This will obviously not be as comfortable as a van as you will not have the necessary cooking facilities, a fridge, and other useful utensils.
Buying a van will save you a lot of money on accommodation and food.

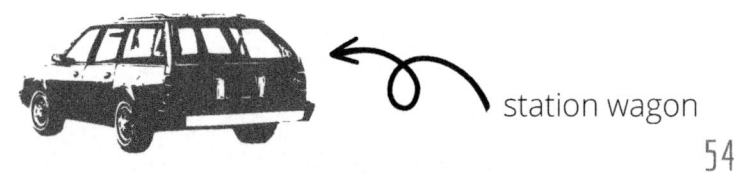

station wagon

ON ARRIVAL : BUYING A VAN

Where to buy a van?

You can reply to classified ads posted on Facebook groups such as: https://www.facebook.com/groups/AustralianCarMarketCarpoolingTravelPartner or on the website Gumtree : www.gumtree.com.au
You can also find ads on the website www.campermanaustralia.com/campervans-for-sale/
It is best to buy a van in the city where you will potentially stay because it will be easier to resell.
In Sydney, visit: www.buyingcampervansydney.com.au
http://sydneytravellerscarmarket.com.au

Parameters to consider before purchasing

- Check the mileage and condition of the van.
- Choose a vehicle with a Bull/Roo bar. In Australia, we avoid driving at night to avoid hitting a kangaroo or a wombat.
- The rego.

You will also need to check that the vehicle is registered with a sticker (regulation or rego) and the validity date of this sticker (3 months, 6 months or 1 year). You will have to renew the rego when it expires. It must be in your name and it is mandatory for driving in Australia.

To transfer the rego from the seller to the buyer, you must go in person with the seller to the prefecture where the vehicle is registered. This is also the time to check that there are no outstanding fines from the seller. If you don't check, you may have to pay the fines yourself! Note that in Western Australia, you don't need to go anywhere. You can do the rego transfer online. The price of the rego depends on the state where you buy your van and ranges from AUD $500 to AUD $900 depending on the weight of the vehicle.

ON ARRIVAL : BUYING A VAN

More information on the details of each state:

New South Wales
https://www.nsw.gov.au/driving-boating-and-transport/vehicle-registration

Western Australia
www.transport.wa.gov.au/licensing/renew-replace-my-vehicle-licence.asp

South Australia :
www.sa.gov.au/topics/driving-and-transport/motoring-fees/vehicle-registration-fees

Australian Capital Territory
www.act.org/content/act/en/products-and-services/the-act/registration/fees.html

Victoria
www.vicroads.vic.gov.au/registration/registration-fees/vehicle-registration-fees

Queensland
www.qld.gov.au/transport/registration/fees/cost

Northern Territory
https://nt.gov.au/driving/rego/fees/registration-fees

Tasmania
https://www.transport.tas.gov.au/online/vehicles

ON ARRIVAL : BUYING A VAN

🔍 Technical inspection

If you are in New South Wales or in Northern Territory, you will have to do the mandatory technical inspection when you renew your rego.
If the vehicle is registered in Victoria, Queensland or Canberra, you will need to have the vehicle inspected at the time of purchase.
The technical inspection is carried out in the state where the vehicle is registered.

🔍 Mandatory information that must be listed on the sales documents:

Brand, model, color, year, plate number, VIN number, vehicle identification number), date and price of sale, names, addresses and signatures of seller and buyer.

🔍 Insurance

You will need to have insurance (CTP: *compulsory third party insurance* or *green slip*) to be covered in case of an accident.
Its cost depends on the state and varies between AUD $20 and AUD $30/month.
This insurance covers third parties injured in an accident, but not the material or your own injuries. You will need additional health insurance for this (see Chapter 4).
If you want peace of mind, you should have Roadside Assistance insurance.
If you break down, you will be towed free of charge by a tow truck to the nearest garage. Beware that some insurances will only tow you within a limited radius of 100 kilometers. For example, NRMA offers rates from AUD $9.99 to AUD $29.99/month depending on the coverage you want: https://www.mynrma.com.au/

57

ADOPTING THE AUSTRALIAN LIFESTYLE

The Australian mindset

The few examples below are only meant to illustrate the Australian mindset in a general way; they cannot capture all the diversity within Australian society and are therefore in no way meant to stereotype all the Australians you might meet!

👉 Friendliness and optimism

The friendliness and openness of Australians is particularly obvious in the sphere of personal relationships.

The best entertainment for them is a gathering with friends in a pub or a house party.

You will find that Australians are very rarely negative and tend to avoid any subject that might be negative. Even if an Aussie is going through a divorce, instead of complaining, he or she will tend to say "Life happens mate!"

Australians appreciate authenticity, sincerity and hate pretentiousness. So you are well advised!

👉 Respect

Australian society is not about class division in terms of wealth and social status. Everyone is treated with an attitude that they deserve, whether they are a wealthy citizen or a service worker. Considering themselves no worse or better than anyone else, Australians are known for treating others with kindness and respect.

👉 A strong connection to their nature

As you may have seen during the massive bushfires, Australians are the first to come to the rescue of their wildlife.
They do not hesitate to save a koala from the flames.

ADOPTING THE AUSTRALIAN LIFESTYLE

Australian habits

👉 Surfing

Australians are known to be excellent surfers. Indeed, early morning surfing is a habit for many Australians. Is it because 4 out of 5 Australians live within 50 km of the coastline? Or is it because Australia has 10,685 beaches?

However, the best time to surf is between September and April because of the spring and summer swells.

👉 The barbecue

Australians love to gather around a barbecue (or *barbie* in their slang) with family or good friends. And for good reason - they do it so well. It's a great opportunity to enjoy their grilled vegetables, sausage, meat, fish or chicken. Whether it's in their backyard, at the local park, at the beach or camping, barbecuing is second nature to Australians.

👉 Waking up at dawn

Australians are used to getting up early and finishing work early. In fact, almost half of Australians are already up before 7am.

In other words, Australians are early risers. They are known for doing sports very early in the morning or during their lunch break. So if you're looking for a job, you'll likely have to set your alarm early!

👉 Drinks

Did you know that Australians drink 1.7 billion liters of beer a year, or about 680 bottles of beer for every adult? In addition, Australia has 60 wine regions.

Currently, about 1.3 billion liters of wine are produced each year in Australia. Be mentally prepared before you go out to party with them!

ADOPTING THE AUSTRALIAN LIFESTYLE

👉 Camping

Australians love to live outside and are big fans of camping. They don't hesitate to go away on weekends or vacations in their 4x4 or van and to take out their swag (a kind of sleeping bag lined with a canvas) to sleep under the stars!
The feeling of freedom in this country is particularly intense.

👉 Sport

Australians are known for playing sports like cricket, rugby, swimming, soccer and tennis. But they also love to watch them on TV in a pub! Cricket and Australian Football League (AFL) are considered the national sports not only because of their popularity, but also because of their sporting history.
The most surprising thing is to see an Australian concentrating on watching a 3 hour cricket match when there is absolutely nothing happening in the game!

Speaking the Australian *slang*

One of the first things you will notice in Australia is the unique way its people speak. Australians speak fast, "chew" words and skip pronouncing letters.
Combine that with their tendency to use slang and abbreviations, and you have a language that is quite difficult to understand!

To help you understand some of the most common slang words and abbreviations used in Australia, I've prepared a short guide.
So the next time someone invites you to a "barbie" or says "chuck a sickie" you'll know exactly what they mean! Here are some examples of Australian slang from A to Z:

SPEAKING AUSTRALIAN SLANG

Aggro : It is the diminutive for aggressive. Someone might get "aggro" if you take the last "Tim Tam" (famous Australian cookie) in the packet.
Ambo : Refers to the ambulance. It can also refer to the ambulance drivers or the service itself.
Ankle biter : A toddler, a small child.
Arvo: Afternoon
Aussie ("ozzie") : Australian.
Back of beyond : Far away in the central outback.
Barbie (barbecue) : Cooking outdoors on a BBQ.
Barrack : means to encourage or support.
Beaut, "bewdie" : Very good.
Bikkie : Biscuit (firm cookie).
Billabong : Watering hole, usually not flowing water.
Bloke : Person, a male.
Blowie : Blow fly.
Bludger : Lazy person.
Bonza : Really good.
Boogie board : Half-sized surf board.
Boomer : Very large male kangaroo.
Brekky : Breakfast.
Brolly : Means umbrella, an essential element in Melbourne where the weather can change quickly.
Brumby : A wild horse.
Buckley's chance/ "You've got Buckley's" : No chance at all.
Bugger off: Go away please.
Bush : In the countryside or away from the city.
Bush telegraph : Gossip network.
Bush tucker : Native foods, usually in the outback.
Bushbash : Bush-walking without a path or along an overgrown track.
Bushranger : Highwayman, outlaw.
Captain Cook : To have a look (reference to the British sailor who founded Australia).
Chippie : Carpenter.
Chokkie : Chocolate.
Chook / Roast chook : A chicken/roaster chicken.

61

SPEAKING AUSTRALIAN SLANG

Chrissie : Christmas.
Chuck a sickie : Take the day off sick when you are perfectly healthy.
Copper : A police officer.
Damper : Bush-oven bread from flour and water.
Digger : Soldier from Australia or New-Zealand.
Dinky-di/true blue : The real thing, genuine.
Dunny : Toilet.
Earbash : Non-stop talk.
Esky : Large insulated chest to keep beer cool. You will probably spot one « esky » or two if you are invited to a « barbie ».
Fair dinkum : Genuine or honest.
Fair go : A chance ("give a bloke a fair go").
Flat out : As fast as possible.
Footy : Soccer.
Gas : Flatulence or bodily gases "downstairs".
G'day : A greeting.
Hard yacka : hard work.
Hooroo : Goodbye.
lollies : Candies or sweets.
Maccas : McDonalds.
Mad as a cut snake : Very angry.
Mate : This usually means a friend; but it can be used to talk to anyone.
Mozzie : Mosquito.
No worries : Everything will be fine.
Outback : The bush, or a remote and uninhabited region.
Oz (or "Straya") : Australia, as in "Oz-tralia" or "...stralia".
Pressie : Gifts.
Rapt : Happy.
Reckon ! : You bet ! Absolutely !
Sanga : sandwich.
Servo : Petrol (gas)/ service station.
She will be apples : It will be alright.
Smoko : Coffee or cigarette break
Snag : Sausage.

SPEAKING AUSTRALIAN SLANG

Sparky : Electrician.
Spit the dummy : Get very upset about something.
Stoked : Happy
Strine : The Australian slang.
Sunnies: Sunglasses.
Swimmers : Swimming costume.
Ta : Australians will often say "Ta" to simply say thank you.
Tall poppies : Achievers, often a disparaging term.
Telly : The television.
The lucky country : Australia ! Where else?
Thingo/thingy : An item that you can't remember the name of when you want it.
This arvo : This afternoon.
Thongs : Rubber sandals, flip-flops.
Tim Tam : A brand of chocolate cookies which are very appreciated in Australia.
To have a pash : To kiss someone passionately, usually someone you don't know very well.
To put your foot down : To accelerate a car, to hurry up, or (confusingly) to bring things to a halt.
Tucker : Food.
Tucker-bag : Food bag.
Tradie : A tradesman.
Underdaks, undles : Underwear.
Ute : Commercial vehicle.
Up a gumtree : In a quandary that's hard to resolve.
Veg out : To relax.
Walkabout : Lengthy walk with no set destination.
Whinge, to have to : To complain or whine about something.
Woop woop : It means that you are in the middle of nowhere. Some people also use this word to describe isolated country towns.
Zonked : Exhausted, really tired, ready for bed.
Yarn : conversation

ADOPTING THE AUSTRALIAN LIFESTYLE : FOOD

The Australian food

As a modern nation with large-scale immigration, Australia is a unique blend of culinary influences and adaptations from various cultures around the world, including indigenous Australians, Asians, Europeans and Pacific Islanders.

For those who are addicted to European cheese or their gluten-free bread, you should know that these products are not the most consumed in Australia, well, at least in the small towns! It is difficult to find very good bread. You will see a lot of sandwich bread and the traditional cheese is cheddar! If you can't do without your favorite products, it might cost you a few extra dollars. Australians eat a lot of fast food and sugar-laden coffee to go.

The farther away you are from the big cities, the more fried the food will be! You will find fish and chips everywhere.

For healthier food, you can find Japanese maki rolls in the main cities for a few dollars.

The 3 most popular dishes in Australia:

🍽 Fish & chips (or "feesh and cheeps")

This dish is on the menu everywhere in Australia! It is a real institution; first because fish is easy to find (the vast majority of Australians live near the water) but also because they tend to fry everything.

If you order for example a fish basket in a pub, don't be surprised that all the fish is fried!

Fish & chips is mainly served in pubs, with a beer.

On the west coast of Australia (around Perth), you can have fish & chips with shark!

However, the most common fish used is hoki (from New Zealand) or cod.

Fish & chips is regularly served in paper because it's a meal that Australians often take for a picnic or a barbie.

ADOPTING THE AUSTRALIAN LIFESTYLE : FOOD

🍴 Chicken Parmigiana
This classic Australian chicken dish - with roots in Italian-American cuisine - is a staple on the menu in almost every restaurant in the country. Originally made with eggplant (and this option is still available to vegetarians), it has evolved into a chicken schnitzel topped with tomato sauce, melted cheese and, if you're inclined, prosciutto ham. The dish is usually served with salad and fries.

🍴 Barbecued snags (aka sausages)
It's no surprise that Australians love to grill, and nothing is more important to a good barbie (you already know the meaning of that slang!) than a decent sausage. Traditional Australian sausages are usually made from pork or beef, but if you're feeling adventurous, there are other animals to try too!

Vegemite: A spread that Australians love!

Every trip to Australia includes a jar of vegemite on the breakfast table. You can't escape it.

It is a brownish paste that Australians spread on toast. They can also mix it into a pasta dish.

Vegemite has a salty taste. It is the little sister of Marmite (British version), made from leftover brewers' yeast extract with vegetables and spice.

A piece of advice: avoid spreading too much on your toast before tasting it!

The recipe has remained unchanged and secret for 100 years.

Nine out of ten Australians eat it, that's how rooted it is in their eating habits!

SYDNEY

How can one not fall in love with Sydney?
The sun shines every day, the people are beautiful, so welcoming and so cheerful!
It's almost impossible to be at a loss for things to do in Sydney; you'll always be up to something: you can take a ferry to Manly for the day, then come back to the city to see an amazing sunset over the Opera House and Harbour Bridge, have a coffee in front of the Opera House, take your surf board and go to Bondi beach, enjoy fireworks every Saturday in Darling Harbour or walk around the Chinese market. The cultural diversity in Sydney will make you feel at home. It is very easy to meet people, to be invited to an improvised barbie (barbecue) or join an organized tour.
40% of Sydneysiders are from abroad.
Australians will tell you: Sydney is a place where you feel safe.
Girls can wear short skirts or basically anything they want, and nobody will bother them in the street. You can even dye your hair blue and no-one will notice! Who cares!

Sydney has a vibrant economy and a stable job market, which is a great thing for WHV holders looking for a job.
Sydney has a population of over 5 million, but it's surrounded by national parks that offer a variety of activities such as rock climbing, sailing and paragliding.

SYDNEY | WHAT TO SEE / WHAT TO DO

Climbing the Sydney Harbour Bridge

Amazing views of Sydney Harbour! Climb one of the bridge pylons to reach the Pylon Lookout.
200 steps to reach 87 meters with 3 levels of exhibition that tell the story of the bridge.
If you are walking from the north, use the steps near Milsons Point Railway Station. At the top of the climb, enjoy the view of Sydney and the Opera House !

> **PYLON LOOKOUT AT SYDNEY HARBOUR BRIDGE**
> Cumberland Street, The Rocks | Tel: +61 2 9240 1100
> www.pylonlookout.com.au
> email: pylonlookout@bridgeclimb.com
> Open every day from 10am to 4pm.
> General Admission Price : AUD $19 per adult.

Visit the Sydney Opera House

Enter the Opera House with a guided tour during which the guide will tell you about the extraordinary history of the place, with images projected on the walls of the building.
The visit passes by at least one of the rooms where shows are organized daily (more than 1500 shows each year).

> **THE SYDNEY OPERA HOUSE TOUR**
> 2 Macquarie Street, Bennelong Point
> Tel: +61 2 9250 7111 / +61 2 9250 7777
> www.sydneyoperahouse.com
> email: infodesk@sydneyoperahouse.com
> General Admission Price : AUD $43 per adult (1 hour).
> There is also a backstage tour for AUD $175 (2 hours)

SYDNEY | WHAT TO SEE / WHAT TO DO

Walk around the Royal Botanic Garden

One of the main attractions of Sydney!
Walk to Macquarie Point for a great view of the Sydney Opera House and Harbour Bridge.
Follow the various signs to learn about the history of the Aboriginal people. Opera performances are also offered, with a great view of the Opera House.
A bubble of nature just a stone's throw from the hustle and bustle of the city.

> **The Royal Botanic Garden**
> Mrs Macquaries Road, CBD | Tel : +61 2 9231 8111
> www.rbgsyd.nsw.gov.au | email: feedback@rbgsyd.nsw.gov.au
> Open every day from 7am, closes between 5pm and 7.30pm depending on the season. Free admission.

Getting to Manly by ferry

Take the ferry from Circular Quay and embark for a 20-minute trip to Manly. We go to Manly to surf but also to walk on North Head Scenic Drive to the Bella Vista Café and its breathtaking view of Sydney.
The must is to take the ferry back at the end of the day for a sunset on the Opera House.

> **MANLY FAST FERRY**
> Circular Quay | Tel: +61 2 9583 1199
> Adult: AUD $10,20.
> www.myfastferry.com.au
> Running from 6.15am to 9.15pm.

68

SYDNEY | WHAT TO SEE / WHAT TO DO

Take a surfing lesson in Bondi

Whether you're new to surfing or experienced, head to Bondi, Sydney's surfing mecca.
The one kilometer long beach offers white sand and beautiful waves for a good surfing session. You will find many locals there enjoying this sport.

> **Lets Go Surfing**
> 128 Ramsgate Ave, North Bondi | Tel : +61 2 9365 1800
> https://letsgosurfing.com.au | email: info@letsgosurfing.com.au
> AUD $99 for a 2 hours class.

Have a drink in Darling Harbour

To enjoy Sydney's nightlife or watch the sunset, head to Darling Harbour. There are many bars, restaurants and nightclubs facing the harbour.

Every Saturday night, at 8:30 pm, you can admire the fireworks in the port.

Climb the Sydney Tower for a view

At 305 meters above sea level, in the heart of the business district (integrated into the Westfield shopping center), the Sydney Tower is the highest building in Sydney. It offers an impressive 360° view of the city and the harbour.
A panoramic observation deck at 260 meters high (Observation Deck) and outside (Skywalk).

> **SYDNEY TOWER EYE**
> Wesfield Sydney Shopping Centre, Pitt Street & Market Street
> Tel:1800 258 693 | Online adult admission: AUD $24,80 (with Skydesk: from AUD $82) | www.sydneytowereye.com.au
> Open every day from 9am to 9pm.

SYDNEY | ACCOMMODATION

Upon arrival: short-term accommodation

You will ideally have booked your accommodation for the first few days before your departure.

It is not an obligation but after a 20 hour flight, you may not feel like walking the streets of the city in search of the best hostel.

The easiest way is to book a few nights in your city of arrival, either in a youth hostel or an Airbnb.

Airbnb can be a good solution to have your own private room in a house for example and thus recover from jet lag for the first few days.

Going straight from your flight to a bed in a dormitory can be tough, but on the other hand, you'll be right in the swing of things!

The hostel will then allow you to meet people and to be able to check job offers locally.

The hostels are often very well positioned in the city center, which is obviously a strategic location if you are looking for a job in the city.

Couchsurfing

The reference website to stay for free with locals.

If you have an empty profile, are male and have few references, you will have little chance of being accommodated.

You can ask friends to give their opinion about you in the 'personal opinion' section.

It's a great place to meet locals and sleep on their couch for one or more nights.

In exchange for accommodation, you can, for example, prepare a meal for your host or buy them a drink in town!

Be careful to check the references of each host before asking them for accommodation.

www.couchsurfing.org

SYDNEY | ACCOMMODATION

Hostels

Sydney CBD

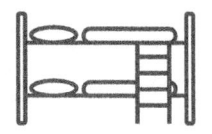

The YHA chain offers a card that you should seriously consider buying if you do a lot of the chain's hostels around Australia. It costs AUD $15 and will pay for itself very quickly.

Please note that the **Railway Square YHA** is temporarily closed for renovation until 2025/26.

Sydney Central YHA
Dormitory: From AUD $47.40.
Private room : From AUD $171.
11 Rawson Place, Angle Pitt St & Rawson Place (in front of the Central Station), Sydney 2000 | Tel: +61(0)2 9218 9000
www.yha.com.au

Wake Up Central
Dormitory: From AUD $54.
509 Pitt Street, Sydney, Australia 2000
Tel: +61(0) 2 9288 7888 | www.wakeup.com.au

Base Backpackers Sydney
Dormitory: From AUD $31
Private room : From AUD $91.
477 Kent Street, Sydney NSW
Tel: +61 (0)2 9267 7718
www.stayatbase.com

Big Backpackers Hostel
One of the cheapest hostels in town.
Dormitory: From AUD $35.
Private room from AUD $177.
212 Elizabeth St, Surry Hills NSW | Tel: +61 2 9281 6030
https://bighostel.com/

SYDNEY | ACCOMMODATION

Long-term accommodation

To find your room in Sydney, go to the following websites:
- Gumtree: https://www.gumtree.com.au
- Flatmates : https://flatmates.com.au
- Airbnb: https://www.airbnb.com
- Facebook groups:
  - https://www.facebook.com/groups/992280484129436 (Sydney - Houseshare / Flatshare / Room for Rent)
  - https://www.facebook.com/groups/817123101728406 (Sydney Houses, Rooms, Rentals)

To check the cost of living in Sydney, see page 25.
Below is a map with the average **monthly rents** by neighborhood. Prices are in Australian dollars.

THE JOB MARKET AND SALARY IN SYDNEY

Sydney is the number one destination for Working Holiday Visa holders. With about 220 000 - 250 000 young workers arriving in Australia every year, you can easily imagine what competition is like in the jobs market. It can be easier if you drive a few kilometres outside the city, look for jobs in the hospitality sector or in call centres and in fruit picking.

SYDNEY | WORK

For qualified jobs, you can maybe find something in IT or engineering. There are a lot of job offers on the internet.

It is not uncommon to hear someone say that he/ she found a job just by talking to the right person at the right moment.

So be brave and tell people that you are looking for a job. Creating a network in Sydney is your main asset in job hunting.

You will probably be told that most companies don't hire Working Holiday Visa holders, but don't let that stop you sending off your resume.
You never know!

It is not uncommon to meet people who have found a sponsor thanks to having a Working Holiday Visa, and who have managed to stay in Australia, so be opportunistic and get talking.

To avoid wasting your time and money when you arrive in Sydney, prepare your resume before coming.
(See page 40 for help with your resume/CV)

Sydney is the major economic hub of Australia, and its most populous city. It is home to a cosmopolitan and international population, Sydneysiders, as the people of Sydney are known, have the second highest earnings among major cities of the world. Living and working here is an exciting and fulfilling experience thanks to its international living standards, multi-cultural society, and splendid infrastructure.

Sydney is the most important port in the South Pacific, and therefore an important industrial centre, generating one third of all jobs in Australia. The following is the national percentage of employment provided by various sectors in Sydney:

Finance and insurance (7.4%), retail (10.7%), manufacturing (10.1%), professional and technical services (9.8%), health care and social assistance (10.1%), and education (7.6%).

SYDNEY | WORK

For a clearer idea of the companies which need people with your profile, get your qualification assessed and recognised by the appropriate authority in Australia:
www.homeaffairs.gov.au/trav/work/work/skills-assessment-and-assessing-authorities/skilled-occupations-lists

If you can secure a job in the foreign branch of an Australian company, that can be very convenient for you in Sydney.

Getting the assistance of an employment agent is another smart way of securing a job in Sydney. Before leaving for Australia, register with good employment agencies, and explain your requirements and qualifications to an agent.

Australia has its own standards in civil engineering and in the medical professions, so overseas job profiles in medicine and civil engineering might need to be approved by the Australian authorities.

Before turning up for any interview, make sure you've done your homework on the company. Learn as much as you can before the interview; this will not only help you in performing well but also in impressing the interviewers, and ultimately in helping you get the job.

Walk around the offices and ask if there are any openings, and leave your resume with the appropriate person.

If you are lucky, you will be invited to go through the selection process immediately; if not, you may be contacted later.

Many vacancies are not advertised, so go directly to the companies.

Go for it and don't hesitate to ask companies directly. If the job hasn't been posted, there won't be as many candidates to compete with!

You will give the company the impression that you are a go-getter, which will probably be highly appreciated.

The minimum wage is AUD $21.38/hour. However, the average wage is AUD $23.45/hour. This can rise to AUD $78.76/hour for a highly skilled job, such as a graphic designer.

SYDNEY | WORK

WEBSITES FOR FINDING A JOB

www.hays.com.au
This is a very popular site for international recruitment, and a good source for the latest job postings in Sydney.

www.infrontstaffing.com
This company is a specialist in the recruitment of workers for industries such as logistics, construction and warehousing.

https://www.experis.com.au/
Recruitment agency specialized in the technology sectors for permanent or temporary contracts.

www.citirecruitment.com
A popular recruiting site in the field of new technologies. The site also offers advice to employers on business intelligence.

www.workingin-australia.com
This is a very useful site that provides comprehensive information on important aspects of Australian life such as education, business, taxes and insurance. There is a section with job offers in health, marketing, IT, sales and advertising.

www.seek.com.au
This is a very informative site about employment. Here employers are required to declare the maximum and minimum salary for each job posting. The site uses this information to provide relevant posts based on the salary requirements and professional profile of each registered member.

SYDNEY | WORK

www.adecco.com.au
This is one of the most reliable HR organizations in the world, and it deals with a large number of employers and job hunters.

www.airtasker.com
These are one-time assignments offered by individuals.
For example, you can be asked to help carry a mattress for AUD $50 or to help with a move. You can apply for each mission by trying to sell yourself as much as possible.

INTERVIEW WITH DAVID : LANDING A JOB IN SYDNEY

David spent one year in Australia on a WHV.
He has been travelling around the world for about ten years and in this interview he explains how he found a job in Sydney.

Marie: How did your job hunting go in Sydney?
David: I was very lucky actually. I just put an ad on Gumtree !

Marie: What did you write in the ad?
David: It was a bit cheeky but simple. I said: 'Hi guys, I'm looking for a job, I am willing to do anything'. I was a bit scared of the answers I might receive, but this young 25-year-old entrepreneur called me. He was looking for a cook to work on a catamaran. And it all began like that. It was then around Christmas and the New Year, and I knew that most companies would be preparing something for the occasion, so I reckoned I would get a job as a cook. So I contacted caterers by email to ask if they needed anyone to work for their Christmas events. I told them that I had a bit of experience as a cook, including in Australia, and that I was available for work.

SYDNEY | WORK

Marie: So your technique was to send an application direct to companies. You also mentioned Gumtree. How did they help?

David: Well, when I arrived in Sydney, I didn't want to work as a cook at first. I had only planned to stay there for five weeks, and my target was to earn AUD $7000 in that time. So when I posted this ad on Gumtree, I said that I had some experience as a cook, but I put more emphasis on the fact that I was willing to be more flexible than my past work experiences.

I said that I was effective, I understood things quickly and that I liked a job well done. But In the end, it was the young guy who offered me the job as a cook who called me first. During that call, I thought 'well why not work as a cook?', and I started sending out unsolicited applications to various caterers. And it worked.
As I said before, I was very lucky, because sometimes I was offered so much work that I had to ask other cooks to step in for me.
So, it all worked out very well for me. I worked 7 days a week.

Over New Year in Sydney the pay is very good, because nobody wants to work. They pay the staff more to make sure they come to work. If the employer only pays AUD $200 or $300 for the evening, the staff might prefer to go partying instead of working.
So, if you work in Sydney over New Year, you can earn at least AUD $800 for the evening.

The guy who offered me the job on the catamaran booked me for New Year's Eve, so I didn't have to look for anything else!. But as I had sent out unsolicited applications in the meantime, I was offered lots of other opportunities to work over the New Year.

Marie: About the unsolicited job requests that you sent to companies. Did you go and see them personally, or did you do it all by email?

SYDNEY | WORK

David: I only sent my resume by email. I googled 'catering companies in Sydney', went on their websites, found the contact details and sent them a resume. And it worked very well. It was very interesting, but you do need to have a good dose of self-confidence and even cheek.

Marie: Really? Australians like people with cheek?
David: Not necessarily but they don't have time to waste, and you need to be self-confident enough to show them that you are flexible. They have to be able to trust you very quickly to do the job.

Marie: Did you do a trial before starting work?
David: They didn't have time! The first guy who called me for the catamaran just showed me the menu, where the food was and I started. But I wasn't alone; the other staff knew the job already so they showed me the ropes.
On another job, I worked in the kitchen for two weeks before going onto the boat.
They don't usually have time to try you out. They call you because one of their staff members hasn't shown up, so they give you the menu and you begin to work straight away. They have no choice. It's you or nobody.

Marie: Do you think it is easy to find a job in Sydney?
David: People say that it is easy to find work in catering, but I met some cooks in Sydney who couldn't get jobs. I arrived on November 30th, and on December 1st I was already working, but that's because I am very flexible, I negotiate and I'm a go-getter sort of person.
After a while in Sydney I had lots of contacts, and when I told some cooks to call an employer, they said: 'I'm not sure; maybe I'll call tomorrow'.

SYDNEY | WORK

I noticed that some people were maybe being too cautious, but I think that If you want something you have to go for it. But if you don't really know what you want, you'll just go round in circles.

I met a lot of hesitant people who wanted to know the size of the kitchen before applying!

I go to the trouble of visiting the place and meeting the manager, and then sometimes they offer me something and sometimes they don't.

Marie: How many resumes did you send out?

David: Hard to say... because I sent them out at different times. Fifteen in all I think, but they didn't all reply.

Marie: Fifteen is not that many.

David: No, it isn't. But I didn't only work as a cook. I worked in a tee-shirt factory, and I even helped a carpenter to build a roof. I was paid AUD $23 an hour.

Marie: And as a cook?

David: AUD $28. For Christmas, I was paid AUD $600 a day and for New Years Eve, AUD $800- $1000.

My objective was to get AUD $7000 in five weeks, so I didn't think too much and just got straight into action.

In five weeks, I only had four days off. I often got last minute jobs.

SYDNEY | WORK | THE RSA

LANDING A JOB QUICKLY IN HOSPITALITY

What is RSA and how do I get it in Sydney?
The RSA is a certificate that shows you know the rules about alcohol.

RSA: Responsible Service of Alcohol
This certificate is essential to work in an establishment that serves alcohol: bars, restaurants, hotels. You will be required to have it, so you might as well get it before you start looking for a job.
It is possible that an establishment will agree to hire you without the RSA but you will then have a one month delay to pass it.
So you may as well give yourself the best possible chance by being prepared!

The RSA is easily done online. Payment is made when you have successfully validated it. The price varies depending on the state.
Online: www.eot.edu.au/online-courses/RSA/australia/
Please note that in the state of New South Wales, you will have to choose the **AUD $129** option. This is the state where the certificate is the most expensive. The test takes a maximum of 3 to 6 hours.
If you are not sure if you are going to stay and work in Sydney and plan to visit several states during your WHV, you can opt to take the RSA that is valid in all states for AUD $183.

To find a job very quickly in Sydney, we advise you to send your CV in bulk to the hotel and restaurant listings in this guide.
Emailing will allow you to send your resume to hundreds of establishments in one or two mailing sessions.
If you want to customize your emails for each company, you can choose from the list here.
If you choose to email, here is the detailed method:

SYDNEY | WORK

The method for sending your CV to hundreds of companies

1- Create an account on MailChimp: www.login.mailchimp.com

2- On the "Audience" tab, go to "Add contacts" and "import contacts" then "copy/paste from the "Audience", go on "Add contacts" and "import contacts" then "copy/paste from file"

3- Open the following link: https://www.dropbox.com/sh/vrw9s7n1vwli84c/AAClygpD27_DEP3oked_3EcPa?dl=0 and download the file.

4- Copy/paste emails from the excel spreadsheet to MailChimp (be careful, you are limited to 1000 contacts. If you want to send more than 1000 emails, you will simply have to delete your contacts after your first sending and import the new ones).

5- Go to the "Create" tab, then "email". Name the campaign "Application". In the "To" section, choose the contact list you have created. In "From", indicate your name and your email address.

In the "Subject" section, indicate "Application for a job". In the "content" section, copy and paste the email you downloaded from Dropbox, adapting it to your background, and your name.

Don't forget to attach your resume or a link to your LinkedIn profile!

"Dear Hiring Manager,

Please accept my enthusiastic application for a position in your hotel (or restaurant). I am happy to offer you my experience in the food industry, strong customer service skills, and my ability to work under pressure.

I believe I fulfill all of these requirements and am therefore an excellent candidate for you.

I have an extensive background in hospitality. I worked for two years at a fast-food restaurant. During this time I gained experience in nearly every aspect of food service. I took orders and served customers their meals, handled the cash register, and performed daily inventory checks.

I could assist not only in taking orders and serving customers but also in a variety of other capacities in which you might require assistance. I also worked in customer service for a number of years. As a cashier at a grocery store for two years, I assisted as many as one hundred customers daily.

My experience in the food industry and in customer service, and my ability to thrive under pressure make me an excellent candidate for you. I have enclosed my resume and will call within the next week to see if we might arrange a time to speak together.

Thank you so much for your time and consideration.

Sincerely,

Your name"

> **The cover letter**
>
> The cover letter does not need to be very long but it should highlight your experience in a few lines.
>
> If you have no experience in the catering industry and your English is average, don't panic. Australians are usually happy to give beginners a chance.
>
> You should then emphasize your qualities in your letter but also in your CV (see page 40, how to write an Australian CV).

SYDNEY | WORK

Hotels in Sydney

QT BONDI
6 Beach Rd, Bondi Beach
+61 2 8362 3900
reservations_qtbondi@evt.com

The Chee Bondi
30-32 Hall St, Bondi Beach
+61 410 345 068
info@thecheebondi.com

The York by Swiss-Belhotel
5 York St
+61 2 9210 5000
restysb@swiss-belhotel.com

Veriu Central
75 Wentworth Ave
+61 1300 964 821
veriucentral@veriu.com.au

Veriu Broadway
35 Mountain St
+61 2 8379 7880
veriubroadway@veriu.com.au

Liv Apartments Haymarket
93-105 Quay St
+61 2 8937 2322
bookings@liv.apartments

The Branksome Hotel
60 Robey St, Mascot
+61 2 8338 3288
ben.chandwani
@thebranksome.com.au

The Urban Newtown
52-60 Enmore Rd, Newtown
+61 2 8960 7800
reservations@theurbanhotel.com.au

Regents Court Sydney
18 Springfield Ave
+61 2 9331 2099
info@regentscourtsydney.com.au

Excelsior Serviced apartments
101 Bridge Rd, Glebe
+61 2 9660 3040
info@excelsiorservicedapartments.com.au

APX World Square
2 Cunningham St
+61 2 9291 1900
sales@apxhotelsapartments.com

Meriton Suites Bondi Junction
97 Grafton St, Bondi Junction
+61 2 9277 1125
stay@meriton.net.au

Harbourside Apartments
2A Henry Lawson Ave
+61 2 9963 4300
stay@
harboursideapartments.com.au

Coogee Sands Hotel
161 Dolphin St, Coogee
+61 2 9665 8588
info@coogeesands.com.au

SYDNEY | WORK

Bondi 38 Serviced Apartments
38 Campbell Parade, Bondi
+61 409 946 313
reservations@bondi38.com.au

Zara Tower
61-65 Wentworth Ave
+61 2 8228 7659
bookings@zaratower.com.au

Adge Apartment Hotel
222 Riley St, Surry Hills
+61 2 8093 9888
concierge@adgehotel.com.au

Fraser Suites Sydney
488 Kent St, Sydney
+61 2 8823 8888
sales.sydney@frasershospitality.com

QT Sydney
49 Market St, Sydney
+61 2 8262 0000
media@evt.com

Mantra 2 Bond Street
Bond Street Cnr George St
+61 2 9250 9555
2bondst.res@mantra.com.au

Mantra on Kent
433 Kent St
+61 2 9284 2300
kent.res@mantra.com.au

Annam Serviced Apartments
21 Ward Ave, Potts Point
+61 2 9331 4633
admin@annamapartments.com.au

Amora Hotel Jamison Sydney
11 Jamison St
+61 2 9696 2500
res@sydney.amorahotels.com

Primus Hotel Sydney
339 Pitt St
+61 02 8027 8000
hr@primushotelsydney.com

Sydney Harbour B&B
140-142 Cumberland St
+61 2 9247 1130
stay@bbsydneyharbour.com.au

The Old Clare Hotel
1 Kensington St
+61 2 8277 8277
email@theoldclarehotel.com.au

DD Apartments on Broadway
16-18 Broadway, Ultimo
+61455595559
hello@ddapartments.com.au

1831 Boutique Hotel
631-635 George St
+61 2 9265 8888
sydney@1831.com.au

SYDNEY | WORK

Astra Parramatta
140 Church St
+61299682401
mike.kring@astraapartments.com.au

Astra North Sydney
Angelo St, North Sydney
+611300797321
nthsyd@astraapartments.com.au

Astra Sydney CBD
3 Hosking Pl
+61411230099
sydneycbd@astraapartments.com.au

Astra Penrith
Aviators Way, Penrith
+61421112408
rener@astraapartments.com.au

Swissôtel Sydney
68 Market St, Sydney
+61 2 9238 8888
sydney@swissotel.com

Grace Building
77 York St, Sydney
+61 2 9272 6888
grace@gracehotel.com.au

Pullman Sydney Hyde Park
36 College St
+61 2 9361 8400
H8763@accor.com

Harbour Rocks Hotel
34 Harrington St
+61 2 8220 9999
H8758@accor.com

The Sebel Quay West
98 Gloucester St
+61 2 9240 6000
reservations_H8764@accorpacific.net

Rendez vous Hotel Sydney
75 Harrington St
+61 2 9251 6711
reservations@tfehotels.com

Hyatt Regency Sydney
161 Sussex St
+61 2 8099 1234
sydney.regency@hyatt.com

Sofitel Darling Harbour
12 Darling Dr
+61 2 8388 8888
H9729-SM2@sofitel.com

Shangri-La Hotel Sydney
176 Cumberland St
+61 2 9250 6000
recruitment@shangri-la.com

Sir Stamford Circular Quay
93 Macquarie St
+61 2 9252 4600
reservations@stamford.com.au

SYDNEY | WORK

Sheraton on the Park
161 Elizabeth St
✆ +61 2 9286 6000
✉ sheratononthepark@sheraton.com

InterContinental Sydney
117 Macquarie St
✆ +61 2 9253 9000
✉ intercontinental.sydney@ihg.com

Four Seasons Hotel Sydney
199 George St, The Rocks
✆ +61 2 9250 3100
✉ helen.radic@fourseasons.com

Holiday Inn
203 Victoria St, Potts Point
✆ +61 2 9368 4000
✉ holidayinnoldsydney@ihg.com

Hilton Sydney
488 George St
✆ +61 2 9266 2000
✉ sydney@hilton.com

The Fullerton Hotel Sydney
1 Martin Pl, Sydney
✆ +61 2 8223 1111
✉ fsy.talent@fullertonhotels.com

Hyatt Sydney park
7 Hickson Rd, The Rocks
✆ +61 2 9256 1234
✉ sydney.park@hyatt.com

PARKROYAL Darling Harbour
150 Day St
✆ +61 2 9261 1188
✉ gm.prsyd@parkroyalhotels.com

Langham Sydney
89-113 Kent St
✆ +61 2 9256 2222
✉ tlsyd.info@langhamhotels.com

Ovolo 1888 Darling Harbour
139 Murray St, Pyrmont
✆ +61 2 8586 1888
✉ 1888@ovolohotels.com

Hotel Bondi
178 Campbell Parade, Bondi
✆ +61 2 9130 3271
✉ reception@hotelbondi.com.au

SKYE Hotel Suites
30 Hunter St, Parramatta
✆ +61 2 7803 2388
✉ info@skyehotels.com.au

The Darling at the Star
80 Pyrmont St, Pyrmont
✆ +61 2 9777 9000
✉ starreservations@star.com.au

CKS Sydney Airport
35 Levey St, Wolli Creek
✆ +61 2 9556 1555
✉ cksreservations@ckssydneyairport.com.au

SYDNEY | WORK

Dive Hotel
234 Arden St, Coogee
+61 2 9665 5538
info@divehotel.com.au

Manly Paradise Motel
54 N Steyne, Manly
+61 2 9977 5799
enquiries@manlyparadise.com.au

Glenferrie Lodge
12 Carabella St, Kirribilli
+61 2 9955 1685
mail@glenferrielodge.com

Ryals Hotel - Broadway
253 Broadway, Glebe
+61 2 9640 6888
camperdown@ryalsapartments.com.au

57Hotel
57 Foveaux St, Surry Hills
+61 2 9011 5757
57@57hotel.com.au

Macleay Hotel
28 MacLeay St, Elizabeth Bay
+61 2 9357 7755
mail@themacleay.com

The Royal Hotel
370 Abercrombie St Darlington
+612 9698 8557
admin@royal.com.au

The Sydney Boulevard Hotel
90 William St
+61 2 9383 7222
admin@sydneyboulevard.com.au

Nesuto Woolloomooloo
88 Dowling St, Woolloomooloo
+61 2 8356 1500
reception.woolloomooloo@nesuto.com

Value Suites Green Square
16 O'Riordan St, Alexandria
+61 2 9699 9666
bookingsgs@valuesuites.com.au

Value Suites Penrith
Billington Pl Emu Plains
+61 22 4735 4433
penrith@valuesuites.com.au

Royal Exhibition Hotel
86-88 Chalmers St, Surry Hills
+61 2 9698 2607
functions@royalexhibition.com.au

Radisson Hotel & Suites
72 Liverpool St, Sydney
+61 2 8268 8888
rebecca.wheeler@radisson-sydney.com.au

Radisson Blu Plaza Hotel
27 O'Connell St, Sydney
+61 2 8214 0000
res.sydplaza@radisson.com

SYDNEY | WORK

Larmont Sydney
2/14 Kings Cross Rd Potts Point
+61 2 9295 8888
info@larmontsydney.com.au

Randwick Lodge
211 Avoca St, Randwick
+61 2 9310 0700
randwick@sydneylodges.com

Big Hostel Sydney
212 Elizabeth St, Surry Hills
+61 2 9281 6030
reception@bighostel.com

Mariners Court Hotel
44-50 McElhone St
+61 2 9320 3888
reservations@marinerscourt.com.au

Wake Up Sydney
509 Pitt St
+61 2 9288 7888
david.draffin@wakeup.com.au

Sydney Harbour YHA
110 Cumberland St, The Rocks
+61 2 8272 0900
sydneyharbour@yha.com.au

Sydney Railway Station YHA
8-10 Lee St
+61 2 9281 9666
railway@yha.com.au

Vulcan Hotel
500 Wattle St, Ultimo
+61 2 9211 3283
info@vulcanhotel.com.au

Great Southern Hotel
717 George St
+61 2 9289 4400
reservations
@greatsouthernhotel.com.au

Hyde Park Inn
271 Elizabeth St, Sydney
+61 2 9264 6001
enquiries@hydeparkinn.com.au

Megaboom City Hotel
93 York St
+61 2 9996 8888
sales@megaboomhotel.com.au

MGSM Executive Hotel
99 Talavera Rd
+61 2 9850 9300
reception.hotel@mgsm.edu.au

The Charrington of Chatswood
22 Centennial Ave, Chatswood
+61 2 9419 8461
enquiries@charringtonhotel.com

Castlereagh Boutique Hotel
169 Castlereagh St
+61 2 9284 1000
reservations
@thecastlereagh.com.au

SYDNEY | WORK

McLaren Hotel
25 McLaren St, North Sydney
+61 2 9965 9500
admin@pacrimhotels.com.au

Neutral Bay Lodge
45 Kurraba Rd, Neutral Bay
+61 2 9953 4199
bookings@neutralbaylodge.com.au

Hotel Urban
194 Pacific Highway
+61 2 9439 6000
stay@hotelurbanstleonards.com.au

North Sydney Harbourview
17 Blue St, North Sydney
+61 2 9955 0499
enquiries@viewhotels.com

Coogee Bay Hotel
253 Coogee Bay Rd, Coogee
+61 2 9665 0000
info@coogeebayhotel.com.au

Morgans Boutique Hotel
304 Victoria St, Darlinghurst
+61 2 8354 3444
info@morganshotel.com.au

Silkari Suites at Chatswood
88 Archer St, Chatswood
+61 2 8188 1818
hello@silkarihotels.com.au

Avonmore on the Park
34 The Avenue, Randwick
+61 2 9399 9388
info@avonmoreonthepark.com.au

Crowne Plaza Coogee
242 Arden St, Coogee
+61 2 9315 7600
reservations.crowneplazacoogee@ihg.com

The Sebel Sydney Chatswood
37 Victor St, Chatswood
+61 2 9414 1600
H8800-GM@accor.com

Holiday Inn Sydney Airport
O'Riordan Street & Bourke Rd
+61 2 9330 0600
holidayinnsydneyairport@ihg.com

Pier One Sydney Harbour
Walsh Bay, 11 Hickson Rd
+61 2 8298 9999
AffiliateManager@marriott.com

Darcys Hotel
2 Abbotsford Rd, Homebush
+61 2 9746 3663
info@darcyshotel.com.au

Watsons Bay Boutique Hotel
1 Military Rd, Watsons Bay
+61 2 9337 5444
info@watsonsbayboutiquehotel.com.au

SYDNEY | WORK

East Sydney Hotel
Cnr Crown &, Cathedral St
+61 2 9358 1975
bookings@eastsydneyhotel.com

The Hughenden Boutique Hotel
14 Queen St, Woollahra
+61 2 9363 4863
reservations@thehughenden.com.au

The Hills Lodge Grand Mercure
1 Salisbury Rd, Castle Hill
+61 2 9680 3800
bookings@hillslodge.com.au
Belinda@hillslodge.com.au

Novotel Sydney Rockford Darling Harbour
17 Little Pier St, Darling Harbour
+61 2 8217 4000
H3021@accor.com

Pullman at Sydney Olympic Park
9 Olympic Blvd, Sydney Olympic Park
+61 2 8762 1700
h6411@accor.com

Pullman Quay Grand Sydney Harbour
61 Macquarie St, Sydney
+61 2 9256 4000
H8779@accor.com

Hotel Sofitel Wentworth
61-101 Phillip St
+61 2 9228 9188
h3665@sofitel.com

The Sebel Manly
8/13 S Steyne, Manly
+61 2 9977 8866
res.sebelmanly@accorvacationclub.com.au

Pullman Sydney Airport
191 O'Riordan St, Mascot
+61 2 8398 4600
H9522@accor.com
marco.warren@accor.com

Novotel Sydney Central
169-179 Thomas St, Sydney
+61 2 9281 6888
H8781@accor.com

Novotel Manly Pacific
55 N Steyne, Manly
+61 2 9977 7666
h5462@accor.com

Novotel Olympic Park
11a Olympic Blvd, Sydney
+61 2 8762 1111
H2732@accor.com

Novotel Sydney Parramatta
350 Church St, Parramatta
+61 2 9630 4999
H8787@accor.com

SYDNEY | WORK

Mercure Penrith
Mulgoa Rd, Penrith
+61 2 4721 7700
h9877@accor.com

MERCURE SYDNEY
818-820 George St, Chippendale
+61 2 9217 6666
H2073@accor.com

Novotel Sydney International Airport
22 Levey St, Wolli Creek
+61 29518 2000
H5603@accor.com

Mercure Sydney Parramatta
106 Hassall St, Rosehill
+61 2 8836 1000
H2123@accor.com

IBIS SYDNEY AIRPORT
205 O'Riordan St, Mascot
+61 2 8339 8500
H3058@accor.com

IBIS DARLING HARBOUR
70 Murray St, Pyrmont
+61 2 9563 0888
H1757@accor.com

IBIS KING STREET WHARF
22 Shelley St, Sydney
+61 2 8045 0000
h6412-re01@accor.com

IBIS SYDNEY OLYMPIC PARK
11 Olympic Blvd, Sydney Olympic Park
+61 28762 1100
H2734@accor.com

IBIS SYDNEY WORLD SQUARE
382/384 Pitt St, Sydney
+61 2 8267 3111
h2132@accor.com

IBIS BUDGET SYDNEY AIRPORT
191-201 William St, Darlinghurst
+61 29326 0300
H5675@ACCOR.COM

IBIS BUDGET SYDNEY OLYMPIC PARK
8 Edwin Flack Ave, Sydney
+61 2 9648 3862
h6582-re@accor.com

Arts Hotel
21 Oxford St, Paddington
+61 2 9361 0211
res@artshotel.com.au

SYDNEY | WORK

French restaurants in Sydney

La guillotine
518 Kent St
+61 2 9264 1487
laguill@bigpond.com

HUBERT
15 Bligh St
+61 2 9232 0881
pastis@restauranthubert.com

Four Frogs
1 Macquarie Pl
+61 2 9241 2277
info@fourfrogs.com.au

Bistro Papillon
98 Clarence St
+61 2 9262 2402
bonjour@bistropapillon.com.au

The little Snail restaurant
3/50 Murray St, Pyrmont
+61 2 9212 7512
restaurant@thelittlesnail.com.au

Bistro Moncur
116A Queen St, Woollahra
+61 2 9327 9713
reservations@bistromoncurmosman.com.au

Claires Kitchen
35 Oxford St, Surry Hills
+61 2 9283 1891
marc@claireskitchen.com.au

Bistro Rex
50 Macleay St, Potts Point
+61 2 8045 0000
hello@bistrorex.com.au

Macleay St Bistro
73A MacLeay St, Potts Point
+61 2 9358 4891
reservations@macleaystbistro.com.au

Felix
2 Ash St
+61 2 9114 7303
feedback@merivale.com

Bistro St Jacques
96 Pitt St, Redfern
+61478705704
info@bistrostjacques.com.au

Loluk Bistro
2/411 Bourke St, Surry Hills
+61 2 7900 6251
manager@loluk.com.au

Atelier by Sofitel
Level 3, 12 Darling Drive
+61 2 8388 8888
atelier.sydney@sofitel.com

Le Petit Flot
97 Pitt St
+61 2 8222 1270
info@lepetitflot.com

SYDNEY | WORK

Le Coq Healthy Rotisserie
758 Darling St, Rozelle
📞 +61 2 9818 4333
✉ lecoqrotisserie@gmail.com

Frenchies Brasserie
3/54 Kalang Rd, Elanora Heights
📞 +61 2 9907 2528
✉ facebook@frenchiesbrasserie.com.au

Bronte Road Bistro
280 Bronte Rd, Waverley
📞 +61 2 9389 3028
✉ bronteroadbistro@gmail.com

Brasserie l'Entrecôte
1047 Pacific Hwy, Pymble
📞 +61 2 8021 2433
✉ resv@brasserielentrecote.com.au

Quartier Sydney
98 Gloucester St, The Rocks
📞 +61 2 9240 6036
✉ quartier.sydney@accor.com

The Rendez Vous Crepe
Lower Ground, 271 Pitt St
📞 +61451164833
✉ therendezvouscrepes@gmail.com

Chez Pascal
440 Rocky Point Rd
📞 +61 2 9529 5444
✉ chezpascal440@gmail.com

Sous le Soleil
60A Clanville Rd, Roseville
📞 +61 2 9880 8816
✉ INFO@SLSHOME.COM.AU

Bistro Cocotte
78 Ramsay St, Haberfield
📞 +61 2 8964 1301
✉ bistrococotte@gmail.com

Saveur Restaurant
11 Hill Street, Roseville
📞 +61 2 9412 3999
✉ admin@saveur.com.au

Bistro Boulevard
40 Avalon Parade, Avalon Beach
📞 +61 2 9918 8933
✉ eat@bistroboulevard.com.au

Bistro Vatel
188 Lyons Rd, Drummoyne
📞 +61 2 9181 3961
✉ eat@vatelrestaurant.com.au

Bistro Mosman
76 Middle Head Rd, Mosman
📞 +61 2 8287 2968
✉ dine@bistromosman.com.au

Garden Court Restaurant
61/101 Phillip St
📞 +61 2 9228 9188
✉ h3665@sofitel.com

SYDNEY | WORK

Rustic French Bistro
Shop 1/87-95 Victoria St, Potts Point
+61 2 9184 7948
info@rusticfrench.com.au

Métisse Restaurant
5-9 Roslyn St, Potts Point
+61 2 8590 7698
metisse@metisse.com.au

Creperie Suzette
34 Harrington St, The Rocks
+61 2 8220 9999
h8758-fb@accor.com

Frenchies Bistro and Brewery
6/61-71 Mentmore Ave, Rosebery
+61 2 8964 3171
contact@frenchiesbistroandbrewery.com.au

Gavroche
1/2-10 Kensington St, Chippendale
+61 2 9281 6668
reservations@gavroche.com.au

The Naked Duck
Shop 4, 175 Liverpool St
+61 2 9267 8010
hydepark@thenakedduck.com.au

The Little French Patisserie
840 Military Rd, Mosman
+61 29969 4599
info@tlfp.com.au

French Fare Catering
+61425362583
raphael@frenchfare.com.au

Bitton Cafe & Restaurant
36/37A Copeland St, Alexandria
+61 2 9519 5111
info@bittongourmet.com.au

Franca Brasserie
2/81 MacLeay St, Potts Point
+61 2 9167 2921
hello@francabrasserie.com.au

The Local Bar
161 Castlereagh St
+61 2 9269 0050
161castlereaghst@thelocalbar.com.au

La Renaissance Patisserie
47 Argyle St, The Rocks
+61 2 9241 4878
orders@larenaissance.com.au

Kittyhawk
16 Phillip Ln
+61455041172
info@thekittyhawk.com.au

François Artisan Baker
91 Bondi Rd, Bondi
+61 2 8403 4014
info@francoisartisanbaker.com

SYDNEY | WORK

Australian restaurants in Sydney

Aria Restaurant Sydney
1 Macquarie St
📞 +61 2 9240 2255
✉ ariasydney@solotel.com.au

Botanic House
1 Mrs Macquaries Rd
📞 1300558980
✉ hello@botanichouse.com.au

Bentley Restaurant + Bar
27 O'Connell St
📞 +61 2 8214 0505
✉ info@thebentley.com.au

nel. Restaurant
75 Wentworth Ave
📞 +612 9212 2206
✉ info@nelrestaurant.com.au

Ester Restaurant
46-52 Meagher St
📞 +61 2 8068 8279
✉ esterrestaurant@gmail.com

O Bar and Dining
264, level 47 George St
📞 +61 2 9247 9777
✉ events@obardining.com.au

Blackbird Cafe
Level 1, Cockle Bay Wharf
Darling Harbour
📞 +61 2 9283 7385
✉ blackbird@blackbirdcafe.com.au

Cafe Sydney
31 Alfred St
📞 +61 2 9251 8683
✉ reservations@cafesydney.com

The Ternary
100 Murray St, Pyrmont
📞 +61 2 9934 0000
✉ theternary.sydney@accor.com

Kingsleys Australian Steakhouse
29a King St, Sydney
📞 +61 2 9295 5080
✉ info@kingsleysauststeak.com.au

Seans
270 Campbell Parade, North Bondi
📞 +61431133352
✉ help@resy.com

The Canopy
1/157 Liverpool St
📞 +61 2 9264 3007
✉ canopy@thecanopy.com.au

Gowings Bar & Grill
1/49 Market St
📞 +61 2 8262 0062
✉ host_gowings@evt.com

NOMAD
16 Foster Street, Surry Hills
📞 +61 2 9280 3395
✉ eat@nomad.sydney

SYDNEY | WORK

TreeHouse Hotel
60 Miller St, North Sydney
📞 +61 2 8458 8980
✉ info@thetreehousehotel.com.au

glass brasserie
level 2/488 George St
📞 +61 2 9265 6068
✉ glass.sydney@hilton.com

The Law Society of NSW
Level 2/170 Phillip St
📞 +61 2 9926 0224
✉ recruitment@lawsociety.com.au

Ripples Milsons Point
1 Olympic Drive, Milsons Point
📞 +61 2 9929 7722
✉ careers@sydneyrestaurantgroup.com.au

Catalina Restaurant
Lyne Park, New South Head Rd, Rose Bay
📞 +61 2 9371 0555
✉ reservations@catalinarosebay.com.au

Rockpool Bar & Grill
66 Hunter St
📞 +61 2 8099 7077
✉ Apply directly on the website
www.rockpooldininggroup.com.au

Barangaroo House
35 Barangaroo Ave, Barangaroo
📞 +61 2 8587 5400
✉ barangaroohouse@solotel.com.au

Bennelong Restaurant
Bennelong Point Sydney Opera
📞 +61 2 9240 8000
✉ Apply directly on the website
www.finkgroup.com.au/sector/restaurant/

Strangers' Restaurant
6 Macquarie St
📞 +61 2 9230 2124
✉ sales.catering@parliament.nsw.gov.au

Pony Dining The Rocks
Cnr Argyle Street & Kendall Ln, The Rocks
📞 +61 2 9252 7797
✉ recruitment@ponydining.com.au

City Extra 24 Hour
E4 East Podium
Between Wharf 3 & 4
📞 +61 2 9241 1422
✉ eat@cityextra.com.au

Chophouse Sydney
25 Bligh St
📞 +61 2 9231 5516
✉ chophousesydney@solotel.com.au

The Bucket List
Bondi Pavilion, Shop, 1 Queen Elizabeth Dr, Bondi Beach
📞 +61 2 9365 4122
✉ sarah@thebucketlistbondi.com

SYDNEY | WORK

80 Bar & Cafe
Building 8/28/14 Ultimo Rd, Ultimo
📞 +61 2 9280 4212
✉ hello@cafe80.com.au

The Apollo Restaurant
44 MacLeay St, Potts Point
📞 +61 2 8354 0888
✉ enquiries@theapollo.com.au

Planar Restaurant
ICC Sydney, Shop C08, Ground Floor/14
📞 +61 2 9212 6789
✉ info@planarrestaurant.com.au

Settlement On Quay
33 Alfred St
📞 +61 2 9241 4010
✉ info@settlementonquay.com

Eastbank Cafe.bar.pizzeria
61-69 Macquarie St
📞 +61 2 9241 6722
✉ info@eastbank.com.au

Q Dining
61 Macquarie St
📞 +61 2 9256 4000
✉ qdining.sydney@accor.com

Silvester's
1 Bulletin Pl
📞 +61 2 9259 7330
✉ mhrs.sydmc.silvesters@marriotthotels.com

The Fenwick
2-8 Weston St, Balmain East
📞 +61 2 9159 4700
✉ reservations@thefenwick.com.au

Portside Sydney Opera House
Western Broadwalk Sydney Opera
📞 +61 2 9250 7220
✉ reservations@portsidesydney.com.au

Boilerhouse Restaurant & Bar
1 N Head Scenic Dr, Manly
📞 +61 2 9466 1511
✉ H8773@accor.com

Roll'd Australia Square
4/264 George St
📞 +61 2 9247 8725
✉ info@rolld.com.au

Mazzaro Restaurant
271-279 Elizabeth St
📞 +61 2 9267 0605
✉ mazzaro3@bigpond.com

Kitchen by Mike CBD
1/7 Bent St
📞 +61 2 9252 5550
✉ info@kitchenbymike.com.au

Altitude
176 Cumberland St
📞 +61 2 9250 6000
✉ Apply on this link:
http://www.shangri-la.com/sydney/shangrila/contact-us/email-us/

SYDNEY | WORK

Steersons Steakhouse
17 Lime St
+61 2 9295 5060
functions@steersons.com.au

Fix Wine Bar + Restaurant
111 Elizabeth St
+61 2 9232 2767
reservations@fixwine.com.au

Sails on Lavender Bay
2 Henry Lawson Ave, McMahons Point
+61 2 9955 5998
Info@sailslavenderbay.com

GRAZE MCA
140 George St, The Rocks
+61 2 9245 2452
grazemca@grazemca.com.au

Barzura
62 Carr St, Coogee
+61 2 9665 5546
barzura@barzura.com.au

Summer Salt Restaurant
66 Mitchell Rd, Cronulla
+61 2 9523 2366
info@summersalt.com.au

The Australian Heritage
100 Cumberland St, The Rocks
+61 2 9247 2229
info@australianheritagehotel.com

Cafe Paci
131 King St, Newtown
+61 2 9550 6196
info@cafepaci.com.au

The Australian Club
165 Macquarie St
+61 2 9229 0400
reception@australianclub.org

The Dining Room
7 Hickson Rd, The Rocks
+61 2 9256 1661
phsydney.diningroom@hyatt.com

Sixpenny
83 Percival Rd, Stanmore
+61 2 9572 6666
info@sixpenny.com.au

Memento Bar and Bistro
2 Bond St
+61 2 9250 9661
memento@mantra.com.au

The Local Eatery
1/127 Kent St, Millers Point
+61 2 9251 1011
info@casadelvino.com.au

The Farmhouse
4/40 Bayswater Rd, Rushcutters Bay
+61448413791
eat@farmhousekingscross.com.au

SYDNEY | WORK

Caffe Amici
1/355 Kent St
+61 2 9279 0953
info@caffeamici.com.au

Drake Eatery
Curlewis St &, Gould St, Bondi Beach
+61 2 9130 3218
hello@drakeeatery.com.au

Fish at the Rocks
29 Kent St
+61 2 9252 4614
reservations@fishattherocks.com.au

Bathers' Pavilion
4 The Esplanade, Mosman
+61 2 9969 5050
eat@batherspavilion.com.au

Wild Sage
Shop 17 & 18, Stocklands
+61 2 9929 8455
dine@wildsage.com.au

The Gantry Restaurant
11 Hickson Rd, Walsh Bay
+61 2 8298 9910
info@thegantry.com.au

Chunoma109 Cafe
109 Glebe Point Rd, Glebe
+61 2 8541 7302
chunoma109@gmail.com

Public Dining Room
2A The Esplanade, Mosman
+61 2 9968 4880
chef@publicdiningroom.com.au

Automata Restaurant
5 Kensington St, Chippendale
+61 2 8277 8555
info@automata.com.au

LuMi Bar and Dining
56 Pirrama Rd, Pyrmont
+61 2 9571 1999
INFO@LUMIDINING.COM

Harry's Café
shop 4/14 Darling Dr
+61 2 9211 7294
enquiries@harryscafedewheels.com.au

Arthur Surry Hills
544 Bourke St, Surry Hills
+61468991088
hello@arthurrestaurant.com

Walsh Bay Kitchen
22 Hickson Rd, Walsh Bay
1300368801
hello@walshbaykitchen.com.au

Estuary Restaurant and Bar
1420 Pacific Hwy, Brooklyn
+61 2 9985 7881
events.estuaryrestaurant@gmail.com

SYDNEY | WORK

Rose of Australia
1 Swanson St, Erskineville
📞 +61 2 9565 1441
✉ enquiries@roseofaustralia.com

love.fish
7/23 Barangaroo Avenue,
Wulugul Walk, Barangaroo
📞 +61 2 8077 3700
✉ eat@lovefish.com.au

Cafe Birkenhead
19 Roseby St, Drummoyne
📞 +61 2 9181 4339
✉ eat@cafebirkenhead.com.au

Brew Bros Licenced Eatery
252 Sussex St
📞 +61 2 9261 2829
✉ david@brewbros.net.au

Zest Kitchen
City Tattersalls Club, 198 Pitt St
📞 +61 2 9267 9421
✉ functions@citytatts.com.au

Lachlan's Old Government House
Parramatta Park Cnr Pitt St &, Macquarie St
📞 +61 2 9687 2662
✉ Apply directly on the website: www.lachlans.com.au/employment/

The Pantry Manly
Ocean Promenade, N Steyne, Manly
📞 +61 2 9977 0566
✉ info@thepantrymanly.com

6HEAD
7-27 Circular Quay W, The Rocks
📞 +61 2 8629 8866
✉ sydney@6head.com.au

Yellow
57 MacLeay St, Potts Point
📞 +61 2 9332 2344
✉ kitchen@thebentley.com.au

Bopp & Tone
60 Carrington St
📞 +61 2 9299 9997
✉ info@boppandtone.com.au

Helm Bar & Bistro
Aquarium Wharf, 7 Wheat Rd
📞 +61 2 9290 1571
✉ bookings@helmbar.com.au

Rubyos Restaurant
18-20 King St, Newtown
📞 +61 2 9557 2669
✉ enquiries@rubyos.com.au

Manta Restaurant
6/6 Cowper Wharf Roadway, Woolloomooloo
📞 +61 2 9332 3822
✉ reservations@mantarestaurant.com.au

SYDNEY | WORK

Greenwood Hotel
36 Blue St, North Sydney
+61 2 9964 9477
drink@greenwoodhotel.com

Four Ate Five
485 Crown St, Surry Hills
+61 2 9698 6485
info@fouratefive.com

North Bondi Fish
120 Ramsgate Ave, North Bondi
+61 2 9130 2155
hello@northbondifish.com.au

Mercado
4 Ash St
+61 2 9221 6444
employment@mercadorestaurant.com.au

Charcoal Fish
670 New South Head Road, Rose Bay
hello@charcoalfish.com

Ursula's
92 Hargrave Street, Paddington
0499 525 235
info@ursulas.com.au

Woodcut
Crown Sydney, Level 1/1 Barangaroo Ave, Barangaroo
+61 2 8871 7171
Apply directly at the restaurant, in person.

Avenue on Chifley
2 Chifley Square
+61 2 9221 7599
info@avenueonchifley.com.au

Mode Kitchen & Bar
199 George Street Ground Floor
+61 2 9250 3160
hello@modekitchenandbar.com.au

Harbour Bar & Kitchen
2-10 Darling Drive, Darling Harbour
+61 2 9280 2029
dine@harbourbarandkitchen.com.au

I'm Angus Steakhouse
T.109 Cockle Bay Wharf
1 300 989 989
restaurant@imangussteakhouse.com.au

Baba's Place
20 Sloane St, Marrickville
+61 2 9090 2925
info@babasplace.com.au

Margaret
30-36 Bay St, Double Bay
+61 2 9068 8888
info@margaretdoublebay.com

Firedoor
23-33 Mary Street, Surry Hills
02 8204 0800
info@firedoor.com.au

SYDNEY | WORK

Bars in Sydney

Papa Gede's Bar
348 Kent St
📞 +61 2 9299 5671
✉ drink@papagedes.com

The Lobo Plantation
1/209 Clarence St
✉ info@thelobo.com.au

The Baxter Inn
152-156 Clarence St
✉ pretzels@thebaxterinn.com

Ramblin Rascal Tavern
199 Elizabeth St
✉ bailey@ramblinrascal.com

PS40
40 King St Enter, Skittle Ln
✉ bookings@ps40bar.com

Palmer & Co
Abercrombie Ln
📞 +61 292643004
✉ drinks@grandmasbarsydney.com.au

Burrow Bar
Basement/96 Clarence St
📞 +61450466674
✉ curious@burrowbar.com.au

The Duke of Clarence
Laneway, 152, 156 Clarence St
📞 +61 2 8999 3850
✉ contact@thedukeofclarence.com

Employees Only
9a Barrack St
📞 +61 2 8084 7490
✉ info@employeesonlysyd.com

Old Mates Place
level 4/199 Clarence St
✉ seeyou@oldmates.sydney

Stitch Bar
61 York St
📞 +61 2 9279 0380
Apply directly on the website :
www.houseofpocket.com.au/careers

The Swinging Cat
44 King St
📞 +61458145394
✉ info@theswingingcat.com

The Rook
level 7/56-58 York St
📞 +61 2 8322 2008
✉ info@therook.com.au

Shady Pines Saloon
4/256 Crown St, Darlinghurst
📞 +61405624944
✉ peanuts@shadypinessaloon.com

Hyde Hacienda
61 Macquarie St
📞 +61 2 9256 4083
✉ bookings@hydehaciendasydney.com

SYDNEY | WORK

Cantina OK!
Council Pl
✉ happy@cantinaok.com.au

Mojo Record Bar
73 York St
📞 +61 2 9262 4999
✉ dan@mojorecordbar.com

Uncle Mings
Basement 49 York St
✉ info@unclemings.com.au

Door Knock
Basement 70 Pitt St
✉ knockknock@doorknock.com.au

Blu Bar on 36
176 Cumberland St
✉ dine.slsn@shangri-la.com

Jacoby's Tiki Bar
154 Enmore Rd
✉ info@jacobys-tiki-bar.com

Cheers Bar
561 George St
Apply directly on the website:
https://cheersbar.com.au/careers

The Doss House
77/79 George St
📞 +61457880180
✉ info@thedosshouse.com.au

Tio's Cerveceria
4/14 Foster St, Surry Hills
✉ kieran@tios.com.au

Highlander Whisky Bar
93 Macquarie St
📞 +61 2 9252 4600
✉ helenxu@stamford.com.au

O Bar and Dining
264, level 47 George St
📞 +61 2 9247 9777
✉ events@obardining.com.au

The Wild Rover
75 Campbell St, Surry Hills
📞 +61 2 9280 2235
✉ drinks@thewildrover.com.au

The Cidery Bar & Kitchen
389 Pitt St
📞 +61 2 8268 1888
✉ sales_worldsquare@evt.com

Alleyway
shop 3/200 George St
📞 +61 2 8964 5727
✉ info@avenuegroup.com.au

Continental Deli Bar Bistro
210 Australia St, Newtown
📞 +61 2 8624 3131
✉ enquiries@continentaldelicatessen.com.au

SYDNEY | WORK

Assembly Bar & Restaurant
488 Kent St
+61 2 9261 0552
reservations@assemblybar.com.au

Grain
199 George St
+61 2 9250 3118
hello@grainbar.com.au

Zeta Bar
level 4/488 George St
+61 2 9265 6070
zetaenquiries.sydney@hilton.com

Dear Sainte Éloise
5/29 Orwell St Potts Point
+61 2 9326 9745
hello@dearsainteeloise.com

Marble Bar
Level B1/488 George St
+61 2 9266 2000
marblebarenquiries.sydney@hilton.com

Archie Rose Distilling Co.
85 Dunning Ave, Rosebery
+61 2 8458 2300
events@archierose.com.au

Champagne Bar
Sofitel, Level 3/12 Darling Dr
+61 2 8388 8888
Champagnebar.Sydney@Sofitel.com

MAYBE SAMMY
115 Harrington St, The Rocks
+61 2 9241 4970
cocktails@maybesammy.com

Banchō
10 Thomas Ln, Haymarket
+61 2 8097 9512
info@tokyobird.com.au

The Edinburgh Castle
294 Pitt St
+61 2 9264 8616
edinburghcastle@solotel.com.au

Side Bar
509 Pitt St
+61 2 9288 7878
hello@sidebarsydney.com.au

The Smoking Panda
5-7 Park St
+61 2 9264 4618
info@thesmokingpanda.com.au

Zephyr
Level 12/161 Sussex St
+61 2 8099 1234
zephyrbarsydney@hyatt.com

Bar Luca
52 Phillip St
+61 2 9247 9700
info@barluca.com.au

SYDNEY | WORK

Ryan's Bar
264-278 George St
+61 2 9252 4369
info@ryansbar.com.au

Tokyo Bird
Commonwealth St & Belmore Ln, Surry Hills
+61 2 8880 0788
info@tokyobird.com.au

The Captains Balcony
46 Erskine St
+61 2 9299 3526
captain@thecaptainsbalcony.com.au

Three Bottle Man
1 Bulletin Pl
+61 2 9259 7279
hello@threebottleman.com.au

Verandah
55/65 Elizabeth St
+61 2 9239 5888
mail@verandah.com.au

3 Wise Monkeys
555 George St
+61 2 9283 5855
careers@3wisemonkeys.com.au

Republic Hotel
69-73 Pitt St
+61 2 9252 6522
info@republichotel.com

Gin Lane
16A Kensington St, Chippendale
hello@ginlanesydney.com

Spawn Point Small Bar
199 Clarence St
+61437374968
info@spawnpoint.com.au

Chamberlain Hotel (C-Bar)
428 Pitt St
+61 2 9288 0888
c-bar@reservehotels.com.au

Shelbourne Hotel
200 Sussex St
+61 2 9267 3100
enquiry@shelbournehotel.com.au

Solander Dining and Bar
65 Sussex St
+61 2 8297 6500
solander_enquiries@hilton.com

The Morrison Bar
225 George St
+61 2 9247 6744
info@themorrison.com.au

SYDNEY | WORK

Darlo Bar
306 Liverpool St, Darlinghurst
📞 +61 2 9331 3672
✉ book.darlobar@solotel.com.au

NOLA Smokehouse and Bar
100 Barangaroo Ave
📞 +61 2 9188 3039
✉ info@nolasydney.com

York Lane
56 Clarence St
📞 +61 2 9299 1676
✉ info@yorklane.com

P.J.O'Brien's
57 King St
📞 +61 2 9290 1811
✉ sydney@pjobriens.com.au

Mjølner
267 Cleveland St, Redfern
📞 +61 2 8646 4930
✉ info@mjolner.com.au

ABODE Bistro & Bar
150 Day St
📞 +61 2 9260 2945
✉ rsvp@abodebistro.com

Solera Bar
36 Hickson Rd, Millers Point
📞 +61423882131
✉ info@solera.bar

Cohibar
10 Darling Dr
📞 +61 2 9282 9444
✉ events@thewatershedhotel.com.au

Big Poppa's
96 Oxford St, Darlinghurst
📞 +61499052201
✉ cheese@bigpoppa.com.au
Apply directly on the website:
www.bigpoppa.com.au/careers

Shell House
37 Margaret St
📞 +61 2 8262 8888
✉ reservations@
shellhouse.com.au

Philter Brewing
98 Sydenham Road Marrickville
📞 +61 2 9199 9655
✉ work@philterbrewing.com

The Barrie
107-109 Regent St, Chippendale
✉ chips@thebarrie.com.au

Apollonia
5-7 Young Street
📞 (02) 7228 1400
Apply directly on the website
https://hinchcliffhouse.com/work-with-us/

SYDNEY | WHERE TO GO OUT

GOING OUT AND MEETING PEOPLE IN SYDNEY

The pub crawl

The concept: you go out to 4 different bars for about 50 dollars, with a drink in each bar + free pizza. Meet between 8 and 8:30 pm in the first bar to validate your ticket.
Book your ticket at:
www.eventbrite.com/d/australia--sydney/bar-crawl
You will go in groups to 4 bars. This can include the following venues:

Side Bar
509 Pitt St, Sydney | www.wakeup.com.au/sydney/side-bar
This is the basement of the Wake Up Hostel. The biggest and most frequented bar in the city by backpackers.

Mojo Record Bar
73 York St, Sydney | www.mojorecordbar.com

Cargo Bar
52-60 The Promenade, King Street Wharf, Darling Harbour
https://cargobar.com.au

Scary Canary
469 Kent St, Sydney | www.scarycanary.net/

3 Wise Monkeys
555 George St, Sydney | www.3wisemonkeys.com.au/

80 Proof @ Cheers Bar
561 George St | www.eightyproof.com.au/

SYDNEY | WHERE TO GO OUT

Couchsurfing website

Go to the "events" section at www.couchsurfing.com and meet people from all over the world.
The meeting place is usually the Helm Bar.

Weekly CS Drinks/Socialising & Making New Friends
Helm Bar, Aquarium Wharf, 7 Wheat Rd, Sydney NSW 2000, Australia
Du 07 fév. 2020, 18:30 au 08 fév. 2020, 06:30 (AEDT)
1 participant(s)

Inscription

Partagez cet événement avec vos amis :

Weekly CS Drinks/Socialising & Making New Friends
Helm Bar, Aquarium Wharf, 7 Wheat Rd, Sydney NSW 2000, Australia
Du 31 jan. 2020, 18:30 au 01 fév. 2020, 06:30 (AEDT)
27 participant(s)

Inscription

Facebook groups

https://www.facebook.com/groups/WorkandTravelAustraliaMeetUpParty
https://www.facebook.com/groups/414130922091016
https://www.facebook.com/groups/CSSydney

Another useful website:

Meet Up: https://www.meetup.com/en-AU/find/au--sydney/

Getting around Sydney with the OPAL card

This is a reloadable card that allows you to travel by train, bus, ferry and light rail without paying more than AUD $15/day (travel limited to AUD $2.50 on Sundays).
The card is sold everywhere in the city and can also be recharged online: https://transportnsw.info/trip#/opal-retailers
and https://transportnsw.info/tickets-opal/opal#/login
Be careful, you have to validate it when you get on and off the bus. Failing to do so might mean you end up paying more than you need to.

MELBOURNE

Melbourne, the capital of the state of Victoria, is Australia's second largest urban area with a population of just over 4.5 million.
Melbourne used to be bigger than Sydney, and the two cities have been rivals for almost 200 years!
People from Melbourne will tell you that Sydney only built its opera house in response to Melbourne being selected to host the Olympics in 1956. The Sydneysiders will tell you that their weather is much better than Melbourne's and that their beaches are more beautiful.
Melbourne was only founded in 1835, yet it has been named the most liveable city in the world for three years running based on three criteria: education, transportation, and the cost of living.
In the 1850s, big gold rocks were found in Victoria. The gold rush brought people from all over the world to this part of Australia, which explains the diversity of nationalities and the fact that Melbourne has the third-largest Chinatown in the world (after China, obviously, and San Francisco). You can find incredible food from everywhere, including Italy, Japan, China, Greece, Spain, and more. The result is that there are many professional opportunities in hospitality.
If you come to Australia for a year, you may want to consider the weather when choosing your city. The weather in Melbourne is not the same as in Sydney, so you won't get the year-long summer that you were maybe hoping for. The weather is a lot like Europe's, and you can even have four seasons in one day!

MELBOURNE | WHAT TO SEE/ WHAT TO DO

WHAT TO SEE/ WHAT TO DO IN MELBOURNE

Free guided tour of Melbourne

Every day at 10:30 am and 2:30 pm, meet the guide in the green T-shirt! You will find him in front of the Victoria State Library for a free walking tour of the city!
At the end of the tour, tip the guide.
This tour will give you a very good overview of the city.
Be prepared to walk around the city for almost three hours.
The guide always has an interesting anecdotes about the history of Australia and Australians in general. No need to book.
https://www.imfree.com.au/melbourne/
Tel : +61 405 515 654 | email address : melbourne@imfree.com.au

Skydiving

Jump from a plane at 14,000m in tandem! After only fifteen minutes of preparation, you are in free fall for 60 seconds at 200km/hour! Then enjoy five minutes of descent to admire the scenery. You can buy the video and/or photos of your jump.

Skydive Melbourne
42A Marine Parade, St Kilda | Tel: +61 1300 663 634
www.skydive.com.au/melbourne
Jump from AUD $449. Decreasing rate from 4 persons.

Walk around the Royal Botanic Garden

Located in the centre of Melbourne, it is an oasis of greenery in the heart of the city!
Take the guided tour and learn about the Aborigines and their heritage.
You can also relax at one of the two cafes;
Tan Garden or The Terrace overlooking the lake.
Birdwood Avenue, Melbourne
http://www.rbg.vic.gov.au/

MELBOURNE | WHAT TO SEE/ WHAT TO DO

A cruise on the Yarra river

Discover Melbourne from its river: The Yarra River.
Listen to the captain tell the story of the Yarra and Melbourne while drinking coffee or tea on board.
Tickets can be purchased at Southgate Riverfront Arts & Leisure Precinct.

Melbourne River Cruises
5-Berth Kiosk or at Federation Wharf.
www.melbcruises.com.au
✉ info@melbcruises.com.au | Tel: +61 3 8610 2600

Eureka Skydeck 88

Climb the tallest tower in the southern hemisphere to enjoy a view of Melbourne by day or night.
88th floor, 297 meters high. Great view.

Eureka Skydeck 88
Admission: From AUD $28/adult.
7 Riverside Quay, Southbank. Tickets on sale at the entrance.
www.eurekaskydeck.com.au
Open from 10am to 10 pm every day.
Email: www.eurekaskydeck.com.au

National Sports Museum

Visit the Australian Sports Museum and discover the legend behind Australia's largest stadium.
You can even relive some of the greatest moments in Australian sporting history.
Buy your ticket at http://www.nsm.org.au/

ACCOMMODATION IN MELBOURNE

On arrival: short-term accommodation

Ideally, you will have booked your accommodation for the first few days before you left home.
It is not obligatory, but after 20 hours of flying, you may not feel like wandering the streets of the city in search of the best hostel.
Booking a few nights in your city of arrival before arriving, either in a hostel or in Airbnb, is a good idea.
An Airbnb can be a good solution to get your own private room in a house and recover from jet lag for the first few days.

Going straight from your flight to a bed in a dormitory can be tough, but on the other hand, you'll be right in the swing of things! The hostel will then allow you to meet people and to be able to check job offers locally.
The hostels are often very well positioned downtown, which is obviously a strategic location if you are looking for a job in the city.

Couchsurfing

The website of reference for free accommodation with locals.
If you have an empty profile, are male and have few references, you will have little chance of being accommodated.
You can ask friends to share their opinion about you in the 'personal reviews' section.
It's a great way to meet locals and sleep on their couch for one or more nights.
In exchange for accommodation you can, for example, prepare a meal for your host or buy them a drink in town!
Be careful to check the references of each host before asking them for accommodation.
www.couchsurfing.org

MELBOURNE | ACCOMMODATION

Hostels

Melbourne Central YHA
Very clean rooms. Located right in front of the train station and the Free City Circle (Line 35 that goes around the city for free).
Free WiFi. Dormitory: From AUD $42.
Private room from AUD $107.
562 Flinders St Melbourne | Tel: +61 31 9621 2523
Email : melbcentral@yha.com.au
www.yha.com.au/hostels/vic/melbourne-hostels/melbourne-central-hostel/

Claremont Guest House
Dormitory: From AUD $42.50.
Private room : From AUD $135. Breakfast included.
189 Toorak Road, South Yarra, Melbourne| Tel: +61 3 9826 8000
https://www.hotelclaremont.com

Base St Kilda
Dormitory from AUD $30 | Private room from AUD $123.50.
www.stayatbase.com/hostels/base-backpackers-melbourne
17 Carlisle Street, St Kilda, Melbourne, Australie
Tel: +61(0)3 8598 6200 | Email: melbourne@stayatbase.com

The Nunnery Accommodation
Dormitory: From AUD $32 | Private room from AUD $105.
http://nunnery.com.au/
116 Nicholson St, Fitzroy VIC 3065 | Tel: 1800 032 635
Hostel well located, although a little noisy. Free breakfast.

Melbourne City Backpackers
Dormitory: From AUD $37.
www.melbournecitybackpackers.com.au
197-199, King Street, Melbourne | Tel: +61 33 9670 1111
Free breakfast, free pancakes every Sunday, pasta party every Wednesday. Free WiFi.
This hostel is conveniently located just a ten-minute walk from Southern Cross Station.

MELBOURNE | ACCOMMODATION | WORK

Long-term accommodation

To find your room in Melbourne, go to :
- Gumtree: https://www.gumtree.com.au
- Flatmates : https://flatmates.com.au
- Airbnb: https://www.airbnb.com (negotiate the price directly with the owner for a several months rental).
- Try to post an ad on the following Facebook groups:

"Melbourne Flatmates and sharehouse search"
"Melbourne Rent a room / house / apartment / flat / accommodation"

THE JOB MARKET AND SALARY IN MELBOURNE

The main sectors that recruit in Melbourne are hospitality, fruit-picking (in Victoria more generally), wwoofing (you work on a farm in exchange for food and accommodation), call centres, construction and babysitting (nannies).

The hostel is certainly the first place where you will see job offers. In many hostels, you will see a big wall sign with job offers. **Get up early** to check it every morning (before everyone else does!).

Here are some of the offers posted at Melbourne City Backpackers Hostel.

Labouring jobs available

Labourers for commercial relocation are required.
Ongoing casual work, flexible days and hours |Based in Footscray
Call on (03)96874488 during business hours.
More info: www.egans.com.au

ROOM ATTENDANTS | HOUSEKEEPERS |CHAMBER MAIDS

We are recruiting now fo casual room attendants to work ongoing regular shifts. Immediate start- Must have previous experience in a four or five-star hotel! Immediate start and top hourly rates of pay.
Tel : 03 8624 1777 | www.pinnaclepeople.com.au
390 Flinders Street Melbourne VIC |melb@pinnaclepeople.com.au

MELBOURNE | WORK

⚠️ Some job offers may seem really attractive, but before you start working, always check the number of hours worked per week and the salary/hourly rate.

The minimum wage in Victoria is AU$21.38/hour.

TIPS FROM MARIE B. | HR MARKETING CONSULTANT.

Marie is French and spent six months in Australia. She arrived in Melbourne, fell in love with the city, and tells us about her job-hunting experience.

« Landing a qualified job is the best way for those who come to Australia on a Working Holiday Visa to do the W to enjoy the H.
If Australia was a job-finding paradise ten years ago, things are very different today. There is still work around, but there is also much more competition.
Here are some tips and tools to prepare for your job hunting.

A few candidates prepare their resumes in English before arriving in the country.
Prepare it ! It's less stressful and you can attack the market as soon as you have recovered from your jetlag.
Agencies, backpacker hostels, the web, networking, all means are valid depending on what you're looking for. There are lots of forums and groups on Facebook that give tips on how to find work, but some people quickly get discouraged and give up, but I say hang in there; some people look for a job for two months or more without finding anything to start with.

Where there's a will there's a way! However, if you arrive in the middle of summer in December/ January, it is the school holidays so you will be up against a lot of competition from Australian students, but that doesn't mean you won't find something. But don't approach the job market as though the world owes you something and you own the place.

MELBOURNE | WORK

Saying 'Have you got a job for me?' probably won't go down very well.
You might be lucky and another WHV holder might give you their job because they are returning home or moving on to another city, but don't sit around waiting for something to fall into your lap.
Get into action.

Hospitality, construction, street marketing, tourism…
If you want to go into the hospitality sector and work in a place where alcohol is served, you will have to pass the RSA certificate (Responsibility Service of Alcohol), and then look for work by knocking on doors.
Don't restrict your search to the Central Business District (the CBD) or St Kilda; go out into the suburbs: Malvern, Carlton or even the docklands at the Port of Melbourne.

Dishwasher, Barista, Runner …
Many job offers are advertised in the windows of restaurants and bars, and even if they aren't, don't be afraid to go in and ask the manager if they need help. They may offer you a trial.

Talking about money is slightly taboo in some parts of the world (especially in Europe), but in Australia it's important to ask straight away what the hourly pay is. Some places will take advantage of you if you're not careful, and a lot of young backpackers with a Working Holiday Visa do not get their trial day paid.
Don't accept anything under AUD $20 an hour cash in hand, with general team tips on top.

You can also work in the construction industry doing plumbing or carpentry, or in clothes stores, in street marketing or as a paper boy. Ask your hostel or even some travel agencies if they need anyone. These jobs are usually casual jobs for a few hours a week, but you can also work in a hostel tidying the kitchen, or making beds etc. This might lead to a discount on the price of your accommodation or in some cases even free accommodation.

MELBOURNE | WORK

If you have experience in tourism, try the travel agencies (Peterpans Adventure Travel have offices everywhere), especially on the east coast; you could work on a ship bound for the Whitsunday Islands, or in a resort on the Paradise Islands in which case go and get a diving certificate or a certificate in health and safety to enhance your CV and give yourself a competitive edge.

My personal experience
From head hunter to freelancer

After doing my master's and a four-year stint in human resources in Canada and Morocco, I wanted to look for a job in Australia in my field. I arrived, I had my resume in English, I had contacts and all the goodwill in the world. Having been a recruiter myself, I had a few tricks up my sleeve, but I knew I had to tread carefully in the Australian market.

My initial contact was a childhood expat friend who was working at Ikea. He had already sent my CV to the HR department, but unfortunately, without having worked in Ikea in my home country, they wouldn't take me on. That would have been too easy, but the recruiter did kindly direct me to agencies and other specialized sites.

I arrived in Melbourne on a Friday, and immediately sent my resume to two recommended agencies: **www.tandempartners.com.au** and **www.hrpartners.com.au**. The following Monday morning, I already had an interview scheduled for the Thursday. I stressed a bit over having an interview in English, but things seemed to be going pretty well, and in fact it turned out to be a prospecting interview to get to know me. I needn't have worried about my accent; recruiters are used to interviewing Europeans or Asians and they're not particularly fussy about grammatical mistakes when you speak. BUT, she was fussy about the kind of visa I had.

From there, I read on her face that it was going to be difficult, and the recruiter was totally clear about that.

MELBOURNE | WORK

I had no problems with a working holiday visa in Canada. On the contrary, there it is used as a way in to finding a sponsor and permanent residency. It is also less restrictive.

In Australia, you can only work for the same employer for six months, so I had to find a job with a short-term contract rather than a long- term one. 'Seek' is the best website for this, and you can filter by using keywords like the name of the district, your specialism or the type of contract you require.

Everything happens through networking, and the more you network, the better because it shows that you have gone out of your way to meet people. A Belgian friend of mine advised me to go to a 'rec to rec' agency (recruiters who find you recruitment jobs). It had worked for her.

One week, five interviews and five job offers later, she signed a contract with a sponsorship organization. Yes, there are some success stories!

Her secret to success was her positive attitude and her apparent self-confidence during the interviews! But my profile was different and I did not want to work in sales.

Too demanding?

Well, I know what I don't want and what I'm comfortable with.

I played the French card and went to the French- Australian Chamber of Commerce and Industry (FACCI). They gave me a directory of all the French companies based in Melbourne. Thanks to them, I went to a networking evening for AUD $20 where I got the name of an agency that specializes in HR consulting and whose founder is French. After three meetings in French with a consultant in Melbourne, the founder and the IT Recruitment Specialist in Sydney, I was on my way to getting a job that would eventually be based in Sydney.

MELBOURNE | WORK

To adapt to the Australian way of life, show that you're enthusiastic. This is the land of 'no worries', Australians avoid stress and conflict.
Some employers take advantage of vulnerable backpackers who are prepared to do anything to earn a bit of money, or of those who will do three months' Wwoofing to get a second visa, but undoubtedly, this country will change you, teach you to excel and, even if it is more difficult now than it was, get ready to experience your best ever Australian dream!
The experience is not only about work but also about confronting a new environment, a new culture, and meeting people who will change your life ...»

Advice :
Use **LinkedIn**,
Add people who contact you by email or phone to your network.
Target companies that interest you, and follow them on LinkedIn.

Job boards. The best is '**seek**':
If the recruiter number is mentioned in the ad, pick up the phone and call!
First come first served!

Move out beyond the CBD ; canvas the neighbourhoods or the suburbs.
Use your network and Facebook groups.

WEBSITES TO FIND A JOB

www.hays.com.au
This is a very popular world-wide recruitment site, and is a good source of the latest jobs in Melbourne.

www.experis.com.au
Recruitment agency specialized in the technology sectors for permanent or temporary contracts.

MELBOURNE | WORK

www.citirecruitment.com
A popular recruitment company for IT; the company also provides employment solutions for data warehousing, business intelligence, and enterprise integration.

www.workingin-australia.com
This is a very helpful site which gives comprehensive information on important aspects of Australian life like education, business, taxes and insurance. Of course, there is a job section with job listings in healthcare, marketing, IT, sales, and advertising.

www.seek.com.au
This is a very informative job website. Here, employers are required to state the maximum and minimum salary for every job posted by them. The website uses this information to provide relevant job vacancies according to the salary requirement and professional profile of every registered member.

www.adecco.com.au
This is one of the most reliable HR organizations in the world, and it deals with a large number of employers and job aspirants.

www.airtasker.com
These are one-time assignments offered by individuals.
For example, you may be asked to help carry a mattress for AUD $50 or to help with a move. You can apply for each mission and try to sell yourself as much as possible.

INTERVIEW WITH CLÉMENT : HIS FRUIT PICKING EXPERIENCE

Marie: How did you find a job on a farm?
Clément: There are books and forums which give the addresses of farms listed according to season and state. I went directly to the farms in the morning to introduce myself and offer my services, including for fruit picking.

MELBOURNE | WORK

I asked to see the boss. I went to about ten farms and left my name and phone number saying that I was available immediately.

I arrived early in the season so that I had a chance of being the first to be called. On the Saturday evening, I got a phone call from a farmer in the Melbourne area who offered me an initial 1-month contract as a farm labourer. He offered my friend a job as a raspberry picker.

Farm work is very much dependent on the weather, so farmers don't always hire, but in general, once you're working, you can save money quickly and then get on your way to the next place.

Marie: Can you describe a typical day?

Clément: The boss would call us the day before, and we would start work sometime between 7:30 am and 8 am in the field. The fruit pickers picked as much fruit as possible (theirs was performance pay) and my colleague and I helped the boss with the maintenance of the farm installing anti-bird nets on the cherry trees, putting up tarpaulins to protect the fruit from the rain, weeding and pruning, etc. It is a busy day with 30 minutes for lunch unpaid and a 10-minute paid break around 10:30. The end of the day was around 5.30 - 6 pm.

There was no official accommodation on our farm, but most farmers will provide you with a space to kip down (you can sleep in your own van and use a bathroom and toilet, thus saving fuel and camping).

Marie: This was your first experience on a farm. What were the advantages and disadvantages?

Clément: The advantages: It allows you to meet Australian farmers, learn their way of life and get work experience abroad. It also allows you to practise your English (if you are not native from an English-speaking country) and learn new expressions listening to that famous Australian accent!

You get to meet backpackers from all over the world (French, German, Italian, Korean, and Japanese).

121

MELBOURNE | WORK | THE RSA

You spend beautiful evenings after work, and in no time save enough money to be able to set off again on the Aussie roads. You don't necessarily need any experience in farming but it's an advantage if you have some.

The drawbacks: finding the right farm that will give you full time work, or at least five days work a week. Finding a big farm is best because there will be a lot of fruit to pick and more money to earn. Some farms don't have accommodation, so you have to find a campsite not too far away and that isn't too expensive (try not to spend one week's pay on housing).

LANDING A JOB IN THE HOSPITALITY INDUSTRY

What is the RSA and how do I get it in Melbourne?
The RSA is a certificate that shows you know the rules about alcohol.
RSA: Responsible Service of Alcohol
This certificate is essential to work in an establishment that serves alcohol: bar, restaurant, hotel. You will be required to have it, so you might as well get it before you start looking for a job.
It is possible that an establishment will accept to hire you without the RSA but you will then have a one month delay to pass it. You might as well put all your chances on your side by anticipating!

It is easily done online:
www.eot.edu.au/online-courses/RSA/australia/
Be aware that in the state of Victoria, it will cost you **AUD $64**.
The test takes between 3 and 6 hours maximum.
If you are not sure if you are going to stay and work in Victoria and plan to work in several Australian states, you can pass the RSA valid in all states for AUD $183.

MELBOURNE | WORK

To find a job very quickly in Melbourne, we advise you to send your CV in bulk to the hotel and restaurant listings in this guide.

Doing an email shot will allow you to send your resume to hundreds of establishments in one or two mailings.

If you want to customize your mailings for each company, you can choose from the list below.

If you choose emailing, here is the detailed method:

The method to send your CV to hundreds of companies

1- Create an account on MailChimp: www.login.mailchimp.com
2- On the button "Audience", go on "Add contacts" and "import contacts" then "copy/paste from file"
3- Open the following link and download the file.
https://www.dropbox.com/sh/kz5g75winugmjwz/AAD5Ma0X95SFJRUSKS5CMkxOa?dl=0
(if you can't open the file, send us an email at contact@helpstage.com and we will email it to you).
4- Copy/paste the emails from the excel spreadsheet to MailChimp (be careful, you are limited to 1,000 contacts. If you want to send more than 1,000 emails, you will simply have to delete your contacts after your first sending and import the new ones).
5- Go to the button "Create", then "email". Name the campaign "Application". In the part "To", choose the created contact list.
In "From", indicate your name and email address.
In the part "Subject", state "Application for a job". In the part "content", copy and paste the email template you downloaded into Dropbox, adapting it to your background and name.
Don't forget to attach your CV!

MELBOURNE | WORK

Example of a cover letter

"Dear Hiring Manager,

Please accept my enthusiastic application for a position in your hotel (or restaurant). I will be happy to bring my experience in the food industry, strong customer service skills, and my ability to work under pressure. I believe I fulfill all of these requirements and am therefore an excellent candidate for you.

I have an extensive background in hospitality. I worked for two years at a fast-food restaurant. During this time I gained experience in nearly every aspect of food service. I took orders and served customers their meals, handled the cash register, and performed daily inventory checks.

I could assist not only in taking orders and serving customers but also in a variety of other capacities in which you might require assistance. I also worked in customer service for a number of years. As a cashier at a grocery store for two years, I assisted as many as one hundred customers daily.

My experience in the food industry and in customer service, and my ability to thrive under pressure make me an excellent candidate for you. I have enclosed my resume and will call within the next week to see if we might arrange a time to speak together.

Thank you so much for your time and consideration.

Sincerely,

Your name"

> The cover letter doesn't have to be very long, but it should highlight your experience in a few lines. If you have no experience in the catering industry and your English is average, don't panic. Australians are usually happy to give beginners a chance
> You will have to emphasize your qualities in your letter but also in your CV.

MELBOURNE | WORK

Hotels in Melbourne

Pegasus Apart'Hotel
206 A'Beckett St
+61 3 9284 2400
reservations@pegasussuites.com.au

IMAGINE MARCO
42/48 Balston St, Southbank
+61 1300 062 726
marco@imaginehotelsresorts.com
drift@imaginehotelsresorts.com
info@imaginehotelsresorts.com

Aura on Flinders
534 Flinders St
+61 3 8648 4178
info@auraonflinders.com.au

Citadines on Bourke `
131/135 Bourke St
+61 3 9039 8888
careers@the-ascott.com

Punthill Apartment Hotel Northbank
560 Flinders St
+61 3 8548 7979
info@punthill.com.au

Experience Bella Hotel Apartments
250 City Rd, Southbank
+61 3 9020 9999
bella@experiencehotels.com.au

Oaks on William
350 William St
+61 1300 554 275
events@theoaksgroup.com.au
reservations@theoaksgroup.com.au

Mantra on Little Bourke
471 Little Bourke St
+61 3 9607 3000
littlebourke.res@mantra.com.au

Mantra 100 Exhibition
100 Exhibition St
13 15 17
100exhibition.res@mantra.com.au

Mantra City Central
318 Little Bourke St
+61 3 9664 2000
citycentral.res@mantra.com.au

Mantra on Russell
222 Russell St
+61 3 9915 2500
russell.res@mantra.com.au

Mantra Southbank
31 City Rd, Southbank
+61 3 8696 7222
southbankmel.res@mantra.com.au

BreakFree on Collins
6/233 Collins St
+61 3 9867 5200
collinsmel.res@breakfree.com.au

MELBOURNE | WORK

Peppers Docklands
679 La Trobe St, Docklands
+61 3 9190 0000
docklands@peppers.com.au

Adina Apartment Hotel Melbourne Flinders Street
88 Flinders Street
+61 3 8663 0000
careers@tfehotels.com

Melbourne SkyHigh
568 Collins St
+61424756588
apartments568collins@gmail.com

Docklands Private Collection Digital Harbour
7/198 Harbour Esplanade, Docklands
+61 3 9642 4220
info@docklandsprivatecollection.com.au

Dominion Apartments
285 City Rd, Southbank
+61 3 9020 9999
aria@experiencehotels.com.au

Park Regis Griffin Suites
604 St Kilda Rd
+61 3 8530 1800
griffin@parkregishotels.com

Best Western Riverside Apartments
474 Flinders St
+61 3 9619 9199
info@riversideservicedapartments.com.au

District South Yarra
10 Claremont St, South Yarra
+61 3 8825 8488
info@districtsouthyarra.com.au

District Apartments Fitzroy
160 Argyle St, Fitzroy
+61 3 9487 7498
info@districtfitzroy.com.au

Carlson View Apartments
315 La Trobe St
+61455030323
info@carlsonview.com

Jade Resorts
241 City Rd, Southbank
+61478068912
rsvp@jaderesorts.com.au

Adara Richmond
185 Lennox St, Richmond
+61 3 9267 1000
reservations@adara.com.au

Tribeca Serviced Apartments
9c/166 Albert St, East Melbourne
+61 3 9412 2100
info@tribecaservicedapartments.com.au

MELBOURNE | WORK

Hawthorn Gardens Serviced Apartments
750 Toorak Rd, Hawthorn East
+61 3 9822 7699
hgardens@bigpond.com

Milano Serviced Apartments
8 Franklin St
+61 3 9926 8200
info@milanoservicedapartments.com.au

ALT Tower Apartments
18 Mt Alexander Rd, Travancore
+61 3 9376 7555
reception@altsienna.com.au

Clarion Suites Gateway
1 William St
+61 3 9296 8888
yukikoc@clarionsuitesgateway.com.au

Crest on Park Apartments
46 Park St, St Kilda West
+61 3 9525 4139
info@crestonpark.com.au

Birches Serviced Apartments
160 Simpson St, East Melbourne
+61 3 9417 2344
info@birches.com.au

City Limits Hotel Apartments
Little Bourke St
+61 3 9662 2544
res@citylimits.com.au

Tyrian Serviced Apartments Fitzroy
91 Johnston St, Fitzroy
+61 3 9415 1900
fitzroy@tyrian.com.au
albertparklake@tyrian.com.au

Corporate Keys - Freshwater Place
1 Freshwater Pl, Southbank
+61 3 9279 7200
reservations@corporatekeys.com.au

Seasons Botanic Gardens
348 St Kilda Rd
+61 3 9685 3000
reservations.sbg@sahg.com.au

Quality Suites Beaumont Kew
7 Studley Park Rd, Kew
+61 3 9853 2722
enquiry@beaumontkew.com.au

Sixty Two On Grey Serviced Apartments
62 Grey St, St Kilda
+61423686699
enquiries@sixtytwogrey.com.au

381 Cremorne
381 Punt Road Cremorne
+61 3 9421 1500
reception@381cremorne.com.au

MELBOURNE | WORK

Adara Collins
182 Collins St
📞 +61 3 9639 1811
✉ collins@adaraapartments.com.au

Fraser Place Melbourne
19 Exploration Ln
📞 +61 3 9669 6888
✉ reservations.melbourne@frasershospitality.com

Carlton Lygon Lodge Studio Apartments
220 Lygon St, Carlton
📞 +61 3 9663 6633
✉ email@lygonlodge.com.au

Knightsbridge Apartments
101 George St, East Melbourne
📞 +61 3 9973 9868
✉ book@knightsbridgeapartments.com.au

Amity Apartment Hotels
27-29 Claremont St, South Yarra
📞 +61 3 8825 3700
✉ reservations@amityhotels.com.au

Mövenpick Hotel Melbourne
160 Spencer Street
📞 +61 3 9600 5400
✉ HB6L9@MOVENPICK.COM

W Melbourne
408 Flinders Ln, Melbourne
📞 +61 3 9113 8800
✉ reservations.melbourne@whotels.com

Serviced Apartments Melbourne - Platinum
45 Clarke St, Southbank
📞 +61411882588
✉ info@serviced-apartments-melbourne.com.au

Harbour Escape Apartments Docklands
5 Caravel Ln, Docklands
📞 +61407771760
✉ enquiry@harbourescape.com.au

Canvas Suites on Flinders
560 Flinders St
📞 +61414628518
✉ emelyn.taing@canvas-suites.com.au

Brighton Bay Apartments
197 Bay St, Brighton
📞 +61 3 9595 6099
✉ enquiries@brightonbay.com.au

Hiigh Apartments
153B High St, Prahran
📞 +61 3 9533 6558
✉ info@hiighapartments.com.au

Melbourne Metropole Central
44 Brunswick St, Fitzroy
📞 +61 3 9411 8100
✉ reservations@metropolecentral.com.au

Hotel Grand Chancellor Melbourne
131 Lonsdale St
📞 +61 3 9656 4000
✉ reshgc@hgcmelbourne.com.au

MELBOURNE | WORK

The Jazz Corner Hotel
352 William St
📞 +61 3 9454 9000
✉ enquiries@jazzcornerhotel.com

The Hotel Windsor
111 Spring St
📞 +61 3 9633 6000
✉ hr@thw.com.au

Brady Hotels Central Melbourne
30 Little La Trobe St
📞 +61 3 9650 9888
✉ res.cm@bradyhotels.com.au

Jasper Hotel
489,Elizabeth Street
📞 +61 3 8327 2777
✉ stay@jasperhotel.com.au

Space Hotel
380 Russell St
📞 +61 3 9662 3888
✉ stay@spacehotel.com.au

Causeway Inn On The Mall
327 Bourke St
📞 +61 3 9650 0688
✉ reservations@causeway.com.au

Grand Hyatt Melbourne
123 Collins Street
📞 +61 3 9657 1234
✉ melbourne.grand@hyatt.com

North Pier Hotel
5 The Esplanade, Cowes
📞 +61 3 5951 4488
✉ info@northpierhotel.com.au

Novotel on Collins
270 Collins Street
📞 +61396675800
✉ H1587@accor.com

Wyndham
199 William St
📞 +61 3 8692 8900
✉ Mycareer@Wyndham.com

Cosmopolitan Hotel
6 Carlisle St
📞 +61 3 8598 6700
✉ book@cosmostkilda.com

Langham Melbourne
1 Southgate Ave
📞 +61 3 8696 8888
✉ tlmel.info@langhamhotels.com

Mercure Welcome
265 Little Bourke Street
📞 +61 396390555
✉ H3031@accor.com

Atlantis
300 Spencer St
📞 +61 3 9600 2900
✉ sales@atlantishotel.com.au

MELBOURNE | WORK

Mercure Melbourne Therry Street
43 Therry Street
📞 +61 396376666
✉ info@mercuretherrystreet.com.au

Miami Hotel Melbourne
13 Hawke St, West Melbourne
📞 +61 3 9321 2444
✉ desk@themiami.com.au

Ibis Melbourne - Hotel & Apartments
15-21 Therry Street
📞 +61 396660000
✉ H1564@accor.com

Novotel Melbourne Central
399, rue Little Lonsdale
📞 +6199298888
✉ HA0B1@ACCOR.COM

Grand Hotel Melbourne
33 Spencer St
📞 +61396114567
✉ stay@grandhotelmelbourne.com.au

Ibis Styles Kingsgate
131 King Street
📞 +61 396294171
✉ info@kingsgatehotel.com.au

Selina - Melbourne Central
250 Flinders St, Melbourne
📞 +61 422 716 090
✉ yoav@selina.com

Best Western Plus Travel Inn Carlton
Corner Grattan & Drummond Streets Carlton
📞 +6139347 7922
✉ res@travelinn.net.au

Arrow on Spencer
585 Latrobe Street
📞 +61 3 9321 0900
✉ reception@arrowonspencer.com.au

IFSuites EQ Tower
135 A'Beckett St
📞 +61426878268
✉ ifstays.service@gmail.com

Winston Apartments
568 Collins Street Melbourne
📞 +61426437888
✉ info@winstonapartments.com.au

Richmond Hill Hotel
353 Church St
📞 +61 3 9428 6501
✉ rhhotel@bigpond.net.au

Treasury on Collins
394 Collins Street
✉ enquiries@treasuryoncollins.com.au

Somerset on Elizabeth Melbourne
250 Elizabeth St
📞 +61 3 8665 8888
✉ somerset.australia@the-ascott.com

MELBOURNE | WORK

Rydges on Swanston
701 Swanston St, Carlton
+61 3 9347 7811
reservations_rydgesswanston@evt.com

Adara Brunswick
343 Sydney Road, Brunswick
+61 3 8590 8584
brunswick@adaraapartments.com.au

Adara St Kilda
135 Inkerman Street
+61 3 9525 5300
stkilda@adaraapartments.com.au

Adara Richmond
185 Lennox Street
+61 3 9267 1000
richmond@adaraapartments.com.au

Stamford Plaza Melbourne
111 Little Collins St
+61 3 9659 1000
sales@spm.stamford.com.au

Citiclub Hotel
113 Queen St
+61 3 9602 1800
info@cqmelbourne.com.au

Quay West Suites
26 Southgate Ave, Southbank
+61 3 9693 6000
h8804@accor.com
kanupriya.mathur@accor.com

The Eminence
145 Queensberry Street, Carlton
+6139347 7788
info@theeminence.com.au

Pan Pacific Melbourne
2 Convention Centre Pl
+61 3 9027 2000
enquiry@pphg.com

Melbourne Metro YHA
78 Howard St
+61 3 9329 8599
melbmetro@yha.com.au

ibis Melbourne Swanston
609 Swanston Street
+61393473027
HA3N5@ACCOR.COM

Mantra on Jolimont
133 Jolimont Road East Melbourne
+61 7 5665 4450
jolimont.res@mantra.com.au

Sofitel Melbourne on Collins
25 Collins Street
+61396530000
H1902@sofitel.com
Shane.Douglas@sofitel.com

Pullman Swanston
195 Swanston St
+61 3 9663 4711
h3028-re6@accor.com

MELBOURNE | WORK

Adelphi Hotel
187 Flinders Lane
+613 8080 8888
info@adelphi.com.au

Crown Towers Melbourne
8 Whiteman St, Southbank
+61 3 9292 6868
reservations.mct@crownhotels.com.au

ROYCE HOTEL MELBOURNE
379 St Kilda Rd
+61396779900
info@roycehotel.com.au

Pullman Melbourne
65 Queens Road
+613 95294300
H8788@accor.com

The Sebel Melbourne
321 Flinders Ln
+61 3 9629 4088
res.flinders@accorvacationclub.com.au

Mercure Melbourne
43 Therry St
+61 3 9637 6666
reservations@mercuretherrystreet.com.au

MERCURE NORTH MELBOURNE
Cnr Flemington Road And, Harker St
+61 3 9329 1788
sarah_macandrew@mercurenorthmelbourne.com.au
jayesh_bala@mercurenorthmelbourne.com.au
emma_williams@mercurenorthmelbourne.com.au

IBIS STYLES MELBOURNE, THE VICTORIA HOTEL
215 Little Collins St
+61 3 9669 0000
stay@victoriahotel.com.au
samantha.eise@victoriahotel.com.au

HOTEL LINDRUM MELBOURNE
26 Flinders St
+61 3 9668 1111
h8757-re@accor.com

The Como Melbourne, MGallery by Sofitel
630 Chapel St, South Yarra
+61 3 9825 2222
h8801@accor.com
john.korkou@accor.com

Pullman Melbourne
192 Wellington Parade
+61 3 9419 2000
h9875-re@accor.com
h9875-sl1@accor.com

MELBOURNE | WORK

French restaurants in Melbourne

The French Brasserie
2 Malthouse Ln
+61 3 9662 1632
info@thefrenchbrasserie.com.au

Philippe
115 Collins St
+61 3 8394 6625
admin@philipperestaurant.com.au

Bistro Guillaume
8, Riverside, Crown Melbourne, Whiteman St, Southbank
+61 3 9292 5777
restaurantreservations@crownmelbourne.com.au
privateevents@crownmelbourne.com.au

French Saloon
First Floor, 46 Hardware Ln
+61 3 9600 2142
info@frenchsaloon.com

La Petite Crêperie
Little Collins St &, Swanston St
+61466406404
lapetitecreperiemelbourne@gmail.com

France-Soir
11 Toorak Rd, South Yarra
+61 3 9866 8569
mail@france-soir.com.au

Le Café Flo
709 High St, Thornbury
+61 3 9484 2089
info@lecafeflo.com

Bon Ap' Petit Bistro
193 Brunswick St, Fitzroy
+61 3 9415 9450
info@bonap.com.au

Noir
175 Swan St, Richmond
+61 3 9428 3585
info@noirrestaurant.com.au

Ryne
203 St Georges Rd, Fitzroy
+61 3 9482 3002
reservations@ryne.com.au

Bistro Gitan
52 Toorak Rd West, South Yarra
+61 3 9867 5853
info@bistrogitan.com.au

Paris Go Bistro
116 Rathdowne St, Carlton
+61 3 9347 7507
parisgo@bigpond.net.au

Small French Bar
3/154 Barkly St, Footscray
+61 3 9687 8479
info@smallfrenchbar.com

Chez Bagou
132 Bridport St, Albert Park
+61 3 7012 2102
info@chezbagou.com.au

MELBOURNE | WORK

Mon Ami Paris Grill
144 Nicholson St, Fitzroy
+61 3 9417 3220
dine@monamirestaurant.com.au

Bistro Voliere
129 Fitzroy St, St Kilda
+61 3 9042 5584
info@bistrovoliere.com.au

Chez Dré
285-287 Coventry St,
South Melbourne
+61 3 9690 2688
info@chezdre.com.au

Bistro La Provence
234 Esplanade, Brighton
+61 3 9592 2000
info@bistrolaprovence.com.au

BISTRO SOUSOU
153 Gertrude St, Fitzroy
+61 3 9417 0400
info@bistrosousou.com.au

Mandoline
432 Glen Huntly Rd, Elsternwick
+61 3 9532 7353
mandoline432@outlook.com

L'Hotel Gitan
32 Commercial Rd, Prahran
+61 3 9999 0990
info@lhotelgitan.com.au

Frédéric
9-11 Cremorne St, Cremorne
+61 3 9089 7224
hello@frederic.com.au

The Little French Deli
524 Nepean Hwy, Bonbeach
+61 3 9776 0855
thelittlefrenchdeli@gmail.com

Breizoz French Crêperie
Entrance On, 2/49 Brunswick St.,
Gertrude St, Fitzroy
+61 3 9415 7588
eat@breizoz.com.au

Vue de monde
Rialto Towers, 525 Collins St
+61 3 9691 3888
vuedemonde@vuedemonde.com.au

Chez Olivier Le Bistro
268 Toorak Rd, South Yarra
+61 3 9525 2273
olivier@chezolivier.com.au

Franco-Belge
9 Evans Pl, Hawthorn East
+61 3 9191 7370
info@francobelge.com.au

Hell of the North
135 Greeves St, Fitzroy
+61 3 9417 6660
dine@hellofthenorth.com.au

MELBOURNE | WORK

Roule Galette
Scott Alley, 237/241 Flinders Ln
+61 3 9639 0307
michel@roulegalette.com.au

Entrecôte Parisian
131-133 Domain Rd, South Yarra
+61 3 9804 5468
dine@entrecote.com.au

Boilermaker House
209-211 Lonsdale St
+61 3 8393 9367
info@boilermakerhouse.com.au

Krimper Cafe
20 Guildford Ln
+61 3 9043 8844
info@krimper.com.au

Bar Margaux
Basement/111 Lonsdale St
+61 3 9650 0088
reservations@barmargaux.com.au

Kirk's Wine Bar
46 Hardware Ln
+61 3 9600 4550
info@kirkswinebar.com

Le Feu
145 Nepean Hwy, Aspendale
+61 3 9580 5990
info@lefeu.com.au

Australian restaurants in Melbourne

Taxi Kitchen
Flinders Street &, Swanston St
+61 3 9654 8808
groupbookings@sovhotels.com

Punch Lane Wine Bar
43 Little Bourke St
+61 3 9639 4944
bookings@punchlane.com.au

Cutler & Co
55/57 Gertrude St, Fitzroy
+61 3 9419 4888
info@cutlerandco.com.au

Henry and The Fox
525 Little Collins St
+61 3 9614 3277
reservations@henryandthefox.com.au

Supernormal
180 Flinders Ln
+61 3 9650 8688
info@supernormal.net.au

Sirocco Restaurant & Bar
575 Flinders Ln
+61 3 9612 5788
reception.melsf@ihg.com

MELBOURNE | WORK

Mr. Hive Kitchen & Bar
Crown Melbourne, 8 Whiteman St, Southbank
+61 3 9292 5777
careers@crownmelbourne.com.au
enquiries@crowncollege.edu.au

Schnitz
QV Melbourne, 28 Artemis Ln
+61 3 9663 3497
hello@schnitz.com.au

Pure South Dining
3 Southgate Ave, Southbank
+61 3 9699 4600
ps@puresouth.com.au

The European
161 Spring St
+61 3 9654 0811
info@theeuropean.com.au

Spoonbill Restaurant and Bar
637/641 Chapel St, South Yarra
+61 3 9040 1333
careers@artserieshotels.com.au

Attica
74 Glen Eira Rd, Ripponlea
+61 3 9530 0111
phil@attica.com.au
alice@attica.com.au

Restaurant Dans le Noir
701 Swanston St, Carlton
+61 3 9347 7811
melbourne@danslenoir.com

Greasy Zoes
shop 3/850 Heidelberg-Kinglake Rd, Hurstbridge
+61 3 9718 0324
info@greasyzoes.com.au

Encore Restaurant & Bar
131 Lonsdale St, Melbourne
+61 3 9656 4000
reshgc@hgcmelbourne.com.au

ALIBI - Urban Gastropub
Ground Floor/471 Little Bourke St
+61 3 9607 3011
alibi.restaurant@mantra.com.au

Coda
141 Flinders Ln
+61 3 9650 3155
info@codarestaurant.com.au

Stones of the Yarra Valley
12 St Huberts Rd, Coldstream
+61 3 8727 3000
careers@stonesoftheyarravalley.com

Maha
21 Bond St
+61 3 9629 5900
admin@maharestaurant.com.au

Miznon
59 Hardware Ln
+61 3 9670 2861
enquiries@miznonaustralia.com

MELBOURNE | WORK

The Moat
176 Little Lonsdale St
+61 3 9094 7820
info@themoat.com.au

Max on Hardware
54-58 Hardware Ln
+61 3 9600 1697
info@maxonhardware.com.au

Daughter In Law
37/41 Little Bourke St
+61 3 9242 0814
goodtimes@daughterinlaw.com.au

Pilgrim Bar
15-19 Federation Wharf
+61 3 9654 9575
functions@pilgrimbar.com.au

Longrain Restaurant
40-44 Little Bourke St
+61 3 9653 1600
melbourneinfo@longrain.com

Om Nom Kitchen
187 Flinders Ln
+61 3 8080 8827
omnom@adelphi.com.au

Embla
122 Russell St
+61 3 9654 5923
ask@embla.com.au

Lûmé
226 Coventry St, South Melbourne
+61 3 9690 0185
contact@restaurantlume.com

Natural History Public Bar
401 Collins St
+61 3 9982 1811
info@naturalhistorypublicbar.com.au

The Baths Upstairs
251 Esplanade, Brighton
+61 3 9539 7000
enquiry@middlebrightonbaths.com.au

Blu By Australian Seafood
146 Gaffney St, Coburg North
+61 3 9350 3200
patsiotis@live.com

Home Kitchen & Bar
1/222 Russell St
+61 3 9915 2528
events@leftbankmelbourne.com.au

Essence on Exhibition
Corner Exhibition &, Lonsdale St
+61 3 9660 1183
mhrs.melmc.ays@marriotthotels.com

Auterra
1160 High St Armadale
+61 3 8529 2660
hello@auterrawinebar.com.au

MELBOURNE | WORK

New York Minute
190 Coventry St, South Melbourne
+61 3 9699 3586
info@newyorkminute.com.au

Mr Hobson
9 Waterfront Pl, Port Melbourne
+61 3 9646 6299
functions@mrhobson.com.au

Time Out Fed Square
Federation Square, 2 Swanston St
+61 3 9671 3855
info@timeoutmelbourne.com.au

HQ's on William Restaurant
380 William St
+61 3 9322 8000
resmelb@radisson.com

Radii Restaurant & Bar
1 Parliament Pl
+61 3 9224 1211
melbourne.park@hyatt.com

Cumulus Inc.
45 Flinders Ln
+61 3 9650 1445
info@cumulusinc.com.au

Bars in Melbourne

Union Electric Bar & Rooftop Gin Garden
13 Heffernan Ln
+61450186466
info@unionelectric.com.au

Beneath Driver Lane
basement/3 Driver Ln
drink@driverlanebar.com

Gin Palace
10 Russell Pl
+61 3 9654 0533
teandra@ginpalace.com.au

Romeo Lane
1A Crossley St
+61457673647
info@romeolane.com.au

Arbory Bar & Eatery
1 Flinders Walk
+61 3 9614 0023
hello@arbory.com.au

1806
169 Exhibition St
+61 3 9663 7722
drinks@1806.com.au

Madame Brussels
59 Bourke St
+61 3 9662 2775
pearls@madamebrussels.com

Heartbreaker
234A Russell St
+61 3 9041 0856
info@heartbreakerbar.com.au

MELBOURNE | WORK

Trinket Bar Melbourne
87 Flinders Ln
+61 3 9810 0044
info@trinketbar.com.au

Bombabar
103 Lonsdale St
+61 3 9650 5778
info@bombabar.com.au

Bar Ampere
16 Russell Pl
+61 3 9663 7557
functions@barampere.com

Arlechin
Mornane Pl
info@arlechin.com.au

The Everleigh Melbourne
150-156 Gertrude St, Fitzroy
+61 3 9416 2229
info@theeverleigh.com

GoGo Bar
125 Flinders Ln
+61 3 8663 2020
info@gogobar.com.au

Loch & Key
34 Franklin St
+61408140043
cheers@lochandkey.com.au

Movida
1 Hosier Lane
+61 3 9663 3038
info@movida.com.au

Whisky and Alement
270 Russell St
+61 3 9654 1284
info@whiskyandale.com.au

House of Correction
Denyers, Building,
Level 4/264 Swanston St
admissions@houseofcorrection.com.au

State of Grace
27 King Street
+61 3 8563 0020
info@stateofgracemelbourne.com.au

Joe Taylor
7 Errol St, North Melbourne
+61 3 9329 4669
joetaylorbar@gmail.com

Bar Lourinhã
37 Little Collins St
+61 3 9663 7890
matt@barlourinha.com.au
drinks@barlourinha.com.au

Kirk's Wine Bar
46 Hardware Ln
+61 3 9600 4550
info@kirkswinebar.com

MELBOURNE | WORK

Ferdydurke
31 Tattersalls Ln
+61 3 9639 3750
info@ferdydurke.com.au

Cookie
252 Swanston St
+61 3 9663 7660
info@cookie.net.au

Section 8
27-29 Tattersalls Ln
+61430291588
media@section8.com.au

Gerald's Bar
386 Rathdowne St, Carlton North
+61 3 9349 4748
info@geraldsbar.eu

Mjølner Melbourne
106 Hardware St
+61 3 8393 9367
melbourne@mjolner.com.au

Whitehart Bar
22 Whitehart Ln
+61 3 9602 2260
drink@whitehartbar.com.au

Chuckle Park Bar
322 Little Collins St
+61 3 9650 4494
janelle@newguernica.com.au

TRAPT Bar & Escape Rooms
377 Lonsdale St
+61 3 9077 7941
bookings@trapt.in

The Elysian Whisky Bar
113 Brunswick St, Fitzroy
+61 3 9417 7441
info@theelysianwhiskybar.com.au

Jungle Boy
96 Chapel St, Windsor
+61 3 9943 7653
info@jboy.com.au

Berlin Bar
level 2/16 Corrs Ln
info@berlinbar.com.au

Bad Frankie
141 Greeves St, Fitzroy
+61 3 9078 3866
hello@badfrankie.com

Bar Liberty
234 Johnston St, Fitzroy
goodtimes@barliberty.com

Ponyfish Island
Pedestrian Bridge
manager@ponyfish.com.au

European Bier Cafe & Rooftop
120 Exhibition St
+61 3 8563 0080
info@ausvenueco.com.au

MELBOURNE | WORK

Fiftyfive
55 Elizabeth St
+61 3 9620 3899
enquiries@fifty-five.com.au

Murmur Piano Bar
17 Warburton Ln
+61 3 9640 0395
info@murmur.com.au

Cherry
68 Little Collins St
manager@cherrybar.com.au

The Carlton Club
193 Bourke St
+61 3 9663 3246
manager@thecarlton.com.au

Diesel Bar & Eatery
202 Little Lonsdale St
+61 3 9663 8078
diesel@acemelbourne.com.au

Bartronica
335 Flinders Ln
+61 3 9629 9921
bartronicamelb@gmail.com

Lustre Bar
Level 1/252 Flinders Ln
+61 3 9671 3371
bar@lustrebar.com.au

Paradise Alley
25 Easey St, Collingwood
+ 61 3 9029 8484
drink@paradisealley.com.au

Good Heavens Rooftop Bar
level 2/79 Bourke St
+61 3 9453 2882
info@goodheavens.com.au

Double Happiness
21 Liverpool St
+61 3 9650 4488
drink@double-happiness.com.au

Leonards House Of Love
3 Wilson St, South Yarra
+61428066778
admin@leonardshouseoflove.com.au

Robot Bar
12 Bligh Pl
+61 3 9620 3646
info@robotbar.com.au

GG EZ Bar
Basement 93/95 Queen St
+61 3 8539 6190
lachlan@ggezbar.com

Rooftop Campari House
23-25 Hardware Ln
+61 3 9600 1574
info@camparihouse.com.au

Galah
216 High St, Windsor
+61 3 9521 5325
info@galah.melbourne

MELBOURNE | WORK

Workshop
1/413 Elizabeth St
+61 3 9326 4365
enquiries@workshopbar.com.au

Storyville
185 Lonsdale St
+61 3 9993 9034
info@storyvillemelbourne.com.au

The Drunken Poet
65 Peel St, West Melbourne
+61 3 9348 9797
info@thedrunkenpoet.com.au

The Moon
28A Stanley St, Collingwood
+61 3 9089 0239
wine@themooninmelbourne.com

Golden Monkey
Basement, 389 Lonsdale Street
+61 3 9602 2055
down@goldenmonkey.com.au

Bodega Underground
55 Little Bourke St
+61 3 9650 9979
enquiries@bodegaunderground.com.au

The Joint Bar
35 Elizabeth St
+61 3 8614 5719
info@thejointbar.com.au

Captain Melville
34 Franklin St
+61 3 9663 6855
enquiries@captainmelville.com.au

Bar Clara
87 Little Bourke St
hello@barclara.com

Juliet Melbourne
37/41 Little Bourke St
+61 3 9639 4944
enquire@julietmelbourne.com.au

Atrium on 35
25 Collins St
+61 3 9653 7744
H1902@sofitel.com

Republica St Kilda Beach
10/18 Jacka Blvd, St Kilda
+61 3 8598 9055
info@republica.net.au

Fable
Level 13, 168 Lonsdale St, Melbourne
+61 (03) 9662 2629
info@fablemelbourne.com.au

Waxflower
153 Weston Street, Brunswick
+61 420 876 574
hello@waxflowerbar.com.au

MELBOURNE | GOING OUT

GOING OUT AND MEETING PEOPLE IN MELBOURNE

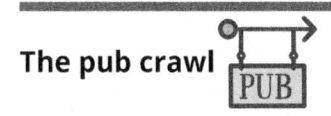

The pub crawl

The concept: you go out to four different bars in the same night for AUD $37, with a drink included in each bar. You can book online easily.

Several websites exist to make reservations:
https://www.melbournebarcrawl.com.au/
https://www.eventbrite.com.au/d/australia--melbourne/pub-crawl/

Couchsurfing website

Go to www.couchsurfing.com in the "events" section and meet people from all over the world.
https://www.couchsurfing.com/events

Facebook groups

https://www.facebook.com/groups/MelbourneBackpacker
https://www.facebook.com/groups/1911181859116003
(BACKPACKERS   Melbourne Australia   )
https://www.facebook.com/groups/melbbackpacker

Other websites

Meet Up: www.meetup.com/fr-FR/pub-crawl-melbourne/

Getting around Melbourne with the Myki card
To travel by train, bus or streetcar in Melbourne, you will need a touch-on/touch-off Myki card. It costs AUD $6.
1800 800 007
For more information: www.ptv.vic.gov.au/tickets/myki

BRISBANE

Brisbane (Brisbie for short) is the capital of Queensland with a population of 2,240,000.

As people say in Brisbane, life and business are more fun when it's sunny! And it's true, the laid-back attitude of the people of Queensland may surprise Europeans who arrive here. When you order a coffee, don't be surprised if the waiter says "too easy!". It just means "ok!".

Brisbane is sometimes called "the little village" because of its small size. Brisbane is the third most popular destination for backpackers in Australia after Sydney and Melbourne. It's a paradise for fruit picking (lots of farms in Queensland) and a must for those traveling along the coast between Sydney and Cairns. It is the ideal place to spend several months.

Brisbane's economy is constantly growing with major Australian companies basing their headquarters or smaller branches in the city. Financial services, information technology, and tourism drive the city's economy.

BRISBANE | WHAT TO SEE/ WHAT TO DO

Lone Pine Koala Sanctuary

This is the first and largest koala sanctuary in the world, with over 130 koalas. Cuddle a koala, feed the kangaroos, and meet a huge variety of Australian wildlife, all in beautiful natural settings.

> **Lone Pine Koala Sanctuary**
> Open every day from 9 am until 5 pm. Price: Adult: AUD$ 49
> 708 Jesmond Rd, Fig Tree Pocket QLD
> More information: http://www.koala.net/

Skydiving

Jump from a plane at 14,000m in tandem! After only fifteen minutes of brief preparation, you are in freefall for 60 seconds at 200km/hour! Then enjoy five minutes of breathtaking views as you descend. You can buy the video and/or photos of your jump.

The Parklands at South Bank

South Bank has Australia's only city centre beach, with panoramic views of the city! http://www.visitsouthbank.com.au/
LVL 3, South Bank House, Stanley St Plaza, South Bank.

Queensland Maritime Museum

Based in South Bank Parklands, the Queensland Maritime Museum is one of the largest of its kind in Australia, featuring the famous HMAS Diamantina (the Royal Australian Navy ship in service in 1945).

> **Queensland Maritime Museum**
> Entry: AUD$18 | Open every day from 9.30 am until 4.30 pm.
> South Brisbane Dry Dock, 412, Stanley Street, South Brisbane
> More information: http://www.maritimemuseum.com.au/

BRISBANE | WHAT TO SEE/ WHAT TO DO

Go and see a game at the Suncorp Stadium

The venue for major sporting events and outdoor concerts, with 52,500 seats, this world-class stadium hosts national and international rugby teams, football matches and concerts.

> **Suncorp Stadium**
> 40 Castlemaine St, Brisbane, Queensland
> www.suncorpstadium.com.au

Story Bridge

On part of the Bradfield Highway, the Story Bridge crosses over the Brisbane River and connects the districts of Fortitude Valley and Kangaroo Point. Watch it all lit up at night.

WHERE TO STAY IN BRISBANE

Upon arrival: short-term accommodation

You will ideally have booked your accommodation for the first few days before your departure.

It is not an obligation but after a 20 hour flight, you may not feel like walking the streets of the city in search of the best hostel.

The easiest way is to book a few nights in your city of arrival, either in a youth hostel or an Airbnb.

Airbnb can be a good solution to have your own private room in a house for example and thus recover from jet lag for the first few days.

Going straight from your flight to a bed in a dormitory can be tough, but on the other hand, you'll be right in the swing of things!

The hostel will then allow you to meet people and to be able to check job offers locally.

The hostels are often very well positioned in the city center, which is obviously a strategic location if you are looking for a job in the city.

BRISBANE | ACCOMMODATION

Couchsurfing

The reference website to stay for free with locals.

If you have an empty profile, are male and have few references, you will have little chance of being accommodated.

You can ask friends to give their opinion about you in the 'personal opinion' section.

It's a great place to meet locals and sleep on their couch for one or more nights.

In exchange for accommodation, you can, for example, prepare a meal for your host or buy them a drink in town!

Be careful to check the references of each host before asking them for accommodation.

www.couchsurfing.org

Hostels

Brisbane City YHA
Dorm: From AUD$ 25,50
Private room from AUD$ 100.
392 Upper Roma ST, Brisbane | Tel: +61 7 3236 1004
http://www.yha.com.au/hostels/

Brisbane Backpackers Resort
Dorm: From AUD$40
110 Vulture St, West End | info@brisbanebackpacker.com.au
Tel: +61 7 3844 9956/ 1 800 626 452
http://www.brisbanebackpackers.com.au/

Brisbane Quarters
Dorm: From AUD$71
Twin room from AUD$ 158.
Spring Hill, 413 Upper Edward St, Brisbane City
Tel: +61 7 3145 6788
http://www.bananabenders.com/

Somewhere To Stay
Dorm: From AUD$24
47 Brighton Road, Highgate Hill | Tel: +61 7 3846 2858
http://www.somewheretostay.com.au

BRISBANE | ACCOMMODATION | WORK

Long term rentals

To find a room in Brisbane, visit the websites below:
- Gumtree: https://www.gumtree.com.au
- Flatmates : https://flatmates.com.au
- Airbnb: https://www.airbnb.com (negotiate the price directly with the owner for a rental of several months)
- Facebook groups:
  - "Brisbane Rent a room/house/apartment/flat/accommodation" https://www.facebook.com/groups/161059968165326
  - "Brisbane Apartment Rentals, Houses, Sublets and Rooms": https://www.facebook.com/groups/438251969841785

FINDING A JOB AND WAGES IN BRISBANE

Finding a job in Brisbane means understanding the city's job requirements and having a detailed knowledge of the main industries and companies that are hiring in Brisbane.

With continued economic growth, the technology and finance industries have become major recruiters in Brisbane. Oil refineries and papermills are also important recruiters in the city.

Brisbane Port is a major employment opportunity; part of the Australian TradeCoast which is also one of the fastest-growing economic development areas in Australia.

In addition to other industries, Brisbane's tourism sector offers great openings for employment. If you have a degree in tourism management, the chances of getting a job are quite high.

There are many platforms available dedicated to finding a suitable job: online job websites, newspapers and recruitment agencies are the preferred and most reliable ways.

BRISBANE | WORK

Fast-growing industries

Brisbane offers a wide range of opportunities for candidates specialising in the services and manufacturing sectors.

The mining industry is also a major industry, but these days the city's focus is on research and development.

If you have skills in clean energy production, information and communication technology, finance, pharmaceuticals, food processing or biotechnology, Brisbane is a great place to find a job fast.

Manufacturing

Brisbane offers many opportunities for skilled workers and expert professionals in sectors such as machinery and equipment, plastics and metals, robotics and microelectronics, packaging and recycling, or marine industries such as shipbuilding.

> Because Brisbane is a port, it handles **37 million tonnes of goods** each year, which opens a multitude of **employment opportunities related to logistics distribution.**

The minimum wage in Queensland is $21.38/hour.

Under the National Employment Standards, the maximum weekly working hours for an employee in full-time employment is 38 hours.

An employer may require an employee to work overtime, as long as it is reasonable to do so.

WEBSITES FOR FINDING A JOB

www.careerone.com.au
This website offers an efficient search engine to help you find a job. Monster was born from the merger of Monster Worldwide and News Corp Australia. The website combines the job search facilities of Monster with the leadership of News Corp Australia.

www.adzuna.com.au
Job search website that works by keyword typed in the search bar. Possibility to upload your CV on the website.

www.seek.com.au
More than 150,000 job offers are online; the website records approximately 25 million visits per month. The website has a strong community that helps each other in their search.

www.adecco.com.au
It is one of the most trusted HR companies in the world, bringing together a large number of employers and job seekers.

www.michaelpage.com.au
It is one of the most reliable agencies in the world with offices on all six continents. Each local branch is adapted to local requirements, resulting in a globally successful organization locally. They focus specifically on matching the right candidate with the right recruiter by region, sector and industry.

www.hays.com.au
Hays is the world leader in placing qualified and skilled professionals. Hays manages a large number of jobs and last year alone placed a record 53,000 people in permanent positions. Hays is present in 33 countries, covering recruitment needs in 20 different specializations.

BRISBANE | WORK

www.airtasker.com
These are one-time projects offered by individuals.
You can be asked for example to help carry a mattress for AU$ 50 or to help with a house move. You can apply for each mission by trying to sell yourself as much as possible

www.australiawide.com.au
It is one of Australia's leading recruitment agencies for engineers, other technical staff and technology.
The company posts permanent and temporary jobs in technical, operations, engineering, and management areas.

www.jobsearch.gov.au
This website is run by the Australian government and advertises job vacancies in all sectors across Australia.
It has many job opportunities from other government agencies such as the Australian Defence Force and the Australian Public Services.

www.brisbane.qld.gov.au/about-council/working-council
This website offers jobs in information technology, communication, human resources management, environmental protection, architecture, administration, etc.

QUICKLY FIND A JOB IN THE HOSPITALITY SECTOR

What is the RSA and how to get it in Brisbane ?
The RSA is a certificate that shows you know the rules about alcohol.
RSA: Responsible Service of Alcohol
This certificate is mandatory to work in an establishment that serves alcohol: bar, restaurant, hotel. You will be asked to have it, so you might as well get it before you start looking for a job.

BRISBANE | WORK | RSA

It is possible that an employer will accept to hire you without the RSA, but you will then have a one-month deadline to pass it. You might as well put all your chances on your side by being prepared! It is easily done online:
www.eot.edu.au/online-courses/RSA/australia/
In the state of Queensland, it will cost you AUD$ 34.
If you don't know yet if you are going to stay and work in Queensland and plan to work in several Australian states, you can obtain the RSA valid in all states for AUD$ 183.

To find a job very quickly in Brisbane, we recommend sending your resume in bulk to the hotel and restaurant listings found in this guide. Emailing will allow you to send your resume to hundreds of establishments in one or two emails.

If you want to customize your emails to each company, you can choose from the list here.

If you choose emailing, here is the detailed method:

The method to send your CV to hundreds of companies

1- Create an account on MailChimp: www.login.mailchimp.com
2- On the "Audience" tab, go to "Add contacts" and "import contacts" then "copy/paste from file"
3- Open the following link and download the file
https://www.dropbox.com/sh/ni0ghaz3fn2lp2k/AAAnADPJ4Ayaadq6wAh7IrnWa?dl=0
4- Copy/paste the e-mail addresses from the excel spreadsheet to MailChimp (be careful, you are limited to 1000 contacts. If you want to send more than 1000 emails, you will just have to delete your contacts after your first sending and import the new ones).
5- Go to the "Create" tab, then "email". Name the campaign "Application". In the "To" part, choose the contact list you created. In "From", enter your name and your email address.
In the "Subject" part, write " Applying for a job ". In the "content" section, copy/paste the email you downloaded from Dropbox and adapt it to your background and name.
Don't forget to attach your CV!

BRISBANE | WORK

Please accept my enthusiastic application for a position in your hotel (or restaurant). I am happy to offer you my experience in the food industry, strong customer service skills, and my ability to work under pressure.

I believe I fulfill all of these requirements and am therefore an excellent candidate for you.

I have an extensive background in hospitality. I worked for two years at a fast-food restaurant. During this time I gained experience in nearly every aspect of food service. I took orders and served customers their meals, handled the cash register, and performed daily inventory checks.

I could assist not only in taking orders and serving customers but also in a variety of other capacities in which you might require assistance. I also worked in customer service for a number of years. As a cashier at a grocery store for two years, I assisted as many as one hundred customers daily.

My experience in the food industry and in customer service, and my ability to thrive under pressure make me an excellent candidate for you. I have enclosed my resume and will call within the next week to see if we might arrange a time to speak together.

Thank you so much for your time and consideration.

Sincerely,

Your name"

> **Cover letter**
> The cover letter does not need to be very long but it should highlight your experience in a few lines.
> If you have no experience in the catering industry and your English is average, don't panic. Australians are usually happy to give beginners a chance.
> You should then emphasize your qualities in your letter but also in your CV (see page 40, how to write an Australian CV).

BRISBANE | WORK

Hotels in Brisbane

PULLMAN BRISBANE AIRPORT
2 Dryandra Road, brisbane
+61 7 3188 7300
h9546-re@accor.com
H9559-SM@ACCOR.COM

NOVOTEL BRISBANE AIRPORT
6-8 the Circuit, Brisbane Airport
+61 7 3175 3100
H9559-SM@ACCOR.COM
renee.brereton@novotelbrisbaneairport.com.au
chris.butcher@novotelbrisbaneairport.com.au

IBIS BRISBANE AIRPORT
2 Dryandra Road, Brisbane
+61 7 3139 8100
H9559-SM@ACCOR.COM
h9546-re@accor.com

SOFITEL BRISBANE CENTRAL
249 Turbot St, Brisbane City
+61 7 3835 3535
H5992@Sofitel.com

PULLMAN BRISBANE KING GEORGE SQUARE
Corner Ann &, Roma St, Brisbane
+61 7 3229 9111
H8784-SL2@accor.com
H8784-RE@accor.com

IBIS BRISBANE
27-35 Turbot St, Brisbane City
+61 7 3237 2333
H2062@ACCOR.COM
h1750@accor.com

THE SEBEL BRISBANE
Cnr Albert and, Charlotte St, Brisbane
+61 7 3224 3500
amanda.balaam@accor.com
H8778@accor.com

NOVOTEL BRISBANE
200 Creek St, Brisbane City
+61 7 3309 3309
peta.hill@accor.com
h1749@accor.com
h1750-sl5@accor.com

MERCURE BRISBANE
85-87 North Quay, Brisbane
+61 7 3237 2300
H1750-RE02@ACCOR.COM
h1750@accor.com

MERCURE BRISBANE KING GEORGE SQUARE
Cnr of Ann & Roma streets
+61 7 3229 9111
H8780@ACCOR.COM
H8784-RE@accor.com

IBIS STYLES BRISBANE ELIZABETH STREET
40 Elizabeth Street, Brisbane
+61 7 3337 9000
H8835@accor.com
H8835-SM@accor.com

154

BRISBANE | WORK

Ibis Budget Windsor
159 Lutwyche Rd, Brisbane City
+61 7 3857 0488
H5403@accor.com

Gambaro Hotel Brisbane
33 Caxton St, Petrie Terrace
+61 7 3369 9500
careers@tfehotels.com

Pacific Hotel Brisbane
345 Wickham Terrace, Spring Hill
+61 7 3831 6177
info@pacifichotelbrisbane.com.au

The Great Southern Hotel
103 George St, Brisbane City
+61 7 3221 6044
reservations103g@greatsouthernhotel.com.au

Mantra Terrace Brisbane
52 Astor Terrace, Brisbane City
+61 7 5665 4450
terrace.res@mantra.com.au

Next Hotel Brisbane
72 Queen St, Brisbane City
+61 7 3222 3222
reservations.brisbane@nexthotels.com

Brisbane Backpackers
110 Vulture St, West End
+61 7 3844 9956
info@brisbanebackpacker.com.au

The Park Hotel Brisbane
551 Wickham Terrace, Spring Hill
+61 7 3058 9333
reservations_theparkhotelbrisbane@evt.com

Rydges South Bank Brisbane
9 Glenelg St, South Brisbane
+61 7 3364 0800
reservations_rydgessouthbank@evt.com

Riverside Hotel SouthBank
20 Montague Rd, South Brisbane
+61 7 3846 0577
reservations@riversidehotel.com.au

Emporium Hotel South Bank
267 Grey St, South Brisbane
+61 7 3556 3333
info@emporiumhotels.com.au

George Williams Hotel
317-325 George St, Brisbane City
+61 7 3308 0700
reservations@georgewilliamshotel.com.au
Tatiano.deoliveira@georgewilliamshotel.com.au

Stamford Plaza Brisbane
39 Edward St, Brisbane City
+61 7 3221 1999
sales@spb.stamford.com.au

Meriton Suites
43 Herschel St, Brisbane City
+61 2 9277 1125
stay@meriton.net.au

BRISBANE | WORK

City Edge Brisbane Hotel
63 Turbot St, Brisbane City
+61 7 3211 3437
info@cityedge.com.au
brisbane@cityedge.com.au

Brisbane Manor Hotel
555 Gregory Terrace, Brisbane City
reservations@brisbanemanor.com

View Brisbane
Kingsford Smith Dr &, Hunt St, Hamilton
+61 7 3862 1800
stay.brisbane@viewhotels.com
brisbane@viewhotels.com

Oaks Felix
26 Felix St, Brisbane City
+61 7 3221 6044
reservations@theoaksgroup.com.au

Capri By Fraser Brisbane
80 Albert St, Brisbane City
+61 7 3013 0088
reservations.brisbane@capribyfraser.com

Nomads Brisbane
308 Edward St, Brisbane City
+61 7 3211 2433
brisbane@nomadsworld.com

Brisbane Skytower
222 Margaret St, Brisbane City
+61 7 3003 0880
admin@brisbaneskytower.com.au

Mantra South Bank Brisbane
161 Grey St, Brisbane
+61 7 3305 2500
southbankbris.res@mantra.com.au

Royal On The Park Brisbane
152 Alice St, Brisbane City
+61 7 3221 3411
stay@royalonthepark.com.au

Brisbane City YHA
392 Upper Roma St, Brisbane
+61 7 3236 1004
brisbanecity@yha.com.au

The Point Brisbane
21 Lambert St, Kangaroo Point
+61 7 3240 0888
reservations@thepointbrisbane.com.au

Mantra Midtown Brisbane
127 Charlotte St, Brisbane City
+61 7 5665 4450
midtown.res@mantra.com.au

Morgan Suites Hotel
14 Merivale St, South Brisbane
+61 7 3018 9404
admin@morgansuites.com.au

Somewhere To Stay
47 Brighton Rd, Highgate Hill
Info@somewheretostay.com.au

Kennigo Hotel Brisbane
22/28 Kennigo St, Spring Hill
richmont.res@mantra.com.au

BRISBANE | WORK

Cathedral Place
41 Gotha St, Fortitude Valley
+61 7 3252 5288
Reservations@cathedralplace.com.au

Bunk Brisbane
11 Gipps St, Fortitude Valley
+61 7 3257 3644
INFO@BUNKBRISBANE.COM.AU

The Manor Apartment Hotel
289 Queen St, Brisbane City
+61 7 3319 4700
info@manorapartments.com.au

Banana Bender Backpackers
118 Petrie Terrace, Brisbane
+61 7 3367 1157
reception@bananabenders.com

The Calile Hotel Brisbane
48 James St, Fortitude Valley
+61 7 3607 5888
reservations@thecalilehotel.com

Bowen Terrace
365 Bowen Terrace, New Farm
+61 7 3254 0458
book@bowenterrace.com.au

Kookaburra Inn
41 Phillips St, Spring Hill
+61 7 3832 1303
accom@kookaburra-inn.com.au

The Johnson Brisbane Art Series
477 Boundary St, Spring Hill
+61 7 3085 7200
careers@artserieshotels.com.au

Mantra on Mary Brisbane
70 Mary St, Brisbane City
+61 7 3503 8000
mary.res@mantra.com.au

The Metropolitan Spring Hill
106 Leichhardt St, Spring Hill
+61 7 3831 6000
info@metropolitanspringhill.com.au

Spicers Balfour Hotel
37 Balfour St, New Farm
reception.balfour@spicersretreats.com

ULTIQA Rothbury Hotel
301 Ann St, Brisbane City
+61 7 3239 8888
reservations@rothburyhotel.com.au

Gabba Central by Vivo
803 Stanley St, Woolloongabba
+61 7 3175 4700
info@gabbacentralapartments.com.au

Breeze Lodge
635 Main St, Kangaroo Point
+61 7 3156 8434
stay@breezelodge.com.au

The Milton Brisbane
55 Railway Terrace, Milton
milton@themiltonbrisbane.com

BRISBANE | WORK

Central Brunswick Apartment Hotel
455 Brunswick St, Fortitude Valley
+61 7 3852 1411
info@centralbrunswickhotel.com.au

Park Regis North Quay
293 N Quay, Brisbane City
+61 7 3013 7200
northquay@parkregishotels.com
confprnq@parkregishotels.com

Kingsford Riverside Inn
114 Kingsford Smith Dr, Hamilton
+61 7 3862 1317
k.r.inn@optusnet.com.au

Sage Hotel Brisbane
70 James St, Fortitude Valley
+61 7 3222 3111
reservations.jamesst@sagehotels.com

Eatons Hill Hotel
646 S Pine Rd, Eatons Hill
+61 7 3325 6777
info@eatonshillhotel.com.au

The Kingsford Brisbane Airport Hotel
510 Kingsford Smith Dr, Hamilton
+61 7 3622 0400
reservations@thekingsford.com.au

FV by Peppers
191 Brunswick St, Fortitude Valley
+61 7 3118 9199
fv.res@peppers.com.au

Royal Albert
167 Albert St, Brisbane City
+61 7 3291 8888
stay@royalalbert.com.au

The Docks on Goodwin
15 Goodwin St, Kangaroo Point
+61 7 3320 1800
info@thedocks.com.au

Kingsford Smith Motel
610 Kingsford Smith Dr, Hamilton
+61 7 3868 4444
bookings@kingsfordsmithmotel.com.au

Airport Ascot Motel
550 Kingsford Smith Dr, Hamilton
+61 7 3268 5266
info@airportascotmotel.com.au

Lancaster Court Motel
521 Ipswich Rd, Annerley
+61 7 3892 5700
admin@lancastercourt.com.au

Sunnybank Hotel
275 McCullough St, Sunnybank
+61 7 3345 1081
sunnybankhotel@alhgroup.com.au

BRISBANE | WORK

Menso at Southbank
68 Cordelia St, South Brisbane
+61 7 3844 1355
reception@mensoatsouthbank.com.au

PRINCE OF WALES HOTEL
100 Buckland Road, Nundah
+61 73266 8077
prince.of.wales.hotel@alhgroup.com.au

Alpha Mosaic Hotel Fortitude Valley
12 Church St, Fortitude Valley
+61 7 3332 8888
enquiries@alphahotels.com.au

Jephson Hotel
63 Jephson St Toowong
+61 7 3736 4400
book@jephsonhotel.com.au

The Airport International
528 Kingsford-Smith Dve, Brisbane
+61732686388
info@airportmotel.com.au

Limes Hotel
142 Constance St, Fortitude Valley
+61 7 3852 9000
booking@limeshotel.com.au

Airport Clayfield Motel
772 Sandgate Rd, Clayfield
+61 7 3862 2966
airportclayfield@live.com

Salisbury Hotel
668 Toohey Rd, Salisbury
+61 7 3051 7642
Info.salisbury@ausvenueco.com.au

Alexandra Hills Hotel
McDonald Rd & Finucane Rd, Alexandra Hills
+61 7 3824 4444
alexmanagers@mcguireshotels.com.au

Airport Motel Brisbane
638 Kingsford Smith Dr, Hamilton
+61 7 3868 2399
airport-motel@bigpond.com

Hotel Chino
19 O'Keefe St, Woolloongabba
+61 7 3896 4000
stay@hotelchino.com.au

Waterloo Bay Hotel
75 Berrima St, Wynnum
+61 7 3893 2344
info@waterloobayhotel.com.au

Chill Backpackers
328 Upper Roma St, Brisbane City
+61 7 3236 0088
info@chillbackpackersbrisbane.com.au

BRISBANE | WORK

French restaurants in Brisbane

Prive249
249 Turbot St, Brisbane City
+61 7 3835 3535
H5992@sofitel.com

Boucher French Bistro
365 Honour Ave, Graceville
+61 7 3716 0388
info@boucher.com.au

La Vue Waterfront Restaurant
1/501 Queen St, Brisbane City
+61 7 3831 1400
manager@lavuerestaurant.com.au

Greenglass
336 George St, Brisbane City
+61403966671
336@greenglasswine.com

Haig Rd. Bistro
111 Haig Rd, Auchenflower
+61 7 3706 3381
hello@haigrdbistro.com.au

French Martini
Little Stanley St, South Brisbane
+61 7 3844 5541
robert@broofa.com

Les Bubbles Steakhouse
144 Wickham St, Fortitude Valley
+61444573955
info@lesbubbles.com.au

AQUITAINE
Sidon St, Brisbane City
+61 7 3844 1888
enquiries@aquitainebrasserie.com.au

Miss Claudes Crepes
400 Newmarket Rd, Newmarket
+61 7 3156 8407
crepes@missclaudes.com.au

Lutèce Bistro & Wine Bar
60 MacGregor Terrace, Bardon
+61 7 3161 1858
bookings@lutece.com.au

Libertine Restaurant
5/61 Petrie Terrace, Brisbane City
+61 7 3367 3353
info@libertine.net.au

French & Mor
shop 1/2 Dawn Rd, Albany Creek
+61 7 3264 1555
pauljones@frenchandmor.com.au

C'est Bon & Le Bon Bar
609/611 Stanley St, Woolloongabba
+61 7 3891 2008
bonjour@cestbon.com.au

The Kitchen
21 Kittyhawk Dr, Chermside
+61 7 3359 9122
kwsc_marketing@kedron-wavell.com.au

BRISBANE | WORK

The Walnut Restaurant and Lounge Bar
152 Alice St, Brisbane City
+61 7 3112 1650
webmaster@thewalnutrestaurant.com.au

Bisou Bisou
458 Brunswick Street, Fortitude Valley
+61 (07) 3131 8900
info@bisou-bisou.com.au

La Cache à Vín
215 Wharf St, Spring Hill
+61 7 3924 0501
lcavwine@outlook.com

Alchemy Restaurant
175 Eagle St, Brisbane City
+61 7 3229 3175
mail@alchemyrestaurant.com.au

Australian restaurants in Brisbane

Bacchus
Podium Level, Rydges South Bank, Glenelg Street & Grey Street, South Brisbane
+61 7 3364 0837
info@bacchussouthbank.com.au

Port Office Dining Room
40 Edward St, Brisbane City
+61 7 3003 4700
functions@portofficehotel.com.au

Customs House
399 Queen St, Brisbane City
+61 7 3365 8999
info@customshouse.com.au

Wooden Horse Restaurant
278 Junction Rd, Clayfield
+61 7 3857 3893
info@woodenhorserestaurant.com.au

Lennons Restaurant & Bar
2/72 Queen St, Brisbane City
+61 7 3222 3232
lennons.brisbane@nexthotels.com

The Lab
130 William St, Brisbane City
+61 7 3306 8888
treasuryfunctions@star.com.au

Montagues Restaurant The Riverside Hotel
20 Montague Rd, South Brisbane
+61 7 3846 0577
reservations@riversidehotel.com.au

Outback Steakhouse Aspley
815 Zillmere Rd, Aspley
+61 7 3862 8199
mike@outbacksteakhouse.com.au

BRISBANE | WORK

Six Acres Restaurant
601 Gregory Terrace, Bowen Hills
+61 7 3188 3000
sixacresrestaurant_rydgesfortitudevalley@evt.com

Portabella
24/720 Albany Creek Rd, Albany Creek
+61 7 3264 8044
info@portabella.com.au

Hobby Lane
4/43 Blackwood St, Mitchelton
+61 7 3355 7990
hobbylanecafe@gmail.com

Restaurant Dan Arnold
10/959 Ann St, Fortitude Valley
+61 7 3189 2735
contact@restaurantdanarnold.com

Little Big House
18 Southpoint, 271 Grey St, South Brisbane
+61 7 3727 3999
res.littlebighouse@solotel.com.au

Vine Restaurant Bar
5/158 Moray St, New Farm
+61 7 3358 6658
info@vinerestaurant.com.au

Blackbird Bar & Grill
Riverside Centre,
123 Eagle St, Brisbane City
+61 7 3229 1200
info@blackbirdbrisbane.com.au

Alchemy Restaurant
175 Eagle St, Brisbane City
+61 7 3229 3175
mail@alchemyrestaurant.com.au

Kennigo Social House
Ground Floor, 28 Kennigo St, Spring Hill
+61 7 3096 1622
kennigosocialhouse@mantra.com.au

Three Blue Ducks
W Brisbane, Level 3/81 N Quay, Brisbane City
+61 7 3556 8833
enquiries@threeblueducks.com

Malt Dining
28 Market St, Brisbane City
+61 7 3236 4855
enquiries@maltdining.com.au

hundred acre bar
Carawa St, St Lucia
+61 7 3870 3433
enquiries@hillstonestlucia.com.au

Putia Pure Food Kitchen
4/17 Royal Parade, Banyo
+61 7 3267 6654
eat@putiapurefood.com.au

Kookaburra Cruises
Eagle Street Pier, 1 Eagle Street, Brisbane City
+61 7 3221 1300
bookings@kookaburrariverqueens.com

BRISBANE | WORK

Bars in Brisbane

Brooklyn Standard
Eagle Ln, BrisbaneCity
+61 7 3221 1604
management@brooklynstandard.com.au

Mr Chester Wine Bar
2/850 Ann St, Fortitude Valley
info@mrchesterwine.com

Next Episode
5 Cordelia St, South Brisbane
nxtepisodebar@gmail.com

The Scratch Bar
8/1 Park Rd, Milton
+61 7 3107 9910
info@scratchbar.com

The Plough Inn
29 Stanley St Plaza, Brisbane
+61 7 3844 7777
events@ploughinn.com.au

Friday's Riverside
Riverside Centre, 123 Eagle St, Brisbane City
+61 7 3051 7622
info@fridays.com.au

Baedeker - Wine Bar
Fortitude Valley
+61 7 3257 4482
enquiries@baedeker.com.au

The Gresham Bar
308 Queen St, Brisbane City
+61437360158
gatherings@thegresham.com.au

Criterion
239 George St, Brisbane City
+61 7 3221 7411
functions@criteriontavern.com.au

Jabiru Cafe & Bar
Brisbane Club Tower, Post Office Square, Level 1, 241 Adelaide St, Brisbane City
+61 7 3062 0245
jabiru.cbd@fibonaccicoffee.com.au

Southbank Beer Garden
30ba Stanley St Plaza,
South Brisbane
+61 7 3844 2866
manager@southbankbeergarden.com.au

Tippler's Tap
5/182 Grey St, South Brisbane
info@tipplerstap.com.au

Lychee Lounge
2/94 Boundary St, West End
+61411888561
vicky@lycheelounge.com.au

BRISBANE | WORK

Super Whatnot
48 Burnett Ln, Brisbane City
+61 7 3210 2343
hello@superwhatnot.com

Suzie Wongs Good Time Bar
678 Ann St, Brisbane
+61 7 3252 0202
info@thebowery.com.au

Mr & Mrs G Riverbar
1 Eagle St, Brisbane City
+61 7 3221 7001
functions@mrandmrsg.com.au

Bar Pacino
175 Eagle St, Brisbane City
+61 7 3221 2397
events@barpacino.com.au

Eleven Rooftop Bar
757 Ann St, Fortitude Valley
+61 7 3067 7447
functions@elevenrooftopbar.com.au

Sixteen Antlers Rooftop Bar
Level 16 Pullman & Mercure Hotel
Cnr Ann &, Roma St, Brisbane City
+61466463742
hello@sixteenantlers.com.au

Byblós
39 Hercules St, Hamilton
+61 7 3268 2223
brisbane@byblosbar.com.au

John Mills Himself
40 Charlotte St, Brisbane City
+61434064349
cafe@johnmillshimself.com.au
bar@johnmillshimself.com.au

Embassy Bar & Kitchen
214 Elizabeth St, Brisbane City
+61 7 3221 7616
emerybasil@yahoo.com

Canvas Club
16B Logan Rd, Woolloongabba
+61 7 3891 2111
info@canvasclub.com.au

Riverland Brisbane
167 Eagle St, Brisbane City
+61 7 3051 7655
info.riverland@ausvenueco.com.au

Soleil Pool Bar
9 Glenelg St, South Brisbane
+61 7 3364 0838
info@soleilpoolbar.com.au

Gerard's Bar
13a/23 James St, Fortitude Valley
+61 7 3252 2606
info@gerardsbar.com.au

The Fox Hotel
71-73 Melbourne St, South Brisbane
+61 7 3844 2883
manager@thefox.com.au

BRISBANE | WORK

Riverland Brisbane
167 Eagle St, Brisbane City
+61 7 3051 7655
info.riverland@ausvenueco.com.au

The Terrace
Emporium Hotel South Bank,
Level 21/267 Grey St, Brisbane
+61 7 3556 3333
info@emporiumhotels.com.au

Eagles Nest Brisbane
21 Lambert St, Kangaroo Point
+61 1800 088 388
info@eaglesnestbrisbane.com.au

The Pool Terrace + Bar
Next Hotel Brisbane, Level 4,
72 Queen Street, Brisbane City
+61 7 3222 3222
reservations.brisbane@nexthotels.com

Platform Bar
270 Ann St, Brisbane City
+61 7 3220 2061
functions@grandcentralhotel.com.au

Brew Cafe & Wine Bar
Lower, Burnett Ln, Brisbane City
+61 7 3211 4242
stuff@brewcafewinebar.com.au

CRU Bar & Cellar
1/22 James St, Fortitude Valley
+61 7 3252 2400
functions@crubar.com

Proud Henry
Wine bar and ginoteca
153 Wickham St, Brisbane City
+61 7 3102 1237
info@proudhenry.com.au

Fitz + Potts
1180 Upstairs, Sandgate Rd, Nundah
+61 7 3061 6205
bookings@fitzandpotts.com.au

Jade Buddha Bar & Kitchen
14/1 Eagle St, Brisbane City
+61 7 3221 2888
info@jadebuddha.com.au
jaelle@jadebuddha.com.au

Brewski Bar
22 Caxton St, Brisbane City
+61 7 3369 2198
hello@brewskibar.com.au

Mr Percival's
5 Boundary St, Brisbane City
+61 7 3188 9090
contact@mrpercivals.com.au

Aquilea Brisbane
G/82 Eagle St, Brisbane City
+61 7 3221 2228
hello@aquila.net.au

Dutch Courage
51 Alfred St, Fortitude Valley
+61 7 3852 4838
info@dutchcourage.com.au

BRISBANE | WORK

Botanic Bar
P Block, Level 3, 2 George Street, Brisbane City
+61 7 3138 8392
pcanning@qutguild.com

Buffalo Bar
169 Mary St, Brisbane City
+61 7 3051 7620
info@buffalobar.com.au

Irish Murphy's
175 George St, Brisbane City
+61 7 3221 4277
brisbane@irishmurphys.com.au
danielle@irishmurphys.com.au

Semi-Pro Brewing Co
65 Manilla St, East Brisbane
beer@semiprobrewing.com.au

The Victory Hotel
127 Edward St, Brisbane City
+61 7 3221 0444
victory.hotel@alhgroup.com.au

HOPE & ANCHOR
267 Given Terrace, Paddington
+61 7 3367 8300
reservations@hopeandanchor.net.au

The Bavarian Eagle Street
1/45 Eagle St, Brisbane City
+61 7 3339 0900
reservations@thebavarian.com.au

Jungle Tiki Bar
76 Vulture St, West End
+61448925912
manager@junglewestend.com.au

Cowch Dessert Cocktail Bar South Bank
2/179 Grey St, South Brisbane
+61 7 3844 1559
chermside@cowch.com.au

Greaser
259 Brunswick St, Fortitude Valley
+61 7 3648 9036
info@greaser.com.au

Saccharomyces Beer Cafe
Fish Ln, South Brisbane
+61 7 3846 0718
beerdeity@sbcbar.com

Verve Restaurant
109 Edward St, Brisbane City
+61 7 3221 5691
info@vervecafe.com.au

BRISBANE | GOING OUT

GOING OUT AND MEETING PEOPLE IN BRISBANE

Pub crawls

The idea: you go out to 4 different bars in the same evening (from AUD $27), with a drink included in each bar. Meet between 8pm and 8:30 pm in the first bar to validate your ticket.
You can book directly on the website:
https://www.eventbrite.com.au/d/australia--brisbane-city/bar-crawl/

Couchsurfing

Go to www.couchsurfing.com in the "events" section and meet people from all over the world.
https://www.couchsurfing.com/events
There is also a section : "Hangouts" where you can see who wants to go out in the city.

Facebook groups

"Brits in Brisbane" : www.facebook.com/groups/822469084431830
"BRISBANE Australia   Backpacker / Traveler" :
https://www.facebook.com/groups/BrisbaneBackpackerTraveler

Other websites

Meet Up:
www.meetup.com/fr-FR/allmyfriends/?chapter_analytics_code=UA-32831841-1

Going around Brisbane with the Go Card
Called the BUZ, the buses operate from 6 am to 11 pm and run every 10 to 15 minutes depending on the time of day.
There is a free bus that runs around the CBD.
Plus d'informations: http://translink.com.au

CAIRNS

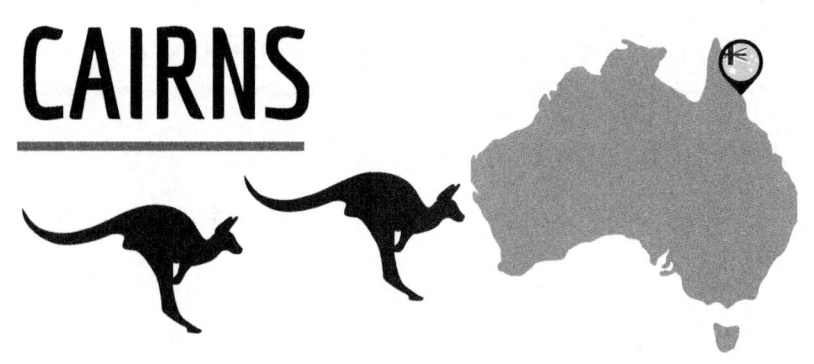

Cairns is located in the far north of Queensland, 1700 kilometers from Brisbane. It has a population of approximately 150,000.
It is **the 13th largest city in Australia** and one of the largest in Queensland. It was originally built to help Australian miners get to the Hodgkinson River goldfield. Today the area has been transformed into a port city.
It is a human-sized town where it is easy to do everything on foot.
The climate is tropical, with a wet season and its monsoons (from November to May) and a dry season (from June to October).
It is a touristic town because of its access to the Great Barrier Reef and the cruises that go there for diving or snorkeling.
The cost of living in Cairns is lower than in other major Australian cities, making it an attractive city to live in.
Hostel accommodation costs around AUD$30 per night, often including a free meal or vouchers for drinks in the bars where you'll meet many travellers.
If you arrive by bus or plane, a free shuttle will pick you up at the train station or airport and take you to your hostel. This is a service offered by most accommodations.
If you are looking for a job in Cairns, **look for opportunities in the hospitality and tourism sector.**

CAIRNS | WHAT TO SEE/ WHAT TO DO

The lagoon

There are no beaches in Cairns, but there is the lagoon! It is located along the Esplanade and offers crystal clear water! If you go there very early in the morning, you will probably see locals doing their daily exercise in the water.

Skydiving

Jump from a plane at 14,000m in tandem! After only fifteen minutes of training, you will be in freefall for 60 seconds at 200km/hour! Then enjoy five minutes of descent to take in the scenery. You can buy the video and/or photos of your jump.

Skydive Cairns
52/54 Fearnley St, Portsmith | 1300 663 634
From AUD$299.
More information: https://www.skydive.com.au/cairns/

Bungy jumping

The Cairns bungee jumping site is the only one in Australia where you can jump off a high-rise building.
Try one of 16 different jumps!
Jump from 50 meters high into a dense rainforest, surrounded by trees and natural waterfalls. From the top, enjoy the view of the beaches and the Great Barrier Reef!
More information: https://www.skyparkglobal.com/au-en/cairns

Skypark Cairns by AJ Hackett
End of McGregor Rd, Smithfield | +61 7 4057 7188
À partir de AUD$139
https://www.skyparkglobal.com/au-en/cairns

CAIRNS | WHAT TO SEE/ WHAT TO DO

Crystal Cascades and Lake Morris

Twenty kilometres from Cairns, the Crystal Cascades are a succession of waterfalls and pools accessible from a footpath (1.2km).
You can get to Lake Morris from Crystal Cascades by walking through the rainforest (three hours round trip).

The Great Barrier Reef

The Great Barrier Reef is the longest coral reef in the world and stretches for 2600 km!
Many tour companies offer a day trip (or longer) to explore the area.
You can even learn to dive and get a certificate on one of these cruises. An instructor shows you the basics on the boat before taking you out into the water as a duo.
The trip costs about $100. You will need to add another $100 for the diving option.
The boats leave from the Marina.

> **Is the Great Barrier Reef going to disappear?**
> The Great Barrier Reef is a multi-billion dollar tourist industry, but due to pollution, it could be gone by 2050. Its slow death is caused by warming waters and coral bleaching.
> Want to know more? http://www.gbrmpa.gov.au

ACCOMMODATION IN CAIRNS

Upon arrival: short-term accommodation

You will ideally have reserved your accommodation for the first few days before your departure.
It is not an imperative but after 20 hours of flight, you may not feel like walking the streets of the city in search of the best hostel.

CAIRNS | ACCOMMODATION

The easiest way is to book a few nights in your city of arrival, either in a youth hostel or an Airbnb.

Airbnb can be a good solution to have your own private room in a house for example and thus recover from jet lag for the first few days.

Going straight from your flight to a bed in a dormitory can be tough, but on the other hand, you'll be right in the swing of things!

The hostel will then allow you to meet people and to be able to check job offers locally.

The hostels are often very well positioned in the city center, which is obviously a strategic location if you are looking for a job in the city.

Couchsurfing

The reference website to stay for free with locals.

If you have an empty profile, are male and have few references, you will have little chance of being accommodated.

You can ask friends to give their opinion about you in the 'personal opinion' section.

It's a great place to meet locals and sleep on their couch for one or more nights.

In exchange for accommodation, you can, for example, prepare a meal for your host or buy them a drink in town!

Be careful to check the references of each host before asking them for accommodation.

www.couchsurfing.org

Hostels

YHA Cairns Central
Dorm: From AUD$ 42.20.
20-26 McLeod St, Cairns | Tel: +61 7 4051 0772
www.yha.com.au/hostels/qld/cairns-and-far-north-queensland/

CAIRNS | ACCOMMODATION

Mad Monkey Backpackers Village
Dorm: From AUD$ 32
Double room from AUD$ 121.
141 Sheridan St, Cairns City | Tel: +61 7 4231 9612
https://www.madmonkey.com.au/

Summer House Backpackers Cairns
Dorm: From AUD$ 32.
Double room from AUD$ 140.
341 Lake St, cairns | Tel: +61 7 4221 3411
http://www.staysummerhouse.com/

Gilligan's
Dorm: from AUD$26
Private room (twin or double) from AUD$ 159.
57-89 Grafton St, Cairns City | Tel: +61 7 4041 6566
https://gilligans.com.au/

The Jack Hotel & Backpackers
Dorm: From AUD$ 28.
Private room from AUD$ 40/person.
Sheridan St &, Spence St, Cairns City | Tel: +61 7 4051 2490
https://thejack.com.au/

Long-Term Rentals

To find a room in Cairns, visit the websites below:
- Gumtree: https://www.gumtree.com.au
- Flatmates : https://flatmates.com.au
- Airbnb: https://www.airbnb.com (price to be negociated with the landlord for a long-term stay)
- Facebook groups:

https://www.facebook.com/groups/Cairns.Room1
"Flatmates Cairns" :
https://www.facebook.com/groups/191155877573571/
"CAIRNS   - Rent a House, Villa, Apartment, Flat, etc"
https://www.facebook.com/groups/1985933561423258

CAIRNS | ACCOMMODATION | WORK

FINDING A JOB AND SALARY IN CAIRNS

Cairns is a city full of opportunities. With its cosmopolitan atmosphere and tranquil waterfront lifestyle, Cairns attracts tourists. Its rapid pace of growth and modernisation continues, and in its wake comes employment opportunities. Cairns' urban growth has brought with it new jobs in technology and management, as well as employment opportunities in more traditional areas.

Its tropical climate and coastal location make Cairns a popular destination for tourists. The Cairns Regional Council offers a fair amount of employment in the health and social services sector. These two sectors employ about 14% of the total workforce.

Finding the right job requires the use of every possible job search tool. The most important ones are: job boards, employment agencies, newspapers and personal networking. There are many job websites that can be used easily.

The minimum wage in Queensland is AUD$ 21.38/heure.
Under national employment standards, the maximum weekly working time for an employee in full-time employment is 38 hours. An employer may require an employee to work overtime, as long as it is reasonable.

WEBSITES FOR FINDING A JOB

www.careerone.com.au
This website offers an efficient search engine to help you find a job. Monster was born from the merger of Monster Worldwide and News Corp Australia. The website combines the job search facilities of Monster with the leadership of News Corp Australia.

CAIRNS | WORK

www.adzuna.com.au
Job search website that works by keyword typed in the search bar. Possibility to upload your CV on the website.

www.seek.com.au
More than 150,000 job offers are online; the website records approximately 25 million visits per month. The website has a strong community that helps each other in their search.

www.adecco.com.au
It is one of the most trusted HR companies in the world, bringing together a large number of employers and job seekers.

www.michaelpage.com.au
It is one of the most reliable agencies in the world with offices on all six continents. Each local branch is adapted to local requirements, resulting in a globally successful organization locally. They focus specifically on matching the right candidate with the right recruiter by region, sector and industry.

www.hays.com.au
Hays is the world leader in placing qualified and skilled professionals. Hays manages a large number of jobs and last year alone placed a record 53,000 people in permanent positions. Hays is present in 33 countries, covering recruitment needs in 20 different specializations.

www.airtasker.com
These are one-time assignments offered by individuals.
For example, you can be asked to help carry a mattress for AUD $50 or to help with a move. You can apply for each mission by trying to sell yourself as much as possible.

CAIRNS | WORK

www.australiawide.com.au
It is one of Australia's leading recruitment agencies for engineers, other technical staff and technology.
The company posts permanent and temporary jobs in technical, operations, engineering, and management areas.

www.jobsearch.gov.au
This website is run by the Australian government and advertises job vacancies in all sectors across Australia.
It has many job opportunities from other government agencies such as the Australian Defence Force and the Australian Public Services.

https://cairnsqld.mercury.com.au
The Regional Council always offers some opportunities. It offers competitive salaries and a range of attractive perks.

QUICKLY FIND A JOB IN THE HOSPITALITY SECTOR

What is the RSA and how to get it in Cairns ?
The RSA is a certificate that shows that you know the rules related to alcohol.
RSA: Responsible Service of Alcohol

This certificate is mandatory to work in an establishment that serves alcohol: a bar, restaurant, or hotel. You will be asked to have it, so you might as well get it before you start looking for a job. It is possible that an employer will accept to hire you without the RSA, but you will then have a one-month deadline to pass it. You might as well put all your chances on your side by being prepared! It is easily done online: www.eot.edu.au/online-courses/RSA/australia/
In Queensland, it will cost you AUD $34.
The test takes betweem 3 and 6 hours maximum.

CAIRNS | WORK | RSA

If you don't know yet if you are going to stay and work in Queensland and plan to work in several Australian states, you can obtain the RSA valid in all states for AUD$ 183.

To find a job quickly in Cairns, we recommend sending your resume in bulk to the hotel and restaurant listings found in this guide.

Emailing will allow you to send your resume to hundreds of establishments in one or two emails.

If you want to customize your emails to each company, you can choose from the list here.

If you choose emailing, here is the detailed method

The method to send your CV to hundreds of companies:

1- Create your account on MailChimp: www.login.mailchimp.com

2- On the "Audience" tab, go to "Add contacts" and "import contacts" then "copy/paste from file"

3- Open the following link on www.dropbox and download the file.
https://www.dropbox.com/sh/wz1zjs3ouav4rl0/AACvNCFwAf72IBqOACBU2fkia?dl=0
(If this doesn't work, send us an email at contact@helpstage.com and we will send you a link).

4- Copy/paste the e-mail addresses from the excel spreadsheet to MailChimp (be careful, you are limited to 1000 contacts. If you want to send more than 1000 emails, you will just have to delete your contacts after your first sending and import the new ones).

5- Go to the "Create" tab, then "email". Name the campaign "Application". In the "To" part, choose the contact list you created. In "From", enter your name and your email address.
In the "Subject" part, write " Applying for a job ". In the "content" section, copy/paste the email you downloaded from Dropbox and adapt it to your background and name.

Don't forget to attach your CV!

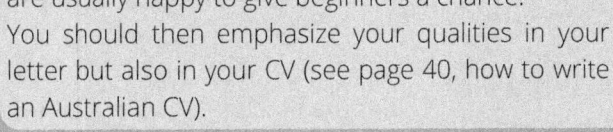

CAIRNS | WORK

"Dear Hiring Manager,

Please accept my enthusiastic application for a position in your hotel (or restaurant). I am happy to offer you my experience in the food industry, strong customer service skills, and my ability to work under pressure.

I believe I fulfill all of these requirements and am therefore an excellent candidate for you.

I have an extensive background in hospitality. I worked for two years at a fast-food restaurant. During this time I gained experience in nearly every aspect of food service. I took orders and served customers their meals, handled the cash register, and performed daily inventory checks.

I could assist not only in taking orders and serving customers but also in a variety of other capacities in which you might require assistance. I also worked in customer service for a number of years. As a cashier at a grocery store for two years, I assisted as many as one hundred customers daily.

My experience in the food industry and in customer service, and my ability to thrive under pressure make me an excellent candidate for you. I have enclosed my resume and will call within the next week to see if we might arrange a time to speak together. Thank you so much for your time and consideration.

Sincerely,

Your name"

> **Cover letter**
> The cover letter does not need to be very long but it should highlight your experience in a few lines.
> If you have no experience in the catering industry and your English is average, don't panic. Australians are usually happy to give beginners a chance.
> You should then emphasize your qualities in your letter but also in your CV (see page 40, how to write an Australian CV).

CAIRNS | WORK

Hotels in Cairns

Ibis Styles Cairns
15 Florence Street, Cairns City
+61 7 4051 5733
manager@ibisstylescairns.com.au
info@ibisstylescairns.com.au

Pullman Cairns International
17 Abbott St, Cairns City
+61 7 4031 1300
H8772@accor.com
H8772-RE@accor.com

Pullman Reef Hotel Casino
1/35/41 Wharf St, Cairns
+61 7 4030 8888
res@reefcasino.com.au
sales@reefcasino.com.au

Novotel Cairns Oasis Resort
122 Lake St, Cairns City
+61 7 4080 1888
h0534@accor.com
stay@novotelcairnsresort.com.au

Cairns Harbour Lights Hotel
1 Marlin Parade, Cairns City
+61 7 4057 0800
H8777@accor.com

Sunshine Tower Hotel
136 Sheridan St, Cairns City
+61 7 4041 1133
reception@sunshinetowerhotel.com.au

Gilligan's
57-89 Grafton St, Cairns City
+61 7 4041 6566
reservations@gilligans.com.au

The Hotel Cairns
Cnr Abbott And, Florence St
+61 7 4051 6188
reservations@thehotelcairns.com

Pacific Hotel Cairns
43 Esplanade, Cairns City
+61 7 4051 7888
reservations@pacifichotelcairns.com

Rydges Esplanade Resort
209-217 Abbott St, Cairns City
+61 7 4044 9000
reservations_rydgesesplanadecairns@evt.com

Hides Hotel Cairns
87 Lake St, Cairns City
+61 7 4058 3700
res@hideshotel.com.au

Cairns Queens Court
167-171 Sheridan St, Cairns North
+61 7 4051 7722
reception@queenscourt.com.au

Shangri-La Hotel, The Marina
Pier Point Rd, Cairns City
+61 7 4031 1411
recruitment@shangri-la.com

CAIRNS | WORK

The Jack Hotel & Backpackers
Sheridan St &, Spence St, Cairns
+61 7 4051 2490
admin@thejack.com.au

Cairns Plaza Hotel
45 Esplanade, Cairns City
+61 7 4051 4688
res@cairnsplaza.com.au

Riley A Crystalbrook Collection Resort
131-141 Esplanade, Cairns City
+61 7 4252 7777
hello.riley@crystalbrookcollection.com

Cairns Central YHA
20-26 McLeod St, Cairns City
+61 7 4051 0772
cairnscentral@yha.com.au

Hilton Cairns
34 Esplanade, Cairns City
+61 7 4050 2000
reservations.cairns@hilton.com

Mad Monkey Central
100 Sheridan St Cairns City
+61 7 4231 9871
original@madmonkey.com.au

Mad Monkey Waterfront
93A Esplanade Cairns City
+61 7 4229 0888
waterfront@madmonkey.com.au

Mad Monkey Village
141 Sheridan St Cairns City
+61 7 4231 9612
village@madmonkey.com.au

Mad Monkey Tropics
5-9 Digger St Cairns City
+61 7 4031 0910
tropics@madmonkey.com.au

Bounce
117 Grafton St Cairns City
+61 7 3846 0577
cairns@bouncehostels.com

Summer House Backpackers
341 Lake St, Cairns
+61 7 4221 3411
cairns@staysummerhouse.com

Holiday Inn Cairns Harbourside
209-217 the Esplanade
+61 74080 3000
hicairns@ihg.com

Cairns Colonial Club Resort
18-26 Cannon St, Manunda
+61 7 4053 8800
reservations@cairnscolonialclub.com.au

Il Palazzo Boutique Hotel
62 Abbott St, Cairns City
+61 74041 2155
bookme@ilpalazzo.com.au

CAIRNS | WORK

The Reef House Palm Cove
99 Williams Esplanade, Palm Cove
+61 7 4080 2600
reservations@reefhouse.com.au

Kewarra Beach Resort & Spa
80 Kewarra St, Kewarra Beach
+61 7 4058 4000
reservations@kewarrabeachresort.com.au

Comfort Inn Cairns City
183 Lake St, Cairns City
+61 7 4214 5395
info@comfortinncairnscity.com.au

Inn Cairns
71 Lake St, Cairns City
+61 7 4041 2350
enquiries@inncairns.com.au

Cairns Sheridan Hotel
295 Sheridan St, Cairns City
+61 7 4255 9000
sales@cairnssheridan.com.au

Park Regis City Quays
6 Lake St, Cairns City
+61 7 4042 6400
cityquays@parkregishotels.com

Bay Village Tropical Retreat
Lake St & Gatton St, Cairns North
+61 7 4051 4622
reservations@bayvillage.com.au

Coral Tree Inn
166-172 Grafton St, Cairns City
+61 7 4031 3744
reservations@coraltreeinn.com.au

Cairns Central Plaza
58 McLeod St, Cairns City
+61 7 4081 6000
reservations@cairnscentralplaza.com.au

Cairns Rainbow Resort
179 Sheridan St, Cairns North
+61 7 4051 1022
info@rainbowinn.com.au

The Abbott
69-73 Abbott Street, Cairns
+61 7 4220 9961
reservations@theabbott.com.au

Reef Palms
41/47 Digger St, Cairns North
+61 7 4051 2599
info@reefpalms.com.au

Sea Change Beachfront
31-35 Vasey Esplanade, Trinity Beach
+61 7 4057 5822
info@seachangecairns.com

Cairns Queenslander Hotel & Apartments
267 Lake St, Cairns North
+61 7 4051 0122
res@cairnsqueenslander.com.au

CAIRNS | WORK

Southern Cross Atrium Apartments
3/11 Water St, Cairns City
+61 7 4080 2700
info@southerncrossapartments.com

Cairns City Sheridan
157 Sheridan St, Cairns City
+61 74051 3555
info@cairnscitysheridan.com.au

Caravella Backpackers
149 Esplanade, Cairns City
+61 7 40512431
info@caravella.com.au

Travellers Oasis
8/10 Scott St, Cairns City
+61 7 4052 1377
info@travellersoasis.com.au

BreakFree Royal Harbour
71- 75 Esplanade, Cairns City
royalharbour.res@breakfree.com.au

The Balinese Motel
215 Lake St, Cairns City
+61 7 4051 9922
info@balinese.com.au

Sarayi Boutique Hotel
95-97 Williams Esplanade, Palm Cove
+61 74059 5600
info@sarayi.com.au

201 Lake Street
201 Lake St, Cairns City
+61 7 4053 0100
info@201lakestreet.com.au

Paradise On The Beach Resort
119-121 Williams Esplanade, Palm Cove
+61 7 4055 3300
resort@paradiseonthebeach.com

Gecko's Backpackers
187 Bunda St, Parramatta Park
+61 7 4031 1344
geckocairns@gmail.com

Crystal Garden Resort
18/24 James St, Cairns North
+61 7 4031 5888
crystalgardon@gmail.com

Balaclava Hotel
423 Mulgrave Rd, Earlville
+61 7 4054 3588
balaclava.hotel@alhgroup.com.au

Coral Sands Beachfront Resort
Trinity Beach Rd & Moore St, Trinity Beach
+61 74057 8800
frontdesk@coralsands.com.au

Blue Lagoon Resort
22-26 Trinity Beach Rd,Trinity Beach
+61 7 4057 2727
info@bluelagoonresort.com.au

CAIRNS | WORK

Waters Edge Apartments
155 Esplanade, Cairns City
+61 7 4044 2300
info@watersedgecairns.com.au

BIG4 Ingenia Holidays Cairns Coconut
23/51 Anderson Rd, Woree
+61 7 4054 6644
marketing@ingeniaholidays.com.au

Castaways Backpackers
207 Sheridan St, Cairns North
+61 7 4051 1238
jobs@castawaysbackpackers.com.au

Peppers Beach Club
123 Williams Esplanade, Palm Cove
+61 7 4059 9200
palmcove@peppers.com.au

Hotel Grand Chancellor Palm Cove
Coral Coast Dr, Palm Cove
+61 7 4059 1234
stay@hgcpalmcove.com.au

Cairns New Chalon
702 Bruce Hwy, Woree
+61466714672
cairnsnewchalon@gmail.com

Cairns Waterfront
83 Esplanade, Cairns City
+61 7 4000 0860
stay@waterfrontbackpackers.com

The Sebel Palm Cove
Coral Coast Dr, Palm Cove
+61 7 4059 8000
res.coralcoast@accorvacationclub.com.au

Cairns Southside
450 Mulgrave Rd, Cairns City
+61 7 4033 7722
info@southsideinn.com.au

Global Backpackers Cairns
67 Esplanade, Cairns City
+61 7 4031 1545
waterfront@globalbackpackers.com.au

IL Centro Apartment Hotel
26-30 Sheridan St, Cairns City
+61 7 4031 6699
stay@ilcentro.com.au

Mantra Amphora Palm Cove
49-63 Williams Esplanade, Palm Cove
+61 7 5665 4450
amphora.res@mantra.com.au

Koala Beach Resort
137 Lake St, Cairns City
+61 7 4051 4933
info@koalaresort.com.au

CAIRNS | WORK

Restaurants in Cairns

Piato Cairns Restaurant
1 Pierpoint Road Shop G4A,
The Pier Marina, Cairns City
📞 +61 7 4041 4284
✉ YUM@PIATOCAIRNS.COM

Prawn Star
Pier Point Road | Marlin Marina,
E31 Berth, Cairns City
📞 +61497007225
✉ admin@prawnstarcairns.com

Bayleaf Balinese Restaurant
Cnr Gatton St &, Lake St, Cairns City
📞 +61 74047 7955
✉ reservations@bayvillage.com.au

Dundee's at the Cairns Aquarium
5 Florence St, Cairns City
📞 +61 74276 1855
✉ dundees@dundees.com.au

Vivaldis Restaurant
53-57 Esplanade, Cairns City
📞 +61 7 4031 1240
✉ info@vivaldisrestaurant.com

Grill'd Cairns
77 Esplanade, Cairns City
📞 +61 7 4041 4200
✉ feedback@grilld.com.au

Tha Fish
Pier Shopping Centre, G7b
Pier Point Rd, Cairns City
📞 +61 74041 5350
✉ info@thafish.com.au

Cairns Burger Cafe
15 Aplin St, Cairns City
📞 +61 7 4041 4492
✉ cairnsburgercafe@gmail.com

C'est Bon Cairns
20 Lake St, Cairns City
📞 +61 7 4051 4488
✉ nicolas@cestboncairns.com.au

Bushfire Flame Grill
43 Esplanade, Cairns City
📞 +61 7 4044 1879
✉ info@bushfirecairns.com

Waterbar & Grill Steakhouse
1 Pier Point Rd, Cairns City
📞 +61 7 4031 1199
✉ info@waterbarandgrill.com.au

Café Strada
79 Lake St, Cairns City
📞 +61 74028 3860
✉ cafestradacairns@gmail.com

Tamarind Restaurant
35-41 Wharf St, Cairns City
📞 +61 7 4030 8897
✉ tamarind@reefcasino.com.au

CAIRNS | WORK

The Chambers Cafe, Restaurant & Bar
21 Spence St, Cairns City
📞 +61 7 4041 7302
✉ careers@the-chambers.com.au

The Lillipad Cafe
72 Grafton St, Cairns City
📞 +61 7 4051 9565
✉ lillipadcafe@gmail.com

Vitalia's Italian Restaurant
22 Palm St, Holloways Beach
📞 +61 7 4000 0865
✉ infovitaliasrestaurant@gmail.com

Iyara By Sakare
91 Esplanade, Cairns City
📞 +61409682461
✉ iyarasakare@bigpond.com

La Pizza
93 Esplanade, Cairns City
📞 +61 7 4031 2646
✉ lapizzarestaurant@iig.com.au

Zambrero Lake Street
28-30 Oceana Walk,
55 Lake St, Cairns City
📞 +61 7 4051 4637
✉ contactus@zambrero.com

Schnitz
2/77 Esplanade, Cairns City
📞 +61 7 4253 5464
✉ hello@schnitz.com.au

Boatshed
Cairns Harbour Lights,
8/1 Marlin Parade, Cairns City
📞 +61 7 4031 4748
✉ social@boatshedcairns.com.au

The Courtyard Cairns
91 Esplanade, Cairns City
📞 +61 7 4081 4817
✉ info.cairns@thecyard.com.au

Bang & Grind
8/14 Spence St, Cairns City
📞 +61 7 4051 7770
✉ bangandgrind@gmail.com

Mondo on the Waterfront
34 Esplanade, Cairns City
📞 +61 7 4052 6780
✉ CRNHI_FB@hilton.com

Coco's Kitchen + Bar
17 Abbott St, Cairns City
📞 +61 7 4031 1300
✉ h8772@accor.com

Dumpling studio
136 Sheridan St, Cairns City
📞 +61 7 4031 6956
✉ dumplingstudio136@gmail.com

McGinty's Irish Bar
41 Shields St, Cairns City
📞 +61439454537
✉ admin@mcgintys.com.au

CAIRNS | WORK

Mi Piace Espresso Bar
1/119 Sheridan St, Cairns City
+61 7 4041 1955
info@mipiaceespresso.com.au

Nu Nu Restaurant
1 Veivers Rd, Palm Cove QLD
+61 7 4059 1880
info@nunu.com.au

Rocco by Crystalbrook
Level 12, Tower,
131/141 Esplanade, Cairns City
+61 7 4252 7711
rocco@crystalbrookcollection.com

Caffiend
5/72-74 Grafton St, Cairns City
+61 7 4051 5522
hello@caffiend.com.au

NOA Eat Drink Share
1 Pyne St, Edge Hill
+61 7 4032 3117
reservations@noaeat.com.au

Jimmys Burger & Co
66 Shields St, Cairns City
+61 7 4041 6651
manager@jimmysburgerco.com

Bars in Cairns

The Pier Bar
The Pier Shopping Centre,
1 Pier Point Rd, Cairns City
+61 7 4031 4677
gday@thepierbar.com.au

Miss Chief Bar & Eatery
level 1/39-49 Lake St, Cairns City
+61411828953
info@misschief.bar

The Attic Lounge Bar
57-89 Grafton St, Cairns City
+61 7 4040 2777
functions@atticlounge.com.au

Flamingos Tiki Bar
43 The Esplanade, Cairns City
aloha@flamingostikibar.com.au

The Conservatory Bar
12/14 Lake St, Cairns City
+61457641977
theconservatorybar@gmail.com

Red Beret Hotel
411 Kamerunga Rd, Redlynch
+61 7 4055 1249
office@theredberet.com.au

BAR36
35-41 Wharf St, Cairns City
+61 7 4030 8822
reservations@reefcasino.com.au

Three Wolves
32 Abbott St, Cairns City
+61 7 4031 8040
info@threewolves.com.au

CAIRNS | WORK

Salt House
Marina Point, 6/2
Pierpoint Road, Cairns City
+61 7 4041 7733
greatviews@salthouse.com.au

Cock & Bull
6 Grove St, Cairns North
+61 7 4031 1160
info@cocknbull.net.au

The Downunder Bar
102 Lake St, Cairns City
+61 7 4028 3448
info@thedownunder.com.au

P.J.O'Brien's Irish Pub
87 Lake St, Cairns City
+61 7 4031 5333
cairns@pjobriens.com.au

Hemingway's Brewery Cairns Wharf
Wharf St, Cairns City
+61 7 4099 6663
info@hemingwaysbrewery.com

Dunwoody's Tavern
317 Sheridan St, Cairns North
+61 7 3558 3322
admin.dunwoodys
@ausvenueco.com.au

Vivo Palm Cove
49 Williams Esplanade, Palm Cove
+61 7 4059 0944
dine@vivo.com.au

Empire Alternacade & Events
86 Sheridan St, Cairns City
+61 7 3558 3309
tim@empirealternacade.com

The Woolshed
22-24 Shields St, Cairns City
+61 7 4031 6304
marketing@thewoolshed.com.au

The Cotton Club
24 Shields St, Cairns City
+61 7 4041 1400
marketing@thecottonclubcairns.com.au

Gin Social
34 Esplanade, Cairns City
+61 7 4050 2006
hello@ginsocial.com.au

Rattle N Hum
67 Esplanade, Cairns City
+61 7 4031 3011
cairns@rattlenhumbar.com.au

The Bluewater
7 Harbour Dr, Trinity Park
+61 7 4057 6788
info@thebluewater.com.au

The Backyard
Pier Point Rd, Cairns City
+61 7 4052 7670
info@thebackyardcairns.com.au

CAIRNS | WORK

Ultimate Party
10 Shields St, Cairns City
+61 7 4041 0332
info@ultimatepartycairns.com

Tradies Bar
8 Grove St, Cairns City
+61448607114
aj-marlin@hotmail.com

The Bedford Bar
+61400103603
hello@thebedfordbar.com.au

Grand Hotel Cairns
34 McLeod St, Cairns City
+61 7 4051 1007
info@grandhotelcairns.com.au

The Edge Hill Tavern
145 Pease St, Manunda
+61 7 4053 4811
edgehill.tavern@alhgroup.com.au

Coco Mojo Bar & Grill
14 Clifton Rd, Clifton Beach
+61 7 4059 1272
cocomojoclifton@hotmail.com

Ellis Beach Bar & Grill
LOT 13 Captain Cook Hwy, Ellis Beach
+61 7 4055 3534
functions@ellisbeachbarandgrill.com.au

CAIRNS | GOING OUT

GOING OUT AND MEETING PEOPLE IN CAIRNS

Pub crawls

The idea: you go out to 4 or 5 different bars in the same evening (AUD $50), with a drink included in each bar, plus freebies. Meet at 7.30pm outside the first bar, The Jack.
Four pub crawls: Monday, Wednesday, Friday and Saturday.
To book: www.partyincairns.com/pub-crawls

You also have the pub crawl in a bus:
https://www.ultimatepartycairns.com/
More information on the Facebook Group:
https://www.facebook.com/ultimatepartycairns/

Couchsurfing

Go to the "events" tab on www.couchsurfing.com and meet people from all around the world.
https://www.couchsurfing.com/events

Facebook groups

"CAIRNS Australia   Backpacker / Traveler":
https://www.facebook.com/groups/CairnsAustraliaBackpackerTraveler
"Cairns backpacker work/play/stay" :
https://www.facebook.com/groups/backpackingausnz

Other Websites

Meet Up:
https://www.meetup.com/en-AU/find/au--cairns/

Get arount in Cairns
Sunbus (or Kinetic) is the city's public transport service. Most buses leave from the pier.
https://www.sunbus.com.au/welcome-to-sunbus
From AUD$ 2,40 AU$ a ticket.

PERTH

Perth is the capital of Western Australia.
It is the most remote city in the world as it is surrounded by an endless ocean on one side and thousands of kilometers of desert on the other!
This is what makes Perth so special and captivating.
Most backpackers arrive on Australia's east coast choosing Sydney or Melbourne to start their adventure, but Perth is worth considering.

Perth is Australia's fourth largest city with a population of 2 million.
Life in Perth is all about the outdoors. You go camping at the beach, have barbecues, go on boat trips, and so on.
It has some of the most beautiful beaches in Australia, with crystal clear water and white sand.
Kings Park, larger than Central Park in New York, is the most visited place in Western Australia.
The view from the park over Perth and the Swan River is a definite must-see.

The atmosphere in Perth is relaxed and laid back. It is not surprising to see people walking barefoot in the streets, or in swimming costumes on the train with their beach towels over their shoulders.

PERTH | WHAT TO SEE / WHAT TO DO

Kings Park and Botanic garden

Kings Park has an impressive view of the city of Perth. Beware, it's a steep climb to get there!
It's where many Perth locals meet for a picnic overlooking the Swan River.
You can walk high above the trees on the Federation Walk and there is also a bush walk from the botanical gardens (1h to 1h30). Be sure to hydrate before starting any of the walks as it gets very hot in summer.
More information: http://www.bgpa.wa.gov.au

Fremantle

From Perth city center, take the Fremantle line to the terminus.
With a population of around 25,000, Fremantle ('Freo' to the locals) is at the estuary of the Swan River and the Perth harbor.
Interesting historic buildings and parks overlooking the sea make Fremantle one of the best tourist attractions around Perth.
More information about Fremantle : www.fremantle.wa.gov.au/

The Sunset Coast

Perth's coastline offers a choice of 19 white sandy beaches.
So there's plenty of choice when it comes to diving or lounging on your towel!
The most popular beaches are Cottesloe ('Cott' to the locals) and Scarborough, which is best known for its surfing.
Enjoy a sunset over the Indian Ocean!

Swan Valley

This is the place to go for wine and food lovers!
It's a 38-kilometre long route dotted with wine cellars and local food stands.
The Swan Valley is 20 minutes east from Perth and is the most visited wine region in the country.

PERTH | WHAT TO SEE / WHAT TO DO

There is also the option of taking a Swan River Scenic Cruise (from AUD$55). More information:
https://www.captaincookcruises.com.au/cruises/swan-river-scenic-cruise-from-perth

Rottnest Island

Rottnest is a paradise for divers and snorkellers.
It is the ideal place to discover colourful corals and tropical fish. Rottnest also has the most beautiful beaches with turquoise water and white sand.
The best way to explore the island is on a bike!
You can rent your bike and snorkel.
The ferry takes approximately 25 minutes from Fremantle and 90 minutes from Perth.

Rottnest Express
📞 1300 467 688 | ✉ reservations@rottnestexpress.com.au
https://rottnestexpress.com.au/

The Bell Tower

18 bells hanging in a 82.5 metre high copper and glass bell tower in Barrack Square.
It is one of the largest musical instruments in the world.
Climb to the sixth floor for views over the Swan River.

ACCOMMODATION IN PERTH

Upon arrival: short-term accommodation

You will ideally have reserved your accommodation for the first few days before your departure.
It is not an imperative but after 20 hours of flight, you may not feel like walking the streets of the city in search of the best hostel.

PERTH | ACCOMMODATION

The easiest way is to book a few nights in your city of arrival, either in a youth hostel or an Airbnb.

Airbnb can be a good solution to have your own private room in a house for example and thus recover from jet lag for the first few days.

Going straight from your flight to a bed in a dormitory can be tough, but on the other hand, you'll be right in the swing of things! The hostel will then allow you to meet people and to be able to check job offers locally.

The hostels are often very well positioned in the city center, which is obviously a strategic location if you are looking for a job in the city.

Couchsurfing

The reference website to stay for free with locals.

If you have an empty profile, are male and have few references, you will have little chance of being accommodated.

You can ask friends to give their opinion about you in the 'personal opinion' section.

It's a great place to meet locals and sleep on their couch for one or more nights.

In exchange for accommodation, you can, for example, prepare a meal for your host or buy them a drink in town!

Be careful to check the references of each host before asking them for accommodation.

www.couchsurfing.org

Hostels

Billabong Backpackers resort
Dorm: From AUD$30 | Private room for 90 AU$.
381 Beaufort St, Highgate | Tel: +61 8 9328 7720
https://www.billabongresort.com.au/

PERTH | ACCOMMODATION

Fremantle Prison YHA
Dorm from AUD$37.90 | Private room from AUD$106.
6A The Terrace, Fremantle | Tel: +61 8 9433 4305
www.yha.com.au/hostels/wa/perth-surrounds/fremantle-backpackers-hostel/

Western Beach Lodge
Dorm from 34 AU$ | Private room from 75 AU$.
6 Westborough St, Scarborough | Tel: +61 8 9245 1624
https://westernbeach.com/

Long-term rentals

To find a room in Perth, visit the websites below:
- Gumtree: https://www.gumtree.com.au
- Flatmates : https://flatmates.com.au
- Airbnb: https://www.airbnb.com
- Facebook groups:
  - Rentals in Perth "https://www.facebook.com/groups/1627616744145119"

FINDING A JOB AND SALARY IN PERTH

Perth is the capital of Western Australia and the economic backbone of the state.
The minerals and oil industries are the main sources of employment in Perth.
Perth is a good place for skilled expats. Apart from the traditional industries, sectors such as engineering and environmental technologies are a great place to work in Perth. 22.7% of people are employed in the technical, scientific and professional services sectors.
Public administration and defence employs 14.6% of people. The mining industry represents 11.6%.
These three sectors are the most prominent in Perth, employing almost 50% of the workforce in total. In the Perth area, you can find jobs as engineers, site managers, but also jobs in information technology if you are skilled.

PERTH | WORK

Positions such as systems engineer, IT manager, IT officer, Microsoft developer are the most commonly offered on the internet.

The career centre www.jobsandskills.wa.gov.au/jobs-and-careers is a useful place to check what skills are required to work in a specific sector in Perth.

The minimum wage in Western Australia is AUD$ 21.58/hour.

WEBSITES FOR FINDING A JOB

www.careerone.com.au
This website offers an efficient search engine to help you find a job. Monster was born from the merger of Monster Worldwide and News Corp Australia. The website combines the job search facilities of Monster with the leadership of News Corp Australia.

www.adzuna.com.au
Job search website that works by keyword typed in the search bar. Possibility to upload your CV on the website.

www.seek.com.au
More than 150,000 job offers are online; the website records approximately 25 million visits per month. The website has a strong community that helps each other in their search.

www.adecco.com.au
It is one of the most trusted HR companies in the world, bringing together a large number of employers and job seekers.

www.michaelpage.com.au
It is one of the most reliable agencies in the world with offices on all six continents. Each local branch is adapted to local requirements, resulting in a globally successful organization locally.

PERTH | WORK

www.hays.com.au
Hays is the world leader in placing qualified and skilled professionals. Hays manages a large number of jobs and last year alone placed a record 53,000 people in permanent positions. Hays is present in 33 countries, covering recruitment needs in 20 different specializations.

www.airtasker.com
These are one-time projects offered by individuals.
You can be asked for example to help carry a mattress for AUD $50 or to help with a house move. You can apply for each mission by trying to sell yourself as much as possible.

www.australiawide.com.au
It is one of Australia's leading recruitment agencies for engineers, other technical staff and technology.
The company posts permanent and temporary jobs in technical, operations, engineering, and management areas.

www.jobsearch.gov.au
This website is run by the Australian government and advertises job vacancies in all sectors across Australia.
It has many job opportunities from other government agencies such as the Australian Defence Force and the Australian Public Services.

https://www.experis.com.au/
Agency specializing in recruitment and employment in IT, as well as in government, financial and commercial services.

PERTH | WORK

INTERVIEW WITH MATHIEU

Mathieu spent a year in Australia on a Working Holiday Visa. He spent 5 months in Perth and explains in this interview how he found a job and accommodation.

Marie: How did your job search in Perth go?
Mathieu: Mainly on Gumtree and Indeedjob. I also answered a few ads and went to interviews.

Marie: How many interviews did you get out of how many applications?
Mathieu: Two applications and two interviews. I didn't really send many! But the interviews I went to were group interviews, a kind of pre-selection for the job.
The most important thing is to speak English well. If you don't speak English well, employers don't take you seriously at all. I don't think we are well prepared before we come to Australia.
We only see the good sides of this country: the beaches, the surfing, the sports, but things are clearly different in reality: the high cost of living, and if you don't have a good enough level of English, it is very difficult to fit in professionally and socially.

Marie: How long did it take you to find a job?
Mathieu: After 4 months in Australia, I found a job as a kitchen hand. So I didn't need to have an excellent level of English but even for this job, it can be a problem when the chef asks you something and you don't understand...! It was a very interesting experience but also difficult because of the language barrier.

PERTH | WORK

Marie: How long did you work in Australia?
Mathieu: In all, I had three jobs in Australia. Three months in total: two months as a kitchen hand, two weeks in a music festival also as a kitchen assistant, and then two weeks helping a bricklayer.

Marie: Concerning wages, are they higher in Perth than elsewhere?
Mathieu: If you compare it with Europe, then yes, the salaries in Perth are higher but the cost of living is higher too.

Marie: How long did it take you to speak English well?
Mathieu: I would say eight months. For the first four months, I had two weeks of English classes while I was working.
After that, I took online courses on my own.

Marie: Let's go back to your job as a kitchen hand, did you have any experience in this field before?
Mathieu: Yes, a little bit, but I don't think you need experience to work in a kitchen in Australia. They show you the basics and if you do well, they give you more things to do. At the end, I was making the pizzas.

Marie: What do you think is the best way to find a job, on the internet or by taking your CV directly to the employer?
Mathieu: I suggest word of mouth. Tell everyone around you that you are looking for a job. People often find jobs that way.
To maximise your chances, you should use the internet, but also phone calls to different restaurants and bars around you. That's what I did, but I didn't find a job that way.
A lot of people put their CVs in directly.

PERTH | WORK | RSA

QUICKLY FIND A JOB IN THE HOSPITALITY SECTOR

What is the RSA and how to get it in Perth?
The RSA is a certificate that shows that you know the rules related to alcohol.

RSA: Responsible Service of Alcohol
This certificate is mandatory to work in an establishment that serves alcohol: a bar, restaurant, or hotel. You will be asked to have it, so you might as well get it before you start looking for a job.

It is possible that an employer will accept to hire you without the RSA, but you will then have a one-month deadline to pass it. You might as well put all your chances on your side by being prepared!

It is easily done online :
www.eot.edu.au/online-courses/RSA/australia/
In Western Australia, it will cost you AUD$ 34.
The test takes between 3 and 6 hours maximum.

If you don't know yet if you are going to stay and work in Western Australia and plan to work in several Australian states, you can obtain the RSA valid in all states for AUD$ 183.

To find a job quickly in Perth, I recommend sending your resume in bulk to the hotel and restaurant listings found in this guide.

Emailing will allow you to send your resume to hundreds of establishments in one or two emails.

If you want to customize your emails to each company, you can choose from the list here.

If you choose emailing, here is the detailed method :

PERTH | WORK

The method to send your CV to hundreds of companies:

1- Create your account on MailChimp: www.login.mailchimp.com

2- On the "Audience" tab, go to "Add contacts" and "import contacts" then "copy/paste from file"

3- Open the following link and download the file. https://www.dropbox.com/sh/epsf76rua8oyesa/AAB3xbYgGwUy8rSDpF_VaNu1a?dl=0
(If it doesn't work, send us an email at contact@helpstage.com and we will send you the link).

4- Copy/paste the e-mail addresses from the excel spreadsheet to MailChimp (be careful, you are limited to 1000 contacts. If you want to send more than 1000 emails, you will just have to delete your contacts after your first sending and import the new ones).

5- Go to the "Create" tab, then "email". Name the campaign "Application". In the "To" part, choose the contact list you created. In "From", enter your name and your email address.
In the "Subject" part, write " Applying for a job ". In the "content" section, copy/paste the email you downloaded from Dropbox and adapt it to your background and name.

Don't forget to attach your CV!

Cover letter

"Dear Hiring Manager,

Please accept my enthusiastic application for a position in your hotel (or restaurant). I am happy to offer you my experience in the food industry, strong customer service skills, and my ability to work under pressure.
I believe I fulfill all of these requirements and am therefore an excellent candidate for you.

PERTH | WORK

I have an extensive background in hospitality. I worked for two years at a fast-food restaurant. During this time I gained experience in nearly every aspect of food service. I took orders and served customers their meals, handled the cash register, and performed daily inventory checks.

I could assist not only in taking orders and serving customers but also in a variety of other capacities in which you might require assistance. I also worked in customer service for a number of years. As a cashier at a grocery store for two years, I assisted as many as one hundred customers daily.

My experience in the food industry and in customer service, and my ability to thrive under pressure make me an excellent candidate for you. I have enclosed my resume and will call within the next week to see if we might arrange a time to speak together. Thank you so much for your time and consideration.

Sincerely,

Your name"

Cover letter

The cover letter does not need to be very long but it should highlight your experience in a few lines.

If you have no experience in the catering industry and your English is average, don't panic. Australians are usually happy to give beginners a chance.

You should then emphasize your qualities in your letter but also in your CV (see page 40, how to write an Australian CV).

Word of mouth is an invaluable way to find out about job openings that may not be posted on the Internet. HR professionals don't necessarily use job boards to post vacancies, so if you find a job through your contacts, your chances of finally getting the job are quite high.

PERTH | WORK

Hotels in Perth

New York on King
32/82 King St, Perth
+61419916306
annies@iinet.net.au

Duxton Hotel Perth
1 St Georges Terrace, Perth
+61 8 9261 8000
sales@perth.duxton.com.au

Rendezvous Hotel Perth Scarborough
148 The Esplanade, Scarborough
+61 8 9245 1000
res.rscb@rendezvoushotels.com

Crown Towers Perth
Great Eastern Highway
Burswood, Perth
+61 8 9362 7777
reservations.pct@crownhotels.com.au

The Peninsula Riverside Serviced Apartments
53 S Perth Esplanade, South Perth
+61 8 9368 6688
bd@thepeninsula.net
reception@thepeninsula.net

Billabong Backpackers Resort Hostel
381 Beaufort St, Highgate
+61 8 9328 7720
info@billabongresort.com.au

Pension Of Perth
3 Throssell St, Perth
+61 8 9228 9049
stay@pensionperth.com.au

Cottesloe Beach Hotel
104 Marine Parade, Cottesloe
+61 8 9383 1100
reception@cottesloebeachhotel.com.au
social@cottesloebeachhotel.com.au

Indian Ocean Hotel
23 Hastings St, Scarborough
+61 8 9341 1122
info@ioh.com.au
rachel@ioh.com.au

Pagoda Resort
112 Melville Parade, Como
+61 8 9367 0300
Jocelyn.Thien@pagoda.com.au

Fraser Suites
10 Adelaide Terrace, East Perth
+61 8 9261 0000
kylie.sullivan@frasershospitality.com
lulu.fox@frasershospitality.com

Pan Pacific Perth
207 Adelaide Terrace, Perth
+61 8 9224 7777
gm.ppper@panpacific.com

PERTH | WORK

QT Perth
207 Adelaide Terrace, Perth
+61 8 9224 7777
qt_perth@evt.com

Tribe Perth
4 Walker Ave, West Perth
+61 8 6247 3333
stayinperth@tribehotels.com.au
inthepapers@tribehotels.com.au

International on the Water
1 Epsom Ave, Ascot
+61 8 9429 8088
reservations@internationalonthewater.com.au
sales@internationalonthewater.com.au

Country Comfort Perth
249-263 Great Eastern Hwy, Belmont
+61 8 9478 0888
reservations.perth@countrycomfort.com

Hyatt Regency Perth
99 Adelaide Terrace, Perth
+61 8 9225 1234
perth.regency@hyatt.com

Pensione Hotel Perth
70 Pier St, Perth
+61 8 9325 2133
perth@pensione.com.au

The Sebel West Perth
659 Murray St, West Perth
+61 8 6147 8388
reservations@thesebelwestperth.com.au

The Melbourne Hotel
33 Milligan St, Perth
+61 8 9320 3333
hello@melbournehotel.com.au

European Hotel by Miss Maud
97 Murray St, Perth
+61 8 9325 3900
admin@missmaud.com.au

CityLights Perth
137 Newcastle St, Perth
+61 8 9227 7372
reservations@citylightshotel.com.au

Holiday Inn West Perth
1309 Hay St, West Perth
+61 8 6500 9100
reservations.perth@sage-hotels.com

Airport Apartments by Aurum
100 Coolgardie Ave, Redcliffe
+61 8 9475 3400
reservations@airport-apartments.com.au

Crowne Plaza Perth
54 Terrace Rd, Perth
+61 8 9270 4200
cpp.reservations@ihg.com

Mont Clare Boutique
190 Hay St, Perth
+61 8 9224 4300
reservations@montclareapartments.com

PERTH | WORK

Batavia Apartments
166 Palmerston St, Perth
+61 8 9227 1598
enquiries@bataviawa.com.au

Flag Motor Lodge
129 Great Eastern Hwy, Rivervale
+61 8 9277 2766
accom@flagmotorlodge.com.au

Citadines St Georges Terrace
185 St Georges Terrace, Perth
+61 8 9226 3355
enquiry.perth@the-ascott.com

Peppers Kings Square Hotel
621 Wellington St, Perth
+611300987600
kingssquare.res@peppers.com.au

Ingot Hotel Perth, an Ascend Hotel Collection member
285 Great Eastern Hwy, Belmont
+61 8 9259 3888
enquiries@ingothotel.com.au

Mercure Perth
10 Irwin St, Perth
+61 8 9326 7000
H1754-OM@accor.com

Quest East Perth
176 Adelaide Terrace, East Perth
+61 8 6210 6000
questeastperth
@questapartments.com.au

Ibis Perth
334 Murray St, Perth
+61 8 9322 2844
matt.juniper@accor.com

All Suites Perth
12 Victoria Ave, Perth
+61 8 9318 4444
info@allsuitesperth.com.au

Quest South Perth Foreshore
22 Harper Terrace, South Perth
+61 8 6559 5500
questspforeshore@questapartments.com.au

Ramada by Wyndham VetroBlu Scarborough Beach
48A Filburn St, Scarborough
+61 8 6248 7000
guestservice@ramadavetroblu.com

Nightcap at Belgian Beer Cafe
Cnr King &,Murray St, Perth
+61 8 9321 4094
belgianbeercafe@nightcaphotels.com.au

Hotel Northbridge
210 Lake St, Perth
+61 8 9328 5254
fom@hotelnorthbridge.com.au

Quality Resort Sorrento Beach
1 Padbury Cir, Sorrento
+61 8 9246 8100
reservations@
sorrentobeach.com.au

PERTH | WORK

InterContinental Perth City Centre
815 Hay St, Perth
+61 8 9486 5700
reservations.perha@ihg.com

Quest Scarborough
4 Brighton Rd, Scarborough
+61 8 6140 3500
questscarborough@questapartments.com.au

Seashells Scarborough
178 The Esplanade, Scarborough
+61 8 9341 9600
scarborough@seashells.com.au

COMO The Treasury
1 Cathedral Ave, Perth
+61 8 6168 7888
como.thetreasury@comohotels.com

St Catherine's on Park
2 Park Rd, Perth
+61 8 9442 0400
reservations@stcatherines.uwa.edu.au

Kangaroo Inn
123 Murray St, Perth
+61 8 9325 3508
gday@kangarooinn.com.au

Fremantle Prison YHA
6A The Terrace, Fremantle
+61 8 9433 4305
fremantle@yha.com.au

Hostel G
80 Stirling St, Perth
+61402067099
reservations@hostelgperth.com

Spinners Backpackers
342 Newcastle St, Perth
+61 8 9328 9468
admin@spinnershostel.com.au

Sorrento Beach Manor
54A Kempenfeldt Ave, Sorrento
+61402072078
admin@sorrentobeachmanor.com

Kings Park Motel
255 Thomas St, Shenton Park
+61 8 9381 0000
bookings@kingsparkmotel.com.au

Restaurants in Perth

Hiss & Smoke
Horseshoe Lane
Yagan Sqaure, Perth
+61 8 6507 3031
hissandsmoke@gmail.com

Short Order Burger Co
800 Hay St, Perth
burgers@shortorderburgerco.com.au

PERTH | WORK

C Restaurant in the Sky
Level 33/44 S Georges Terrace, Perth
+61 8 9220 8333
general@crestaurant.com.au

Petition
State Buildings, St Georges Tce &, Barrack St, Perth
+61 8 6168 7771
HI@PETITIONPERTH.COM

Bivouac Canteen & Bar
198 William St, Perth
+61 8 9227 0883
info@bivouac.com.au

Amano Restaurant
Pier, 1 Barrack St, Perth
+61 8 9325 4575
bookings@amanorestaurant.com.au

Balthazar
6 The Esplanade, Perth
+61 8 9421 1206
info@balthazar.com.au

Angel Falls Grill
Shop/16 Shafto Ln, Perth
+61 8 9468 7177
hola@angelfallsgrill.com.au

Maruzzella Restaurant
63 Bennett St, East Perth
+61 8 9225 5591
info@maruzzellarestaurant.com

Sen5Es Restaurant
221 Adelaide Terrace, Perth
+61 8 9221 1200
H1764-fb@accor.com

Wildflower
COMO The Treasury, Level 4/1 Cathedral Ave, Perth
+61 8 6168 7855
careers.thetreasury@comohotels.com

Friends Restaurant
Cloisters, 200 St Georges Terrace, Perth
+61 8 9221 0885
friends@iinet.net.au

Uma Restaurant
207 Adelaide Terrace, Perth
+61 8 6211 7221
umaperth@panpacific.com

Hunter & Barrel Raine Square
Raine Square Shopping Centre, 119 William St, Perth
+61 8 6163 8889
info@hunterandbarrel.com

Riverside Cafe
Eastern Pavilion, Barrack Square Barrack St, Perth
+61 8 9221 3703
info@riversidecafeperth.com.au

PERTH | WORK

Matilda Bay Restaurant
3 Hackett Dr, Crawley
+61 8 9423 5000
matbay@matbay.com.au

Epicurean Crown Towers
Crown Towers, Crown Perth, Great Eastern Hwy, Burswood
+611800556688
careers@crownperth.com.au

Post
1 Cathedral Ave, Perth
+61 8 6168 7822
post.thetreasury@comohotels.com

Sentinel Bar & Grill
111 St Georges Terrace, Perth
+61 8 6103 0507
info@sentinelbar.com.au

My Bayon
313 William St, Northbridge
+61 8 9227 1331
mybayon@gmail.com

Andaluz Bar & Tapas
21 Howard St, Perth
+61 8 9481 0092
info@andaluzbar.com.au

Lalla Rookh
77 St Georges Terrace, Perth
+61 8 9325 7077
info@lallarookh.com.au

Mount Street Breakfast Bar
42 Mount St, West Perth
+61 8 9213 9057
contact@mountstreetbreakfastbar.com

Sayers Sister
236 Lake St, Perth
+61 8 9227 7506
sayerssister@westnet.com.au

Garum
480 Hay St, Perth
+61 8 6559 1870
garum@westin.com

Fraser's Restaurant
Kings Park and Botanic Garden, 60 Fraser Ave, West Perth
+61 8 9481 7100
reservations@frasersrestaurant.com.au

Prego restaurant
440 Cambridge St, Perth
+61 8 9287 2700
info@pregorestaurant.com.au

BamBamBoo
25/140 William St, Perth
+61 8 6388 8900
info@bambamboo.com.au

Bread in Common
43 Pakenham St, Fremantle
+61 8 9336 1032
info@breadincommon.com.au

PERTH | WORK

The George
216 St Georges Terrace, Perth
+61 8 6161 6662
info@thegeorgeperth.com.au

Blackbird Restaurant
4/10 Eastbrook Terrace, Perth
+61481990888
info.blackbird410@gmail.com

Public House
263 Adelaide Terrace, Perth
+61 8 6117 0675
info@publichouseperth.com.au

Santini Bar & Grill
133 Murray St, Perth
+61 8 9225 8000
santini_qtperth@evt.com

Toastface Grillah
Grand Lane Rear,
143 Barrack St, Perth
+61409115909
marica@toastfacegrillah.com

Gusti Restaurant
54 Terrace Rd, East Perth
+61 8 9270 4200
gusti@ihg.com

Outback Jacks Northbridge
124 James St, Northbridge
+61 8 9227 7346
info@outbackjacks.com.au

Coco's Restaurant
85 S Perth Esplanade, South Perth
+61 8 9474 3030
functions@cocosperth.com

Il Lido Italian Canteen
88 Marine Parade, Cottesloe
+61 8 9286 1111
bookings@illido.com.au

Wassup Dog
113 Royal St, Perth
+61 8 9221 5436
catering@wassupdog.com.au

Tony Roma's
919 Hay St, Perth
+61 8 9481 8152
perthreservations@tonyromas.com.au

Hearth Restaurant & Lounge
1 Barrack St, Perth
+61 8 6559 6888
hearth.perth@ritzcarlton.com

Old Faithful Bar & BBQ
86 King St, Perth
+61439467035
general@oldfaithfulbar.com.au

The Meat & Wine Co Perth
Ground Floor, 108 St Georges Terrace, Perth
+61 8 6163 8880
perth@themeatandwineco.com

PERTH | WORK

Mister Walker Restaurant
Mends Street Jetty, South Perth
📞 +61 8 9367 1699
✉ info@mrwalker.com.au

Rambla On Swan
South Shore Shopping Centre, 39/85 S Perth Esplanade, South Perth
📞 +61 8 9367 2845
✉ info@ramblaonswan.com.au

Ascua Spanish Grill
King Street (opposite His Majesty's Theatre), Perth
📞 +61 8 9486 5700
✉ hola@ascua.com.au

Restaurant 1903
1/37 Robinson Ave, Perth
📞 +61 8 9228 8238
✉ christina.perth@gmail.com

The Boatshed Restaurant
1L Coode St, South Perth
📞 +61 8 9474 1314
✉ bookings@boatshedrestaurant.com

Lulu La Delizia
5/97 Rokeby Rd, Subiaco
📞 +61 8 9381 2466
✉ info@lululadelizia.com.au

Perugino Restaurant
77 Outram St, West Perth
📞 +61 8 9321 5420
✉ scaramellaa@hotmail.it

Manuka Woodfire Kitchen
134 High St, Fremantle
📞 +61 8 9335 3527
✉ manuka@manukawoodfire.com.au

Clarke's
97 Flora Terrace, North Beach
📞 +61 8 9246 7621
✉ clarkesofnorthbeach@hotmail.com

Julio's Italian Restaurant
1309 Hay St, West Perth
📞 +61 8 6500 9111
✉ info@tockhq.com

Bars in Perth

The Stables
888 Hay St, Perth
📞 +61 8 6314 1300
✉ info@thestablesbar.com.au

Ezra Pound
189 William St, Northbridge
📞 +61401347471
✉ ezra@epbar.com.au

PERTH | WORK

Hula Bula Bar
12 Victoria Ave, Perth
+61 8 9225 4457
bookings@hulabulabar.com

Helvetica
Rear, 101 St Georges Terrace, Perth
+61 8 9321 4422
info@helveticabar.com.au

Mechanics Institute
REAR, 222 William St, Northbridge
+61 8 9228 4189
ruckus@mechanicsinstitutebar.com.au

399 Small Bar
399 William St, Perth
+61420922716
sohan@399bar.com.au

Bob's Bar
Print Hall Building Brookfield Place,
125 St Georges Terrace, Perth
+61 8 6282 0077
info@printhall.com.au

The Aviary Perth
140 William St, Perth
+61 8 9460 9959
info@theaviaryperth.com.au

Frisk
103 Francis St, Northbridge
frisksmallbar@gmail.com

Badlands Bar
1/3 Aberdeen St, Perth
+61498239273
goodtimes@badlands.bar

Prince Lane Bar
356 Murray St, Perth
+61 8 9481 3222
info@princelane.com.au

The Lucky Shag
Ferry Route Barrack St Jetty,
Riverside Dr, Perth
+61 8 9221 6011
info@luckyshagbar.com.au

The Standard
28 Roe St, Northbridge
+61 8 9228 1331
info@thestandardperth.com.au

Hadiqa
Hibernian Place, Top Floor,
(Cnr Hay Street, 40 Irwin St, Perth
+61 8 6277 0387
info@hadiqa.com.au

Strange Company
5 Nairn St, Fremantle
fremantle@strangecompany.com.au

43 Below Bar & Restaurant
43 Barrack St, Perth
+61 8 9421 1333
info@43below.com.au

PERTH | WORK

Bar Lafayette
Brookfield Place, 125 St Georges Terrace, Lower Georges Lane, Perth
+61416816355
functions@barlafayette.com

Bobeche
Basement/131 St Georges Terrace, Perth
+61 8 9226 5596
imbibe@bobeche.com.au

Varnish on King
75 King St, Perth
+61 8 9324 2237
info@varnishonking.com

Alabama Song Bar
232 William St, Perth
functions@alabamasong.com.au

The Flour Factory
16 Queen St, Perth
+61 8 9485 1711
info@theflourfactory.com

Caballitos
26 Queen St, Perth
+61 8 9321 8305
info@caballitos.com.au

Tiny's
QV1 Plaza, enter via, Milligan St, Perth
+61 8 6166 9188
events@tinysbar.com.au

The Court
50 Beaufort St, Perth
+61 8 9328 5292
info@thecourt.com.au

Public House
263 Adelaide Terrace, Perth
+61 8 6117 0675
info@publichouseperth.com.au

The Royal on the Waterfront
60 Royal St, East Perth
+61 8 9221 0466
info@theroyaleastperth.com

Sneaky Tony's
Northbridge
+61432444090
info@sneakytonys.com

Goody Two's
Basement/40 Irwin St, Perth
+61 8 9221 9545
goodtimes@goodytwos.com.au

Universal Bar
221 William St, Perth
+61 8 9227 6771
functions@universalbar.com.au

The Palace Arcade
84 Beaufort St, Perth
+61 8 9227 7439
contact@thepalacearcade.com.au

PERTH | WORK

Mayfair Lane Pub
72 Outram St, West Perth
+61 8 9425 5222
hello@mayfairlane.com.au

Market Grounds
10 Telethon Ave, Perth
+61 8 6148 5600
info@marketgrounds.com.au

The Globe
495/497 Wellington St, Perth
+61 8 9460 9999
info@theglobeperth.com.au

Jack Rabbit Slim's
133 Aberdeen St, Perth
+61 8 9325 6677
info@jackrabbitslims.net

Belgian Beer Cafe
Cnr King & Murray Sts, Perth
+61893214094
belgianbeercafeperth@alhgroup.com.au

GOING OUT AND MEETING PEOPLE IN PERTH

Pub crawl

The concept: you go out to 3 different bars in the same night (AUD$ 38.50), with a drink included in each bar, plus freebies. On Saturday nights, the "Perth Saturdays".
To book: https://www.theperthpubtour.com.au/

Couchsurfing

Go to www.couchsurfing.com in the "events" tab and meet people from all over the world.
https://www.couchsurfing.com/events

Facebook Groups

- PERTH Australia - Backpackers and Travellers :
https://www.facebook.com/groups/PerthBackpacker
- Backpackers in Western Australia :
https://www.facebook.com/groups/BackpackersinWesternAustralia

Other websites

Meet Up:
https://www.meetup.com/fr-FR/cities/au/perth/

PERTH | GETTING AROUND

Getting around in Perth

With a Transperth ticket you can travel by train, bus and ferry. Perth has an extensive bus network but the service is rather slow, especially at weekends.
You also have the train which is on time and efficient.
Most buses and trains depart from Elizabeth Quay station.

DARWIN

Darwin is the capital of the Northern Territory.
It is a small, quiet city at the top end of Australia with a population of almost 150,000.
Darwin is a city like no other, very different from other Australian cities. Everything is very green and the air is very humid. The climate is tropical and constantly warm. It is 30 degrees all year round.
People in Darwin are very friendly. You can walk down the street and ask someone how they are, talk to strangers and no one will look at you funny.
Darwinians will tell you that it is almost impossible to walk up to someone on the street in Melbourne and ask them how they are without being taken for a complete nutcase!
The power is out? Never mind, you can head to the local pub to meet your mates and bet on horse or greyhound races! What time does work start? When you get up! As you can see, the atmosphere here is very relaxed.
Darwin is doing well economically. The average salary is higher than in the rest of Australia.
A lot of Aboriginals live here (40%) and stay mainly among themselves and don't really mix with the rest of the population, which can create some sad and disturbing street scenes: alcoholism, and begging.
One last thing, in Darwin, there is the sea. Yes, but you don't swim in it! It is infected with sea crocodiles. The city has therefore provided municipal swimming pools to cope with the heat.

DARWIN | WHAT TO SEE/ WHAT TO DO

See crocodiles up close

Discover some of Australia's largest saltwater crocodiles.
Swim with the crocs or try the famous 'Death Cage' and face a crocodile !

Crocosaurus Cove
📞 +61 08 8981 7522 | ✉ info@croccove.com
58 Mitchell Street, Darwin | https://www.crocosauruscove.com
Entry: AUD$38 | Entry + death cage: AUD$180

Market

Day: The Nightcliff Market is open every Sunday between 8am and 2pm. This is a great place to have breakfast with a nice coffee. Great selection of Asian food.
https://www.facebook.com/Nightcliff-Markets-164673453567229/
Night: The Mindil Beach Sunset Market takes place every Thursday evening during the dry season from May to October between 5pm and 10pm.
The market is located in Mindil Beach on Gilruth Avenue.
http://www.mindil.com.au

Day trips from Darwin

Adelaide River and the "jumping crocs"
Adelaide River is about 110km from Darwin.
Hop on a boat for an hour on the Adelaide River to see crocodiles jumping right in front of you! Scary!
Prix: AUD$ 45
https://www.jumpingcrocodile.com.au/

Two parks not to be missed: Litchfield et Kakadu
Spectacular waterfalls, termite mounds, red soil: a complete disorientation. Don't forget to check the weather forecast before visiting, especially during the wet season.

DARWIN | ACCOMMODATION

Upon arrival: short-term accommodation

You will ideally have booked your accommodation for the first few days before your departure.

It is not an obligation but after a 20 hour flight, you may not feel like walking the streets of the city in search of the best hostel.

The easiest way is to book a few nights in your city of arrival, either in a youth hostel or an Airbnb.

Airbnb can be a good solution to have your own private room in a house for example and thus recover from jet lag for the first few days.

Going straight from your flight to a bed in a dormitory can be tough, but on the other hand, you'll be right in the swing of things! The hostel will then allow you to meet people and to be able to check job offers locally.

The hostels are often very well positioned in the city center, which is obviously a strategic location if you are looking for a job in the city.

Couchsurfing

The reference website to stay for free with local people.

If you have an empty profile, are male and have few references, you will have little chance of being accommodated.

You can ask friends to give their opinion about you in the 'personal opinion' section.

It's a great place to meet locals and sleep on their couch for one or more nights.

In exchange for accommodation, you can, for example, prepare a meal for your host or buy them a drink in town!

Be careful to check the references of each host before asking them for accommodation.

www.couchsurfing.org

DARWIN | ACCOMMODATION

Hostels

Hostels in Darwin are of very average quality.
If you are staying with several people, it is best to book a twin room or an Airbnb. We have selected two hostels here.

Youth Shack Backpackers Darwin
Dorm: From AUD$ 30
69 Mitchell St, Darwin City | Tel: +61 8 8981 5221
https://www.youthshack.com.au/
Beware because this hostel is close to the nightlife. Sensitive ears, avoid!

Melaleuca On Mitchell (MOM)
Dorm from AUD$26.
52 Mitchell Street Darwin | Tel: 08 8941 7800/ 1300 723 437
www.momdarwin.com

Argus Hotel Darwin
13 Shepherd St, Darwin City | Tel: 08 8941 8300
From AUD $107 /night for a double room
https://argusaccommodation.com.au/
reservations@argushotel.com.au

Darwin City Hotel
59 Smith St, Darwin City | Tel : 08 7981 5125
www.darwincityhotel.com/ email : stay@darwincityhotel.com
From AUD $105/night for a double room.

Coconut Grove Holiday Apartments
146 Dick Ward Dr, Coconut Grove | Tel: 08 8985 0500
From AUD$ 110.
www.coconutgroveapartments.com.au

Long-term Rentals

To find a room in Darwin, visit the websites below:
- Gumtree: https://www.gumtree.com.au
- Flatmates : https://flatmates.com.au
- Facebook group: "Darwin Houses, Rooms, Rentals" : https://www.facebook.com/groups/772903339490844

DARWIN | WORK

FINDING A JOB AND WAGES IN DARWIN

Darwin has a thriving economy with a strong reputation for having the most skilled professionals in Australia. Currently, Darwin is experiencing huge economic growth, and the employment rate in Darwin is the highest in the country. So, with the right qualification, it is quite easy to find a job in Darwin.

What makes finding a job in Darwin even more attractive is that the city offers higher salaries than the rest of Australia. Salaries in Darwin are 20 percent higher than the Australian national average.

The average annual salary in Darwin is AUD$ 77,959, while the Australian average annual salary is AUD$ 68,279.

As a result of Darwin's booming economy, there is a real shortage of skilled professionals, so there are many vacancies.

So if you have the right qualifications and professional skills, getting a job in Darwin is relatively easy.

If you have a qualification in the medical field or civil engineering, you will need to have it certified by the Australian authorities. Australia has its own standards for civil engineering and medical studies, and once your qualifications have been assessed and validated, this will be a valuable entry point for presenting yourself to companies.

To assess your qualifications: :http://www.australia.gov.au

If you're looking for seasonal work, you'll find opportunities in fruit picking around Darwin, mainly for mango picking. There are also opportunities in the pearling industry (for the most courageous ones).

Construction and catering are also sectors that are recruiting. You can easily hand out your CV in any of the bars and restaurants that line Mitchell Street, Darwin's main street.

The minimum wage in the Northern Territory is $21.38/hour. The average hourly rate is AUD $37.

DARWIN | WORK

WEBSITES FOR FINDING A JOB

www.careerone.com.au
This website offers an efficient search engine to help you find a job. Monster was born from the merger of Monster Worldwide and News Corp Australia. The website combines the job search facilities of Monster with the leadership of News Corp Australia.

www.adzuna.com.au
Job search website that works by keyword typed in the search bar. Possibility to upload your CV on the website.

www.seek.com.au
This is a very informative job website. Here, employers are required to state the maximum and minimum salary for every job posted by them. The website uses this information to provide relevant job vacancies according to the salary requirement and professional profile of every registered member.

www.adecco.com.au
It is one of the most trusted HR companies in the world, bringing together a large number of employers and job seekers.

www.michaelpage.com.au
It is one of the most reliable agencies in the world with offices on all six continents. Each local branch is adapted to local requirements, resulting in a globally successful organization locally. They focus specifically on matching the right candidate with the right recruiter by region, sector and industry.

www.hays.com.au
Hays is the world leader in placing qualified and skilled professionals. Hays manages a large number of jobs and last year alone placed a record 53,000 people in permanent positions. Hays is present in 33 countries, covering recruitment needs in 20 different specializations.

www.airtasker.com
These are one-time assignments offered by individuals.
For example, you may be asked to help carry a mattress for AUD $50 or to help with a move. You can apply for each mission and try to sell yourself as much as possible.

www.australiawide.com.au
It is one of Australia's leading recruitment agencies for engineers, other technical staff and technology.
The company posts permanent and temporary jobs in technical, operations, engineering, and management areas.

www.jobsearch.gov.au
This website is run by the Australian government and advertises job vacancies in all sectors across Australia.

https://www.experis.com.au/
Recruitment agency specialized in the technology sectors for permanent or temporary contracts.

Do not hesitate to post an ad on the website
www.gumtree.com.au

LANDING A JOB QUICKLY IN HOSPITALITY

What is RSA and how do I get it in Darwin?
The RSA is a certificate that shows you know the rules about alcohol.

RSA: Responsible Service of Alcohol
This certificate is essential to work in an establishment that serves alcohol: bars, restaurants, hotels. You will be required to have it, so you might as well get it before you start looking for a job.

DARWIN | WORK | THE RSA

It is possible that an establishment will accept to hire you without the RSA but you will then have a one month delay to pass it. You might as well put all your chances on your side by anticipating!

The RSA is easily done online :
www.eot.edu.au/online-courses/RSA/australia/
In the state of Northern Territory, it will cost you AUD$ 34.
If you don't know yet if you are going to stay and work in Northern Territory and plan to work in several Australian states, you can obtain the RSA valid in all states for AUD$ 183.

To find a job very quickly in Darwin, we advise you to send your CV in bulk to the hotel and restaurant listings in this guide.
Emailing will allow you to send your resume to hundreds of establishments in one or two mailing sessions.
If you want to customize your emails for each company, you can choose from the list here.
If you choose to email, here is the detailed method:

The method to send your CV to hundreds of companies

1- Create an account on MailChimp: www.login.mailchimp.com
2- On the "Audience" tab, go to "Add contacts" and "import contacts" then "copy/paste from file"
3- Open the following link and download the file :
https://www.dropbox.com/sh/w9x23e14mulstaq/AACKikvGxixGz5AbfYlq3z8Ma?dl=0
4- Copy/paste emails from the excel spreadsheet to MailChimp (be careful, you are limited to 1000 contacts. If you want to send more than 1000 emails, you will simply have to delete your contacts after your first sending and import the new ones).
5- Go to the "Create" tab, then "email". Name the campaign "Application". In the "To" section, choose the contact list you have created. In "From", indicate your name and your email address.

DARWIN | WORK

In the "Subject" section, indicate "Application for a job". In the "content" section, copy and paste the email you downloaded from Dropbox, adapting it to your background, and your name. **Don't forget to attach your resume or a link to your LinkedIn profile!**

Example of a cover letter

"Dear Hiring Manager,

Please accept my enthusiastic application for a position in your hotel (or restaurant). I will be happy to bring my experience in the food industry, strong customer service skills, and my ability to work under pressure. I believe I fulfill all of these requirements and am therefore an excellent candidate for you.
I have an extensive background in hospitality. I worked for two years at a fast-food restaurant. During this time I gained experience in nearly every aspect of food service. I took orders and served customers their meals, handled the cash register, and performed daily inventory checks.
I could assist not only in taking orders and serving customers but also in a variety of other capacities in which you might require assistance. I also worked in customer service for a number of years. As a cashier at a grocery store for two years, I assisted as many as one hundred customers daily.

My experience in the food industry and in customer service, and my ability to thrive under pressure make me an excellent candidate for you. I have enclosed my resume and will call within the next week to see if we might arrange a time to speak together. Thank you so much for your time and consideration.
Sincerely,

Your name"

DARWIN | WORK

The cover letter

The cover letter doesn't have to be very long, but it should highlight your experience in a few lines. If you have no experience in the catering industry and your English is average, don't panic. Australians are usually happy to give beginners a chance

You will have to emphasize your qualities in your letter but also in your CV.

Word of mouth is an invaluable way to find out about job openings that may not be posted on the Internet. HR professionals don't necessarily use job boards to post vacancies, so if you find a job through your contacts, your chances of finally getting the job are quite high.

Hotels in Darwin

Novotel Darwin Airport
2 Sir Norman, Brearley Drive, Darwin
+61 (8) 8920 7800
ha209-sl@accor.com
ha207@accor.com

Mercure Darwin Airport Resort
1 Sir Norman, Brearley Drive, Darwin
+61 (8)8920 3333
HA209@ACCOR.COM

Alatai Holiday Apartments
7 Finniss St, Darwin City
+61 8 8981 5188
info@alataiapartments.com.au

Hilton Darwin
32 Mitchell St, Darwin City NT
+61 8 8982 0000
hiltondarwin.info@hilton.com

Palm City Resort
64 Esplanade, Darwin City
+61 88982 9200
Manager@palmscityresort.com

DARWIN | WORK

Mercure Kakadu Crocodile
1 Flinders Street, Jabiru
+61 (8) 8979 9000
reservations@crocodilehotel.com.au

Cooinda Lodge Kakadu
Kakadu National Park, Jabiru
+61 (8) 8979 1500
reservations@yellowwater.com.au

Argus Hotel Darwin
13 Shepherd St, Darwin City
+61 8 8941 8300
reservations@argushotel.com.au

Travelodge Resort Darwin
64 Cavenagh St, Darwin City
+61 8 8946 0111
darwin@travelodge.com.au

Luma Luma Holiday
26 Knuckey St, Darwin City
+61 88981 1899
enquiries@lumaluma.com.au

Vitina Studio Motel
38 Gardens Rd, Darwin City
+61 (08) 8911 0066
reception@vitina.com.au

Coconut Grove Holiday Apartments
146 Dick Ward Dr, Coconut Grove
+61 8 8985 0500
sales@coconutgroveapartments.com.au

Double Tree by Hilton
122 Esplanade, Darwin City
61 8 8943 3600
DoubleTreeDarwin.reservations@hilton.com
teddy.wijaya@hilton.com

Mantra on Esplanade
88 The Esplanade, Darwin City
+61 88943 4333
esplanadedar.res@mantra.com.au

The Leprechaun Resort
378 Stuart Hwy, Winnellie
+61 8 8922 9800
office@theleprechaunresort.com

H on Smith Hotel
81 Smith St, Darwin City
+61 88942 5555
reservations@hhotel.com.au

Casa On Gregory Motel
52 Gregory St, Parap
+61 8 8941 3477
info@casaongregory.com.au

Rydges Palmerston - Darwin
15 Maluka Dr, Palmerston City
+61 8 8983 6666
reservations_rydgespalmerston@evt.com

Down Under Hostels
4 Harriet Pl, Darwin City
+61 4 2734 7102
darwin@downunderhostels.com.au

DARWIN | WORK

RNR Serviced Apartments
Cnr woods &,Gardiner St, Darwin
+61 87970 0138
sales@rnrdarwin.com.au

Paravista Motel
5 Mackillop St, Parap
+61 8 8981 9200
para@paravistamotel.com.au

Frontier Hotel Darwin
3 Buffalo Ct, Darwin City
+61 8 7922 3300
reservations
@frontierdarwin.com.au

City Gardens Apartments
93 Woods St, Darwin City
+61 8 8941 2888
info@citygardensapts.com.au

Club Tropical Darwin
622 Lee Point Rd, Lee Point
+61 88944 8500
reservations@
clubtropicalresortdarwin.com.au

Mindil Beach Casino Resort
Mindil Beach, Gilruth Ave, Darwin
+61 8 8943 8888
MBCR-HumanResources@
delawarenorth.com

Restaurants à Darwin

Damasquino Restaurant
2/57 Marina Blvd, Larrakeyah
+61 8 7981 5278
damasquino.darwin@gmail.com

Shenannigans
1/69 Mitchell St, Darwin City
+61 8 8989 2100
info@shenannigans.com.au

The O.A.K
33 Woods St, Darwin City
+61 8 8981 0888
events@theoaksgroup.com.au

Memories of India
5/2 Sabine Rd, Millner
+61424096804
rajghotrad@yahoo.co.in

Little Miss Korea
aka graffiti laneway, Austin Ln, Darwin City
+61 8 8981 7092
info@littlemisskorea.com

Hot Tamale
F2/19 Kitchener Dr, Darwin City
+61 8 8981 5471
manager@hottamale.net.au

Wisdom Bar & Cafe
48 Mitchell St, Darwin City
+61 8 8941 4866
wisdom@wisdombar.com

Eat-A-Pizza
1/57 Marina Blvd, Larrakeyah
+61 8 8941 0963
eatapizza@bigpond.com

DARWIN | WORK

Hanuman
93 Mitchell St, Darwin City
+61889413500
darwin@hanuman.com.au

PM Eat & Drink
Corner of Knuckey Street & Austin Lane, Darwin City
+61 8 8941 3925
manager@pmeatdrink.com

Pee Wee's at the Point
Alec Fong Lim Dr, East Point
+61 8 8981 6868
INFO@PEEWEES.COM.AU

Sari Rasa
6/24 Cavenagh St, Darwin
+61421347535
rajadrw@yahoo.com.au

Wharf One Food & Wine
Building, 3/19 Kitchener Dr, Darwin Waterfront
+61 8 8941 0033
functions@wharfone.com.au

Manoli's Greek Taverna
64 Smith St, Darwin City
+61 8 8981 9120
manolisgreektaverna@hotmail.com.au

Tim's Surf & Turf
10 Litchfield St, Darwin
+61 8 8981 1024
tims.darwin@westnet.com.au

Good Thanks Burger and bar
33 Knuckey St, Darwin City
+61447566878
goodthanksdarwin@gmail.com

Lazy Susan's Eating House
9/21 Cavenagh St, Darwin
+61 8 8981 0735
info@lazysusansdarwin.com.au

CHOW!
D1 &, D2/19 Kitchener Dr, Darwin
+61 8 8941 7625
info@chowdarwin.com.au

Char Restaurant
70 Esplanade, Darwin
+61 8 8981 4544
bdm@chardarwin.com.au

Yots Greek Taverna
4/54 Marina Blvd, Larrakeyah
+61 8 8981 4433
yots@yots.com.au

Moorish Cafe
37 Knuckey St, Darwin City
+61 8 8981 0010
gertrude@moorishcafe.com.au

The Precinct
7 Kitchener Dr, Darwin
+61 8 8941 9000
functions@theprecincttavern.com.au

DARWIN | WORK

Crustaceans on the Wharf
45 Stokes Hill Wharf, Stokes Hill Rd, Darwin City
+61 8 8981 8658
info@crustaceans.net.au

Alfonsino's
20/69 Mitchell St, Darwin
+61 8 8942 1586
admin@alfonsinos.com

Oyster Bar Darwin
19 Kitchener Dr, Darwin City
+61 8 8981 2242
darwin@oysterbar.com.au

Roast & Noodles 328
Shop 15, The Galleria Shopping Centre, 37-39 Smith St, Darwin City
+61 8 8981 6598
info@roastandnoodle.com

The Jetty Restaurant
39 Stokes Hill Rd, Darwin
+61 8 8942 1500
thejettyrestaurant@outlook.com

Rendez vous Cafe
22 Mitchell St, Darwin City
+61 8 8981 9231
eat@rendezvouscafedarwin.com.au

The Kebab and MoMo House
3/4 Edmunds St, Darwin City
+61 8 8981 0264
kebabs.momo@gmail.com

Three Mums Kitchen
38 The Mall, Darwin City
+61 8 8941 5808
threemumskitchen@gmail.com

Darwin Tandoor
Shop 21/69 Mitchell St, Darwin
+61 8 8900 7742
darwintandoor@gmail.com

Saffrron Restaurant
14/34 Parap Rd, Parap
+61 8 8981 2383
info@saffrron.com

Lizards Bar & Restaurant
105 Mitchell St, Darwin City
+61 8 8946 3000
info@lizardsbar.com.au

Zzan on Cullen Bay
Shop 1/52 Marina Blvd, Darwin
+61 8 7978 6111
info@zzan.com.au

Uncle Sam's Take Away Food
5/109 Smith St, Darwin City
+61 8 8981 3797
unclesams1238@gmail.com

Bamboo Lounge
17/90 Frances Bay Dr, Stuart Park
+61 8 8942 2501
info@bamboolounge.com.au

DARWIN | WORK

The Lost Arc
89 Mitchell St, Darwin City
+61 8 8942 0873
info@discoverydarwin.com.au

Laneway Specialty Coffee
4/1 Vickers St, Parap
+61 8 8941 4511
eat@lanewaycoffee.com.au

Fiddlers Green
19 Kitchener Dr, Darwin City
+61 8 8981 2222
fiddlersdarwin@bigpond.com.au

The Foreshore Restaurant
259 Casuarina Dr, Nightcliff
+61 8 8948 4488
info@foreshorecafe.com.au

Spice Garden Eating House
2 Pavonia Pl, Nightcliff
+61 8 8900 8068
book@spicegarden.com.au

Besser Kitchen & Brew Bar
6/116 Coonawarra Rd, Winnellie
+61 8 8984 3254
eat@besserbrewbar.com.au

Noodle House
84 Mitchell St, Darwin City
+61 8 8942 1888
noodlehouse@bigpond.com

Snapper Rocks
B2/7 Kitchener Dr, Darwin City
+61 8 8900 6928
info@snapper.rocks

Bars in Darwin

Parap Tavern
15 Parap Rd, Parap
+61 8 8981 2191
paraptavern@alhgroup.com.au

Four Birds
2/32 Smith St, Darwin City
+61408729708
fourbirdscafe@gmail.com

Palmerston Tavern
1110 Chung Wah
Terrace, Palmerston City
+61 8 8932 1567
palmerstontavern@alhgroup.com.au

Virginia Tavern
30 Virginia Rd, Virginia
+61 88983 2996
virginia.hotel@bigpond.com

Monsoons Darwin
46 Mitchell St, Darwin City
+61 8 8989 2171
admin@
monsoonsdarwin.com.au

DARWIN | WORK

the tap ON MITCHELL
58 Mitchell St, Darwin City
+61 8 8981 5521
info@thetap.com.au

The Trader Bar
3 Harriet Pl, Darwin City
+61416084326
info@thetraderbar.com

The Deck Bar
22 Mitchell St, Darwin City
+61 8 8942 3001
info@thedeckbar.com.au

Stone House wine bar
33 Cavenagh St, Darwin City
+61481069657
hello@stonehousedarwin.com.au

Elements Poolside Bar Bistro
901 Stuart Hwy, Pinelands
+618 8935 0888
bookings@darwinfreespiritresort.com.au

Buff Club
57 Stuart Hwy, Stuart Park
+61 8 8981 3201
raobclub@bigpond.net.au

The Bell Bar & Bistro
127 Flynn Cct, Bellamack
+61 8 7917 8926
thebell@alhgroup.com.auau

Dollys Bar
8 Leanyer Dr, Leanyer
+61 8 8927 6388
functions@hibiscustavern.com

Airport Tavern
227 McMillans Rd, Jingili
+61 8 8985 4555
airporttavern@alhgroup.com.au

D Bar & Restaurant
81 Smith St, Darwin City
+61 8 8942 5555
reservations@hhotel.com.au

One Mile Brewery
8/111 Coonawarra Rd, Winnellie
+61429782870
admin@onemilebrewery.com.au

Pint Club
165 Abala Rd, Marrara
+61 8 8945 2452
admin@pintclub.com.au

Cossies Poolside Bar and Bistro
1 Sir Norman Brearley Dr, Marrara
+61 8 8920 3429
ha207@accor.com

Discovery Darwin
89 Mitchell St, Darwin City
+61 8 8942 3300
info@discoverydarwin.com.au

DARWIN | WORK

Eva's Cafe
Gardens Rd, The Gardens
📞 +61447474776
✉ events@botanicgardenscafe.com.au

Beaver Brewery
2/14 Tang St, Coconut Grove
📞 +61412089948
✉ chris@beaverbrewery.com.auu

Dom's Bar & Lounge
Shop 7/60 Aralia St, Nightcliff
📞 +61418259467
✉ domsdarwin@gmail.com

Howard SpringsTavern
280 Whitewood Rd,
Howard Springs
📞 +61 8 8983 1463
✉ howardspringstavern@ntpubco.com.au

Roma Bar
9 Cavenagh St, Darwin City
📞 +61 8 8981 6729
✉ catering@romabar.com.au

GOING OUT AND MEETING PEOPLE IN DARWIN

Pub crawl

The concept: you go out to 4 different bars in the same evening with a drink included in each bar, plus gifts. More information on the Facebook groups:
https://www.facebook.com/darwinpubcrawls/
https://www.facebook.com/groups/207944959637747/
The Monsoons bar on Mitchell Street is Darwin's ultimate bar for socialising and entertainment.
Check out the events: www.facebook.com/MonsoonsDarwinNT/

Couchsurfing

Go to www.couchsurfing.com in the "events" tab and meet people from all over the world.
https://www.couchsurfing.com/events

Facebook group

- DARWIN Australia   Backpacker / Traveler
https://www.facebook.com/groups/DarwinAustraliaBackpackerTraveler

DARWIN | GOING OUT/ GETTING AROUND

Other websites

Meet Up: www.meetup.com/cities/au/darwin/

Getting around in Darwin

The centre of Darwin is small and you can walk everywhere, but if you have to go to the suburbs, it is better to go by car, as the travelling distances are considerable.

There are 7 bus routes to Darwin, Casuarina, Palmerston and Mindil Beach market.

www.nt.gov.au/driving/public-transport-cycling/public-buses

ADELAIDE

Adelaide is the capital of South Australia.
Despite its small size, Adelaide is a vibrant and dynamic city with a high-quality food industry. Not only is Adelaide a great place to live, but it is also very safe and offers a wide range of activities.
For example, it hosts great music festivals, a food and wine festival in April, and the famous Fringe Festival in March (Mad March)!
One of the benefits of living in Adelaide is that you don't have to spend a lot of money on transport as everything is close by.
With a single north-south tram line, it's really easy to get from one point to another without getting lost.
Another advantage is that if you get bored of the city, just a few tram stops away and you're on a beautiful beach in Glenelg.
The sunsets there are stunning!

Adelaide is also next to the famous Barossa Valley wine region. A three-hour drive from the city center takes you through the vineyards, with kangaroos hopping along the road! Speaking of kangaroos, Adelaide is the gateway to Kangaroo Island. Take the SeaLink ferry and enjoy this island still well unspoiled by mass tourism, with incredible Australian wildlife.

The climate in Adelaide is Mediterranean. It is the driest of all Australian capital cities with the hottest summer and coldest winter of all Australian cities!

ADELAIDE | WHAT TO SEE/ WHAT TO DO

The Art Gallery

Main entrance is free. Some exhibitions may be subject to a fee. Discover the impressive collection of 38,000 pieces of art from Australia, Europe, America and Asia: paintings, sculptures, drawings, photos, ceramics, jewellery, etc.

> ☎ +61 8 8207 7000 | North Terrace, Adelaide
> https://www.agsa.sa.gov.au/

South Australian Museum

Explore the museum with its exhibitions and dozens of videos about Aboriginal history. Don't miss the Australian Aboriginal culture gallery.
Free admission. Free guided tours are available daily at 11 am on weekdays, and 2 pm and 3 pm on weekends and public holidays.

> ☎ +61 8 8207 7500 | North Terrace, Adelaide
> https://www.samuseum.sa.gov.au

Adelaide Central Market

44 – 60 Gouger Street, Adelaide.
It is the most visited place in Adelaide, with over 80 stalls, cafes and restaurants. It is the largest market in Australia.
http://www.adelaidecentralmarket.com.au

Botanical gardens

North Terrace, Adelaide. Free admission.
http://www.environment.sa.gov.au/botanicgardens/home

Glenelg, town and beach

Just eleven kilometers from the city center, Glenelg is a small seaside town worth visiting! Have a drink on Jetty Road or at Holdfast Marina to watch an incredible sunset!

ADELAIDE | ACCOMMODATION

Upon arrival: short-term accommodation

You will ideally have booked your accommodation for the first few days before your departure.

It is not an obligation but after a 20 hour flight, you may not feel like walking the streets of the city in search of the best hostel.

The easiest way is to book a few nights in your city of arrival, either in a youth hostel or an Airbnb.

Airbnb can be a good solution to have your own private room in a house for example and thus recover from jet lag for the first few days.

Going straight from your flight to a bed in a dormitory can be tough, but on the other hand, you'll be right in the swing of things!

The hostel will then allow you to meet people and to be able to check job offers locally.

The hostels are often very well positioned in the city center, which is obviously a strategic location if you are looking for a job in the city.

Couchsurfing

The reference website to stay for free with local people.

If you have an empty profile, are male and have few references, you will have little chance of being accommodated.

You can ask friends to give their opinion about you in the 'personal opinion' section.

It's a great place to meet locals and sleep on their couch for one or more nights.

In exchange for accommodation, you can, for example, prepare a meal for your host or buy them a drink in town!

Be careful to check the references of each host before asking them for accommodation.

www.couchsurfing.org

# ADELAIDE | ACCOMMODATION

Hostels

Adelaide Central YHA
Dorm: From AUD$ 50
135 Waymouth St, Adelaide | Tel: +61 8 8414 3010
www.yha.com.au/hostels/sa/adelaide/adelaide-backpackers-hostel/

Tequila Sunrise Hostel
Dorm: From AUD$ 58 (AUD$ 48 on booking.com)
123 Waymouth St, Adelaide | Tel: +61 451 434 627
http://tequilasunrisehostel.com/

Glenelg Beach Hostel
1/7 Moseley St, Glenelg | Tel : +61 8 8376 0007
http://www.glenelgbeachhostel.com.au/
From AUD $25 /night for a bed in a dorm.

Port Adelaide Backpackers
24 Nile St, Port Adelaide | Tel: +61 8 8447 6267
From AUD $25/night for a night in a dorm
From AUD $70/night for a private double room.
https://portadelaidebackpacker.com.au/

Long-term rentals

To find a room in Adelaide , visit the websites below:
- Gumtree: https://www.gumtree.com.au
- Flatmates : https://flatmates.com.au
- Facebook groups:
    - Adelaide Houses, Rooms, Rentals : https://www.facebook.com/groups/867931493244186
    - Adelaide Rentals/Sublets/Housemates V2
      https://www.facebook.com/groups/386327910253317/

FINDING A JOB AND WAGES IN ADELAIDE

Adelaide is Australia's fifth largest city. It is home to major government organisations and private-sector businesses.
The fastest growing industries in Adelaide are:
• n. of employees in security and public administration - 25,326 /21%

234

ADELAIDE | WORK

- n. of employees in health and social work - 16,039 / 14%
- n. of employees in technical and scientific services - 12,647 / 11%
- n. of employees in administrative support services - 11,725 / 10%
- n. of employees in hotel/restaurant services - 10,744 / 9%

Adelaide is also home to many defence-related industries, and therefore a good place to find jobs in this sector. The city is home to Saab Systems and Raytheo; BAE Systems Australia; Lockheed Martin Australia; and the Defence Science and Technology Organisation.
These companies alone generate a total revenue of A$1 trillion!
Adelaide is a great city where you can find jobs in pearl farming and wine production. 65% of Australia's wine is produced in South Australia. The education, transport, tourism, and car manufacturing sectors are also important recruiters in the Adelaide area.

The minimum wage in South Australia is $21.38/hour.

WEBSITES FOR FINDING A JOB

www.adzuna.com.au
Job search website that works by keyword typed in the search bar. Possibility to upload your CV on the website.

www.robertwalters.com.au/jobs-in-adelaide.html
In Adelaide, Robert Walters offers jobs in new technology, marketing, accounting, sales or secretarial work. Specialist teams will match your profile with the right jobs.

www.careerone.com.au
This website offers an efficient search engine to help you find a job. Monster was born from the merger of Monster Worldwide and News Corp Australia. The website combines the job search facilities of Monster with the leadership of News Corp Australia.

ADELAIDE | WORK

www.seek.com.au
This is a very informative site about employment. Here employers are required to declare the maximum and minimum salary for each job posting. The site uses this information to provide relevant posts based on the salary requirements and professional profile of each registered member.

www.adecco.com.au
This is one of the most reliable HR organizations in the world, and it deals with a large number of employers and job hunters.

www.michaelpage.com.au
It is one of the most reliable agencies in the world with offices on all six continents. Each local branch is adapted to local requirements, resulting in a globally successful organization locally. They focus specifically on matching the right candidate with the right recruiter by region, sector and industry.

www.hays.com.au
Hays is the world leader in placing qualified and skilled professionals. Hays manages a large number of jobs and last year alone placed a record 53,000 people in permanent positions. Hays is present in 33 countries, covering recruitment needs in 20 different specializations.

https://www.experis.com.au/
Recruitment agency specialized in the technology sectors for permanent or temporary contracts.

ADELAIDE | WORK

www.airtasker.com
These are one-time assignments offered by individuals.
For example, you can be asked to help carry a mattress for AUD $50 or to help with a move. You can apply for each mission by trying to sell yourself as much as possible.

www.australiawide.com.au
t is one of Australia's leading recruitment agencies for engineers, other technical staff and technology.
The company posts permanent and temporary jobs in technical, operations, engineering, and management areas.

www.jobsearch.gov.au
This website is run by the Australian government and advertises job vacancies in all sectors across Australia.
It has many job opportunities from other government agencies such as the Australian Defence Force and the Australian Public Services.

Do not hesitate to post an ad on the website
www.gumtree.com.au

LANDING A JOB QUICKLY IN HOSPITALITY

What is RSA and how do I get it in Adelaide?
The RSA is a certificate that shows you know the rules about alcohol.
RSA: Responsible Service of Alcohol
This certificate is essential to work in an establishment that serves alcohol: bars, restaurants, hotels. You will be required to have it, so you might as well get it before you start looking for a job.

ADELAIDE | WORK | THE RSA

It is possible that an establishment will agree to hire you without the RSA but you will then have a one month delay to pass it.
So you may as well give yourself the best possible chance by being prepared! It is easily done online:
www.eot.edu.au/online-courses/RSA/australia/
In South Australia, it will cost you AUD$ 34.
The test takes between 3 and 6 hours maximum.
If you don't know yet if you are going to stay and work in South Australia and plan to work in several Australian states, you can obtain the RSA valid in all states for AUD$ 183.

To find a job very quickly in Adelaide, we advise you to send your CV in bulk to the hotel and restaurant listings in this guide.
Emailing will allow you to send your resume to hundreds of establishments in one or two mailing sessions.
If you want to customize your emails for each company, you can choose from the list here.
If you choose to email, here is the detailed method:

The method to send your CV to hundreds of companies:
1- Create an account on MailChimp: www.login.mailchimp.com
2- On the "Audience" tab, go to "Add contacts" and "import contacts" then "copy/paste from file"
3- Open the following link and download the file.
https://www.dropbox.com/sh/ip601ef05mfgn8y/AACl7N1ITyBJFjBl9lxRTsGma?dl=0
(If this doesn't work, send us an email at contact@helpstage.com and we will send you a link)
4- Copy/paste the e-mail addresses from the excel spreadsheet to MailChimp (be careful, you are limited to 1000 contacts. If you want to send more than 1000 emails, you will just have to delete your contacts after your first sending and import the new ones).

ADELAIDE | WORK

> **5-** Go to the "Create" tab, then "email". Name the campaign "Application". In the "To" section, choose the contact list you have created. In "From", indicate your name and your email address.
> In the "Subject" section, indicate "Application for a job". In the "content" section, copy and paste the email you downloaded from Dropbox, adapting it to your background, and your name.
> **Don't forget to attach your resume or a link to your LinkedIn profile!**

"Dear Hiring Manager,

Please accept my enthusiastic application for a position in your hotel (or restaurant). I am happy to offer you my experience in the food industry, strong customer service skills, and my ability to work under pressure.
I believe I fulfill all of these requirements and am therefore an excellent candidate for you.
I have an extensive background in hospitality. I worked for two years at a fast-food restaurant. During this time I gained experience in nearly every aspect of food service. I took orders and served customers their meals, handled the cash register, and performed daily inventory checks.

I could assist not only in taking orders and serving customers but also in a variety of other capacities in which you might require assistance. I also worked in customer service for a number of years. As a cashier at a grocery store for two years, I assisted as many as one hundred customers daily.
My experience in the food industry and in customer service, and my ability to thrive under pressure make me an excellent candidate for you. I have enclosed my resume and will call within the next week to see if we might arrange a time to speak together.
Thank you so much for your time and consideration.
Sincerely,

Your name"

ADELAIDE | WORK

The cover letter

The cover letter doesn't have to be very long, but it should highlight your experience in a few lines.
If you have no experience in the catering industry and your English is average, don't panic. Australians are usually happy to give beginners a chance
You will have to emphasize your qualities in your letter but also in your CV.

Word of mouth is an invaluable way to find out about job openings that may not be posted on the Internet.
HR professionals don't necessarily use job boards to post vacancies, so if you find a job through your contacts, your chances of finally getting the job are quite high.

Hotels in Adelaide

The Playford
120 North Terrace, Adelaide South
+61 (8) 8213 8888
reservations@theplayford.com.au

Mercure Adelaide Grosvenor
125 North Terrace, Adelaide
+61 (8) 8407 8888
stay@mercuregrosvenorhotel.com.au

Rockford Adelaide
164 Hindley Street, Adelaide
+61 (8) 8211 8255
adelaide@rockfordhotels.com.au

Ibis Adelaide
122 Grenfell Street, Adelaide
+61 (8) 8159 5588
H8822@ACCOR.COM

Pullman Adelaide
16 Hindmarsh Square, Adelaide
+61 (8) 8206 8888
HB217@ACCOR.COM

Adelaide Travellers Inn
220 Hutt St, Adelaide
+61 8 8224 0753
bookings@adelaidebackpackers.com.au

ADELAIDE | WORK

Hilton Adelaide
233 Victoria Square, Adelaide
📞 +61 8 8217 2000
✉ adelaide@hilton.com

Adelaide Central YHA
135 Waymouth St, Adelaide
📞 +61 8 8414 3010
✉ adlcentral@yha.com.au

Hotel Grand Chancellor
65 Hindley St, Adelaide
📞 +61 8 8231 5552
✉ stay@hgcadelaide.com.au

InterContinental Adelaide
North Terrace, Adelaide
📞 +61 8 8238 2400
✉ recruitsafe@ihg.com
✉ global.ecareers@ihg.com

Rydges Adelaide
1 South Tce, Adelaide
📞 +61 8 8216 0300
✉ reservations_rydgesadelaide@evt.com

The Hotel Metropolitan
46 Grote St, Adelaide
📞 +61 88231 5471
✉ functions@hotelmetro.com.au

Adelaide Paringa
15 Hindley St, Adelaide
📞 +61 8 8231 1000
✉ info@adelaideparinga.com.au

Glenelg Beach Hostel
1/7 Moseley St, Glenelg
📞 +61 8 8376 0007
✉ glenelgbeachhostel@bigpond.com

Adabco Boutique Hotel
219/223 Wakefield St, Adelaide
📞 +61 8 8100 7500
✉ reception@adabcohotel.com.au

Stamford Plaza Adelaide
150 North Terrace, Adelaide
📞 +61 8 8461 1111
✉ sales@spa.stamford.com.au

Adelaide Riviera Hotel
31-34 North Terrace, Adelaide
📞 +61 8 8212 1700
✉ reservations@adelaideriviera.com.au

Peppers Waymouth
55 Waymouth St, Adelaide
📞 +61 8 8115 8888
✉ waymouth@peppers.com.au

BreakFree Adelaide
255 Hindley St, Adelaide
✉ adelaide.res@breakfree.com.au

Sage Hotel Adelaide
208 South Tce, Adelaide
📞 +61 8 8223 2800
✉ reservations.adelaide@sage-hotels.com

ADELAIDE | WORK

Adelaide Inn
160 O'Connell St, North Adelaide
+61 8 8267 5066
reception@adelaideinn.com.au

Adelaide Meridien Hotel & Apartments
21-39 Melbourne St, North Adelaide
+61 8 8267 3033
info@adelaidemeridien.com.au

Hotel Richmond
128 Rundle Mall, Adelaide
+61 8 8215 4444
reception@hotelrichmond.com.au

Majestic Minima Hotel
146 Melbourne St, North Adelaide
minima@majestichotels.com.au

Mantra Hindmarsh Square
55-67 Hindmarsh Square, Adelaide
+61 7 5665 4450
hindmarsh.res@mantra.com.au

The Franklin Hotel
92 Franklin St, Adelaide
+61 8 8410 0036
info@thefranklinhotel.com.au

Atura Adelaide Airport
1 Atura Cct, Adelaide Airport
+61 8 7099 3300
reservations_aturaadelaideairport@evt.com

Cosmo on Bank Hotel
25 Bank St, Adelaide
+61 8 8231 8881
info@cosmoonbank.com.au

Chifley on South Terrace
226 South Tce, Adelaide
+61 8 8223 4355
frontoffice.southterrace@chifleyhotels.com

Adelaide Royal Coach
24 Dequetteville Terrace, Kent Town
+61 8 8362 5676
info@royalcoach.com.au

The Highlander Hotel
647 North East Road, Gilles Plains
+61 8 8261 5288
admin@highlanderhotel.com.au

Esplanade Hotel
135 Esplanade, Brighton
+61882967177
esplanadehotel@alhgroup.com.au

Arkaba Hotel
150 Glen Osmond Rd, Fullarton
+61 8 8338 1100
reception@arkabahotel.com.au

Mile End Hotel
30 Henley Beach Rd, Mile End
+61 88443 4756
Postuler directement sur la page
www.mileendhotel.com.au/work-us

ADELAIDE | WORK

Ambassadors Hotel & Function Rooms
107 King William St, Adelaide
+61 8 8231 4331
functions@theambassadorshotel.com.au

The Watson Adelaide - Art Series
33 Warwick St, Walkerville
+61 8 7087 9666
info@artserieshotels.com.au

Oaks Plaza Pier
16 Holdfast Promenade, Glenelg
events@theoaksgroup.com.au

North Adelaide Boutique Stays
190-194 Gover St, North Adelaide
+61 8 8267 2500
reception@nabsa.com.au

Lockleys Hotel
493 Henley Beach Rd, Fulham
+61 8 8356 4822
info@lockleyshotel.com.au

Hendon Hotel
120 Tapleys Hill Rd, Royal Park
+61 8 8445 6161
hendon.hotel@alhgroup.com.au

Rex Hotel
172-176 Richmond Rd, Marleston
+61 88443 8188
rex.hotel@alhgroup.com.au

Adelaide Backpackers and Travellers Inn
262 Hindley St, Adelaide
+61 88231 9524
westend@adelaidebackpackers.com.au

Haven Marina
6/10 Adelphi Terrace, Glenelg North
+61883505199
reservations@haveninn.com.au

Princes Lodge Motel
73 Lefevre Terrace, North Adelaide
+61 8 8267 5566
princeslodge@outlook.com.au

Nightcap at Rose & Crown
100 Philip Hwy, Elizabeth South
+61 8 8255 2233
info@nightcaphotels.com

Port Adelaide Backpackers
24 Nile St, Port Adelaide
+61 88447 6267
info@portadelaidebackpackers.com

Walkers Arms Hotel
36 North East Road, Walkerville
+61 8 8344 8022
reception@walkersarms.com.au

Serafino
39 Kangarilla Rd, McLaren Vale
+61883238911
vince@mclarenvalebottlers.com.au
reservations@serafinomclarenvale.com.au

ADELAIDE | WORK

The Manor Basket Range
762 Lobethal Rd, Basket Range
+61 87200 2397
functions@
themanorbasketrange.com.au

Mansfield Park Hotel
426 Grand Jct Rd, Mansfield Park
+61 8 8445 3300
info@mansfieldparkhotel.com.au

Morphett Arms Hotel
138 Morphett Rd, Glengowrie
+61 8 8295 8371
office@
morphettarms.com.au

Restaurants in Adelaide

Golden Boy
309 North Terrace, Adelaide
+61 8 8227 0799
info@golden-boy.com.au

Apoteca
118 Hindley St, Adelaide
+61882129099
drink@apoteca.com.au

The Playford Restaurant
120 North Terrace, Adelaide
reservations@theplayford.com.au

Jolleys Boathouse
1 Jolleys Ln, Adelaide
+61 8 8223 2891
management@jolleysboathouse.com

Mayflower Restaurant
45 King William St, Adelaide
+61 8 8210 8899
events@mayfairhotel.com.au

Star of Siam
67 Gouger St, Adelaide
+61 8 8231 3527
starofsiamadelaide@gmail.com

Gin Long Canteen
42 O'Connell St, North Adelaide
+61 8 7120 2897
ginlongcanteen@gmail.com

Coal Cellar + Grill
233 Victoria Square, Adelaide
+61882370697
info@coalcellarandgrill.com.au

La Rambla Tapas Bar
28 Peel St, Adelaide
+61 8 8410 0020
shout@laramblatapas.com.au

ADELAIDE | WORK

Africola
4 East Terrace, Adelaide
+61 8 8223 3885
info@africola.com.au

Press* Food & Wine
40 Waymouth St, Adelaide
+61 8 8211 8048
eat@pressfoodandwine.com.au

Shiki Japanese Restaurant
Upper Lobby, North Terrace, Adelaide
+61882382400
reservations.adelaide@ihg.com

ORSO Restaurant
36 Kensington Road, Rose Park, Adelaide
+61 8 8364 1008
Bookings@orsokensington.com.au

Penfolds Magill Estate
78 Penfold Rd, Adelaide
+61 8 8301 5551
magillestaterestaurant@penfolds.com.au

Georges on Waymouth
20 Waymouth St, Adelaide
+61 8 8211 6960
info@georgesonwaymouth.com.au

Marrakech Restaurant
91 O'Connell St, North Adelaide
+61883619696
marrakech@post.com

Herringbone Restaurant
72-74 Halifax St, Adelaide
+61428926977
hello@herringbonerestaurant.com.au

Social Street S2
174A Hutt St, Adelaide
+61 451 166 576
s2team17@gmail.com

Chianti
160 Hutt St, Adelaide
+61 8 8232 7955
chianti@chianti.net.au

Botanic Gardens Restaurant
Plane Tree Dr, Adelaide
+61 8 8223 3526
restaurant@botanicgardensrestaurant.com.au

Soi38 Regional Thai
54 Pulteney St, Adelaide
+61 8 8223 5472
eat@soi38.com.au

B'Churrasco Brazilian BBQ
12 East Terrace, Adelaide
+61 8 8232 5111
adelaide@bchurrasco.com.au

Lenzerheide Restaurant
146 Belair Rd, Hawthorn
+61 8 8373 3711
info@lenzerheide.com.au

ADELAIDE | WORK

Hill of Grace Restaurant
War Memorial Dr, North Adelaide
+61 8 8205 4777
reservations@hillofgracerestaurant.com.au

Estia Greek Restaurant
255 Seaview Rd, Henley Beach
+61 8 8353 2875
eatatestia@outlook.com

Von thai
264 Flinders St, Adelaide
+61 8 7081 5878
info@vonthai.com.au

Culshaw's Restaurant
55 Frome St, Adelaide
+61 8 8100 4495
functions@majestichotels.com.au

Sean's Kitchen
North Terrace, Adelaide
+61882184244
marketing@adelaidecasino.com.au

Osteria Oggi
76 Pirie St, Adelaide
+61 8 8359 2525
eat@osteriaoggi.com.au

Windy Point Restaurant
Windy Point Lookout, Belair Rd, Belai
+61 8 8278 8255
info@windypoint.com.au

Parlamento
140 North Terrace, Adelaide
+61 8 8231 3987
info@parlamento.com.au

Skyline Restaurant
1 South Tce, Adelaide
+61 8 8216 0388
functions_rydgesadelaide@evt.com

MaiKitchen
1/5/34 Wright St, Ferryden Park
+61 8 7226 6591
maikitchen@outlook.com.au

Gaucho's Argentinian Restaurant
91 Gouger St, Adelaide
+61882312299
Postuler directement sur le site www.gauchos.com.au/contact/#employment

Allegra Dining Room
L1/125 Gilles St, Adelaide
hello@allegradiningroom.com

New India Restaurant
167 Hindley St, Adelaide
+61 8 8212 8212
eat@newindiarestaurant.com.au

ADELAIDE | WORK

The Gallery
30 Waymouth St, Adelaide
+61 8 8211 8820
info@galleryadelaide.com.au

Raj on Taj Hyde Park
109 King William Rd, Unley
+61 8 8271 7755
rajontajhydepark@yahoo.com

Delicatessen Kitchen & Bar
12 Waymouth St, Adelaide
+61 8 8211 8871
hello@delicatessenbar.com.au

2KW Bar and Restaurant
2 King William St, Adelaide
+61 8 8212 5511
Postuler directement sur le site
http://2kwbar.com.au/employment/

La Boca Bar and Grill Adelaide
150 North Terrace, Adelaide
+61 8 8461 0860
bookings@laboca.com.au

Red Ochre Grill
War Memorial Dr, North Adelaide
+61 8 8211 8555
info@redochrebarrelandgrill.com.au

Krung Thep Thai adelaide
147 O'Connell St, North Adelaide
+61 8 8367 0932
krungthep147@gmail.com

Borsa Pasta Cucina
1/25 Grenfell St, Adelaide
+61882116572
eat@borsapastacucina.com

Lucky Lupitas
1/163-169 O'Connell St,
North Adelaide
+61458882605
luckylupitas@gmail.com

Kafana
27 Gilbert Pl, Adelaide
+61 8 7132 1816
info@kaffana.com.au

Ruby Red Flamingo
142 Tynte St, North Adelaide
+61 8 8267 5769
rubyredflamingo@opusnet.com.au

River Cafe
War Memorial Dr, North Adelaide
+61 8 8211 8666
info@rivercafe.com.au

ADELAIDE | WORK

Lantern by Nu
10 Selby St, Adelaide
+61 491 173 802
admin@lanternbynu.com.au

Level One Restaurant @ Electra House Hotel
131/135-139 King William St, Adelaide
+61 8 7123 4055
info@electrahouse.com.au

Amalfi Pizzeria Ristorante
29 Frome St, Adelaide
+61 8 8223 1948
info@amalfipizzeria.com.au

NAGOMI Japanese Kitchen
Shop5/242 Hutt St, Adelaide
+61 8 8232 0944
info@nagomijapanesekitchen.com.au

The Greek on Halifax
75/79 Halifax St, Adelaide
+61 8 8223 3336
info@thegreek.com.au

Cantina Sociale
108 Sturt St, Adelaide
+61 8 8410 6246
info@cantinasociale.com.au

Bars in Adelaide

BRKLYN
260-262 Rundle St, Adelaide
info@brklyn-adl.com

Hennessy Rooftop Bar
45 King William St, Adelaide
events@mayfairhotel.com.au

The Bibliotheca Bar and Book Exchange
1/27 Gresham St, Adelaide
+61 8 8212 6979
bar@bibliotheca.com.au

Urban Wine Room
33/37 Wright St, Adelaide
+61 8 8212 6959
urbanwineroom@gmail.com

Alfred's Bar
14 Peel St, Adelaide
hello@alfredsbar.com.au

Rob Roy Hotel
106 Halifax St, Adelaide
+61 8 8223 5391
enquiries@robroyhotel.com.au

Casablabla
12 Leigh St, Adelaide
+61 8 8231 3939
bookings@casablabla.com

Mary's Poppin
5 Synagogue Pl, Adelaide
info@maryspoppin.com

ADELAIDE | WORK

Clever Little Tailor
19 Peel St, Adelaide
✉ hello@cleverlittletailor.com.au

Maybe Mae
15 Peel St, Adelaide
✉ hello@maybemae.com

Pink Moon Saloon
21 Leigh St, Adelaide
✉ hello@pinkmoonsaloon.com.au

Hains & Co
23 Gilbert Pl, Adelaide
☎ +61884107088
✉ ahoy@hainsco.com.au

Mother Vine
22-26 Vardon Ave, Adelaide
☎ +61 8 2227 2273
✉ wine@mothervine.com.au

The Collins Bar
233 Victoria Square, Adelaide
☎ +61 8 8237 0760
✉ info@thecollins.com.au

The HandleBar Adelaide
140 Gray St, Adelaide
☎ +61421858153
✉ info@handlebaradelaide.com

Proof Bar
9 Anster St, Adelaide
☎ +61 8 8212 0708
✉ drink@proof-bar.com

La Buvette Drinkery
27 Gresham St Adelaide
☎ +61 8 8410 8170
✉ info@labuvettedrinkery.com.au

El Cheeky Flamingo
40/33 Vardon Ave, Adelaide
☎ +61421672043
✉ info@thecheekyflamingo.com.au

Bank Street Social
48 Hindley St, Adelaide
✉ hello@bankstreetsocial.com.au

Bar Torino
158 Hutt St, Adelaide
☎ +61 8 8155 6010
✉ hello@bartorino.com.au

The Little Pub
17 Hindley St, Adelaide
☎ +61 8 8231 3225
✉ contact@thelittlepub.com.au

Mr. Goodbar
12 Union St, Adelaide
☎ +61 8 8223 7574
✉ hello@mrgoodbar.com.au

Hellbound Wine Bar
Basement/201 Rundle St, Adelaide
☎ +61420322715
✉ drink@hellboundwinebar.com

ADELAIDE | WORK

Nineteen Ten
Rooftop 143 Hindley Street
Rooftop, Adelaide
📞 +61478770292
venuemanager@nineteenten.com.au

Fumo Blu
270 Rundle St, Adelaide
📞 +61 8 8232 2533
✉ fumo@fumoblu.com

GOING OUT AND MEETING PEOPLE IN ADELAIDE

Pub crawl

The concept: you go out to 4 different bars in the same evening with a drink included in each bar.
All events are on the page
https://www.eventbrite.ca/d/australia--adelaide/bar-crawl/

Couchsurfing

Go to www.couchsurfing.com in the "events" tab and meet people from all over the world.
https://www.couchsurfing.com/events

Facebook group

ADELAIDE Australia   Backpacker / Traveler:
https://www.facebook.com/groups/AdelaideBackpacker

Other websites

Meet Up: https://www.meetup.com/en-AU/find/au--adelaide/

Getting aroung in Adelaide
Getting around in Adelaide by tram is really easy. It's impossible to get lost as there is only one tram line running from Glenelg to the Entertainment Centre. The one-way ticket costs AUD$5.90 | https://www.adelaidemetro.com.au/
By train, there are about ten routes to the Adelaide suburbs: Belair, Blackwood, Gawler, Gawler Central, Grange, Osborne, Outer Harbor, Salisbury, Seaford, and Tonsley.
By train, there are about ten routes to the Adelaide suburbs: Belair, Blackwood, Gawler, Gawler Central, Grange, Osborne, Outer Harbor, Salisbury, Seaford, and Tonsley.

HOBART

Tasmanian Devil

Hobart is the capital of Tasmania (nicknamed 'Tassie'), a small island in South-East Australia. It is the twelfth largest city in Australia with a population of just over 220,000.

Tasmania is not usually an attractive destination for a Working Holiday because it is far from the big cities. However, it is a great place to go if you want to do some *fruit picking* as its oceanic climate is perfect for many fruits and vegetables to grow all over the island. Winters are mild and summers are cool.

Tasmania is well worth a visit for nature lovers, open spaces or just to see the Tasmanian devil! You will also have the opportunity to see wombats in the wild. The advantage of Hobart is that as soon as you leave the city, you are quickly in the wild.

The other three main towns in Tasmania are Devonport, Launceston, and Strahan.

Mount Wellington overlooks the city of Hobart. Many outdoor activities await you in this mountainous setting with landscapes very similar to those of New Zealand. Lakes, forests, vineyards, and endless meadows are all part of Tasmania and provide employment opportunities in tourism (travel agents, mountain bike tours, hiking guides, grape harvesting, fruit picking, hotel reception, and waitressing in Hobart's many restaurants).

As with all islands, the further you will get from Hobart, the more you will feel the need to have a car, for work and/or for travel.

HOBART | WHAT TO SEE/ WHAT TO DO

Mount Wellington

For a spectacular view of Hobart city, climb Mount Wellington (called 'The Mountain' by the locals) on its 22-kilometre tarmac road. With snow on top, even in summer, Mount Wellington offers many options for nature lovers, including hiking or mountain biking if you're a thrill-seeker!

> **Mount Wellington Descent Cycle Tour**
> From AUD $95 for a Descent Cycle Tour.
> https://underdownunder.com.au/tour/mount-wellington-descent/

Museum of Old and New Art

MONA is a contemporary art museum on three floors.
The atmosphere is a bit unusual as there are no windows and some of the works on display may be shocking to the most sensitive. You will discover the giant mural of a rainbow snake made up of 1620 paintings by Sidney Nolan.

> +61 3 6277 9900 | 655 Main Rd, Berriedale TAS
> Open Thursday to Monday between 10 am and 5 pm.
> https://www.mona.net.au/ | Entry AUD $35.

Salamanca Market

Salamanca Pl, Hobart TAS | Open every Saturday from 8:30 am to 3 pm. To sample the local specialties or stroll through the stands in a friendly and relaxed atmosphere. You will find everything you can think of.
https://www.salamancamarket.com.au/Home

Battery Point

Residential area of Hobart, to visit in order to discover historical buildings and the oldest buildings of Hobart. You will experience a little time travel. It is the most authentic and charming area of Hobart, offering many small cafes and restaurants to eat.

HOBART | ACCOMMODATION

On arrival: short-term accommodation

You will ideally have reserved your accommodation for the first few days before your departure.

It is not an imperative but after 20 hours of flight, you may not feel like walking the streets of the city in search of the best hostel.

The ideal is to book a few nights in your arrival city, either in a hostel or in an Airbnb.

Airbnb can be a good solution to have your own private room in a house for example and help you recover from jet lag the first few days.

Going straight from your flight to a bed in a dormitory can be tough, but on the other hand, you'll be right in the swing of things! The hostel will then allow you to meet people and to be able to check job offers locally.

The hostels are often very well positioned in the city center, which is obviously a strategic location if you are looking for a job in the city.

Couchsurfing

The website of choice for free accommodation with locals.

If you don't have a profile, if you are a man and if you have only a few references, you will have limited chances to be accommodated.

You can ask your friends to give their opinion about you in the 'personal reviews' section.

It's a great website to meet locals and sleep on their couch one or more nights.

In exchange for the accommodations, you can for example prepare a meal for your host or buy him/her a drink in town!

Be careful though to check the references of each host before asking them for hosting.

www.couchsurfing.org

HOBART | ACCOMMODATION

Hostels

Narrara Backpackers
Dorm: From AUD $26.
88 Goulburn St, Hobart TAS | Tel: +61 3 6234 8801
https://www.narrarabackpackers.com/

Hobart Central YHA
Dorm: From AUD $44.60
19 Argyle St, Hobart | Tel: +61 3 6231 2660
https://www.yha.com.au/hostels/tas/hobart-surrounds/

MONTACUTE BOUTIQUE BUNKHOUSE
1 Stowell Ave, Battery Point | Tel : +61 3 6212 0474
https://montacute.com.au/
From AUD $37/night for a bed in a dorm.

Long-Term Rentals

To find a room in Hobart, visit the websites below:
- Gumtree: https://www.gumtree.com.au
- Flatmates : https://flatmates.com.au
- Facebook group: "Rentals in Tasmania"

FINDING A JOB AND WAGES IN HOBART

If you have a background in healthcare, you will have many opportunities to work in Hobart as this is the industry that hires the most.
The administrative and service sectors are next.
However, if you are interested in working in construction or have an electrician qualification, you will also have a chance to find work. Construction work requires physical fitness!
Engineering is also hiring, especially in the field of renewable energy.
Also, you should know that tourism in Tasmania represents 15% of the economy, so there are many opportunities, despite the health crisis.

HOBART | WORK

Outdoor tourism is very popular in Australia, so you can apply to be a hiking guide for example.

When you arrive with a Working Holiday Visa in Hobart, you can also aim for anything related to agriculture and aquaculture.

Tasmania is nicknamed "Apple Isle" because of its exceptional apple industry.

Livestock, dairy, viticulture, and crop production are growing steadily throughout the state, and farms regularly advertise for workers. Tasmanian farms are always in need of pickers, drivers, pruners, sorters, and packers.

In the meantime, working in agriculture is a fantastic way to explore rural areas and enjoy the outdoors while earning money. Other benefits of working in agriculture include job diversity, industry growth, and improved mental health (agricultural careers are proven to reduce stress, anxiety, and depression !)

The minimum wage in Tasmania is AUD$ 21.38/hour.

WEBSITES FOR FINDING A JOB

www.adzuna.com.au
Job search website that works by keyword typed in the search bar. Possibility to upload your CV on the website.

https://www.jobs.tas.gov.au/
This website gathers job offers in the medical sector, including positions at the Hobart Hospital.

https://tasmania.com/work-with-us/
This website is dedicated to job opportunities in the tourism sector. You will find positions as a writer or digtal marketing for example.

HOBART | WORK

www.careerone.com.au
This website offers an efficient search engine to help you find a job. Monster was born from the merger of Monster Worldwide and News Corp Australia. The website combines the job search facilities of Monster with the leadership of News Corp Australia.

www.seek.com.au
More than 150,000 job offers are online; the website records approximately 25 million visits per month. The website has a strong community that helps each other in their search.

www.adecco.com.au
It is one of the most trusted HR companies in the world, bringing together a large number of employers and job seekers.

www.michaelpage.com.au
It is one of the most reliable agencies in the world with offices on all six continents. Each local branch is adapted to local requirements, resulting in a globally successful organization locally.

www.hays.com.au
Hays is the world leader in placing qualified and skilled professionals. Hays manages a large number of jobs and last year alone placed a record 53,000 people in permanent positions. Hays is present in 33 countries, covering recruitment needs in 20 different specializations.

https://www.experis.com.au/
Agency specializing in recruitment and employment in IT, as well as in government, financial and commercial services.

www.harvesttrail.org.au/ for agricultural jobs.

HOBART | WORK

www.airtasker.com
These are one-time projects offered by individuals.
You can be asked for example to help carry a mattress for AUD$ 50 or to help with a house move. You can apply for each mission by trying to sell yourself as much as possible.

www.australiawide.com.au
It is one of Australia's leading recruitment agencies for engineers, other technical staff and technology.
The company posts permanent and temporary jobs in technical, operations, engineering, and management areas.

www.jobsearch.gov.au
This website is run by the Australian government and advertises job vacancies in all sectors across Australia.
It has many job opportunities from other government agencies such as the Australian Defence Force and the Australian Public Services.

Feel free to post an ad on this website **www.gumtree.com.au**

QUICKLY FIND A JOB IN THE HOSPITALITY SECTOR

What is the RSA and how to get it in Hobart?
The RSA is a certificate that shows that you know the rules related to alcohol.
RSA: Responsible Service of Alcohol

This certificate is mandatory to work in an establishment that serves alcohol: bar, restaurant, hotel. You will be asked to have it, so you might as well get it before you start looking for a job.

HOBART | WORK | RSA

It is possible that an employer will accept to hire you without the RSA, but you will then have a one-month deadline to pass it. You might as well put all your chances on your side by being prepared! It is easily done online:
www.eot.edu.au/online-courses/RSA/australia/
In the state of Tasmania, it will cost you AUD $45.
The test takes between 3 and 6 hours maximum.
If you don't know yet if you are going to stay and work in Tasmania and plan to work in several Australian states, you can obtain the RSA valid in all states for AUD $183.

To find a job very quickly in Hobart, we recommend sending your resume in bulk to the hotel and restaurant listings found in this guide.
Emailing will allow you to send your resume to hundreds of establishments in one or two emails.
If you want to customize your emails to each company, you can choose from the list here.
If you choose emailing, here is the detailed method:

The method to send your CV to hundreds of companies:

1- Create an account on MailChimp: www.login.mailchimp.com
2- On the "Audience" tab, go to "Add contacts" and "import contacts" then "copy/paste from file"
3- Open the following link and download the file.
https://www.dropbox.com/scl/fo/orzpq99kt648gtgsf9t89/h?dl=0&rlkey=zfec650meurpyafftt7dbwy0l
(If this doesn't work, send us an email at contact@helpstage.com and we will send you a link.)
4- Copy/paste the e-mail addresses from the excel spreadsheet to MailChimp (be careful, you are limited to 1000 contacts. If you want to send more than 1000 emails, you will just have to delete your contacts after your first sending and import the new ones).

HOBART | WORK

5- Go to the "Create" tab, then "email". Name the campaign "Application". In the "To" part, choose the contact list you created. In "From", enter your name and your email address.
In the "Subject" part, write " Applying for a job ". In the "content" section, copy/paste the email you downloaded from Dropbox and adapt it to your background and name.
Don't forget to attach your CV!

"Dear Hiring Manager,

Please accept my enthusiastic application for a position in your hotel (or restaurant). I will be happy to bring my experience in the food industry, strong customer service skills, and my ability to work under pressure. I believe I fulfill all of these requirements and am therefore an excellent candidate for you.
I have an extensive background in hospitality. I worked for two years at a fast-food restaurant. During this time I gained experience in nearly every aspect of food service. I took orders and served customers their meals, handled the cash register, and performed daily inventory checks.

I could assist not only in taking orders and serving customers but also in a variety of other capacities in which you might need assistance. I have also worked in customer service for years. As a cashier at a grocery store for two years, I assisted as many as one hundred customers daily.
My experience in the food industry and in customer service, and my ability to thrive under pressure make me an excellent candidate for you. I have enclosed my resume and will call within the next week to see if we might arrange a time to speak together. Thank you so much for your time and consideration.
Sincerely,
Your name"

HOBART | WORK

Cover letter

The cover letter does not need to be very long, but it should highlight your experience in a few lines.

If you have no experience in the restaurant industry and your English is average, don't panic.

Australians easily give beginners a chance.

You should then emphasize your strengths in your letter but also in your CV (see page 40, how to write an Australian CV).

Word of mouth is an invaluable way to find out about job vacancies that may not be posted on the Internet. HR professionals don't necessarily use job websites to post vacancies, so if you hear of a job through your contacts, your chances of finally getting the job are quite high.

Hotels in Hobart

Hobart Central YHA
9 Argyle St, Hobart
+61 3 6231 2660
hobartcentral@yha.com.au

MONTACUTE BOUTIQUE BUNKHOUSE
1 Stowell Ave, Battery Point
+61 3 6212 0474
hello@montacute.com.au

Hotel Grand Chancellor
1 Davey St, Hobart
+61 3 6235 4535
reservations@hgchobart.com.au

Narrara Backpackers
88 Goulburn St, Hobart
+61 3 6234 8801
info@narrarabackpackers.com

MACq 01 Hotel
18 Hunter St, Hobart
+61 3 6210 7600
hello@macq01.com.au

The Henry Jones Art Hotel
25 Hunter St, Hobart
+61 3 6210 7700
reservations@thehenryjones.com

HOBART | WORK

Hadley's Orient Hotel
34 Murray St, Hobart
+61 3 6237 2999
marketing@hadleyshotel.com.au

Lenna Of Hobart Hotel
20 Runnymede St, Battery Point
+61 3 6232 3900
enquiries@lenna.com.au

Salamanca Wharf Hotel
17A Castray Esplanade, Battery Point
+61 3 6224 7007
info@salamancawharfhotel.com

The Alabama Hotel
72 Liverpool St, Hobart
+61 499 987 698
reservations@alabamahobart.com.au

Mayfair on Cavell
17 Cavell St, West Hobart
+61 3 6231 1188
mayfair@mayfaironcavell.com.au

Hobart City Apartments
80 Elizabeth St, Hobart
+61 3 6240 5585
res@hobartcityapartmenthotel.com

Quest Waterfront
3 Brooke St, Hobart
+61 3 6224 8630
contact@questapartments.com.au

RACV Hobart Hotel
154-156 Collins St, Hobart
+61 3 6270 8600
hobart@resorts.racv.com.au

Galleria Salamanca
31-35 Salamanca Pl, Hobart
+61 447 033 272
salamancagalleria@outlook.com

Somerset on the Pier Hobart
1 Elizabeth Street Pier, Hobart
+61 3 6220 6600
somerset.australia@the-ascott.com

Travelodge Hotel Hobart
167 Macquarie St, Hobart
+61 3 6220 7100
hobart@travelodge.com.au

The Old Woolstore Apartment Hotel
1 Macquarie St
+61 3 6235 5355
reservations@oldwoolstore.com.au

ibis Styles Hobart
173 Macquarie St, Hobart
+61 3 6289 8500
HB040@accor.com

The Tasman, a Luxury Collection
12 Murray St, Hobart
+61 3 6240 6000
hobart@luxurycollection.com

HOBART | WORK

Vibe Hotel Hobart
36 Argyle St, Hobart
+61 3 6240 5600
hobart@vibehotels.com.au

Best Western Hobart
156 Bathurst St, Hobart
+61 3 6232 6255
reservations97434@bestwestern.com.au

Mantra on Collins Hobart
58 Collins St, Hobart
collins.res@mantra.com.au

Sullivans Cove Apartments
21 Hunter St, Hobart
+61 3 6234 5063
stay@sullivanscoveapartments.com.au

Zero Davey Boutique Apartments
15 Hunter St, Hobart
+61 3 6270 1444
zerodavey@escapesresorts.com.au

Mövenpick Hotel Hobart
28 Elizabeth St, Hobart
+61 3 6235 9888
HB7N8@ACCOR.COM

Macquarie Manor Hotel
172 Macquarie St, Hobart
+61 3 6289 6711
stay@macquariemanor.com.au

The Tasmanian Inn
172 Campbell St, Hobart
+61 3 6295 3360
info@tasmanianinn.com.au

Salamanca Inn
10 Gladstone St, Battery Point
+61 3 6223 3300
reservations@salamancainn.com.au

The Lodge on Elizabeth
249 Elizabeth St, Hobart
+61 3 6231 3830
reservations@thelodge.com.au

Moss Hotel
39 Salamanca Pl, Hobart
+61 (0)3 6281 3600
HELLO@MOSSHOTEL.COM.AU

Harrington's 102
102 Harrington St, Hobart
+61 3 6234 9277
info@harringtons102.com.au

Salamanca Terraces
93 Salamanca Pl, Hobart
+61 3 6232 3900
enquiries@salamancaterraces.com.au

Backpackers Imperial Hotel
138 Collins St, Hobart
+61 3 6223 5215
info@backpackersimperialhobart.com.au

HOBART | WORK

The Quarry House Luxury Retreat
95 Brooker Highway, Glebe
+61 418 341 126
info@thequarryhouseluxuryretreat.com

Roxburgh House
162 Elizabeth St, Hobart
+61 447 572 007
info@roxburghhouse.com.au

Central Hotel - Bar, Bistro, Gaming & Accommodation
73 Collins St, Hobart
+61 3 6234 4419
admin@centralhotelhobart.com.au

Grand Old Duke
31 Hampden Rd, Battery Point
61 413 040 403
stay@grandoldduke.com.au

Astor Private Hotel
157 Macquarie St, Hobart
+61 3 6234 6611
bookings@astorprivatehotel.com.au

Allurity Hotel
96 Bathurst St, Hobart
+61 3 6128 3636
info@allurityhotel.com.au

White Room Apartments
Goulburn St, Hobart
+61 438 132 939
info@whiteroomapartments.com

Corinda's Cottages
17 Glebe St, Hobart
+61 3 6169 9577
julian@corinda.com.au

Sanctum Boutique Apartments
156 Harrington St, Hobart
+61 438 540 291
clair@sanctumboutique.com

Jenatt Apartments Salamanca
7/15 Salamanca Mews,
Gladstone St, Battery Point
+61 437 083 477
stay@jenatt.com.au

Trinity Hill Apartments
21 Paternoster Row, Hobart
+61 (0) 468 352 930
reservations@trinityhillapartmentsandco.com.au

Hobart Cityscape
43 and 47 Molle Street, Hobart
+61 434 762 311
stay@hobartcityscape.com.au

Apartments Portsea Place
62 Montpelier Retreat,
Battery Point
+610 409 649 158
trevor@portseaplace.com.au

The Rox
160-162 Elizabeth St, Hobart
+61 419 805 465
hello@theroxhobart.com

HOBART | WORK

Restaurants in Hobart

Peacock and Jones
33 Hunter St, Hobart
+61 3 6210 7730
sayhello@peacockandjones.com.au

Fico
151A Macquarie St, Hobart
+61 3 6245 3391
federica@ficofico.net

The Astor Grill
157 Macquarie St, Hobart
+61 3 6234 3122
info@astorgrill.com.au

Templo
98 Patrick St, Hobart
+61 3 6234 7659
mail@templo.com.au

Frank Restaurant
1 Franklin Whrf, Hobart
+61 3 6231 5005
info@frankrestaurant.com.au

Maldini
47 Salamanca Pl, Hobart
+61 3 6223 4460
maldinirestaurant@outlook.com

Dier Makr
123 Collins St, Hobart
+61 3 6288 8910
diermakr.hobart@gmail.com

Landscape Restaurant & Grill
23 Hunter St, Hobart
+61 3 6210 7712
info@thehenryjones.com

Aloft
Pier one, Brooke St, Hobart
+61 3 6223 1619
info@aloftrestaurant.com

Urban Greek
103 Murray St, Hobart
+61 3 6169 1129
info@urbangreekhobart.com

The Lounge by Frogmore Creek
18 Hunter St, Hobart
+61 3 6274 5876
admin@frogmorecreek.com.au

Cultura Espresso Bar & Restaurant
123 Liverpool St, Hobart
+61 3 6234 7111
eat@culturahobart.com.au

Filoxenia
322 Elizabeth St, North Hobart
+61 455 930 842
filoxeniahobart@gmail.com

Tasman Restaurant
Ground Floor, 1 Davey St, Hobart
+61 3 6235 4547
restaurant01@hgchobart.com.au

HOBART | WORK

Rude Boy
130 Elizabeth St, Hobart
+61 429 904 133
info@rudeboyhobart.com.au

Drunken Admiral
17/19 Hunter St, Hobart
+61 3 6234 1903
info@drunkenadmiral.com.au

Kosaten Japanese Restaurant
17 Castray Esplanade, Battery Point
+61 3 6135 4018
info@kosaten.com.au

Hearth Pizza & Small Plates
37 Montpelier Retreat, Battery Point
+61 3 6223 2511
info@hearthpizza.com.au

The Glass House Hobart
Brooke Street Pier, Franklin Whrf, Hobart
+61 3 6223 1032
info@theglass.house

Tesoro
28 Elizabeth St, Hobart
+61 3 6235 9840
tesoro.hobart@movenpick.com

AURA Hobart
Level 12/110 Liverpool St, Hobart
+61 3 6236 9001
info@aurahobart.com.au

Mures Upper Deck
Victoria Dock, Davey St, Hobart
+61 3 6231 1999
upperdeck@mures.com.au

Dāna Eating House
131 Murray St, Hobart
+61 416 161 756
info@danaeatinghouse.com.au

Tavern 42 Degrees South (T42)
Ground Level Elizabeth Street Pier, Unit 59/4 Franklin Whrf, Hobart
+61 418 568 636
bookings@t42hobart.com.au

Bar Wa Izakaya
216-218 Elizabeth St, Hobart
+61 3 6288 7876
barwaizakaya@gmail.com

Rockwall Bar and Grill
89 Salamanca Pl, Hobart
+61 3 6224 2929
info@rockwallbarandgrill.com.au

The Duke
192 Macquarie St, Hobart
+61 3 6223 5206
duke@theduke.com.au

Brooke Street Pier
Brooke Street Pier, 12 Franklin Whrf, Hobart
+61 3 6135 5457
hellosailor@brookestreetpier.com

HOBART | WORK

Monsoon Shabu Shabu
120 Elizabeth St, Hobart
+61 3 6289 6329
monsoonshabu@gmail.com

Pearl + Co
Mures Building Victoria Dock, Franklin Whrf, Hobart
+61 3 6231 1790
pearl@mures.com.au

Stockmans Restaurant at The Old Woolstore Hotel
1 Macquarie St, Hobart
+61 3 6235 5355
reservations@oldwoolstore.com.au

Amici
310 Elizabeth St, North Hobart
+61 3 6234 7973
eat@amici-restaurant.com.au

Tacos Mexican Restaurant
11 Morrison St, Hobart
+61 3 6223 5666
tacosmexican2018@gmail.com

Medici
67 Murray St, Hobart
+61 3 6234 8848
medicipizzeria@gmail.com

Belvedere Hobart
36 Argyle St, Hobart
+61 3 6240 5600
reservations@tfehotels.com

Preachers
5 Knopwood St, Hobart
+61 3 6223 3621
bars.preachers@gmail.com

THE DECK
Level 4/110 Liverpool St, Hobart
+61 3 6213 4200
crowneplazahobart@ihg.com

Harbour Lights Cafe
29 Morrison St, Hobart
+61 3 6224 2138
info@harbourlightscafe.com.au

Blue Eye Seafood Restaurant
1 Castray Esplanade, Battery Point
+61 3 6223 5297
office@thenoshcompany.com

Peppina
2b Salamanca Pl, Hobart
+61 3 6240 6053
peppina@luxurycollection.com

Amigos Mexican Restaurant
237 Elizabeth St, North Hobart
+61 3 6234 6115
amigos.mexican.hobart@gmail.com

Birdsong Restaurant
10 Gladstone St, Hobart
+61 3 6220 0404
restaurant@salamancainn.com.au

HOBART | WORK

The Brooke Street Stock Market Restaurant + Bar
8 Brooke St, Hobart
+61 3 6128 3353
info@stocmarketrestaurant.com.au

Grape Food and Wine Bar
55 Salamanca Pl, Hobart
+61 3 6224 0611
info@grapebar.com.au

Ball & Chain Grill
87 Salamanca Pl, Battery Point
+61 3 6223 2655
hello@ballandchain.com.au

Billy's Burgers and Bar
1 Elizabeth St, Hobart
+61 448 548 088
bookings@billysburgers.com.au

Restaurant Collins
58 Collins St, Hobart
+61 3 6226 1111
collins.res@mantra.com.au

Hog's Breath Cafe Hobart
2 Macquarie St, Hobart
+61 3 6236 9955
bosshog@hogsbreath.com.au

Post Street Social
11-13 Franklin Whrf, Hobart
+61 3 6231 6600
poststreetsocial@pubbanc.com.au

Marquis Bistro & Buffet
209 Brisbane St, West Hobart
+61 3 6200 8861
marquisbuffet@gmail.com

The Orient Bar
34 Murray St, Hobart
+61 3 6237 2999
reservations@hadleyshotel.com.au

Zambrero Hobart
80 Liverpool St, Hobart
+61 3 6234 4561
contactus@zambrero.com

Fish Frenzy
Sullivans Cove, Elizabeth Street Pier, Hobart
+61 3 6231 2134
info@fishfrenzy.com.au

Kopitiam Singapore Cafe
86 Collins St, Hobart
+61 450 588 761
kopitiamsingaporecafe@hotmail.com

Sush
Wellington Ct, Hobart T
+61 3 6234 6650
sushi@sush.com.au

Paesano Pizza & Pasta
108 Lansdowne Cres, West Hobart
+61 3 6234 2111
paesanopizzapasta@bigpond.com

HOBART | WORK

Bars in Hobart

IXL Long Bar
25 Hunter St, Hobart
+61 3 6210 7700
reservations@thehenryjones.com

The Story Bar
18 Hunter St, Hobart
+61 3 6210 7602
hello@macq01.com.au

Amor Bar
217/215-219 Elizabeth St, Hobart
+61 418 393 532
info@amorbar.com.au

Post Street Social
11-13 Franklin Whrf, Hobart
+61 3 6231 6600
poststreetsocial@pubbanc.com.au

Irish Murphy's
21 Salamanca Pl, Hobart
+61 3 6223 1119
infohobart@irishmurphys.com.au

The Brick Factory
55 Salamanca Pl, Hobart
+61 3 6224 3667
info@thebrickfactory.com.au

Derwent Bar
Murray St, Hobart
+61 3 6234 6645
reception@customshousehotel.com

Hope & Anchor Tavern
65 Macquarie St, Hobart
+61 3 6236 9982
hopeandanchortavern@hotmail.com

Grinners Dive Bar
132-134 Elizabeth St, Hobart
+61 439 190 031
info@grinnersdivebar.com

Pablos Cocktails & Dreams
101-103 Harrington St, Hobart
+61 409 230 801
pabloscocktails@gmail.com

Grape Food and Wine Bar
55 Salamanca Pl, Hobart
+61 3 6224 0611
grape@thebrickfactory.com.au

The Glass House Hobart
Brooke Street Pier,
Franklin Whrf, Hobart
+61 3 6223 1032
info@theglass.house

Forty Spotted Gin Bar
Level 1/30 Argyle St, Hobart
+61 428 059 192
hello@ginbarhobart.com

Sonny
120a Elizabeth St, Hobart
mail@sonny.com.au

HOBART | WORK

Lucinda Wine Bar
123 Collins St, Hobart
+61 3 6288 8910
hey@lucindawine.com

New Sydney Hotel
87 Bathurst St, Hobart
+61 3 6234 4516
hello@maybemae.com

Replay Bar
level 1/37 Elizabeth Mall, Hobart
+61 3 6200 1478
info@replaybar.com.au

Republic Bar & Cafe
299 Elizabeth St, North Hobart
+61 3 6234 6954
republicbar@pubbanc.com.au

Lark Distillery
14 Davey St, Hobart
+61 3 6231 9088
info@larkdistilling.com

The Grand Poobah
142 Liverpool St, Hobart
+61 498 951 173
thegrandpoobahbar@gmail.com

Jack Greene Bar
49 Salamanca Pl, Battery Point
+61 3 6224 9655
resumes@pubbanc.com.au

In The Hanging Garden
112 Murray St, Hobart
+61 8 8410 8170
info@inthehanginggarden.com.au

The Whaler
Salamanca Pl, Battery Point
+61 3 6200 1854
info@thewhaler.com.au

AURA Hobart
Level 12/110 Liverpool St, Hobart
+61 3 6236 9001
info@aurahobart.com.au

Willing Brothers. Wine Merchants
390 Elizabeth St, North Hobart
+61 8 8155 6010
willingbros@gmail.com

Altar
112 Murray St, Hobart
info@altarhobart.com.au

Providence Cafe
12 Union St, Adelaide
+61 414 679 006
hello@liveatprovidence.com.au

Hobart Cat Cafe
269 Elizabeth St, North Hobart
+61 3 6285 9971
contact@hobartcatcafe.com.au

HOBART | MEETING PEOPLE & GETTING AROUND

GOING OUT AND MEETING PEOPLE IN HOBART

The pub tour
The idea: you go out to 1 or more pubs and learn about the history of the city. AUD $36/person.
All events are on the page
https://hobarthistorictours.com.au/tour/old-hobart-pub-tour/

Couchsurfing website
Go to www.couchsurfing.com in the "events" tab and meet people from all over the world.
https://www.couchsurfing.com/events

Facebook groups
https://www.facebook.com/groups/TasmaniaBackpackerTraveler
https://www.facebook.com/groups/1278007408944773 (Tasmania Backpackers

Other websites
Meet Up: https://www.meetup.com/find/?location=au--Hobart&source=EVENTS

Getting around in Hobart
Taking the bus in Hobart is very easy with MetroTas.
A ticket costs AUD $3.50.
https://www.metrotas.com.au/
That being said, the city being relatively small makes it easy to get around on foot.
GreenCard is a rechargeable card that allows you to take the bus and get discounts (you will pay your ticket AUD $2.80 instead of AUD $3.50). It can be reloaded on the link
https://www.metrotas.com.au/corporate/campaigns/top-up-your-greencard/

WORKING ON A SOLAR FARM

The basics

Getting a white card

This document allows you to work in the construction industry.

To obtain it, you must complete OHS induction training with an approved training organisation. The RTO will then issue a 'Statement of Achievement' to WorkSafe as proof that you have satisfactorily completed the training and provided proof of identity.

You can do the training online. It's convenient, easy, much cheaper than face-to-face training, and fully accredited (except for South Australia and Northern Territory: it is only available face-to-face).

The cost is AUD $35-AU$220 (depending on the state), which is due at the end of the fifth unit.

It takes about 2-4 hours to complete the course content and about 1-2 hours to complete the assessments.

Here is the link to get started:
https://www.eot.edu.au/online-courses/white-card/

Be patient and flexible

It is possible that a recruiter will tell you that you are going to start in 2 weeks' time and that you will end up waiting 3 months!

Just as you may be called on the day to go to work the next day, you may have to wait months for that call.

Once you are called, you will need transportation to get to the solar farm, often in very remote areas.

Be clean

If you're a big party animal who likes drugs and alcohol, don't bother, because you will have your blood tested before you are hired. There are often even breath tests in the morning before you start work.

Long hours of hard work

Be prepared to work 10-12 hours a day and do repetitive work, with no opportunity for distraction in the evening.

WORKING ON A SOLAR FARM

A decent salary and good savings

Solar farms are in high demand as it is a job that pays very well. **You could earn up to AUD $2000/week**. So it's worth waiting several months/weeks to get the job. Plus, since you'll be in the middle of nowhere with no distractions and your only expense is a weekly rent of about AUD $100, imagine the savings you can make in a few months!

Possible types of jobs

The following are examples of possible positions in a solar farm:
- Supervisors
- Operators
- Mechanical fitters
- Maintenance fitters
- Electrical installers
- Coded welders
- Boilermakers
- Carpenters, etc.

Where to find a job on a solar farm

You can apply online:
https://www.seek.com.au/solar-farm-jobs
https://au.indeed.com/Solar-Farms-Jobs-jobs
For unsolicited applications, you can send your CV to the contacts in the following directory.

Solar farm directory

New South Wales

Solar power is becoming increasingly important in New South Wales, with 14 more projects of over 50MW expected to join the existing six in the next few years. Here is the list in ascending order. There are few solar farms in the country, so there are many applicants for limited places.

272

WORKING ON A SOLAR FARM

Broken Hill Solar Plant
Barrier Hwy, Broken Hill
AGLCommunity@agl.com.au
www.agl.com.au/about-agl/how-we-source-energy/broken-hill-solar-plant

Moree Solar Farm
Moree NSW 2400
+61 1800 337 490
infoaustralia@frv.com

Parkes Solar Farm
Parkes NSW
www.parkessolarfarm.com.au
contact@parkessolarfarm.com.au

Goonumbla Solar Farm
10km west of Parkes and 280km northwest of Sydney.
www.goonumblasolarfarm.com
info@australia@frv.com

Metz Solar Farm
www.metzsolarfarm.com
+61 3 9239 8088

Springdale Solar Farm
www.springdalesolarfarm.com.au
info@renewestate.com

Bomen Solar Farm
10 km northeast of Wagga Wagga
info@bomensolarfarm.com.au
www.bomensolarfarm.com.au

Beryl Solar Farm
245 Beryl Rd, Gulgong
berylsolarfarm@firstsolar.com.au
+61 2 9002 7700

Nyngan Solar Plant
Nyngan NSW
AGLCommunity@agl.com.au

Coleambally Solar Farm
44-18 Ercildoune Rd, Coleambally
+61 1300 872 699
contact@coleamballysolarfarm.com
https://coleamballysolarfarm.com.au

Nevertire Solar Farm
Mitchell Hwy, Nevertire
biosar@biosar.gr
+61 398 636 212
www.biosar.gr

Maryvale Solar Farm
Maryvale
http://www.photonenergy.com.au
careers.aus@photonenergy.com
maryvalesolarfarm@photonenergy.com

Gunnedah Solar Farm
Orange Grove Road, Gunnedah
info.aus@photonenergy.com
http://www.photonenergy.com.au

Sapphire Renewable Energy Hub
+61 2 4013 4640
ed.mounsey@cwpr.com.au

WORKING ON A SOLAR FARM

Finley Solar Farm
198 Canalla Rd, Finley
📞 +61 499 888 521
www.escopacific.com.au
✉ info@escopacific.com.au

Limondale Solar Farm
Balranald NSW
www.overlandsunfarming.com.au

Darlington Point Solar Farm
336 Donald Ross Dr, Darlington Point
✉ darlingtonpointsolar@workpac.com

Sunraysia Solar Storage Facility
c/o Maoneng Australia Level 4,
5 Talavera Rd Macquarie Park
https://sunraysiasolarfarm.com.au/

Victoria

Victoria currently has five solar farms over 50MW. This is less than in other states, perhaps due to the limited availability of suitable locations where the sun is abundant.

Gannawarra Solar Farm
Lalbert-Kerang Rd, Bael Bael
📞 +61 2 8790 4000
https://edifyenergy.com/
✉ hello@edifyenergy.com

Wemen Solar Farm
Booth Rd, Liparoo
📞 +61 1300 816 410
✉ info@wirsol.com.au
✉ info@womensolarfarm.com.au

Bannerton Solar Park
Bannerton
✉ bannerton@foresightgroupau.com
www.bannertonsolarfarm.com.au

Carwarp Solar Farm
✉ shanem@createenergy.com.au
www.altenergy.com.au/listing/carwarp-solar-farm/

Karadoc Solar Farm
Iraak
📞 +61 3 9429 5629
https://www.baywa-re.com.au

Numurkah Solar Farm
Suite 1 – Level 10/227 Elizabeth St, Sydney
📞 +61 2 9267 7203
✉ numurkahsolarfarm@downergroup.com
www.numurkahsolarfarm.com.au

Winton Solar Farm
📞 +61 418 142 173
✉ infoaustralia@frv.com
http://wintonsolarfarm.com/

Yatpool Solar Park
Yatpool
✉ peter.mcpherson@baywa-re.com
www.altenergy.com.au/listing/yatpool-solar-farm/

WORKING ON A SOLAR FARM

Queensland

The state is called the Sunshine State for an obvious reason: the sun! Indeed, Queensland is leading the way in large-scale solar power generation, with some of its largest farms located in the north, near Townsville.

Hayman Solar Farm
Springlands QLD
+61 2 8790 4000
https://edifyenergy.com/
hello@edifyenergy.com

Childers Solar Farm
Isis River, South of Bundaberg, CHILDERS
+61 1300 734 318
shannae.Brydon@corelogic.com.au
www.corelogic.com.au/careers

Whitsunday Solar Farm
Curringa Rd, Springlands
+61 2 8790 4000
https://edifyenergy.com/
hello@edifyenergy.com
darlingtonpointsolar@signalenergy.com

Hamilton Solar Farm
Springlands QLD
+61 2 8790 4000
https://edifyenergy.com/
hello@edifyenergy.com

Susan River Solar Farm
Maryborough Hervey Bay Rd, SUSAN RIVER
+61 1300 734 318
shannae.Brydon@corelogic.com.au

Lilyvale Solar Farm
Oaky Creek Mine Access, Lilyvale
infoaustralia@frv.com
www.lilyvalesolarfarm.com.au

Clare Solar Farm
Clare QLD
+61 447 057 435
claresolarfarm@frv.com
www.claresolarfarm.com.au/

Darling Downs Solar Farm
Kogan QLD
supplier.enquiries@apa.com.au
https://www.apa.com.au

Ross River Solar Farm
Kelso Dr, Kelso
hannah.willson@palisadeims.com.au
www.rossriversolarfarm.com.au

Sun Metals Solar Farm
1 Zinc Rd, Stuart QLD
+61 7 4726 6600
administration@sunmetals.com.au
http://www.sunmetals.com.au/

Daydream Solar Farm
Springlands QLD
+61 2 8790 4000
hello@edifyenergy.com
https://edifyenergy.com/

WORKING ON A SOLAR FARM

Warwick Solar Farm
3 Sandstone Ct, Warwick
+61 404 839 069
www.warwicksolarpanels.com.au/
office@warwicksolarpanels.com.au

Rugby Run Solar Farm
Moranbah, Queensland
enquire@ehpartners.com.au
https://www.ehpartners.com.au/careers/

Oakey Solar Farm
12871 Warrego Hwy, Oakey
https://oakeysolarfarm.com.au/
https://arena.gov.au/projects/oakey-solar-farm/
+61 481 008 408.

Clermont Solar Farm
info@wirsol.com.au
+61 1300 815 970
www.clermontsolarfarm.com.au/

Yarranlea Solar Farm
+61 423 954 792
Samantha.McCarthy@torquejobs.com
https://yarranleasolar.com.au/

Aramara Solar Farm
Peak Downs Highway, Coppabella
enquire@ehpartners.com.au
https://www.ehpartners.com.au/careers/

Rodds Bay Solar Farm
+61 2 8459 9704
info@renewestate.com
www.roddsbaysolarfarm.com.au/

Clarke Creek Solar Farm
150km northeast of Rockhampton and 150km south of Mackay
info@goldwindaustralia.com
www.clarkecreekwindandsolar.com.au

Haughton Solar Farm
Upper Haughton QLD
enquiries@pacifichydro.com.au
https://www.tangoenergy.com/pacific-hydro
1800 730 734

Harlin Solar Farm
d'Aguilar Highway, Harlin
enquire@ehpartners.com.au
https://www.ehpartners.com.au/careers/

South Australia

Although South Australia cannot accommodate the same volume of solar farms as other states, it is worth noting that the largest operational solar farm in Australia, the Bungala Solar Power Project, is located in this state.

276

WORKING ON A SOLAR FARM

Vena Energy Australia
au-enquiries@venaenergy.com
https://www.venaenergy.com.au/contact-us/
+61 7 3708 1420

Bungala Solar Power Project
Wami Kata SA
openinnovability-support@enel.com
https://www.wsp.com/en-AU
Check the available positions :
https://www.wsp.com/en-au/careers/join-our-team?country=AU

Kingfisher Solar Storage
Olympic Way, Roxby Downs
enquire@ehpartners.com.au
https://www.ehpartners.com.au/careers/

Whyalla Solar Farm
Level 24 Westpac House,
91 King William St, Adelaide
+61 1300 130 303
https://www.whyalla.sa.gov.au/our-city/news-and-events/latest-news/whyalla-solar-farm-opened

Solar River Project
Goyder Highway, Warnes,
enquire@ehpartners.com.au
https://www.ehpartners.com.au/careers/

Lake Bonney Battery Energy Storage System
+61 2 8031 9900
reception@infigenenergy.com
www.infigenenergy.com/lake-bonney

Cultana Solar Farm
1284 South Road, Tonsley
info@cultanasolarfarm.com.au
1300 988 098

Riverland Solar Farm and Storage
Goyder Highway, Cadell
enquire@ehpartners.com.au
https://www.power-technology.com/marketdata/riverland-morgan-solar-pv-park-battery-energy-storage-system-australia/

Western Australia

Western Australia is home to a number of small solar farms, none of which currently exceed 50 MW. Over the next few years, the state expects two large solar farms to join its ranks.

Merredin Solar Farm
Robartson Rd, Merredin
info@merredinsolar.com.au
+61 3 9795 9601
www.merredinsolar.com.au

Badgingarra Renewable Facility
200 km north of Perth
supplier.enquiries@apa.com.au
https://www.apa.com.au

ROAD TRIPS

Renting or buying a vehicle?

This question is bound to come up if you plan to be on the road for several weeks.
A van can be resold, whereas a rental will cost a fair bit if you plan to travel for more than two months.
To be able to resell your van at a good price, you need to allow a few weeks at the end of your road trip to find a buyer, so you need to have some time to devote to reselling. We recommend renting if you are on the road for less than two months.

Where to rent a van or a car

APOLLO MOTORHOME HOLIDAYS

From AUD $543 per week | https://new.apollocamper.com/
Open every day from 8am to 4pm.
Sydney: 31 Bay Rd, Taren Point, Sydney | 1800 777 779
Melboune: 40-46 Hume Hwy, Somerton | 1800 777 779
Perth: 65 Worrell Ave, High Wycombe | 1800 777 779
Adelaide : 338 South Rd, Croydon Park | 1800 777 779
Alice Springs: 40 Stuart Highway, Alice Springs | 1800 777 779
Brisbane: 733A Nudgee Road, Northgate | 1800 777 779
Broome: 11B Blackman Street, Broome | 1800 777 779
Cairns: 432-434 Sheridan Street, Cairns | 1800 777 779
Darwin:Henry Wrigley Dr, Darwin Airport |1800 777 779
Gold Coast: Gold Coast Highway, Coolangatta | 1800 777 779
Hobart: Airport, 1 Hawkesford Road, Cambridge| 1800 777 779

BRITZ

From AUD $567 per week | www.britz.com/au
Open every day from 8am to 4pm.
Sydney: 1/1801 Botany Rd, Banksmeadow | +61 2 9316 9071
Melboune: 2 Central West Business Park, 9 Ashley St, Braybrook +61 3 8398 8855
Perth: 471 Great Eastern Hwy, Redcliffe | +61 8 9479 5208
Adelaide : 376 Sir Donald Bradman Dr, Adelaide | +61 8 8234 4108

ROAD TRIPS

Alice Springs: Stuart Highway, Power St, Alice Springs
+61 1800 331 454
Brisbane: 21 Industry Ct, Eagle Farm | +61 7 3868 1248
Broome: 10 Livingstone St, Broome | +61 8 9192 2647
Cairns: 419 Sheridan St, Cairns City | +61 1800 331 454
Darwin:17 Bombing Rd, Winnellie | +61 8 8981 2081
Hobart: Airport, 14 Long St, Cambridge | +61 3 6248 4168

WICKED CAMPERS

From AUD $43 per day | www.wickedcampers.com.au
Open from Monday to Friday from 9am - 4pm, Saturday from 9am- 12pm. Closed on Sundays and public holidays.
Sydney: 320 Botany Rd, Alexandria | +61 1800 246 869
Melboune: 195 Kensington Rd, West Melbourne |+611800 246 869
Perth: 28 Charles St, Bentley | +61 1800 246 869
Adelaide: 86 Gibson St, Bowden | +61 1800 246 869
Alice Springs: 9 Hele Cres, Alice Springs | +61 1800 246 869
Brisbane: 100 Longlands St, Woolloongabba | +61 1800 246 869
Broome: 1 Tanami Dr, Broome | +61 1800 246 869
Cairns: 75 Sheridan St, Cairns City | +61 1800 246 869
Darwin: 75 McMinn St, Darwin City| +61 1800 246 869
Hobart : 201 Kennedy Dr, Cambridge | +61 1800 246 869
Other branches: Exmouth, Monkey Mia, Byron Bay, Airlie Beach)

BUDGET (cars and 4x4)

From AUD $130 per week | https://www.budget.com.au/
Sydney: Airport Domestic Terminal 2, Keith Smith Ave, Mascot
+61 2 9207 9165 (Open every day from 5am to 11pm).
Melboune: 8 Franklin St, Melbourne | +61 3 9204 3933
(Open Monday to Friday from 7.30am to 5.30pm, Saturday and Sunday from 8am to 2pm)
Perth: Metro, 960 Hay St, Perth| +61 8 9237 0022 (Open Monday to Friday from 7.30am to 6pm, Saturday and Sunday from 7.30am to 1pm).
Adelaide: 274 North Terrace, Adelaide | +61 8 8418 7300
(Open from Monday to Thursday from 7.30am to 5pm, Friday until 6pm, Saturday and Sunday from 8am to 2pm)

ROAD TRIPS

Canberra : Terminal Building, (Metro), Canberra | +61 2 6219 3040 (Open every day from 7am to 11pm)

Alice Springs: Terminal Building (Remote), Alice Springs +61 8 8955 5899 (Open every day from 9am to 5.30pm)

Brisbane: 53 Albert St, (Cnr Albert & Margaret St), Brisbane +61 7 3247 0599 (Open from Monday to Friday from 8am to 5pm, Saturday from 8am to midday, and Sunday from 8.30am to midday).

Broome: Mcpherson St, Via Broome Airport, Broome +61 8 9193 5355
(Open Monday to Friday from 8am to 5pm, Saturday from 9am to 1pm and Sunday from 9am to 5pm.)

Cairns :153 Lake St, Cairns| +61 7 4048 8166 | (Open Monday to Friday from 7.30am to 5pm, Saturday to Sunday from 8am to midnight)

Darwin : Darwin Airport | +61 8 8945 2011 (Open from 5am to 1.30am)

Hobart: Domestic Terminal (Metro), Hobart | +61 3 6248 5333 (Open every day from 5.30am to midnight)

ENTERPRISE RENT A CAR (cars)
From AUD $315/week|www.enterpriserentacar.com.au

Sydney: Plaza Sydney International Airport In Terminal Building, Airport Dr, Mascot | +61 2 8303 2282 (Open every day from 5am to 11pm)

Melboune: Melbourne Tullamarine Airport | +61 3 9335 1177 (Open every day from 5am to 1am)

Perth: Terminal 1, Horrie Miller Dr, Perth Airport|+61 8 9479 5099 (Open every day from 6am to 12am, Friday from 7.30am to 6pm, Saturday and Sunday from 7.30am to 1pm)

Adelaide: Andy Thomas Cct, Adelaide Airport| +61 8 8234 4822 (Open every day from 6.30am to 10.30pm)

Darwin: Darwin International Airport, Terminal Building, 1 Henry Wrigley Dr, Darwin City | +61 8 8945 3909 (open every day from 5.30am to 1.30am)

Cairns: Terminal Building, Dakota Court, Aeroglen | +61 7 4034 9052 (open every day from 5am to 12.30am).

Hobart: 67 Argyle St, Hobart | +61 3 6231 2752 | (open Monday to Friday from 7.30am to 5.30pm, Saturday and Sunday until midday)

ROAD TRIPS | THE GREAT OCEAN ROAD

10 unmissable road trips

The Great Ocean Road (from Melbourne to Allansford)

One of the most beautiful roads in the world that stretches along 243km of coastline sculpted by the sea.

> The tourist buses make the round trip in one day, but if you want to enjoy the scenery and avoid the crowds at the must-see spots, you'll need 3 days. If you're a slow traveller, you should allow 6 days.

From Melbourne, it's an hour and a half to **Torquay,** Australia's surfing capital. If it's spring, you'll be lucky enough to catch the Bells Beach Rip Curl Pro (in the first half of April), a surfing competition that attracts all the world's best surfers.

Although there are good surf spots all along the coast up to the 12 Apostles, Bells Beach is still the number one!

Torquay is where Doug Warbrick and Brian Singer founded the Rip Curl brand in 1969 (inspired by the expression "rip the curl": surfing the wave).

Surfing lessons in Torquay

There are several surf schools where you can learn to surf or just rent a board.

Torquay Surfing Academy	**Go Ride A Wave**
34A Bell Street, Torquay	1/15 Bell St, Torquay
☏ +61 3 5261 2022	☏ +61 1300 132 441
✉ contact@torquaysurf.com.au	✉ info@gorideawave.com.au
http://www.torquaysurf.com.au	https://gorideawave.com.au
ⓢ AUD $70/person for a lesson (2 hours)	Board rental from AUD $30.	ⓢ AUD $79/person for a lesson (2h)	Board rental from AUD $25.

ROAD TRIPS | THE GREAT OCEAN ROAD

Accommodation in Torquay

One hostel and a few campsites

Anglesea Backpackers
(14 km from Torquay)
40 Noble St, Anglesea
www.angleseabackpackers.com.au
✉ angleseabackpacker@iprimus.com.au
📞 +61 3 5263 2664
Bookings (and price) by email.

Torquay Foreshore Caravan Park
35 Bell St, Torquay
📞 +61 3 5261 2496
www.torquaycaravanpark.com.au
✉ torquay@gorcc.com.au
From AUD $66 per camping pitch.

Jan Juc Park
93 Sunset Strip
Jan Juc, Victoria (7 min drive from Torquay).
📞 +613 5261 2932
✉ admin@janjucpark.com.au
https://www.janjucpark.com.au/
From AUD $50/night for unpowered camping.

Beyond the town of **Lorne**, the scenery along the coastline becomes incredible. A stop at **Kenneth River** is essential if you want to see the koalas in their natural environment. This is simply a small road surrounded by trees where hundreds of koalas live.
It is also possible to see king parrots here, which will land on your shoulder quite comfortably. You can then stop at **Apollo Bay** and visit Great Otway National Park. The park is a few kilometres inland from the coast. If you are a hiker, you can walk to the 12 Apostles from Apollo Bay (and do the Great Ocean Walk in 8 days).
You can also choose to do just one section.

Otway Fly Treetop Adventures
Walk on an elevated walkway 600 metres long and 25 metres high for an unparalleled view of the flora and fauna of the region. Online bookings: AUD $23.40/person | AUD $108 for the zip line.
360 Phillips Track Beech Forest, Weeaproinah
📞 +61 3 5235 9200 | https://www.otwayfly.com.au

ROAD TRIPS | THE GREAT OCEAN ROAD

Accommodation at Apollo Bay

Hostels
Apollo Bay Eco YHA
5 Pascoe St, Apollo Bay
+61 3 5237 7899
apollobay@yha.com.au
https://www.yha.com.au/
From AUD $50 for a bed in a dorm.

Campings

Apollo Bay Recreation Reserve & Camping Ground
70 Great Ocean Rd, Apollo Bay
+61 3 5237 6577
www.apollobaycampground.com.au
From AUD $42 per camping pitch with electricity.
(AUD $60 in high season).

BIG4 Apollo Bay Pisces Holiday Park
311 Great Ocean Rd, Apollo Bay
+61 3 5237 6749
info@big4apollobay.com.au
https://big4apollobay.com.au/
From AUD $56 per camping pitch.

The 12 Apostles are 85 km from Apollo Bay. The road does not run along the coast the whole way. You'll be driving through rainforests with huge trees that are several hundred years old.
Although you've probably seen photos of the 12 Apostles, nothing compares to the moment you come face to face with these huge rocks along the beach. If you want to avoid the crowds, it is best to go early in the morning. It is best to sleep close by to avoid the drive from Apollo Bay.

Accommodation close to The 12 Apostles

The 13th Apostle Backpackers
(7 minutes drive from the site).
28 Old Post Office Rd, Princetown
+61 437 000 751
Book on www.booking.com
From AUD $40 per bed in a dorm.

ROAD TRIPS | THE GREAT OCEAN ROAD

Five minutes from the 12 Apostles, stop at **Loch Ard Gorge.**
This is also best done early in the morning as it is very busy. The selfie sticks will be out! If you're a little too late at the 12 Apostles site, you can choose to stay around an extra night and try Loch Ard Gorge the next morning. In the meantime, you can go for a walk. There are 3 routes on offer. For all of them, allow 3 hours.
Loch Ard Gorge was named after the shipwreck of the same name in 1878 on this particularly dangerous coast.
Continue on to **Port Campbell** for a short 4km walk: the Port Campbell Discovery Trail. Here you will see the eroded arches of The Arch, London Bridge and The Grotto. Finish with Bay of Martyrs, a site that looks a bit like the 12 Apostles.

Accommodation at Port Campbell

Hostels

Sow and Piglets Guesthouse
18 Tregea St, Port Campbell VIC
📞 +61 3 5598 6305
https://sowandpigletsguesthouse.com.au
✉ reception@sowandpigletsguesthouse.com.au
From AUD $36 for a bed in a dorm.

Campsites

NRMA Port Campbell Holiday Park
30 Morris St, Port Campbell
📞 1800 505 466
www.nrmaparksandresorts.com.au
From AUD $42 per camping pitch.

Port Campbell Recreation Reserve
90 Hennessy St, Port Campbell
📞 +61 431 128 790
www.portcampbellcamping.com
✉ info@portcampbellcamping.com
f PortCampbellRecReserve
From AUD $10 to 16.50 per camping pitch.

ROAD TRIPS | FROM SYDNEY TO BRISBANE

From Sydney to Brisbane

Sydney - Port Macquarie - Coffs Harbour - Yamba - Byron Bay - Brisbane (7 days).

This route is very popular. You will meet a lot of people. It will be very easy to find travel mates to join you.

If you are on a tight budget, choose to travel by bus (with Greyhound http://www.greyhound.com.au/) and use the couchsurfing website to stay with locals and save on accommodation.

Port Macquarie (2 days)

Port Macquarie, 420km north of Sydney, offers beautiful beaches and great surfing.

Located between Sydney and Brisbane, this small town is a photographer's paradise. The crystal clear waters and peaceful atmosphere will make you want to stay forever!

Choose from fourteen different beaches, walk in the national parks and visit the koala hospital!

Koala Hospital

Take a tour of the Koala Hospital and hear the stories of koalas who have been admitted due to bushfires, dog attacks or car accidents.

Lord St, Port Macquarie
📞 +61 2 6584 1522 | www.koalahospital.org.au/
Open every day between 8am and 4.30pm.
Visit at meal times at 8am or 3pm | Free entry - donations appreciated.

ROAD TRIPS | FROM SYDNEY TO BRISBANE

Accommodation at Port Macquarie

Hostels

Port Macquarie Backpackers
2 Hastings River Drive,
Port Macquarie
+61(0) 02 6583 1791
sleep@portbackpackers.com.au
www.portbackpackers.com.au
From AUD $37 per bed in a dorm.

Port Macquarie YHA - Ozzie Pozzie Backpackers
36 Waugh St, Port Macquarie
+61 2 6583 8133
https://www.yha.com.au/
From AUD $37 per bed in a dorm.

Beachside Backpackers
40 Church St, Port Macquarie
+61 2 6583 5512
www.beachsidebackpackers.com
From AUD $31 per bed in a dorm.

Campings

Flynns Beach Caravan Park
22 Ocean St, Port Macquarie
+61 2 6583 5754
www.flynnsbeachcaravanpark.com.au
bookings@flynnsbeachcaravanpark.com.au
From AUD $35 per camping pitch.

Lighthouse Beach Holiday Village
140 Matthew Flinders Dr, Port Macquarie
+61 2 6582 0581
www.lighthousebeachholidayvillage.com.au/
From AUD $40/60 per camping pitch depending on the season.

Coffs Harbour (1 day)

A two-hour drive north of Port Macquarie, Coffs Harbour is a small town of about 75,000 people.
You must eat the famous Coffs' bananas!
Take a stroll along the pier and try the fish and chips for lunch!
http://www.visitcoffsharbour.com

ROAD TRIPS | FROM SYDNEY TO BRISBANE

Accommodation in Coffs Harbour

Hostels

Aussitel Backpackers
312 Harbour Dr, Coffs Harbour
+61 2 6651 1871
info@aussitel.com
https://aussitel.com/
From AUD $28 per bed in a dorm.

Campsites

BIG4 Park Beach Park
1 Ocean Parade, Coffs Harbour
+61 2 6648 4888
www.coffscoastholidayparks.com.au
Camping pitches from AUD $48 with electricity.

Banana Coast Caravan Park
429 Pacific Hwy, Coffs Harbour
+61 2 6652 2868
www.bananacoastcaravanpark.com
Camping pitches from AUD $30.

Yamba (1 day)
About two hours from Coffs Harbour heading north.
With a population of just over 6,000 people, Yamba is a very charming town with pristine beaches, national parks and good cafes and restaurants making it a great place to relax.
http://www.yambansw.com.au

Accommodation in Yamba

Hostels

Yamba YHA
26 Coldstream Street, Yamba
+61 2 6646 3997
https://www.yha.com.au/
Dorms: from AUD $32.

ROAD TRIPS | FROM SYDNEY TO BRISBANE

Campsites

Blue Dolphin Holiday Resort
Yamba Rd, Yamba
+61 2 6646 2194
https://bluedolphin.com.au/
info@bluedolphin.com.au
Camping pitches from
from AUD $52 with electricity.

BIG4 Saltwater @ Yamba Holiday Park
286 O'Keefes Ln, Palmers Island
+61 2 6646 0255
www.big4saltwater.com.au
Camping pitches from
from AUD $58 with electricity.

Byron Bay (2 days)

It's a two-hour drive from Yamba to Byron Bay.
The surfing capital of New South Wales, Byron Bay is home to surfing courses and Australia's golden youth who come here to party. There's a hippie vibe in the town with its huge beaches, yoga classes, shops and vegan and healthy restaurants all over the place.

Accommodation in Byron Bay

Hostels

Aquarius Backpackers
16 Lawson St, Byron Bay
+61 2 6685 7663
www.aquariusbyronbay.com.au/
info@aquarius-backpackers.com.au
Dorm from AUD $45.

Byron Bay YHA
7 Carlyle St, Byron Bay
+61 2 6685 8853
https://www.yha.com.au
byronbay@yha.com.au
Dorm from AUD $69.

Backpackers Inn Byron Bay
29 Shirley St, Byron Bay
+61 2 6685 8231
info@backpackersinnbyronbay.com.au
www.backpackersinnbyronbay.com.au
Dorm from AUD $28.

ROAD TRIPS | FROM SYDNEY TO BRISBANE

Campsites

Discovery Parks - Byron Bay
399 Ewingsdale Rd, Byron Bay
📞 +61 2 6685 7378
www.discoveryholidayparks.com.au
Camping pitches from
from AUD $37 with electricity.

First Sun Holiday Park
Lawson St, Byron Bay
📞 +61 2 6685 6544
www.firstsunholidaypark.com.au
Camping pitches from
from AUD $57 without electricity.

Suffolk Beachfront Holiday
143 Alcorn St, Suffolk Park
📞 +61 2 6685 3353
http://suffolkbeachfront.com.au
Camping pitches from
from AUD $60.

Broken Head Holiday Park
184 Beach Road, Broken Head
📞 +61 2 6685 3245
www.brokenheadholidaypark.com.au
Camping pitches from
from AUD $34 without electricity.

Byron Bay's most beautiful beaches
Broken Head Nature Reserve: Kings Beach, Bray Beach and Whites Beach are located on the other side of Cape Byron and are ideal for surfing. Kings Beach is sometimes frequented by nudists.
Main Beach: A huge beach at the end of the shopping street in Byron Bay. You can sit on the grassy strip above it for a picnic or to watch the sunset.
Flynns Beach: More wild than its neighbours, it is the meeting point for surfers early in the morning.

From Brisbane to Cairns

Brisbane - Noosa - Rainbow Beach - Fraser Island - Airlie Beach- Whitsundays - Magnetic Island - Cairns (12 days).

This route is certainly the most popular in Australia as it is on this route that you will find Fraser Island and the Whitsundays Islands. There are a number of hostels and tours to the islands along the way.

ROAD TRIPS | FROM BRISBANE TO CAIRNS

Noosa (1 day)

The small town of Noosa is 130km north of Brisbane on the Sunshine Coast.

It's an upmarket part of Queensland with lots of impressive homes close to the beach. It's a laid-back, health-conscious town with lots of organic shops in the small town centre.

The sunsets over the sea are particularly spectacular. The sky turns dark blue and then pink, giving you the illusion of a completely pink beach.

www.visitnoosa.com.au

Accommodation in Noosa

Hostels

Noosa Heads YHA
2 Halse Ln, Noosa Heads
+61 7 5447 3377
noosaheads@yha.com.au
www.yha.com.au/
Dorm from AUD $47.

Dolphins Beach House
14-16 Duke St, Sunshine Beach
+61 7 5447 2100
https://dolphinsbeachhouse.com/
info@dolphinsbeachhouse.com
Dorm from AUD $42.

Campings

Noosa North Shore Beach Campground
240 Wilderness Track, Noosa North Shore
+61 7 5449 8811
www.noosaholidayparks.com.au
Camping pitches from
from AUD $49.

Noosa River Holiday Park
4 Russell St, Noosaville
+61 7 5449 7050
www.noosaholidayparks.com.au/noosa-river
Camping pitches from AUD $55.

Rainbow Beach- Fraser Island (3 days)

From Noosa, you'll need to drive for about two hours to get to Rainbow Beach.

Fraser Island is the world's largest sand island, stretching 123 kilometers in length. The island is accessible by ferry from Rainbow Beach or Hervey Bay (45 minutes).

ROAD TRIPS | FROM BRISBANE TO CAIRNS

Fraser is a true paradise for lovers of flora and fauna. You will see dingoes (a type of wild dog), the island's unique emblem, on the beach and in the forests.

There are about 100 lakes dotting the island, and the crystal clear water is so pure that bathers are asked not to go into the water with sunscreen on so as not to pollute it!

The white sand has washing and water-softening properties so you can swim in Lake McKenzie to wash yourself!

There are two ways to get the most out of Fraser Island: on your own, or with a tour package, knowing that travel on the island is by 4WD.

If you choose to hire the 4WD yourself, the insurance cover issued by most car rental agencies does not include accidents that might occur on the sand.

Dingos Fraser Island 4WD Tours
3 Day Fraser Island 4WD Tag-Along Adventure: AUD $489.
20 Spectrum St, Rainbow Beach
+61 8 8131 5750 | https://www.dingosfraser.com/

Accommodation in Rainbow Beach

Hostels

Pippies Beachhouse
22 Spectrum St, Rainbow Beach
+61 7 5486 8503
bookings@pippiesbeachhouse.com.au
www.pippiesbeachhouse.com.au
Dorm from AUD $ 32.
This hostel also offers 4x4 rental and tours.

Freedom Rainbow Beach
20 Spectrum St, Rainbow Beach
+61 7 5401 5500
www.freedomrainbowbeach.com
info@dolphinsbeachhouse.com
Dorm from AUD $40.

ROAD TRIPS | FROM BRISBANE TO CAIRNS

Campings

BIG4 Breeze Holiday Parks
308 Carlo Rd, Rainbow Beach
+61 7 5486 3200
stay@rainbowbeachholidaypark.com.au
www.rainbowbeachholidaypark.com.au
Camping pitches from
AUD $35 without electricity,
AUD $45 with electricity.

Rainbow Beach Ultimate Camping
Rainbow Beach
+61 419 464 254
https://ultimatecamp.com.au
bookings@ultimatecamp.com.au
Prices on request.

Airlie Beach- Whitsundays (4 days)

It is about a 12 hour drive from Rainbow Beach to Airlie Beach, so if you are travelling in a van you may find the journey very tedious as there is virtually nothing to see on this road. It is also very dangerous to drive at night due to kangaroos that cross the roads unexpectedly, and can cause a lot of damage to the car!

Airlie Beach is best known as the starting point for cruises to the Whitsunday Islands.

There are several travel agencies that organise these idyllic cruises in the middle of the Great Barrier Reef.

Airlie Beach is very touristy and famous for its party atmosphere, bars and nightclubs. Many hostels line the streets and offer great value for money. Some hostels even have their own bar!

There is also a lagoon in the city which was created to allow people to swim safely.

Accommodation in Airlie Beach

Hostels

Nomads Airlie Beach Hostel
336 Shute Harbour Rd, Airlie Beach
+61 7 4999 6600
info@nomadsairliebeach.com
https://nomadsworld.com/australia
Dorms from AUD $31.33.
There is also a camping available.

Airlie Beach YHA
394 Shute Harbour Rd, Airlie Beach
+61 7 4946 6312
www.yha.com.au/hostels
airliebeach@yha.com.au
Dorms from AUD $45.60.

ROAD TRIPS | FROM BRISBANE TO CAIRNS

Magnums Backpackers
370 Shute Harbour Rd, Airlie Beach
+61 7 4964 1199
https://magnums.com.au/
Dorm : From AUD $35.

Base Backpackers
336 Shute Harbour Rd, Airlie Beach
+61 7 4948 2000
https://www.stayatbase.com
info@stayatbase.com
Dorm from AUD $56,81.
Campsite from AUD $25.

Campings

NRMA Airlie Beach Holiday Park
234 Shute Harbour Rd, Cannonvale
+61 7 4946 6379
www.nrmaparksandresorts.com.au/airlie-beach/
Camping pitches from
From AUD $30 without electricity,
AUD $48 with electricity.

Big4 Holiday Park
25-29 Shute Harbour Road, Airlie Beach
+61 7 4948 5400
https://www.big4.com.au
Camping pitch from AUD $53.

Whitsundays

The islands were named by Captain Cook because he discovered them on Whitsunday.

With turquoise waters and white sands, the Whitsundays are one of Australia's most popular destinations, and a top choice for honeymooners.

This idyllic spot, which you can reach by boat from Airlie Beach, is home to more than 150 species of birds.

You can also go diving in the Coral Sea, and see fish of many colours, as well as rays. Many agencies offer cruises from one to several days. If you want to see more than one island and not just the most famous one, Whitehaven, then book a three day - two night cruise.

ROAD TRIPS | FROM BRISBANE TO CAIRNS

As well as seeing incredible islands, you can dive, kayak or simply sunbathe on the catamaran.

The atmosphere on board will depend on the agency that sold you the cruise, the size of the boat and the number of people on the boat. There are party boats and quieter boats.

> **Sailing Whitsundays**
> Day tour from AUD $99.
> 2 day cruise from AUD $339.
> 4/1 Airlie Esplanade, Airlie Beach
> +61 74914 2425 | https://sailing-whitsundays.com

Magnetic Island (2 days)

3.5 hours north of Airlie Beach is Townsville, the port from which ferries depart for Magnetic Island (AUD $30 return)
http://www.sealinkqld.com.au/

Magnetic Island has become a suburb of Townsville with a population of around 2000 permanent residents.

Accommodation in Magnetic Island

Hostels & campings

Bungalow Bay Koala Village
40 Horseshoe Bay Rd,
Horseshoe Bay
+61 7 4778 5577
info@bungalowbay.com.au
www.bungalowbay.com.au
Camping pitches from AUD $25 per person/ per night (AUD $20 for unpowered campsites)

Nomads Magnetic Island (Base)
1 Nelly Bay Rd, Magnetic Island
+61 7 4778 5777
https://www.stayatbase.com/
Dorm from AUD $42.94.
Camping from AUD $19.

CStay Holiday
32 Picnic St, Picnic Bay
+61 7 4758 1616
https://www.cstay.com.au/
Dorm from AUD $30.
Twin from AUD $30/person.

ROAD TRIPS | FROM PERTH TO ESPERANCE

From Perth to Esperance
Perth - Esperance - Albany - Denmark - Margaret River - Perth (9 days)

There is nothing special to see on this rather monotonous road. This is the longest part of the journey as the road does not follow the coast but goes inland. But wait! The long journey is worth it!

Esperance (3 days)
Located about 720 kilometres south-east of Perth, Esperance has a population of 10,000.

Esperance is a French word and the name of the ship captained by Bruni d'Entrecasteaux. This was the first European ship to arrive in this part of Australia. The part of the coast called Recherche Archipelago was named after the second French ship *Recherche* arrived.

Esperance is renowned for having some of the most beautiful beaches in Australia; a spectacular coastline, an abundance of wildlife, national parks and white sand.

You may even see kangaroos lounging on Lucky Bay beach!

There's not much to do in the evenings if you want to go out. You can always go to the Pier Hotel on the esplanade, which is the largest pub. (www.thepierhotelesperance.com)

Twilight Beach
With seven kilometres of white sand, Twilight Beach is the safest beach for swimming and surfing.

Cape Le Grand National Park
This national park is fifty kilometres southeast of Esperance. Once you're here, you can drive a 4WD along the beach and enjoy incredible views of the ocean!

The first stop you make should be at Hellfire Bay. It's spectacular! Climb Frenchman Peak (262m) with a panoramic view of Cape Legrand and its islands as your reward.

ROAD TRIPS | FROM PERTH TO ESPERANCE

Accommodation in Esperance

Campings

Esperance Bay Holiday Park
162 Dempster St, Esperance
+61 8 9071 2237
www.summerstar.com.au/
Camping pitches from
AUD $42.

Esperance Seafront Caravan Park
Cnr Goldfields and Norseman Roads, Esperance
+61 (08) 9071 1251
www.holidayparksdownunder.com.au

Albany (1 day)

With a population of almost 30,000, Albany is a small town but one of the most visited in Western Australia.

It is a wine growing region but is most popular for its famous beaches: Little Beach, Middleton Beach and Two Sisters Beach.

The climate in Albany is cooler than in Perth. Prices are more competitive and the people are very friendly.

More info: www.albany.wa.gov.au

The Blow Holes:
These are cracks in the granite rocks along the coast. When the waves hit these rocks, they produce geysers and a deafening and surprising noise!

The markets
There's a farmers' market every Saturday morning, voted the best farmers' market in Australia, so it might be worth popping in between beach sessions!

ROAD TRIPS | FROM PERTH TO ESPERANCE

Accommodation in Albany

Hotels
There is one hostel for backpackers in Albany but it has bad reviews. So, the best thing to do is to rent a twin if you are travelling with someone.

Emu Point Motel
1 Medcalf Parade, Emu Point
+61 8 9844 1001
info@emupointmotel.com.au
www.emupointmotel.com.au/
Twin : from AUD $155.

Albany Foreshore Guest House
86 Stirling Terrace, Albany
+61 412 704 794
www.albanyforeshoreguesthouse.com.au/
Twin : from AUD $155.

Campings

Albany Happy Days
1584 Millbrook Rd, King River
+61 8 9844 3267
https://albanycaravanpark.com
Camping pitches from
from AUD $40- 60.

BIG4 Middleton Beach Holiday Park
28 Flinders Parade, Middleton Beach
+61 8 9841 3593
holiday@holidayalbany.com.au
www.holidayalbany.com.au
Camping pitches from
from AUD $58/person.

Acclaim Albany Holiday Park
550 Albany Hwy, Albany
+61 8 9841 7800
www.acclaimparks.com.au/locations/albany
albanyholiday@acclaimparks.com.au
Camping pitches from
AUD $45.

BIG4 Emu Beach Holiday Park
8 Medcalf Parade, Albany
+61 8 9844 1147
https://www.big4.com.au
Camping pitches from AUD $45.

Denmark (2 days)
Denmark is a small hippy town of 2,280 people, 423 kilometres south-east of Perth and only 40 minutes west of Albany. There are many breweries and wineries in the area, as the region is a major wine producer. Beach wise, it's hard to say which is the prettiest! The view of the coast is absolutely magnificent.
Make sure you don't miss Elephant Cove and Greens Pool beaches.
More info at: http://www.denmark.com.au

ROAD TRIPS | FROM PERTH TO ESPERANCE

Accommodation in Denmark

Hostels

Blue Wren Travellers Rest YHA
17 Price St, Denmark
+61 8 9848 3300
info@denmarkbluewren.com.au
www.denmarkbluewren.com.au
Dorm from AUD $35.

Campings

Denmark Rivermouth Caravan Park
Inlet Dr, Denmark
+61 8 9848 1262
admin@denmarkrivermouthcaravanpark.com.au
www.denmarkrivermouthcaravanpark.com.au
Camping pitches from AUD $45.

Denmark Ocean Beach Holiday Park
770 Ocean Beach Rd, Denmark
+61 8 9848 1105
https://www.big4.com.au
Camping pitches from AUD $40.

> **Valley of the Giants Tree Top Walk**
> Not afraid of heights? Explore this forest of gigantic 40 metre trees!
> Entrance fee: Tree Top Walk AUD $21
> Valley of the Giants Rd, Tingledale
> +61 8 9840 8263
> www.treetopwalk.com.au

Riverbend Chalets & Caravan Park
40 Riverbend Ln, Denmark
+61 8 9848 1107
www.riverbend-caravanpark.com.au
Camping pitch from AUD $37-47 (depending on the season).

Margaret River (3 days)

Margaret River (or *Margs* if you're a local) is a three hour drive from Perth (South).
It's a world famous surfing spot but also has a few shark attacks!
Cape Leeuwin Lighthouse is a must see as it is the most south-westerly cape in Australia.
More information on Margaret River: http://www.margaretriver.com

ROAD TRIPS | FROM PERTH TO ESPERANCE

The Wine Route
The Margaret River region produces a very young wine (the first vines were planted only 60 years ago!).
The near-perfect weather conditions have made the wine from this region recognised as some of the best in the world.
Some wineries to stop at:
Voyager Estate (http://www.voyagerestate.com.au),
Xanadu (www.xanaduwines.com),
Deepwood (http://www.deepwoods.com.au),
Leewin Estate (http://www.leeuwinestate.com.au),
Watershed (https://www.watershedwines.com.au),
Evans & Tate (http://www.evansandtate.com.au)

Accommodation in Margaret River

Hostels and campings

RAC Margaret River
Wooditjup National Park, Carters Rd, Margaret River
+61 8 9758 8227
www.parksandresorts.rac.com.au
Book directly on www.hostelworld.com
Dorm: Price on request
Camping: From AUD $44 per pitch.

Margaret River Tourist Park
44 Station Rd, Margaret River
+61 8 9757 2180
https://summerstar.com.au
Camping pitches from AUD $40.

Margaret River Backpackers
66 Town View Terrace, Margaret River
+61 8 9757 9572
stay@margaretriverbackpackers.com.au
www.margaretriverbackpackers.com.au
Book directly on www.hostelworld.com
Dorm from AUD $30.

Riverview Tourist Park
8/10 Willmott Ave, Margaret River
+61 8 9757 2270
https://summerstar.com.au
Camping pitches from AUD $38.

BONUS: THE HARVEST GUIDE

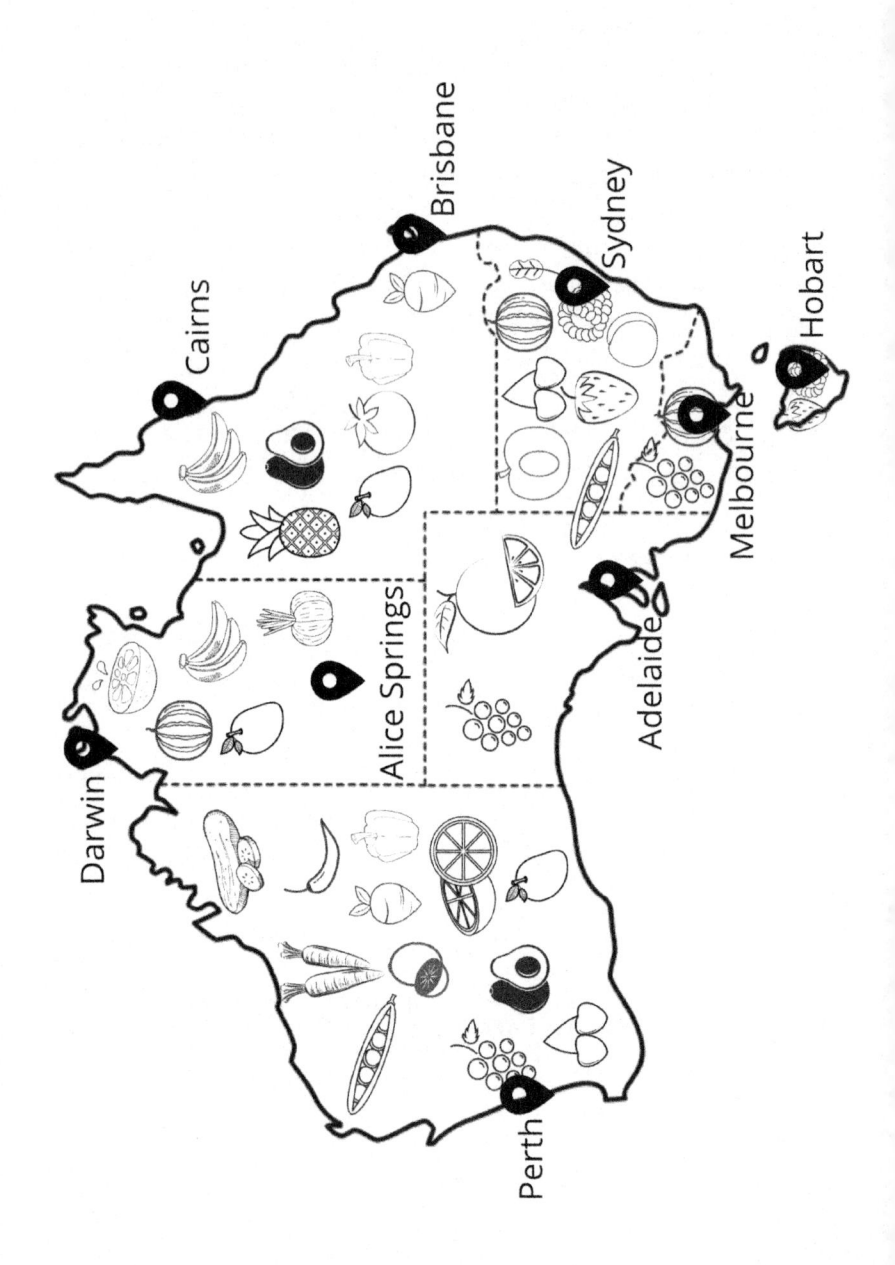

WORKING CONDITIONS AND WAGES

Working Conditions

You will have to leave your comfort zone and probably share some space with other people (for example, sleep in a dorm, share the kitchen and/or the bathroom). Sometimes, the farm will host the employees on site and will deduct the cost from your paycheck. Housing conditions are sometimes sketchy.
If you have a camper van, it will be perfect because you can save on housing.

It is also necessary to cope with the heat, the repetitive nature of the job and the weight of certain fruits, such as bananas for example. Do not accept abusive working conditions, like not being allowed to drink water or use the bathroom for hours. When the temperature is over 40 °C (104 °F) all day, you should drink 3-4 litres of water per day.

Pay Rates

Pay rates vary from one region to another. You can be paid by performance, by basket (bucket or bin) or by kilo, more rarely by the hour. This means that the faster you go, the more you earn! This can be motivating for some people, but very discouraging for others.
If, for example, you work at your maximum level but still earn less than AUD $21.38 an hour (the legal minimum wage), then it's not a good plan.

Nevertheless, you will get faster as time goes on, so your income will increase. Some pickers reach AUD $200 a day -- that's a great way to save money.
If you want to be paid by the hour, opt for packing jobs (fruit packaging).

BEWARE OF SCAMS

Beware of scams: working hostels and contractors

Many seasonal workers are fooled by some working hostels who promise a job as *pickers* just to rent their accommodation.
Never pay in advance for accommodation. If you are asked for a deposit of AUD $150 to work, run away!
Particular attention should be paid to the city of Bundaberg (Queensland), which is sadly renowned for these practices.
Not all working hostels are a scam. Some of them really offer work and provide decent accommodation.
The same applies to contractors who are an intermediary between the farm and you, and therefore take a commission.
In Victoria, many farms work exclusively with a contractor.

If you are asked to pay to apply for a job, just leave. The best thing to do is to go directly onsite to check the farm and ask the owners directly if they need pickers (after confirming what is being harvested at the time).
Some farms take advantage of the fact that you are in the middle of nowhere to sell you their accommodation.

> ### Do I have to go to a working hostel if I don't have a car?
>
> The advantage of a working hostel is that it can take you to your workplace every day. You leave with the team in the morning in a van and come back in the evening. It is very easy for you if you don't have your own transportation.
>
> **So YES, but always check the online reviews before going.**

HOW TO CONTACT THE FARMS

Sign a contract !

This may seem obvious, but it is important to remember it.
To get your second Working Holiday Visa and your 88 days, you will need your pay slips and a contract.
Beware of farmers who say yes and make you stay there until the fruit is mature - some backpackers have waited for weeks without any pay. Check the condition of the fruit yourself, and if after 3 days you haven't started working, move to the next!
If there is no contract, don't stay.

> **What to do in the event of a conflict with an employer?**
> If there are problems with a farm, contact **Fair Work Australia au 13 13 94** (8am - 5.30pm Monday to Friday).

How do I contact the farms ?

To contact the farms, you will have to call them, except for some owners who ask that you apply online with a resume or CV. Usually, it's first come, first served. Don't wait until you're in the middle of the season to call; plan ahead !
"G'day! Are you looking for any pickers? »

If your English is not so good and you have a van, or if you are traveling with several people in a car, you can go directly to the farm to ask them in person if they are looking for any workers. If you don't want to drive too far, text messages work too! If you call and the owner says "ok" on the phone, keep in mind that if another picker arrives before you, you will probably lose your spot.

The essentials

FRUIT PICKING SEASONS | NEW SOUTH WALES

NEW SOUTH WALES

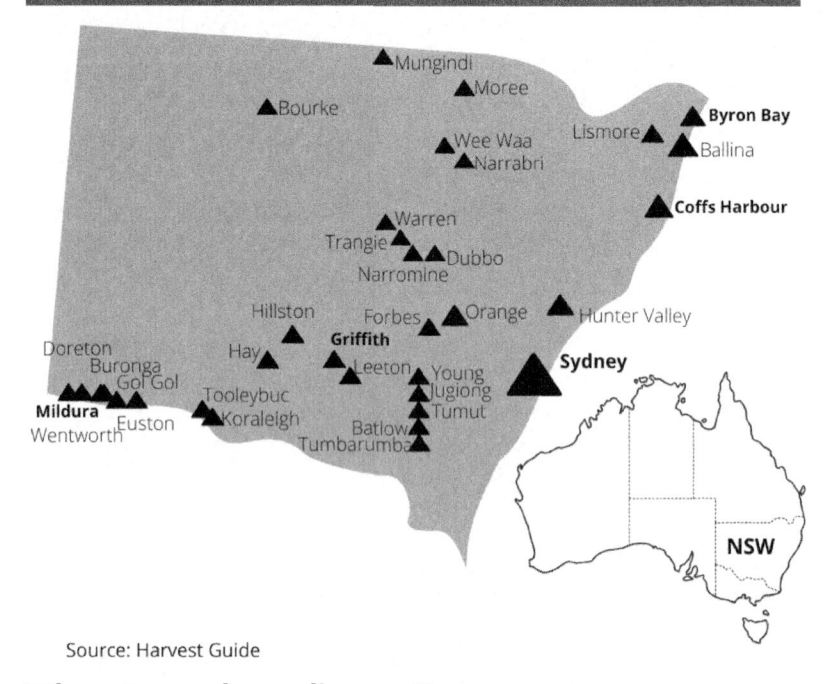

Source: Harvest Guide

Where to go, depending on the season

In Wentworth (1000 km west of Sydney), there is **high demand May through August and October through December** for lemons (average demand in September), and **from February through September** for grapes (average demand in January).
October and November is the peak season for vegetables (average demand in January and February and May through September).

In Young (374 Km west of Sydney) average demand for berries, grapes, and stone fruits February through April; for cherries, November and December, and for plums; June through September.

Contact the farms even if it's not the peak season

FRUIT PICKING SEASONS | NEW SOUTH WALES

In Wee Waa and Warren (600 km and 500 km northwest of Sydney), there is **high demand in April and May** for cotton.

In Tumut (400 km southwest of Sydney), there is **high demand February through May** for apples.

In Tumbarumba (468 km southwest of Sydney), there is **high demand March through May** for apples (average demand for the rest of the year), **February through April** for grapes (average demand June through September), **and January through March** for berries (average demand in April and December).

In Trangie, there is average demand for cotton in April and May.

In Tooleybuc (895 km west of Sydney)**, there is high demand May through August and October through January** for lemons (average demand in September), **December through February** for stone fruit, and for grapes **February through April and June through September** (average demand in January and May). Average demand May through February for vegetables.

In the Sydney area, demand remains average all year: from February to April for apples, avocados from December to February, August to November for lemons, November to January for stone fruit and all year for vegetables, turf and flower nurseries.

In Orange (255 km west of Sydney), there is **high demand February through April** for apples (average demand in May); **February through April, and June through September** for grapes (average demand in December); **November and December** for cherries (average demand in January).

FRUIT PICKING SEASONS | NEW SOUTH WALES

In Narromine (430 km west of Sydney), there is **high demand in April and May** for cotton and **May through October** for lemons (average demand from November through March).

In Narrabri and Mungindi (520 km and 748 km worthwest of Sydney, respectively), there is **high demand in April and May** for cotton (average demand in March in Mungindi).

In Moree (627 km northwest of Sydney), there is **high demand in April and May** for cotton (average demand in March), and **May through July** for olives (average demand in April and August). Average demand April through August for hazelnuts.

In Lismore (740 km north of Sydney), **high demand June through October** for avocados (average demand in November), **September through November** for berries (average demand in December, January, July and August); **October and November** for stone fruits (average demand in December), **May through July** for hazelnuts (average demand in April, August and September).

In Leeton (550 km west of Sydney), **high demand October through March** for lemons (average demand throughout the rest of the year); **in February and March** for grapes, **February through April, November and December** for stone fruits (average demand in January). Average demand for vegetables September through May.

In the Hunter Valley (240 km north of Sydney) **high demand in January and February and June through August** for grapes (average demand in March and September).

FRUIT PICKING SEASONS | NEW SOUTH WALES

In Hillston (680 km west of Sydney), **high demand in November** for cherries; **October through February and May through August** for lemons (average demand in March and April), **from April to June** for cotton; **July, August, November and December** for vegetables (average demand in June and September).

In Hay (720 km west of Sydney), **high demand March through December** for vegetables. Average demand for melons January through March, and for cotton in April and May.

In Griffith (570 km west of Sydney) **high demand October through February and June through August** for lemons (average demand in March, April, May and September); **February through April and June through August** for grapes (average demand in January); **December through February** for vegetables (average demand in November and March).

In Gol Gol (1000 km west of Sydney), **high demand October through January and in June and July** for lemons (average demand in May, August and September), **February through April and June through September** for grapes (average demand in January and May). Average demand for vegetables May through February.

In Forbes (375km west of Sydney), **high demand January through March** for stone fruits (average demand October through December). Average demand May through August for plums.

In Euston (920km east of Sydney) **high demand February through April** for grapes (average demand in January and May), **and May through September** for plums.
Average demand for vegetables May through February.

307

FRUIT PICKING SEASONS | NEW SOUTH WALES

In Dubbo (388 km west of Sydney), **high demand in April and May** for cotton.

In Coffs Harbour (524 km north of Sydney), **high demand July through September** for avocados (average demand in June and October through December); **September through November** for berries (average demand in December, January, July, and August). Average demand for bananas throughout the year.

In Byron Bay (763 km north of Sydney), **high demand in June and July** for avocados (average demand in April, May, August and September); **September through November** for berries (average demand in July, August, December and January); **February and March** for lychees; **May through July** for hazelnuts (average demand in April, August and September). Average demand for stone fruits September through December.

In Bourke (750 km northwest of Sydney), **high demand December through February and May through September** for lemons; **April and May** for cotton; **November through January** for grapes (average demand in May and June); **January through May** for melons; **May and June** for plums.

In Batlow (440 km southwest of Sydney), **high demand March through May** for apples.

In Ballina (735 km north of Sydney), **high demand in June and July** for avocados (average demand in April, May, August and September); **September through November** for berries (average demand in July, August, December and January); **May through July** for hazelnuts (average demand in April, August and September). Average demand for stone fruits September through December.

FRUIT PICKING SEASONS | NEW SOUTH WALES

	Jan.	Feb.	Mar.	April	May	June	July	Aug.	Sept.	Oct.	Nov.	Dec.
High demand				Average demand								
Ballina												
Batlow												
Bourke												
Byron Bay												
Coffs Harbour												
Dubbo												
Euston												
Forbes												
Gol Gol												
Griffith												
Hay												
Hillston												
Hunter Valley												
Leeton												
Lismore												
Moree												
Mungindi												
Narrabri												
Narromine												
Orange												
Sydney région												
Tooleybuc												
Trangie												
Tumbarumba												
Tumut												
Warren												
Wee Waa												
Wentworth												
Young												

FARM ADDRESSES AND CONTACTS | NSW

Farm addresses and contacts

ORANGE

Harvest Information Service
1800 062 332   www.harvesttrail.gov.au

Appledale Processors Co-Operative Ltd.
5 Stephen Pl, Orange NSW
02 6361 4422
www.appledale.com.au

Darley P R & J D
Daydawn, Nashdale NSW
02 6365 3278

Thornbrook Orchard (cherries)
39 Nashdale Ln, Nashdale
Paula : 04 27 269 437
www.thornbrookorchard.com.au
info@thornbrookorchard.com.au

Rossi Orchards Pty Ltd
98, Mount Pleasant La, Orange
02 6365 3106

Kirkwood J W Pty Ltd
Ballykeane, Orange NSW 2800
02 6362 9960

Pearce R S
Orange NSW 2800
02 63 65 82 16

Huntley Berry Farm, Orange non-profit disability enterprise
Huntley Rd, Huntley NSW
02 6365 5282
Mobile : 0427 252 308
www.huntleyberryfarm.com.au
huntleyberryfarm@octec.org.au
f huntleyberryfarm

D & J Vardanega Cherries
610 Pinnacle Road, Orange
02 6365 3242
wvardanega@gmail.com
f D & J Vardanega Cherries

Carinya Orchards Pty Ltd
98 Nancarrow La, Nashdale NSW
02 6365 3317

Gartrell David & Carolyn
"Wattleview"
Mt Lofty Rd, Nashdale NSW 2800
02 6365 3233

B Carthew
Towac Rd, Canobolas NSW 2800
02 63 65 31 38

FARM ADDRESSES AND CONTACTS | NSW

Prudhomme P & A
Ku-Ring-Gai, Nashdale NSW
📞 02 63 65 32 89

Cunich M E
Orange, Nashdale NSW 2800
📞 02 63 65 31 51

Huntley Berry Farm
Huntley Rd via, Orange NSW
📞 02 63 65 52 82
✉ hurtleyberryfarm@otec.org.au
www.huntleyberryfarm.com.au
f huntleyberryfarm

Hillside Harvest
1209 The Escort Way Borenore
📞 02 6365 2247
www.hillsideharvest.com.au
f hillsideharvestorange

McClymont P A
Shed, Springside NSW 2800
📞 0418 350 163

Cunial G & T
Mount View, Nashdale NSW
📞 02 6365 3187

BOURKE

Pitches R.G. & G. A.
Bourke NSW 2840
📞 02 68 72 22 67

Darling River Cotton Pty Ltd
Gorrell Ave, Bourke NSW
📞 0268 708521

NARROMINE

Mumblepeg
Mumble Peg, Narromine NSW 2821
📞 02 6889 6130

BYRON BAY / BALLINA

Blueberry Fields
769 Fernleigh Rd, Brooklet
📞 02 6687 8114
Call only on Wednesdays between 11am and noon. If there is no answer, it means that there is no more jobs available. No email. Blueberry picking all year round with a high season between June and January. No accommodation on site.
www.blueberryfields.com.au

Byron Bay Organic Produce
Cnr Johnston Lane & Pacific Hwy, Ewingsdale
📞 02 6684 7007
Mobile: 0412865423
www.byronbayorganicproduce.com.au

311

FARM ADDRESSES AND CONTACTS | NSW

Cape Byron Bush Foods
Lot 96/ Raywards La, Skinners Shoot
02 66 85 81 12

Aussie Orchards Growers & Packers
206 Warwick Park Rd, Mooball NSW
0421 381 129

Summerland Farm
253 Wardell Rd, Alstonville NSW
02 6628 0610
www.summerlandhousefarm.com.au

Ooray Orchards (35 min north of Byron Bay) - plums
28 Plumtree Pkt, Upper Burringbar
02 66 77 14 66

SYDNEY AREA

First Creek Wine Centre
McDonald Road Pokolbin NSW
02 4998 7293
dstevens@firstcreekwines.com.au
or sales@firstcreekwines.com.au
www.firstcreekwines.com.au

Tyrrell's Wines
1838 Broke Rd, Pokolbin
01800 045 501
www.tyrrells.com.au

Gardiner B
Cornwallis, Windsor NSW 2756
02 4577 3231

Dtharowal Creek Nashi Orchard
Fountaindale Rd, Robertson
04 12 65 02 07

Apple Growers & Merchants Pty Ltd
Flemington NSW 2140
02 9746 8806

Cedar Creek Distributors
(100 km south of Sydney)
210 Mulhollands Rd, Thirlmere
02 46 81 84 57
www.cedarcreekorchards.com.au

Jerian Berry Pty Ltd
(140 km south of Sydney)
14 Kangaroo Valley Rd, Berry
04 08 25 86 16

Bakewell Graeme & Joanne
(316 km south of Sydney)
Peaches and nectarines
Mt George NSW 2424
02 65 50 65 13

Goddard K Stunt Farm
Mitchell Rd, Sackville North
0245791 299

FARM ADDRESSES AND CONTACTS | NSW

Summerfruit Australia
Apricots, nectarines, peaches and plums
Main Rd, Mt George NSW 2424
📞 03 93 29 21 00
✉ ceo@summerfruit.com.au
www.summerfruit.com.au

Montrose Berry Farm
Ormond St, Sutton Forest NSW
📞 02 48 68 15 44
✉ info@montroseberryfarm.com.au
www.montroseberryfarm.com.au

Arcadia Orchard
(154 km south of Sydney)
Penrose NSW 2579
📞 02 48 84 42 31
f www.facebook.com/arcadiaorchard

Wisbeys Orchards
(310 km south of Sydney)
Peaches and nectarines
LOT 1 Majors Creek Araluen Road,
Araluen NSW 2622
📞 02 48 46 40 24

Batinich Barisha & Kathy
Rhodes NSW 2138
📞 0263 843 221

GRIFFITH / LEETON

Aussie Gold Citrus
📞 02 6963 6229
230 Slopes Rd, Tharbogang
f Aussie Gold Citrus

Fruitshack Farm
312 Henry Lawson Drive, Leeton
📞 04 29 866 965

Warburn Estate
700 Kidman Way, Tharbogang
📞 02 6963 8300
www.warburnestate.com.au
Check out open jobs at
www.warburnestate.com.au/vacancies
✉ info@warburnestate.com.au

Catania Fruit Salad Farm
187 Cox Rd, Hanwood NSW
📞 04 27 630 219
www.cataniafruitsaladfarm.com.au

Bindera Orchard Pty Ltd
Farm 873/23 Aylett Rd, Stanbridge
📞 02 69 55 29 00

Harvest Labour Assistance
MADEC Australia | Shop 3, 104 Yambil Street Griffith
📞 1800 062 332 ✉ Griffith@madec.edu.au

FARM ADDRESSES AND CONTACTS | NSW

Mia Vine Improvement Society Inc.
2655 Mallee Point Rd, Yenda NSW
📞 02 6968 1202
✉ miavis@bigpond.com

Hillyer P J (63 km south of Griffith)
Farm 1173, Yanco NSW 2703
📞 02 69 55 72 73

Mammarella D
Yenda NSW 2681
📞 02 69 68 11 86

Williams I J & M P
(40 km south of Griffith)
Stanbridge NSW 2705
📞 02 69 55 12 84

Auddino S & D
(50 km south of Griffith)
Farm 313, Wamoon NSW 2705
📞 02 69 55 94 30

NIANGALA

Koolkuna
144 Koolkuna Rd, Niangala NSW
📞 02 67 69 22 21/ 04 27 28 37 02
✉ koolkuna@ipstarmail.com.au
f Koolkuna-Berries

WENTWORTH

Scopelliti V
Curlwaa NSW 2648
📞 03 50 27 63 60

Medaglia J & J
Dareton NSW 2717
📞 03 50 27 45 96

Webley J
Channel Rd, Dareton NSW
📞 03 50 27 45 38

Shepherd E G & M M
Boronia Crs, Dareton NSW
📞 03 50 27 42 66

Clayson's
Silver City Hwy, Dareton NSW
📞 03 50 27 46 02

Stephens J M & S F
Boeill Creek NSW 2648
📞 0350 23 31 37

Lamshed R G
(50 km south of Wentworth)
Sturt Hwy, Monak NSW 2738
📞 03 50 24 02 12

Voullaire & Sons
Monak NSW 2738
📞 03 50 24 02 18

FARM ADDRESSES AND CONTACTS | NSW

BATLOW

Pineview Orchard Pty Ltd
Kunama Via Batlow Ernis Way, Batlow NSW
02 69 49 18 15
04 29 49 18 15
www.orchardpineview.com
f Orchard Pineview
✉ orchard_pineview@hotmail.com

HAY

Gravina Farms
Maude Rd, 2711
02 69934239

YOUNG

Hallmark Orchard
North Koepang P/L PO Box 1069 YOUNG NSW 2594
www.hallmarkorchards.com
Apply by email :
✉ lucinda@hallmarkcherries.com.au

Big Cherry from Young
0404 536 542 - 02 6382 1278
45 Richens La, Young NSW 2594:
✉ the_big_cherry_young
@hotmail.com
f The-Big-Cherry-from-Young

Anes Cherrygrove Orchard
Wombat Rd, Wombat NSW
0402 077 891

Valley Fresh Cherries and Stonefruits
4179 Olympic Hwy, South Young
02 63 84 32 21
www.valleyfreshcherries.com.au
✉ admin@valleyfreshcherries.com.au
f valleyFreshCherriesStonefruit

Eastlake's family tree
3923 Olympic Highway, Young
02 6384 3403
www.fairfieldsorchard.com.au
✉ admin@eastlakes.net

TOOLEYBUC

Hackett D N & J L
Goodnight NSW 2736
03 50 30 55 42

Wisbeys Orchards
(peaches and nectarines)
LOT 1 Majors Creek Araluen Road, Araluen NSW 2622
02 48 46 40 24

HILLSTON
Rennie Produce (Aust) Pty Ltd
Moora Farm Hillston, NSW 2675
02 6967 4152

315

FARM ADDRESSES AND CONTACTS | NSW

TUMBARUMBA

Costa Group
Send your resume by email to
✉ employment.blueberry@costagroup.com.au
If no answer after 2 weeks, call 0266492784.

Uusitalo A
Courabyra NSW 2653
📞 02 69 48 86 29

Jolly Berries Blueberry Farm
(blueberries, raspberries, blackberries)
181 Wagga Rd, Tumbarumba NSW
📞 02 2 6948 2742
✉ jmcroz@westnet.com.au
www.jollyberries.com.au
f Jolly-berries-blueberries

HUNTER VALLEY

Popeye's Olive Farm
Luskintyre NSW 2321
📞 024930 6132

DUBBO

Bentivoglio Olives
(164 km east of Dubbo)
📞 0263 791 610
034 Tarmons Lue Rd, Rylstone
www.rylstoneolivepress.com.au
✉ rylstoneaustralianorganic@gmail.com
f www.facebook.com/rylstoneolivepress

WALLAROO
(300 km south of Sydney)

Loriendale Organic Orchard
(cherries, nectarines, peaches)
16 Carrington Rd, Wallaroo NSW
📞 02 62 30 25 57
✉ organics@loriendale.com.au
www.loriendale.com.au

FORBES

Girot Greg
Fairhaven, Forbes
📞 0458 287 628

Betland B A & M T
Bundaburrah NSW 2871
📞 02 68 53 22 40

Ellison R G (apples)
South Lead Rd, Forbes NSW
📞 02 6852 1704

Markwort F L (apples)
South Condobolin Rd, Forbes
📞 02 6852 1952

ACCOMMODATION | NEW SOUTH WALES

MOREE

T P Cotton
Moolahway, Manildra NSW
02 6364 5025

Milo Cotton Co Farm Work
Milo, Moree NSW 2400
02 6754 2147

Where to Stay

ORANGE

→ Check if the farm can host you!

Federal Falls campground
Federal Falls Walking Track Canobolas
02 6332 7640
npws.centralwest@environment.nsw.gov.au
www.nationalparks.nsw.gov.au
Free camping; 10 sites available.
Reservations not accepted;
first come, first served.

Canobolas Scout Camp
Lake Canobolas Rd, Nashdale
02 6393 8000
www.nsw.scouts.com.au/groups
council@orange.nsw.gov.au
Fees apply.

Colour City Caravan Park
203 Margaret St, Orange
02 6393 8980
www.orange.nsw.gov.au/contact

BOURKE

Kidman's Camp
Mitchell Hwy, Bourke
02 6872 1612
www.kidmanscamp.com.au
Book directly on the website.

Mitchell Caravan Park
2 Becker St, Bourke
02 6830 0200
www.mitchellcaravanpark.com.au
mcp1@outlook.com.au
From AUD $25/night.

Yanda campground
Yanda Campground Trail, Gunderbooka
02 6393 8980
npws.bourke@environment.nsw.gov.au
10 sites. AUD $6/person.

How to get to Orange
256 km west of Sydney:
🚆 + 🚌 AUD $19 - AU$34 (4h 45min)
🚗 3h 40min

How to get to Bourke
800 km west of Sydney:
🚆 + 🚌 AUD $73 (11h 30min)
🚗 8h 44min

ACCOMMODATION | NEW SOUTH WALES

NARROMINE / DUBBO

Narromine Rockwall Tourist Park
69 Mitchell Hwy, Narromine
0437 656 594
www.narrominerockwalltouristpark.com.au
narrominerockwall@gmail.com

Narromine Tourist Park & Motel
4108 Mitchell Hwy, Narromine
02 6889 2129
mail@narrominetouristpark.com.au
AUD$15-$30/night for a campsite.

Dubbo Holiday & Caravan Park
154 Whylandra Street, Dubbo
02 6884 8633
dubbo@discoveryparks.com.au
www.discoveryholidayparks.com.au
AUD$27-$32/night for a campsite.

Dubbo Midstate Caravan Park
21 Bourke St, Dubbo
02 6882 1155
https://dubbomidstate.com.au/
dubbo@southerncrossparks.com.au
AUD $33/night for camping.

How to get there
400 km west of Sydney:
AUD $36-$50 (6h 30min)
5h

In Narromine and Dubbo, there are no local buses. You should have your own transportation or arrange to be picked up at the station.

BYRON BAY / BALLINA

Backpackers Inn On The Beach
29 Shirley St, Byron Bay
02 6685 8231
www.backpackersinnbyronbay.com.au
info@backpackersinnbyronbay.com.au
From AUD $28/night in a dorm.

Wake Up! Byron Bay
25 Childe St, Byron Bay
02 6685 7868
https://wakeup.com.au/
askup@wakeup.com.au
From AUD $41/night in a dorm.

Reflections Holiday Parks Ballina
1 River St, Ballina
02 6686 2220
www.reflectionsbookings.com.au
From AUD $88 for a campsite for 2 nights.

Flat Rock Tent Park
38 Flat Rock Rd, East Ballina
02 6686 4848
www.flatrockcamping.com.au
AUD$36-$48/night for a campsite.

318

ACCOMMODATION | NEW SOUTH WALES

How to get there
766 km north of Sydney:
🚆 + 🚌 from AUD$77 (14 hrs)
🚗 8.5 hours

POKOLBIN / HUNTER VALLEY

Wine Country Tourist Park Hunter Valley
3 O'Connors Rd, Nulkaba
📞 02 4990 5819
www.winecountrytouristpark.com.au/
From AUD$30/night in low season, AUD $35/night in high season for a campsite.

McNamara Park (camping)
1273 Milbrodale Rd, Broke

How to get there
164 km north of Sydney:
🚆 + 🚌 AUD $41-$56 (4h 10min)
🚗 2 hrs

GRIFFITH / LEETON

Griffith Caravan Village
📞 02 6962 3785
1 Gardiner Rd, Yoogali
www.griffithcaravanvillage.com.au
✉ reservations@griffithcaravanvillage.com.au

Oasis Caravan Park
📞 02 6953 3882
90 Corbie Hill Rd, Leeton

How to get there
About 600 km from Sydney:
🚆 from AUD$60 (7.5 hours)
🚗 6 hrs

WENTWORTH / GOL GOL

Willow Bend Caravan Park
📞 03 5027 3213
14-16 Darling St, Wentworth

Fort Courage Caravan Park
1703 Old Renmark Rd, Wentworth
📞 03 5027 3097

Rivergardens Holiday Park
Cnr Stuart Highway &, Punt Rd, Gol Gol
📞 03 5024 8541
www.rivergardensholidaypark.com.au
Campsite from AUD$36/night.

How to get there
About 1000 km from Sydney:
🚌 AUD $80-$109 (17 hours)
✈ starting at AUD $270

Book train and bus tickets at
www.transportnsw.info/regional

ACCOMMODATION | NEW SOUTH WALES

> No local buses in Batlow. You should get your own transportation or arrange to be picked up at the station.

BATLOW

Batlow Caravan Park
Kurrajong Ave, Batlow
02 6949 1444
www.visitbatlow.com.au/161/775.ashx

Buddong Falls Campground
Hume and Hovell Walking Track, Buddong
02 6947 7025
www.nationalparks.nsw.gov.au
Free campsites.

The Apple Inn (motel)
1 Tumbarumba Rd, Batlow
02 6949 1342
https://www.appleinn.com.au/
reception@appleinn.com.au
Consider this option if you are a party of 2 who can share a room; AUD $94/night.

> **How to get there**
> About 400 km from Sydney:
> 🚆+🚌 AUD $65 (9h 12min)
> 🚗 (4.5 hours)

HAY

Hay Big 4 (camping)
02 6993 1875
4 Nailor St, Hay
www.big4.com.au
AUD $25-$45/night.

> **How to go to Hay**
> 725 km west of Sydney:
> 🚆+🚌 from AUD $81 (12h 15min)
> 🚗 (8h 25min)

YOUNG

Young Tourist Caravan Park
17 Edwards St, Young
02 6382 2190
www.youngcaravanpark.com.au
youngtouristpark@gmail.com
Campsites from AUD $33/night.

Boorowa Caravan Park
93 Brial St, Boorowa
02 6385 3658
www.visitnsw.com/destinations

> **How to get there**
> 374 km west of Sydney:
> 🚆+🚌 From AUD $54 (7h 52min)
> 🚗 (4 hrs)

320

ACCOMMODATION | NEW SOUTH WALES

No local buses in Tooleybuc. To go to the farms, you should have your own transportation or arrange to be picked up from the Swan Hill station.

TOOLEYBUC

Tooleybuc Pet Friendly Caravan Park
63 Murray St, Tooleybuc
03 5030 5025

Tooleybuc Country Roads Motor Inn
78 Cadell St, Tooleybuc
03 5030 5401
www.tooleybuccountryroads.com.au
Two people can share a room for AUD $90.

How to get there
900 km west of Sydney:
AUD $100-193 (15 h)
(9h 10min)

HILLSTON

Billabourie Riverside Tourist Park
Mt Grace Road, (Wallanthry Road), Hillston
0427 674 131

Willandra group campground
02 6966 8100
Yinnagalang Billana Track, Roto
www.nationalparks.nsw.gov.au
AUD $6/person/night.

How to get to Hillston ?
682 km West of Sydney:
No local buses
(7h16)

TUMBARUMBA

Tumbarumba Creek Caravan Park
Lauder St, Tumbarumba
02 6948 3330

Buddong Falls Campground
Hume and Hovell Walking Track, Buddong
02 6947 7025
www.nationalparks.nsw.gov.au/
Free campsite. No reservations accepted; first come, first served.

How to get there
470 km southwest of Sydney:
From AUD $68 (9h 48min)
(5 hrs)

321

FRUIT PICKING SEASONS | NORTHERN TERRITORY

FORBES

BIG4 Forbes Holiday Park
141 Flint St, Forbes
02 6852 1055
www.big4.com.au/caravan-parks/
Campsites for AUD
$26-$49/night.

Apex Riverside Tourist Park
88 Reymond St, Forbes
02 6851 1929

How to get there
386 km west of Sydney:
🚆+🚌 From AUD $44 (6h 43min)
🚗 (4h 45min)

To find a campsite, download the WIKICAMPS app at www.wikicamps.com.au

NORTHERN TERRITORY

- Darwin
- Humpty Doo
- Katherine
- Ti Tri
- **Alice Springs**

NT

Source: Harvest Guide

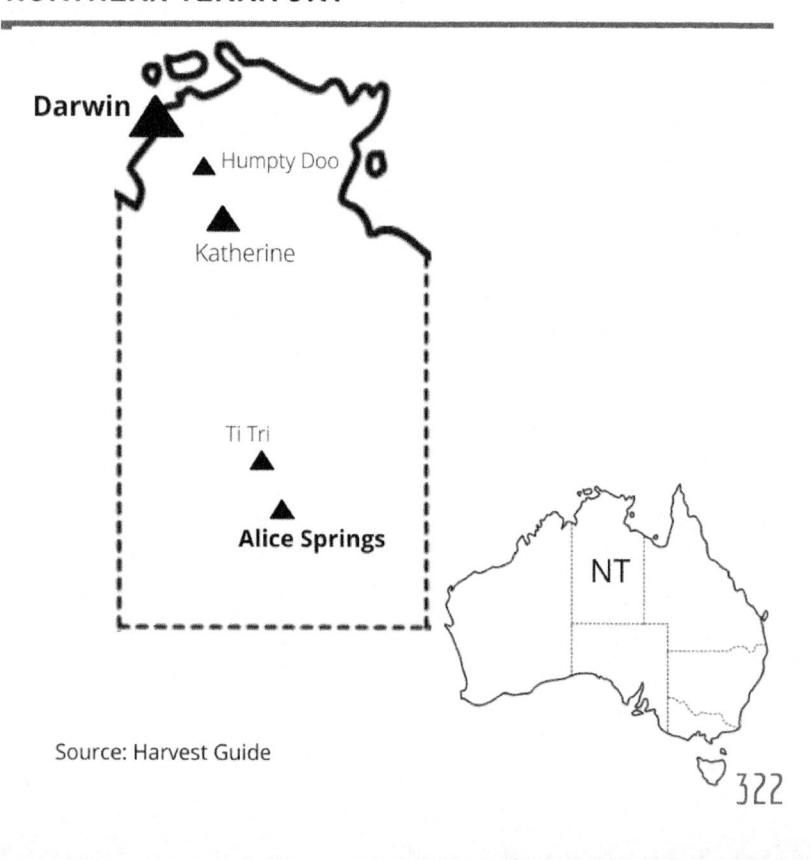

322

FARM ADDRESSES AND CONTACTS | NT

Where to go, depending on the season

In Darwin, there is **high demand from September through November** for mangoes, and average demand from August through October for melons. **In Katherine, high demand from October through December** for mangoes. Average demand for melons from May to November and for vegetables from May to October.

High demand				░░		Average demand		░░				
	Jan.	Feb.	Mar.	April	May	June	July	Aug.	Sept.	Oct.	Nov.	Dec.
Darwin												
Katherine												

Farm addresses and contacts

DARWIN

Harvest Labour Assistance
📞 08 8971 0938 katherine@thejobshop.com.au

Pearl farms
(Year round with peaks in April-May and September-October). The salary is about AUD$150/day. Be aware that this job isn't for everyone. You have to cope with the heat, the fishy smells and the long working hours.
You may be asked to start at 4am. You'll soon be covered in mud and sea water, starting in the morning and for the next ten hours!

Paspaley Pearls
📞 08 8982 5560
✉ recruitment@paspaley.com.au
www.paspaleygroup.com

Fruit picking

Middle Point Farm Pty Ltd
(tropical fruits)
GPO Box 2511, Darwin NT 0801
📞 08 89 83 25 55

Southport Siding Exotic Fruit Farm (70 km south of Darwin)
Lot 4, Head Of Cavenagh, Duddel Rd, Darwin River Dam NT 0822
📞 08 89 88 60 66

Milkwood Tropical Orchards
(100 km south of Darwin)
Mangoes, avocados, lemons
Batchelor NT 0845
📞 04 09 32 54 99
www.milkwoodtropical.com.au

FARM ADDRESSES AND CONTACTS | NT

Acacia Hills Farm PTY Ltd
(63 km south of Darwin)
Mangoes
31 Golding Rd, Acacia Hills NT
📞 08 89 88 14 67

Jabiru Tropical Orchards
(50 km south of Darwin)
Tropical fruits
5 Hopewell Rd, Berry Springs NT
📞 08 89 88 61 50

The Melon patch
(45 km from Darwin) - Melons
1015 Pioneer Drv, Humpty Doo
📞 08 99 88 19 87

Sweet Life
(55 km east of Darwin)
255 Alphatonia Rd, Lambells Lagoon NT 0822
📞 08 99 88 19 99

Tropiculture Australia
(30 km from Darwin)-
Limes, tropical fruits.
110 Horne Rd, Bees Creek
📞 08 99 88 11 1
f Tropiculture Australia

Cdml Ellis Enterprises
(340 km south of Darwin)
470 Cossack Rd, Florina
📞 08 89 72 24 82

KATHERINE

Manbulloo Mangoes Australia Pty Ltd
Victoria Hwy, Katherine NT 0850
📞 08 89 72 25 90
www.manbulloo.com
You can send your resume to
✉ employment@manbulloo.com

ALICE SPRINGS

Rocky Hill Table Grapes
Undoolya Station Alice Springs NT
✉ rockyhillmagic@bigpond.com

TI TREE
(200 km north of Alice Springs)

Red Centre Farm (mangoes)
Stuart Hwy, Ti Tree NT 0872
📞 08 89 56 98 28
✉ ognam@bigpond.com.au

The Desert Fruit Company (dates)
NT Portion 7016, Deepwell
via Alice Springs NT
📞 08 89 56 07 82
✉ info@desertfruitcompany.com.au
sales@desertfruitcompany.com.au
www.desertfruitcompany.com.au

Table Grape Growers Of Australia
Mail Bag 88, Alice Springs NT 0872
📞 08 89 56 97 44

ACCOMMODATION | NORTHERN TERRITORY

Where to stay

Check if the farm can host you!

DARWIN

Hostels in Darwin are of average quality.

Melaleuca On Mitchell (MOM)
Dormitory: From AUD26/night.
52 Mitchell Street Darwin
08 8941 7800/ 1300 723 437
www.momdarwin.com/
From AUD $55/night
for a double room or twin.

A good option is to share a hotel room for more comfort.

Argus Hotel Darwin
13 Shepherd St, Darwin City
08 8941 8300
From AUD $76/night for a twin.
https://argusaccommodation.com.au/
reservations@argushotel.com.au

Darwin City Hotel
59 Smith St, Darwin City
08 7981 5125
https://www.darwincityhotel.com/
stay@darwincityhotel.com
From AUD $69/night for a double room.

Coconut Grove Holiday Apartments
146 Dick Ward Dr, Coconut Grove
08 8985 0500
From AUD $65/night.
www.coconutgroveapartments.com.au

KATHERINE

Pine Tree Motel
3 Third St, Katherine
08 8972 2533
Twin from AUD $69/night.
www.pinetreemotel.com.au
reservations@pinetreemotel.com.au

Riverview Tourist Village
(camping)
440 Victoria Hwy, Katherine
08 8972 1011
www.riverviewtouristvillage.com.au/
info@riverviewtouristvillage.com.au
AU$40-$45/night for a campsite.

How to get there
317 km south of Darwin

🚌 From AUD $78 (4h)
🚗 (3h 20 min)

Book your bus ticket directly at
https://www.greyhound.com.au/book-a-ticket/availability

ACCOMMODATION | NORTHERN TERRITORY

ALICE SPRINGS

Youth hostels in Alice are pretty good.

Alice's Secret Travellers Inn
Dormitory: From AUD $26/night.
Twin room from AUD $65/night.
6 Khalick St, East Side NT
📞 08 8952 8686
https://www.asecret.com.au/
✉ stay@asecret.com.au

Jump Inn Alice Budget Accommodation
Dormitory: From AU$26/night.
Twin room from AU$77/night.
4 Traeger Ave, The Gap NT
📞 08 8929 1609
https://www.jumpinnalice.com/
✉ stay@jumpinnalice.com

Alice Lodge Backpackers
Dormitory: From AUD $25/night
Twin room from AUD $63/night
4 Mueller St, East Side NT
📞 08 8953 1975
https://alicelodge.com.au/
✉ info@alicelodge.com.au

Alice Springs YHA
Dormitory: From AUD $29/night.
Twin room from AUD $95/night.
Cnr Parsons Street and Leichhardt Terrace, Alice Springs
📞 08 8952 8855
www.yha.com.au/
✉ alicesprings@yha.com.au

Alice Springs Tourist Park
70 Larapinta Dr, Araluen
📞 08 8952 2547
www.alicespringstouristpark.com.au
✉ info@alicespringstouristpark.com.au
AUD $25-39/night for a campsite.
From AUD $95/night for a double cabin.

Wintersun Cabin & Caravan Park
Crn. Stuart Highway and Head Street, Alice Springs
📞 08 8952 4080
http://www.wintersun.com.au/
✉ wintersun@wintersun.com.au
From AU$43/night for a campsite.

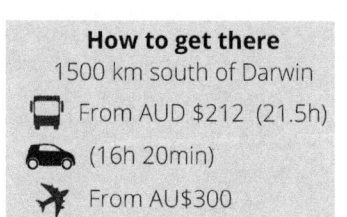

How to get there
1500 km south of Darwin
🚌 From AUD $212 (21.5h)
🚗 (16h 20min)
✈ From AU$300

FRUIT PICKING SEASONS | QUEENSLAND

QUEENSLAND

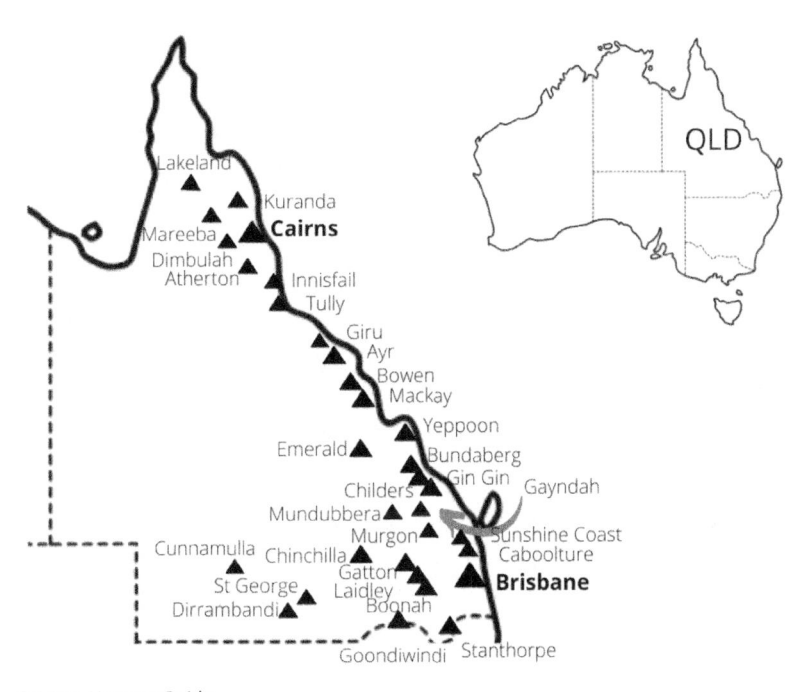

Source: Harvest Guide

Where to go, depending on the season

Around Cairns

In **Tully** (140 km south of Cairns), there is **high demand year-round** for bananas.

In **Innisfail** (88 km south of Cairns), there is **high demand year-round** for bananas.

FRUIT PICKING SEASONS | QUEENSLAND

In Lakeland (250 km north of Cairns), **high demand year-round** for bananas.

In Atherton (95 km southwest of Cairns), **high demand March through May** for avocados (average demand in February and June); from April through June for apples (average demand in March and July), and for vegetables **October through December** (average demand in September).
Average demand year-around for bananas.

In Ayr (435 km south of Cairns on the coast), **high demand May through November** for vegetables; **in November and December** for mangoes **in May and June; then September through December** for melons.
Average demand for tomatoes May through November.

In Bowen (550 km south of Cairns on the coast), **high demand September through November** for melons (average demand in May and June); **December** for mangoes (average demand in November and January); **May through November** for tomatoes.
Average demand May through November for vegetables.

In Dimbulah (113 km west of Cairns), **high demand in December and January** for mangoes (average demand in November).
Average demand from February through April for avocados; November through April for vegetables; November through March for lychees.

In Giru (400 km south of Cairns), **high demand in November and December** for mangoes. Average demand from May through November for vegetables.

FRUIT PICKING SEASONS | QUEENSLAND

In Mareeba (60 km west of Cairns), **high demand in February and March** for avocados (average demand in April and May); **December and January** for mangoes (average demand in February, March and November).
Average demand year-around for bananas and lemons; November through March for lychees; October through February for pineapple and April through September for vegetables.

Around Brisbane

In Bundaberg (360 km north of Brisbane), average demand for avocados April through August; March through July for lemons.
High demand May through July for macadamia (average demand in March, April, August and September); **January and February** for mangoes (average demand in December); **September through November** for melons (average demand in May and June); **April through August and October through December** for tomatoes (average demand in September); **April through December** for vegetables. Average demand year-around for berries.

In Gayndah (324 km northwest of Brisbane), **high demand April through August** for lemons (average demand in September and from November through March); **from June through August** for avocados (average demand in September and October.

In Boonah (86 km southwest of Brisbane), **high demand from November through April** for tomatoes; **December through February** for melons. Average demand year-round for vegetables.

In Dirranbandi (600 km west of Brisbane), average demand March through May for cotton.

FRUIT PICKING SEASONS | QUEENSLAND

In Emerald (870 km northwest of Brisbane), **high demand May through July** for lemons (average demand in March, April, August and September); **November and December** for grapes (average demand in May, June and October), **and in September and October** for melons (average demand April through August, and in November and December).
Average demand for cotton March through May.

In Childers (310 km north of Brisbane), **high demand in February** for mangoes (average demand in January and March); **November and December** for vegetables (average demand in October).
Average demand for avocados from July through April; for lemons March through July; for lychees from December through February and for tomatoes April through September.

In Gatton (92 km west of Brisbane), **high demand September through June** for vegetables (average demand in July and August); **December** for melons (average demand in January and February).
Average demand for tomatoes November through May.

In Gin Gin (347 km north of Brisbane), **high demand March through May** for lemons (average demand from December through February); **January and February** for mangoes (average demand in March and April).
Average demand from February through September for avocados; January through March for dragon fruits, and from April through October for vegetables.

In Goondiwindi (350 km west of Brisbane), average demand March through May for cotton.

In Laidley (86 km west of Brisbane), **high demand year-round** for vegetables; **December through February** for melons.
Average demand November through May for tomatoes.

330

FRUIT PICKING SEASONS | QUEENSLAND

In Mundubbera (360 km northwest of Brisbane), **high demand May through July** for lemons (average demand in April, August and September); **December** for grapes (average demand in June, July and November); **January** for mangoes.
Average demand for berries August through November.

In St George (500 km west of Brisbane), **high demand December through March** for grapes (average demand between June and November); **December through March** for melons (average demand in April and November); **October through December** for vegetables.
Average demand March through June for cotton.

In Stanthorpe (218 km southwest of Brisbane), **high demand February through April** for apples and pears (average demand November through January and in May); **November and December** for stone fruits (average demand in September and October); **January through April** for tomatoes (average demand in May and December); **from November through March** for vegetables (average demand in April, May and October); **February through April and November and December** for strawberries (average demand in January, May and October).

In Chinchilla (300 km west of Brisbane), **high demand in December and April** for melons (average demand January through March). Average demand in November for vegetables.

In Caboolture (50 km north of Brisbane), **high demand July through October** for strawberries (average demand March through June and November); **March through June** for pineapples (average demand in February, September, October and November), and **May through August** for raspberries (average demand in April).

In Cunnamulla (800 km west of Brisbane), **high demand in December and January** for grapes (average demand in May, June, July, September and October).

FRUIT PICKING SEASONS | QUEENSLAND

In Sunshine Coast (100 km north of Brisbane), **high demand August through October** for strawberries (average demand in March, April, July and November). Average demand April through June for apples, in February, March and May and then August through October for ginger; February through May and then September and October for pineapples.

In Yeppoon (655 km north of Brisbane), average demand in January and February for mangoes; November and January for lychees; March and April for apples, and January through March for pineapples.

High demand				Average demand								
	Jan.	Feb.	Mar.	April	May	June	July	Aug.	Sept.	Oct.	Nov.	Dec.
Atherton												
Ayr												
Boonah												
Bowen												
Bundaberg												
Caboolture												
Childers												
Chinchilla												
Cunnamulla												
Dirranbandi												
Emerald												
Gatton												
Gayndah												
Gin Gin												
Giru												
Goondiwindi												
Innisfail												
Laidley												
Lakeland												
Mareeba												
Mundubbera												
Stanthorpe												
St George												
Sunshine Coast												
Tully												
Yeppoon												

FARM ADDRESSES AND CONTACTS | QUEENSLAND

Farm addresses and contacts

BRISBANE

Qld Citrus (lemons)
Southgate Commercial Cntr/
250 Sherwood Rd, Rocklea
073379 3833

Farm Fresh Central
25 Sperling St, Rocklea QLD 4106
07 32 16 65 07

Qld Citrus Growers Incorporate
(lemons)
250 Sherwood Rd, Rocklea QLD
07 33 79 38 33

Randall's Farm Fresh Fruit & Vegies
Birkdale Rd, Birkdale QLD 4159
07 32 07 25 09

CAIRNS

Jonsson's Farm Market
31 Johnston St, Stratford QLD
07 40 58 90 00
www.jonssonsfarmmarket.com.au
f Jonsson's Farm Market

Scomazzons Roadside Stall
(77 km north of Cairns)
Scomazzon Rd, Mossman QLD
07 40 98 34 46

Scomazzons Roadside Stall
(77 km north of Cairns)
Scomazzon Rd, Mossman QLD
07 40 98 34 46

Rainforest Pawpaws
(71 km south of Cairns)
Price Rd, Bartle Frere QLD
07 40 67 64 17

Vanilla Australia
(67 km north of Cairns)
Captain Cook Hwy, Port Douglas
07 40 99 33 80
info@vanillaaustralia.com
ou VanillaAustralia@Gmail.com
www.vanillaaustralia.com

Crystal Brook Exotic Farm
(112 km north of Cairns)
Stewarts Creek Rd, Daintree
07 40 98 62 72

Blushing Acres (apples)
66027 Burke Development Rd,
Dimbulah QLD 4872
07 40 93 51 55
f BlushingAcres
(apply by message on Facebook).

FARM ADDRESSES AND CONTACTS | QUEENSLAND

MAREEBA

Bellview Orchards (avocados)
155 Rains Road, Mareeba
📞 04 0823 1363

Top Of The Range Lychee
(58 km north of Mareeba)
RP 908 Rex Highway, Julatten
📞 07 40 94 13 45

Golden Triangle Avocado
(29 km south of Mareeba)
Kimmins Rd, Tolga QLD 4882
📞 07 4095 4381

Avocado Estates
(29 km south of Mareeba)
535 Beantree Rd, Tolga QLD
📞 07 4095 4587

Rigato Farms Pty Ltd
Kennedy Highway, 4880 Mareeba
📞 07 4093 3555

TULLY

Lissi M A
Mullins Rd, Tully QLD 4854
📞 07 4066 7980

Dores Bananas
(23 km south of Tully)
Dores Road (4854) Murray Upper
📞 07 4066 5561

Chiquita North Queensland
Syndicate Rd, Tully QLD
📞 074066 7945

Pinnacle Hill Lychees
402 Pinnacle Hill Rd, Toobanna
📞 07 47 77 22 77
✉ cjb.phl@lycheesaustralia.com.au
www.lycheesaustralia.com.au/

Collins Farms
8 Bamber St, Tully QLD 4854
📞 07 4068 1268
f Collins-Banana-Farm

G&J Flegler PTY LTD
LOT 1 Davidson Rd, Euramo
📞 07 4066 7577

CNC Banana Co.
798 Davidson Rd, Euramo QLD
📞 07 4066 7810

Dundee Creek Banana
Bruce Hwy, Tully QLD 4854
📞 0740682770

FARM ADDRESSES AND CONTACTS | QUEENSLAND

GIN GIN

McMahon Citrus Pty Ltd
Abbotsleigh, Wallaville QLD
📞 07 41 57 61 70

Monduran Citrus
3245 Monduran Rd, Gin Gin
📞 07 4157 3816

Abbotsleigh Citrus
251 Grahams Rd, Gin Gin
📞 07 4157 6980
www.abbotsleigh.com.au
✉ abbotsleighadmin@nutrano.com.au

GAYNDAH / MUNDUBBERA

Robinson A G
Humphrey Binjour Rd, Gayndah
📞 0741 61 19 55

Burnett Valley Olive Growers Association Inc
(140 km south of Gayndah)
PO Box 382, Kingaroy QLD
📞 07 41 62 58 56

Zipf N & Sons
Glenrae Dip Rd, Mundubbera
📞 07 41 65 43 77

Trott B J & J E & Sons
(38 km west of Gayndah)
Coonambula Rd, Mundubbera
📞 07 41 65 47 55

Gr8 Citrus Pty Ltd (lemons)
196 Mt Lawless Rd, Gayndah
📞 07 41 61 15 32

Two Pine Orchard
Bonaccord Rd, Gayndah QLD
📞 07 41 61 22 85
f Two Pine Orchard

Riverton Orchard (lemons)
Gayndah QLD 4625
📞 07 41 61 61 73

Quebec Orchard
Mundubbera QLD 4626
📞 07 41 65 61 39

Glen Grove Orchard (lemons)
Boomerang Rd, Gayndah QLD
📞 07 41 61 11 96
✉ admin@glengrove.com.au

Auburnvale Citrus Pty Ltd
(lemons)
Hawkwood Rd, Derri Derra QLD
📞 07 41 65 61 65

FARM ADDRESSES AND CONTACTS | QUEENSLAND

Ventnor Grove Pty Ltd (lemons)
Coonambula Rd, Mundubbera
📞 07 41 65 43 60

Glenellen Pty Ltd (lemons)
Humphrey Binjour Rd, Gayndah
📞 07 41 61 19 55

Murray & Averial Benham
«Benyenda», Gayndah QLD
📞 07 41 61 62 49

GIRU / AYR /TOWNSVILLE

R&M Packing
(55 km north of Townsville)
19 Hencamp Creek Rd.Rollingstone
📞 07 47707430

Paradise Estate Produce
27 Lisa Drv, Ayr
📞 0747 834 585

Davco Farming
(24 km west of Ayr)
484 Pelican Rd , Ayr
📞 07 4782 7575
✉ office@davcofarming.com
www.davcofarming.com

Bugeja Cane Farm
Old Clare Rd, Ayr QLD 4807
📞 07 4783 1984

A&JO Felesina
Leibrecht Rd, Airville QLD
📞 07 4782 6869

Ace Mangoes
(82 km north of Ayr and
8 km from Townsville)
14 Tomkins St, Cluden QLD
📞 07 4778 1672

Penruth Produce (tomatoes)
123 Queen St, Ayr QLD 4807
📞 07 4783 6169

Ollera Tropical Orchards
(111 km north of Giru)
Ponderosa Rd, Rollingstone
📞 07 47 70 81 82

BOWEN

Battiston F & Co
Bruce Highway, Gumlu
📞 0747 848 161

Elphinstone & Kirby Pty Ltd
"Leslie", Mt Dangar QLD
📞 07 4785 2244

FARM ADDRESSES AND CONTACTS | QUEENSLAND

GATTON

Gatton Fruit Bowl (tomatoes)
Spencer St, Gatton QLD 4343
07 5462 1435

Windolf Farms Pty Ltd
671 Mount Sylvia Rd, Upper Tenthill
www.windolffarms.com.au
To apply, call between 8am and 4pm from Monday to Friday: 07 5462 6121.

Rugby Farm Pty Ltd
22 Hoods Rd, Gatton QLD
07 5466 3200
www.rugbyfarm.com.au
Apply directly at :
www.rugbyfarm.com.au/employment.html

Kesteven Farms (44 km west of Gatton and 8km from Toowoomba)
07 46 30 14 68

Blackboy Ridge
385 Forestry Rd, Vinegar Hill
07 5462 5202
f blackboyridge

Kiwi Land Orchard
Keys Rd, Hampton QLD 4352
07 46 97 91 68

Wodonga Park Fruit & Nuts
(avocados, madadamia)
45 Mt. Binga Road, Mt. Binga QLD
07 41 63 01 66 (Guy Butler)
wpfn@mail.com
www.wodonga-park.com.au

Bauer's Organic Farm Pty Ltd
1166 Mount Sylvia Rd, Mt Sylvia
hwww.bauersorganic.com
Do not call but only apply via the form here:
www.bauersorganic.com/get-in-touch

YEPPOON

Wilson's Paw Paws-Papayas
(30 km south of Yeppoon)
papayas
Sleipner Rd, Tungamull QLD
07 49 34 42 34

Gemkid (43 km southwest of Yeppoon and 3 km from Rockampton)
10 Craigilee St, The Range QLD
07 49 27 00 68

Talorb Pty Ltd T/A Tropical Pines
Rockhampton Rd, Yeppoon QLD
07 49 39 57 49

FARM ADDRESSES AND CONTACTS | QUEENSLAND

Keppel Orchards (apples, avocados, mangoes, lemons)
414 Keppel Sands Road, Keppel Sands
📞 0438 307 011
f Keppel Orchards

CABOOLTURE

Hermes Strawberries Pty Ltd (strawberries)
490 Newlands Rd, Wamuran
📞 0422 333 071
www.hermesstrawberries.com.au
Apply directly at
http://hermesstrawberries.com.au

Sunray Strawberries
347 King Rd, Wamuran QLD 4512
📞 07 5496 7364
✉ admin@sunraystrawberries.com.au
f SunrayStrawberry

Schiffke Pty Ltd. (strawberries)
210 Stern Rd, Bellmere QLD
📞 07 5495 8274
f TSLFAMILYFARMS

Harvest information Service
📞 1800 062 332
www.harvesttrail.gov.au

R G & R J Forster (apples)
24 km North of Caboolture.
160 Judds Rd, Glass House Mountains QLD 4518
📞 07 54 96 91 29

Piñata Farms
382 Scurr Rd, Wamuran QLD
📞 07 5497 4295
✉ info@pinata.com.au
Apply directly at
www.pinata.com.au/seasonal-opportunities
www.pinata.com.au

Berry Patch farm (strawberries)
Lot 1 O Shea Rd, Wamuran
📞 07 54 96 68 80

Stothart Family Farms
219 Stern Rd, Bellmere, QLD
📞 07 54 95 87 95
https://stothart.wordpress.com/

SUNSHINE COAST

Koogie Downs Strawberry
58 Rainforest Road, Chevallum
📞 07 5445 9100
✉ brsdaniels@iprimus.com.au

338

FARM ADDRESSES AND CONTACTS | QUEENSLAND

Sunfresh Pines (70 km west of Sunshine Coast)
Tunnel Rd, Kandanga QLD 4570
📞 07 5484 3269 / 0419 774 384
✉ sunfresh@spiderweb.com.au
www.sunshinecoastregionalfood.com.au

All About Fruit New Farm
(105 km south of Sunshine Coast)
85 Merthyr Rd, New Farm QLD
📞 07 33 58 63 44
www.allaboutfruitandjuice.com.au/
f www.facebook.com/AllAboutFruit

Kandanga Farm (70 km northwest of Sunshine Coast)
93 Main St, Kandanga QLD 4570
📞 07 5484 3771
www.kandangafarmstore.com.au
f Kandanga-Farm-Store

Avocado Australia Ltd
U8/ 63 Annerley Rd, Woolloongabba QLD 4102
📞 07 38 46 65 66
✉ admin@avocado.org.au
www.avocado.org.au

> **Harvest information Service**
> 📞 1800 062 332
> www.harvesttrail.gov.au

Sunshine Coast Farm
133 Laxton Rd, Palmview
📞 07 54 94 51 46
✉ info@strawberryfields.com.au
www.strawberryfields.com.au
f StrawberryfieldsAustralia

Eumundi Strawberry Farm
(strawberries)
Strawberry La, Eumundi QLD
📞 07 54 42 82 13
✉ eumundistrawberries@bigpond.com
f Eumundi-Strawberry-Picking

STANTHORPE

Tornabene E A
(11 km south of Stanthorpe)
Glen Aplin, QLD 4381
📞 07 46 83 43 33

Patane Transport
«Wallaroo Orchards», Severnlea
📞 07 46 83 52 54

Geoff Farrelly & Sons
(17 km north of Stanthorpe)
Border Gate Rd, Cottonvale
📞 07 46 85 22 25

FARM ADDRESSES AND CONTACTS | QUEENSLAND

A R Allan
173 Kelly Rd, Applethorpe QLD
07 46 83 22 54

Ballandean Estate Wines
(20 km south of Stanthorpe)
354 Sundown Rd, Ballandean QLD
07 4684 1226
info@ballandeanestate.com

W Mann
Emu Swamp Rd, Glen Aplin QLD
07 46 83 43 08

Fast Fruit Sales
Amiens Rd, Thulimbah QLD
07 46 85 21 91

Bent & Haynes Pty Ltd
Ballandean QLD 4382
07 46 84 11 56

Sunstate Fruits Pty Ltd
285 Border Rd, Applethorpe QLD
07 46 83 24 22

Volpato A & W
Newlands Rd, Cottonvale QLD
07 46 85 22 20

A Baronio
113 Matthews La, The Summit
07 46 83 22 86

A & A Gangemi
154 Goodwin Rd, The Summit
07 46 83 23 25

Brisotto I & R (apples)
21 Ann St, Applethorpe QLD
07 46 83 22 93

Belvedere Orchard
Quirks Rd, Amiens QLD
07 46 83 32 08

P Savio
Savio La, Pozieres QLD
07 46 85 33 12

A Filipetto
Amiens Rd, Pozieres QLD
07 46 85 32 09

C Andreatta
Andreatta La, Pozieres QLD
07 46 85 32 53

A & I Nicoletti
61 Nicoletti La, Pozieres QLD
07 46 85 32 31
admin@nicolettiorchards.com.au
www.nicolettiorchards.com.au
f www.facebook.com/nicolettiorchards

T R & A M Carnell
Back Creek Rd, Severnlea QLD
07 46 83 53 65

340

FARM ADDRESSES AND CONTACTS | QUEENSLAND

G & J Mattiazzi (apples)
Halloran Drv, Cottonvale QLD
📞 07 46 85 22 06

BOONAH

Peak Crossing Pawpaw Farm
(28 km north of Boonah)
Washpool Rd, Peak Crossing QLD
📞 07 54 67 20 30
f Peak-Crossing-Pawpaw-Farm

Telemon Orchards (50 km south of Boonah) - lemons
1 Philp Rd, Rathdowney QLD
📞 07 55 44 12 32

Kalfresh
6206 Cunningham Hwy, Kalbar
📞 07 5463 7290
www.kalfresh.com.au
✉ info@kalfresh.com.au
Send your resume to Karl (specifying your visa):
karl@kalfresh.com.au
f Kalfresh Vegetables

> **Harvest information service**
> 📞 1800 062 332
> www.harvesttrail.gov.au

CHILDERS

Simpson Farms Pty Ltd
Goodwood Plantation Goodwood Rd, Childers QLD
📞 07 41 26 82 00
✉ admin@simpsonfarms.com
www.simpsonfarms.com.au
(For applications, fill the form directly on the website)

Sunstate Orchards (86 km south of Childers) - Lemons
Tiaro QLD 4650
📞 07 41 29 25 03

Campbell Partnership
Dallarnil QLD 4621
📞 07 41 27 72 33

BUNDABERG

Mission Beach Bananas
(bananas)
1023 Ten Mile Rd, Sharon QLD
📞 07 41 57 70 14

MacLennan I
(50 km west of Bundaberg)
Bruce Hwy, Wallaville QLD 4671
📞 07 41 57 62 36

FARM ADDRESSES AND CONTACTS | QUEENSLAND

Eden Farms (cucumbers)
324 Dahls Road, Bundaberg
07 41 59 76 09
manager@edenfarms.com.au
www.edenfarms.com.au
f edenfarmsaustralia
Apply between November and March by phone or via this form
www.edenfarms.com.au/employment

Bundaberg Fruit & Vegetable Growers
Unit 13 2 Tantitha St, Bundaberg
07 41 53 30 07
bfvg.info@bfvg.com.au
www.bfvg.com.au
Kylie Jackson Agriculture Workforce Officer
Mob: 0488 533 801
kylie.jackson@bfvg.com.au

Spencer Ranch Pty Ltd
(lemons) 50 km west of Bundaberg.
97 McLennan Drv, Wallaville
07 41 57 62 45

Basacar Produce (apples)
4551 Goodwood Rd, Alloway
07 41 59 78 89

Harvest Informations
1800 062 332
www.harvesttrail.gov.au

INNISFAIL

Wadda Plantation
(22km west of Innisfail)
Pullom Rd, Nerada QLD 4860
0740 645 233 (call to apply)
www.waddabananas.com.au/

Pacific Coast Produce
228 Boogan Rd, Innisfail QLD
0740 642 452
info@eco-banana.com.au
www.eco-banana.com.au

Brighton Banana Farm
787 East Feluga Rd, East Feluga
07 4068 2215

Australian Banana
101 Upper Daradgee Rd, Upper Daradgee QLD
07 4061 6833
LinkedIn :
Australian Banana Company

Hampson Bros
(23 km west of Innisfail)
565 Mount Utchee Creek Rd, Utchee Creek QLD 4871
07 4065 3382

FARM ADDRESSES AND CONTACTS | QUEENSLAND

Rigoni Bros (Bananas)
22 km west of Innisfail
📞 0740 645 181
Gattera Rd Nerada QLD 4860

Robson K G (bananas)
Flying Fish Point Rd, Innisfail
📞 07 4061 4632

Alcock Bananas
645 Palmerston Hwy, Innisfail
📞 07 4061 2971

Fresh Yellow Bananas
291 Boogan Rd, Boogan QLD
📞 07 4064 3000
f Fresh-Yellow

Tropicana Banana
445 Upper Daradgee Rd, Upper Daradgee QLD 4860
📞 02 9746 8348
www.tropicanabanana.com.au
Gavin Eilers: 0447005166
Chris Rummary: 0497013260
For the farm in Mareeba :
Scott Franklin: 0438794667

Gonzos Bananas
Bruce Hwy, Mourilyan QLD 4858
📞 07 4063 2451

ACCOMMODATION | QUEENSLAND

Where to stay

BRISBANE

Summer House Backpackers Brisbane
Dorm : From AUD $22/night
350 Upper Roma St, Brisbane City
07 3236 5007
www.staysummerhouse.com
✉ brisbane@staysummerhouse.com

Brisbane City YHA
Dormitory: From AUD $35/night.
Twin room from AUD $97/night
392 Upper Roma St, Brisbane City
07 3236 1004
www.yha.com.au
✉ brisbanecity@yha.com.au

Bowen Terrace Accommodation
Dorm: From AUD $24/night
Twin room from AUD $66/night
365 Bowen Terrace, New Farm
07 3254 0458
www.bowenterrace.com.au
✉ book@bowenterrace.com.au

Breeze Lodge
Dorm: From AUD $33/night
635 Main St, Kangaroo Point
07 3156 8434
www.breezelodge.com.au
✉ stay@breezelodge.com.au

CAIRNS

Gilligan's Backpacker Hotel & Resort Cairns
Dormitory: From AUD $15/night.
57-89 Grafton St, Cairns City
07 4041 6566
www.gilligans.com.au
✉ reservations@gilligans.com.au

Mad Monkey Backpackers Village
Dormitory: From AUD $18/night
Double room from AUD $61/night
141 Sheridan St, Cairns City
07 4231 9612
www.madmonkey.com.au
✉ village@madmonkey.com.au

Summer House Backpackers Cairns
Dormitory: From AUD $13/night
Twin room from AUD $55/night
341 Lake St, Cairns City
07 4221 3411
hwww.staysummerhouse.com
✉ cairns@staysummerhouse.com

ACCOMMODATION | QUEENSLAND

MAREEBA

Camp Paterson (camping)
540 Shanty Creek Rd, Mareeba
0428 030 885
www.camppaterson.com.au
info@camppaterson.com.au

Riverside Caravan Park
13 Egan St, Mareeba
07 4092 2309

> **How to get there**
> 60 km west of Cairns
> (56 min)

TULLY

Jackaroo Treehouse Mission Beach (29 km from Tully)
13 Frizelle Rd, Bingil Bay
07 4210 6008
Dorm : From AUD $24/night
Double room from AUD $62/night
www.jackarootreehouse.com
info@jackarootreehouse.com

Dunk Island View Caravan Park (camping)
21-35 Webb Rd, Wongaling Beach
07 4068 8248
From AU$36/night for a campsite.
www.dunkislandviewcaravanpark.com
info@dunkislandviewcaravanpark.com

> **How to get to Tully**
> 140 km south of Cairns
> From AUD $29 (2.5h)
> 1h 50min

GAYNDAH / MUNDUBBERA

Riverside Carvan Park
11-15 Dalgangal Rd, Gayndah
07 4161 1911
www.riversidegayndah.com
riversidegayndah@gmail.com
From AUD $26/night for a campsite.

Mundubbera Three Rivers Tourist Park
37 Strathdee St, Mundubbera
07 4165 3000
www.threeriverspark.com.au
admin@threeriverspark.com.au

> **How to get there**
> 324 km of Brisbane
> from AUD $29 (2.5h)
> 3h 53min

TOWNSVILLE

Civic Guesthouse
262 Walker St, Townsville
07 4771 5381
Dorm : From AUD$21/night
Twin from AUD $52/night
www.civicguesthousetownsville.com.au
info@civicguesthouse.com.au

345

ACCOMMODATION | QUEENSLAND

Orchid Guest House
34 Hale St, Townsville
📞 0418 738 867
www.orchidguesthouse.com.au/
✉ fames@bigpond.net.au
Dorm: From AUD $24/night
Twin room from AUD $56/night.

Discovery Parks - Townsville
6 University Rd, Wulguru
📞 07 4778 4555
www.discoveryholidayparks.com.au
From AUD $30/night for a campsite.

> **How to get there**
> 347 km south of Cairns
> 🚌 From AUD $58 (4h 45min)
> 🚗 4h 07min
> ✈ From AUD $140 (1h) with Qantas or Rex

GIN GIN

Gin Gin Hotel
Twin room from AUD $79/night (to share)
66 Mulgrave St, Gin Gin
📞 07 4157 2106

> **How to get there**
> 347 km north of Brisbane
> 🚌 from AUD $113 (7h 20min)
> 🚗 4 hrs

GATTON

Heifer Creek (camping)
2536 Gatton Clifton Rd, Fordsdale

Lake Dyer Caravan & Camping Ground
134 Gatton Laidley Rd E, Laidley Heights
📞 07 5465 3698

> **How to get there**
> 92 km west of Brisbane
> 🚌 from AUD $26 (1h 10min)
> 🚗 1h 10min

YEPPOON

Yeppoon Beachhouse
58 Farnborough Rd, Yeppoon
📞 07 4910 5264
Dorm: From AUD $28/night
Twin room from AUD $80/night
www.yeppoonbeachhouse.com.au

Beachside Caravan Park
45-51 Farnborough Rd, Yeppoon
📞 07 4939 3738
www.beachsidecaravanpark
www.yeppoon.com.au

> **How to get there**
> 655 km north of Brisbane
> 🚆 from AUD $71 (10h 39min)
> 🚗 7h 36min

346

ACCOMMODATION | QUEENSLAND

BOWEN

Tropical Beach Caravan Park
25 Argyle St, Bowen
07 4785 1490
From AU$32/night for a campsite.
info@tropicalbeachcaravanparkbowen.com

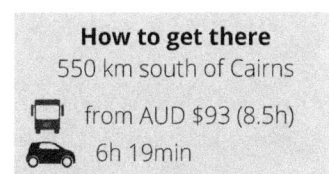

How to get there
550 km south of Cairns
from AUD $93 (8.5h)
6h 19min

CABOOLTURE

Highland House
Twin room from AUD $70 (to share)
277 Victoria Ave, Redcliffe
0416 233 502

How to get there
52 km north of Brisbane
from AUD $7 (47 min)
45 min

SUNSHINE COAST

Noosa Flashpackers
Dormitory from AUD $38/night
102 Pacific Ave, Sunshine Beach
07 5455 4088
www.flashpackersnoosa.com

BIG4 Caloundra Holiday Park
(camping)
44 Maloja Ave, Caloundra
01800 550 138
https://big4caloundra.com.au/
enquiry@big4caloundra.com.au

Cotton Tree Holiday Park
Cotton Tree Parade, Cotton Tree
07 5459 9070
www.sunshinecoastholidayparks.com.au
From AU$43/night for a campsite.

How to get there
105 km north of Brisbane
from AUD $23 (2h 25min)
1h 18min

STANTHORPE

Sommerville Valley Tourist Park
63 Sommerville Ln, Stanthorpe
07 4681 4200
www.sommervillevalley.com.au
info@sommervillevalley.com.au
From AUD $30/night for a campsite.

Book your bus ticket directly at
www.greyhound.com.au

347

ACCOMMODATION | QUEENSLAND

Country Style Caravan Park
27156 New England Hwy, Glen Aplin
📞 07 4683 4358
www.countrystylecaravanpark.com.au
From AUD $35/night for a campsite

> **How to get to Stanthorpe**
> 218 km southwest of Brisbane
> 🚌 from AU$55 (2h 39min)
> 🚗 2h 38min

BOONAH

Frog Buttress
https://qpws.usedirect.com/qpws/
Mount French QLD
📞 0137468

> You can book your accommodation in Boonah contacting the Boonah Visitor Information Centre.
> 📞 07 5463 223

> **How to get there**
> 86 km southwest of Brisbane
> 🚗 1 hour

CHILDERS

Childers Tourist Park & Camp
111 Stockyard Rd, North Isis
📞 07 4126 1371
www.childerstouristparkandcamp.com.au
✉ chilltourpark@gmail.com
Prices on request.

Iron Ridge Park (camping)
1472 Goodwood Rd, Redridge
📞 07 4126 8410
www.ironridgepark.com.au
✉ admin@ironridgepark.com.au
From AUD $28/night for a campsite.

> **How to get there?**
> 310 km north of Brisbane
> 🚌 from AUD $95 (7 hrs)
> 🚗 3h 32min

BUNDABERG

Bunk Inn Hostel
Dorm: from AUD$32/night.
25 Barolin St, Bundaberg Central
📞 0497 055 350
www.bunkinnhostel.com.au
✉ contact@bunkinnhostel.com.au

Palms Hostel
Dorm: from AUD $28/night.
7 Bauer Street, 4670 Bargara
Reservations directly at
www.booking.com

> **How to get there**
> 360 km north of Brisbane
> 🚌 from AUD $97 (7h)
> 🚗 7h-9h

348

FRUIT PICKING SEASONS | SOUTH AUSTRALIA

SOUTH AUSTRALIA

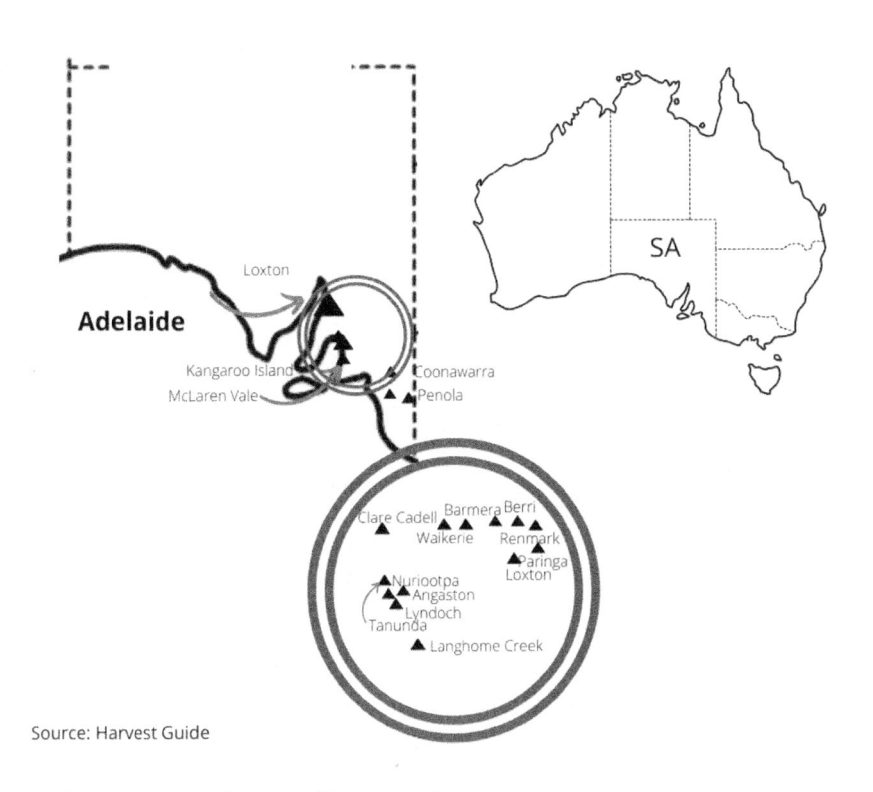

Source: Harvest Guide

Where to go, depending on the season

In Adelaide Hills (30 km from Adelaide), average demand February through May for apples and pears; November through January for cherries; February through April and June through December for grapes.

In Angaston (88 km north of Adelaide), **high demand in February, March, July, August, October and November** for grapes (average demand in April, June, September and December).

FRUIT PICKING SEASONS | SOUTH AUSTRALIA

In Barmera (227 km east of Adelaide), **high demand in October and November** for cherries; **June through November** for lemons (average demand December through February and in May); **February, March, June and July** for grapes (average demand in January, April and August), **and November through February** for stone fruits (average demand in March and October).

In Berri (240 km east of Adelaide), **in Cadell** (185 km northeast of Adelaide), **in Paringa** (260 km east of Adelaide), **in Renmark** (257 km from Adelaide), **and in Waikerie** (180 km east of Adelaide), **high demand June through November** for lemons (average demand December through February and in May); **February, March, June and July** for grapes (average demand in January, April and August), and November through February for stone fruits (average demand in March and October).

In Clare (140 km north of Adelaide) **and in Langhorne Creek** (64 km southeast of Adelaide), **high demand in February, March, July and August** for grapes (average demand in April, June and September).

In Coonawarra (373 km south of Adelaide), **high demand from December through February and April and May** for vegetables (average demand in March and June); **December and January** for cherries, and **from February through August** for grapes.

In Loxton (256 km east of Adelaide), **high demand January through March** for apples (average demand in April and December); **February through April** for grapes (average demand in January and from June through August), and **June through November** for lemons (average demand December through February and in May).
Average demand for stone fruits October through March.

In Lyndoch (59 km northeast of Adelaide), high demand February through April for grapes (average demand June through December).

FRUIT PICKING SEASONS | SOUTH AUSTRALIA

In Lyndoch (59 km northeast of Adelaide), **high demand February through April** for grapes (average demand June through December).

In McLaren Vale (40 km south of Adelaide), **high demand in March, June and July** for grapes (average demand in February, April, May and August).

In Nuriootpa and in Tanunda (80 km and 75 km northeast of Adelaide), **high demand in February, March, July, August, October and November** for grapes (average demand in April, June, September and December).

In Penola (382 km south of Adelaide), **high demand December through June** for vegetables; **December and January** for cherries, and **from February through August** for grapes.

High demand			Average demand									
	Jan.	Feb.	Mar.	April	May	June	July	Aug.	Sept.	Oct.	Nov.	Dec.
Adelaide Hills												
Angaston												
Barmera												
Berri												
Cadell												
Clare												
Coonawarra												
Langhorne Creek												
Loxton												
Lyndoch												
McLaren Vale												
Nuriootpa												
Paringa												
Penola												
Renmark												
Tanunda												
Waikerie												

FARM ADDRESSES AND CONTACTS | SA

Farm addresses and contacts

WIRRABARA / BEETALOO VALLEY (100 km north of Clare, 245 km from Adelaide)

Curtis N A
Wirrabara SA 5481
08 86 68 41 70

Beetaloo Grove (olives)
Beetaloo Gr, Beetaloo Valley SA
0418 844 935
enquiries@beetaloogrove.com.au
www.beetaloogrove.com.au

LANGHORNE CREEK

Thomson J P & J G (50 km from Langhorne Creek)
North Bokara Rd, Mypolonga
08 85 35 41 94

WAIKERIE

Miller D K & M M
Waikerie SA 5330
08 85 43 22 56

Frankleigh Fruits
Carter Rd, Waikerie SA
08 85 41 22 96

Sunlands Produce
Sunlands SA
5322
08 85 41 90 28

Boehm M W & D A
Ramco SA 5322
08 85 41 35 76

Wurst A C (lemons)
72 D Channel Rd, Waikerie SA
08 85 41 20 18

G M Arnold & Son Pty Ltd
Waikerie SA 5330
08 85 41 20 91

Travaglione Q
Waikerie SA 5330
08 85 41 25 29

Red Earth Farms (melons, grapes, lemons, hazelnuts)
PMB 10 Waikerie SA 5330
Stephen : (04) 28 41 91 18
info@redearthfarms.com
www.redearthfarms.com

DeVito A D & P E
Waikerie SA 5330
04 27 41 24 52

FARM ADDRESSES AND CONTACTS | SA

Liebich David L
Morgan-Renmark Rd, Taylorville
📞 08 85 43 22 57

Camerlengo A A
D Channel Rd, Waikerie
📞 08 85 41 29 67

Wurst A C
72 D Channel Rd, Waikerie SA
📞 08 85 41 20 18

Ohlmeyer K E & H A & B K
Sturt Hwy, Waikerie SA
📞 08 85 40 50 50

Noble Gregory J
Sunlands SA 5322
📞 08 85 41 90 57

L & R citrus Pty Ltd (lemons)
Lewis Rd, Waikerie SA 5330
📞 08 85 41 24 70

Murray View Irrigation Pty Ltd
Murray View Rd, Qualco SA 5320
📞 08 85 41 90 37

Jubilee Almonds (hazelnuts)
13923 Goyder Highway WAIKERIE
📞 08 85 89 30 38
✉ brendan@jubileealmonds.com

Ricciuto M A & C (lemons)
Waikerie SA 5330
📞 08 85 41 26 70

AROUND ADELAIDE

Varverakis C & M
(40 km north of Adelaide)
129 Gawler River Rd, Lewiston SA
📞 08 85 24 33 42

Magarey AA & Sons (16 km south of Adelaide) -
plums, pears and apples.
40 Magarey Rd Coromandel Valley
📞 08 82 78 10 34
www.magareyorchard.com
f magareyorchard
✉ admin@magareyorchard.com

Cottonville Farms
(24 km south of Adelaide)
1 Kanbara Rd West, Scott Creek
📞 08 83 88 25 25

Drury Orchards (30 km east of Adelaide) - apples and pears.
Inglewood SA 5133
📞 08 83 80 54 21

Walkers International
(36 km east of Adelaide)
24 Blaser Road, MYLOR, SA 5153
📞 08 83 88 53 90
www.walkerfamilyfarms.com.au

353

FARM ADDRESSES AND CONTACTS | SA

Smith Gully Orchards
(15 km east of Adelaide)
Cherries, apples, lemons, etc.
49 Smiths Gully Rd, Montacute
📞 08 83 90 22 65
✉ smithgullyorchards@ihug.com.au
www.smithgullyorchards.com.au
f Smith-Gully-Orchards

Montacute Valley Orchards
(cherries, stone fruits, lemons, etc)
Institute Rd, Montacute SA 5134
📞 08 83 90 22 13
✉ sales@montacutevalleyorchards.com.au ou
montacute.valley.orchards@gmail.com
www.montacutevalleyorchards.com.au
f MontacuteValleyOrchards

PENOLA

Penola Strawberry Farm
(strawberries, apples)
Church St, Penola SA 5277
📞 08 87 37 29 66

MCLAREN VALE

Blueberry Hill-Glaetzer's
(blueberries)
182 Peel Rd, Pages Flat SA
📞 08 85 56 12 04

> **Harvest Labour Assistance**
> 📞 1800 062 332
> www.harvesttrail.gov.au

The Blueberry Patch
December through February)
36 km south of McLaren Vale
558 Nangkita Rd, Mt Compass
📞 08 85 56 91 00
✉ farm@blueberrypatch.com.au
www.blueberrypatch.com.au
f The-Blueberry-Patch/

Fleurieu Cherries (cherries)
19 km south of McLaren Vale.
159 Pages Flat Rd, Pages Flat
📞 08 85 56 13 14
✉ info@fleurieucherries.com
www.fleurieucherries.com
f www.facebook.com/farmcherries

CADELL

Apold S & H Pty Ltd
PMB 85, Morgan SA 5320
📞 08 85 40 40 53

Rob & Karen Smyth
Cadell SA 5321
📞 08) 85 40 32 08

Walker C A & P A
Ramco Rd, Ramco SA 5322
📞 04 85 41 41 00

> **Harvest Labour Assistance**
> 8 Ral Ral Avenue Renmark SA
> 📞 1800 062 332
> ✉ renmark@madec.edu.au

FARM ADDRESSES AND CONTACTS | SA

Leske M R & P A
Ramco SA 5322
📞 08 85 41 26 05

ADELAIDE HILLS

MacDonald Fruit
Powell Rd, Kersbrook SA 5231
📞 08 83 89 32 03

HarrisVille Orchards
(cherries, apples)
Harris Rd, Lenswood SA 5240
📞 0407 427 747
www.harrisvilleorchards.com
✉ harrisvilleorchards@bigpond.com
f Harrisville-Orchards

Verrall S M Para Dell
(25 km north of Adelaide Hills)
Verrall Rd, Upper Hermitage
📞 08 83 80 52 76

Drury Orchards Pty Ltd
(19 km north of Adelaide Hills)
Paracombe Rd, Inglewood SA
📞 08 83 80 53 01

K & R Filsell & Sons
(apples, pears)
Deviation Rd, Forest Range SA
📞 08 83 89 82 49

Appelinna Hills
Plummers Rd, Forest Range SA
📞 08 83 89 84 13
✉ appelinnahills@gmail.com
www.appelinnahills.com.au

LL Dearman & Sons
Paracombe SA 5132
📞 08 83 80 52 78

Paracombe Premium Perry
169, Murphy Rd, Paracombe
📞 0402 082 532
www.paracombepremiumperry.com.au
f ParacombePremiumPerry
✉ info@paracombepremiumperry.com.au

Aberdeen Orchards
Tiers Rd, Lenswood SA 5240
📞 08 83 89 84 29

I L & K L Plummer
(apples, pears)
Hewlett Rd, Lenswood SA 5240
📞 08 83 89 82 38

Hillview Fruits NPL
Main Rd, Lenswood SA 5240
📞 08 83 89 82 97

Harvest Labour Assistance MADEC Australia
📞 1800 062 332 ✉ mountbarker@madec.edu.au

FARM ADDRESSES AND CONTACTS | SA

Plummers Border Valley Orchards Pty Ltd
Jackson Hill Rd, Gumeracha SA
08 83 89 11 24
Ian : 0407.716.929,
Gavin : 0407.898.318
www.cherry-picking.com.au
(You can contact them by message via the form on their website).

Hillview Fruits NPL
(apples, pears)
Main Rd, Lenswood SA 5240
08 83 89 82 97

Bower Berries
Lot 9 Edward Hill Rd, Lenswood
08 83 89 81 93

BARMERA / RENMARK

Cordaro N & R
Tapalin St, Renmark SA 5341
08 85 95 13 23

Tassios T & T
Renmark Ave, Renmark SA
08 85 95 14 26

> **Harvest Labour Assistance**
> 8 Ral Ral Avenue Renmark SA
> 1800 062 332
> renmark@madec.edu.au

Johnson T E & L J
510 Cobdogla, Barmera SA 5345
04 17 81 42 19

Recchia L
Gallery Tce, Lyrup SA 5343
08 85 83 82 16

Babaniotis G
Twenty-Fourth St, Renmark SA
08 85 86 68 49

Richards A R
Renmark Ave, Renmark SA 5341
08 85 95 13 07

Ekonomopoulos B & C (lemons)
Cooltong Ave, Renmark North SA
08 85 95 31 69

Sims P G & S D
Bookmark Ave, Renmark West SA
08 85 95 16 18

Klingbiel T W & J E
Barmera SA 5345
08 85 88 71 55

B A B S Harvesting & Contracting Pty Ltd
Culgoa St, RENMARK NORTH SA
08 85 95 30 27

FARM ADDRESSES AND CONTACTS | SA

Martinko J
Renmark SA 5341
📞 08 85 95 50 46

Hoffman V R & P L (apples)
Hoffman Rd, Barmera SA 5345
📞 08 85 88 20 84

Beech A G & J A
Cnr Thelma & Evans Rds, Barmera
📞 08 85 88 20 38

Levak F & K
Barmera West SA 5345
📞 08 85 88 70 16

Reed J M
Barmera SA 5345
📞 08 85 88 28 79

Edmonds Rick
Main Rd, Cooltong SA
📞 08 85 95 72 17

Hausler K C
Lot 6/ Hd Renmark I D Renmark West SA
📞 08 85 95 13 17

Mason Brian R
Barmera SA 5345
📞 08 85 88 31 61

Gallo Orchards Pty Ltd
Lot 9/ Ral Ral Ave Renmark North
📞 08 85 95 35 55

Johnson K L & V D
PO Box 76, Moorook SA 5332
📞 08 85 84 90 84

Rapisarda A & M
Moorook SA 5332
📞 08 85 83 92 70

Kypreos A
Mcintosh Ave, Glossop SA 5344
📞 04 19 51 43 52

Kondoprias S & M
Berriman Rd, Monash SA 5342
📞 08 85 83 55 66

Liakos A & A
Trenaman Rd, Monash SA 5342
📞 08 85 83 53 72

Frahn I H
Lobban Rd, Monash SA 5342
📞 08 85 83 53 26

Kollias J & S
Section 804 McKenzie Rd, Loveday
📞 08 85 83 94 00

DelZoppo A R & P G
321 Hunt Rd, Loveday SA 5345
📞 08 85 88 71 25

FARM ADDRESSES AND CONTACTS | SA

Dimou John & Son
Warrego St, Renmark North SA
📞 08 85 95 32 83

A Sourtzis Fruit Growers
Twentysixth St, Renmark West SA
📞 04 38 08 53 73

Grant L W
Teal St, Renmark North SA
📞 08 85 95 33 24

Mystere Orchards
Main Rd, Cooltong SA
📞 08 27 95 72 29

Nobile S
Monash SA 5342
📞 08 85 83 53 73

Edmonds Rick
Main Rd, Cooltong SA
📞 08 85 95 72 17

LOXTON / BERRI

Lawrie R F & M C
Sturt Hwy, Berri SA 5343
📞 08 85 82 14 69

Nagy L & V
Winkie SA 5343
📞 08 85 83 72 62

Lippis T & T
Sykes Rd, Lyrup SA 5343
📞 08 85 83 82 62

Ruediger Bill & Pam
Loxton SA 5333
📞 08 85 82 15 96

Jaeschke D E & J A
Loxton SA 5333
📞 08 85 82 11 29

Brand A J & K L
Brand Drv, Berri SA 5343
📞 08 85 82 29 43

Swanbury A E & M J
Loxton SA 5333
📞 08 85 84 47 69

Lloyd L D & Sons Pty Ltd
Pike Creek Rd, Lyrup, SA 5343
📞 08 85 83 83 48

Wegener C L & B J
Trenamin Rd, Glossop SA 5344
📞 08 85 83 20 64

Plush John & Julie
Winkie SA 5343
📞 08 85 83 73 07

Lindner P R
McKay Rd, Loxton East SA 5333
📞 08 85 84 69 45

358

FARM ADDRESSES AND CONTACTS | SA

Pipinis D
Sturt Hwy, Berri SA 5343
08 85 82 14 80

Panagopoulous I
Gratwick Rd, Loxton East SA
04 85 84 69 64

Jaeschke D E & J A
Loxton SA 5333
08 85 82 11 29

Googee
62 Powell St, Berri SA
08 85 82 18 96

Biddle B R & M A
Cutler Rd, Loxton North SA 5333
08 85 84 12 77

Weaver R A & M K
Balfour-Ogilvy Ave, Loxton North
08 85 84 12 42

Cottee Harold W Pty Ltd
1086, Murtho Rd, Murtho SA
08 85 95 80 43

Gillainey Orchards (lemons)
Lot 58 Murtho Rd Paringa,
08 85 95 52 51
f Gillainey-Orchards

NURIOOTPA

Munzberg & Co Pty Ltd
Research Rd, Tanunda SA 5352
04 18 39 68 41

Kerrsbrook Cherry Farm
(cherries)
Kersbrook Rd, Kersbrook SA 5231
08 83 89 22 31

Permedah Pty Ltd
Paringa SA 5340
08 85 95 50 34

Pike River Produce (grapes)
Loxton Rd, Paringa SA 5340
08 85 95 50 10

> **Harvest information Service**
> 1800 062 332
> www.harvesttrail.gov.au

ACCOMMODATION | SOUTH AUSTRALIA

Where to stay → **Check if the farm can host you !**

WIRRABARA / BEETALOO VALLEY

Ippinitchie Camp Grounds
Wirrabara SA 5481
www.parks.sa.gov.au

> **How to get there**
> 241 km north of Adelaide
> 🚌 From AUD $124 (3h 20min)
> 🚗 2h 45min

ADELAIDE

Adelaide Central YHA
135 Waymouth St, Adelaide
Dorm : from AUD $37/night.
📞 08 8414 3010
www.yha.com.au
✉ adlcentral@yha.com.au

Tequila Sunrise Hostel
123 Waymouth Street, Adelaide
📞 0451 434 627
Dorm : from AUD $23/night.
http://tequilasunrisehostel.com
✉ admin@tequilasunrisehostel.com

Backpack Oz
144 Wakefield St, Adelaide
📞 08 8223 3551
Dorm : from AUD $24/night.
http://backpackoz.com.au/

The Guest House
144 Wakefield Street (Cnr of Pulteney & Wakefield Street), Adelaide
Dormitory from AUD $25/night.
📞 08 8223 3551
http://backpackoz.com.au

Hostel 109 Flashpackers
109 Carrington St, Adelaide
📞 08 8223 1771
Dorm : from AUD $31/night.
www.hostel109.com
✉ stay@hostel109.com.au

WAIKERIE

Waikerie Holiday Park
44 Peake Terrace, Waikerie
📞 08 8541 2651
www.waikerieholidaypark.com.au
✉ stay@waikerieholidaypark.com.au
From AUD $36/night for a campsite.

> **How to get there**
> 184 km east of Adelaide
> 🚌 From AUD $30 (2h 40min)
> 🚗 2h 06min

ACCOMMODATION | SOUTH AUSTRALIA

PENOLA

Coonawarra Bush Holiday Park
242 Comaum School Rd, Comaum
0455 146 647
https://cbhp.com.au/
slm@cbhp.com.au

> **How to get there**
> 382 km south of Adelaide
> From AUD $60 (5h min
> 4 hrs

MCLAREN VALE

McLaren Vale Lakeside Caravan Park
48 Field St, McLaren Vale
08 8323 9255
www.mclarenvalelakesidecaravanpark.com.au
mclarenvalelakeside@bigpond.com
From AUD $34/night for a campsite.

> **How to get there**
> 40 km south of Adelaide
> From AUD $7 (1h 37min)
> 40 min

CADELL

Commercial Hotel Morgan
13 Railway Terrace, Morgan
08 8540 2107
www.commercialhotelmorgan.com
commercialhotelmorgan@outlook.com
From AUD $45/night for a twin.

> **How to get there**
> 189 km northeast of Adelaide
> From AU$39 (4h 13min)
> 2h 11min

ADELAIDE HILLS

Adelaide Brownhill Creek Tourist Park
60 Brown Hill Creek Rd, Adelaide
01800 626 493
www.brownhillcreekcaravanpark.com.au
info@brownhillcreekcaravanpark.com.au
From AUD $29/night for a campsite.

Shiloh Hills Park
354 Pole Rd, Ironbank SA
0428 661 802
www.shilohills.com.au/
From AUD $15/night/person for a campsite.

YHA camp ground
Mount Crawford SA
08 8521 1700
www.forestrysa.com.au

Cromer Shed
Mount Crawford SA
www.forestrysa.com.au
08 8521 1700

361

ACCOMMODATION | SOUTH AUSTRALIA

How to get to Adelaide Hills
40 km east of Adelaide
🚌 From AUD $4 (20 min)
🚗 39 min

How to get to Barmera
261 km east of Adelaide
🚌 From AUD $40 (4h)
🚗 3h 08min

LOXTON / BERRI

BARMERA / RENMARK

Kingston-on-Murray Caravan Park
461 Holmes Rd, 5331 Kingston on Murray
📞 08 8583 0209
www.komcaravanpark.com.au
✉ info@komcaravanpark.com.au
From AUD $55/night for a bungalow.

Riverbend Caravan Park
101 Sturt Hwy, Renmark
📞 08 8595 5131
www.riverbendrenmark.com.au
✉ stay@riverbendrenmark.com.au
From AUD $44/night for a campsite.

BIG4 Renmark Riverfront Holiday Park
Sturt Hwy, Renmark
📞 08 8586 8111
https://big4renmark.com.au
✉ stay@big4renmark.com.au
From AUD $46/night for a campsite.

Berri Hotel
Riverview Drive, 5343 Berri
📞 08 8582 1411
https://www.berrihotel.com.au
✉ info@berrihotel.com.au
From AUD $77/night for a twin.

Booky Cliffs Campground
Winkie SA
📞 08 8204 1910
www.parks.sa.gov.au/booking
From AUD $12,50/night for a campsite.

How to get there
256 km east of Adelaide
🚌 From AUD $40 (3h 45min)
🚗 2h 45min

NURIOOTPA

BIG4 Barossa Tourist Park
Penrice Rd, Nuriootpa
📞 08 8562 1404
www.barossatouristpark.com.au
From AUD $40/night for a campsite.

FRUIT PICKING SEASONS | TASMANIA

TASMANIA

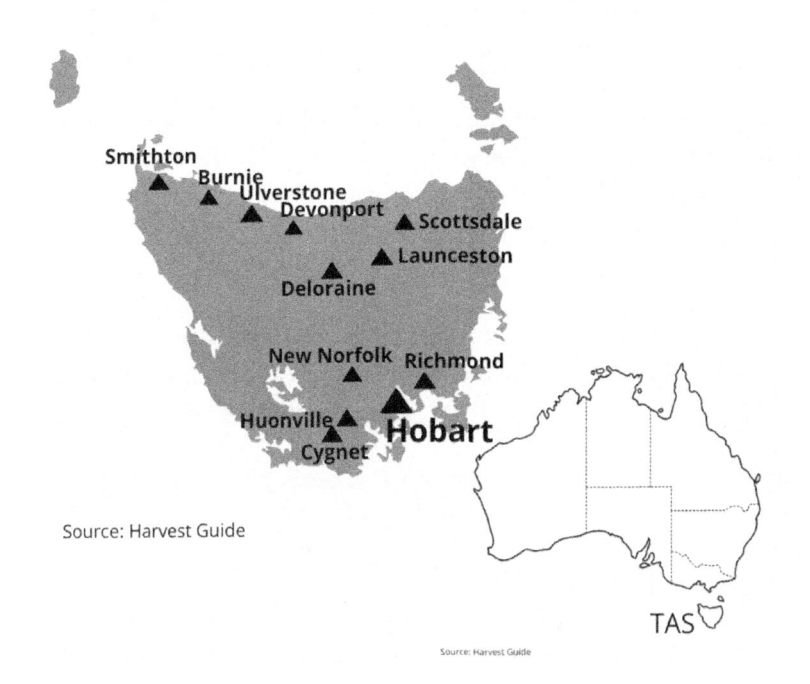

Source: Harvest Guide

Where to go, depending on the season

In Burnie, high demand January through June for vegetables (average demand for the rest of the year); **December through May** for berries (average demand in November).
Average demand for apples February through April, and for cherries December through February.

In Deloraine, high demand December through April for berries (average demand in May), and **January through June** for vegetables (average demand for the rest of the year).

FRUIT PICKING SEASONS | TASMANIA

In Devonport, high demand January through June for vegetables (average demand for the rest of the year).
Average demand for cherries in December and January; for berries December through April and for apples March through May.

In Huonville, high demand March through May for apples; **December and January** for cherries (average demand in February), and **November and May** for strawberries.
Average demand for grapes in March, April and June through August.

In Launceston, high demand in March and April for apples (average demand in February and May), and **in April, July and August** for grapes (average demand in March and May).

In New Norfolk, high demand December through February for cherries, and **in March and April** for hops (average demand in September and October). Average demand for grapes in March, April and June through August.

In Richmond, high demand in December and January for stone fruits (average demand in February, March and April); **January through June** for vegetables (average demand for the rest of the year), and **December and January** for apples and cherries (average demand in February, March and April).
Average demand from March to July for grapes.

In Scottsdale, high demand in March, April and from September through November for hops **and January through June** for vegetables (average demand for the rest of the year).

In Smithton, high demand January through June for vegetables (average demand for the rest of the year).

FRUIT PICKING SEASONS | TASMANIA

In **Ulverstone, high demand January through June** for vegetables (average demand for the rest of the year) **and December through May** for berries (average demand in November).

High demand			Average demand								
	Jan.	Feb.	Mar.	April	May	June	July	Aug.	Sept.	Oct.	Nov.	Dec.
Burnie												
Deloraine												
Devonport												
Huonville												
Launceston												
New Norfolk												
Richmond												
Scottsdale												
Smithton												
Ulverstone												

Farm addresses and contacts

CYGNET

Tahune Fields Nursery
(28 km north of Cygnet)
106 Lucaston Rd, Lucaston
03 62 66 44 74
f Tahune-Fields-Orchard-Farm

Smith R & R
(26 km north of Cygnet)
«Lollara» 54 Lucaston Rd, Grove
03 62 66 43 39
www.rrsmith.com.au
Andrew:
andrew@raworganics.net.au

Lucaston Park Orchards
(28 km north of Cygnet)
apples
33 Lucaston Rd, Lucaston TAS
03 62 66 44 12
f lucastonparkorchards
lucastonparkorchards@gmail.com

Groombridge, Peter
(22 km east of Cygnet)
Trial Bay TAS 7155
03 62 67 44 69

Tassie Blue Blueberries
79 Cygnet Coast Rd, Lymington
03 6295 0082
f Tru-Blu Berries

FARM ADDRESSES AND CONTACTS | TASMANIA

Trial Bay Orchards (apples)
26 km east of Cygnet.
3160 Channel Hwy, Kettering TAS
03 62 67 44 69

Glenburn Orchards Pty Ltd
(apples and cherries)
7254 Channel Hwy, Cygnet
03 62 95 04 35
Apply directly on the website
www.glenburnorchards.com.au
admin@glenburnorchards.com.au

Eden Farmstay
22 Supplice Rd, Cygnet
03 6295 0716
www.edenfarmstay.com.au
edenorchard@bigpond.com

Hartzview Vineyard
70 Dillons Rd, Gardners Bay
03 6295 1623
www.hartzview.com.au
enquiries@hartzview.com.au
f Hartzview Vineyard

HUONVILLE

R J & P C Hankin
(33 km south of Huonville)
450 Sledge Hill Rd, Glendevie TAS
04 28 97 63 42

BW Griggs & Sons (apples)
2873 Huon Hwy, Huonville TAS
03 62 64 14 74
office@fruitgrowerstas.com.au
www.fruitgrowerstas.com.au

Calvert Bros (apples)
Ranelagh TAS 7109
03 62 64 22 67

Cane D T & D M
(11 km south of Huonville)
3238 Huon Hwy, Franklin TAS
03 62 66 31 70
f Cane-D-T-D-M

Scott Brothers
(25 km south of Huonville)
322, Scotts Road, Cairns Bay TAS
03 6297 1230
aw.scott@bigpond.com
www.facebook.com/scottbrosfarm

Francis M & F
(40 km south of Huonville)
Francis Town Rd, Dover TAS 7117
03 62 98 15 19

Lucaston Park Orchards
26 Lucaston Rd, Lucaston
03 6266 4412
f Lucaston Park Orchards
lucastonparkorchards@gmail.com

FARM ADDRESSES AND CONTACTS | TASMANIA

Oaksun Cherries
41 Narrows Rd, Strathblane
📞 03 6298 1420

3rd Rock Agriculture
799 North Huon Rd, Judbury
📞 03 6266 6272

Woodstock Cherries Pty Ltd
8624 Channel Hwy, Woodstock
📞 0408 951 773
www.woodstockcherries.com.au

Home Hill Winery
38 Nairn Rd, Ranelagh
📞 03 6264 1200
www.homehillwines.com.au
✉ info@homehillwines.com.au

Oaksun Cherries Tasmania Pty Ltd (cherries)
48 km south of Huonville.
41 Narrows Rd, Strathblane TAS
📞 03 62 98 14 20

Jildon Farm
(25 km south of Huonville)
190 Cygnet Coast Rd, Petcheys Bay
📞 03 62 95 00 88

Harvest information Service
1800 062 332
www.harvesttrail.gov.au

LAUNCESTON

Crestview Blueberry Farm
(blueberries)
524 Golconda Rd, Lilydale TAS
📞 03 63 95 14 07
✉ crestview3@bigpond.com
f Crestview-Blueberries

Legana Orchards Pty Ltd
(13 km north of Launceston)
61 Jetty Rd, Legana TAS 7277
📞 03 63 30 22 12 or
03 63 30 11 15

Burlington Berries
(40 km south of Launceston)
157 Burlington Rd, Cressy TAS
📞 03 63 97 65 91
✉ hr@burlingtonberries.com.au
www.burlingtonberries.com.au

Windarra Raspberry Farm
(25 km south of Launceston) - Strawberries
Cressy Rd, Longford TAS 7301
📞 04 07 87 74 86
f Windarra-Raspberry-Farm

Aviemore Farm
403 Gravelly Beach Rd, Gravelly Beach
📞 03 6394 4631

FARM ADDRESSES AND CONTACTS | TASMANIA

Miller G C & Sons Pty Ltd
(30 km north of Launceston)
291 Main Rd, Hillwood TAS 7252
03 63 94 81 81

Lees Orchard
(apples, pears and berries)
Dilston TAS 7252
036328 1158
office@leesorchard.com.au
f Lees.Orchard.Dilston

Montague Fresh
38 Jetty Rd, Legana
03 9709 8100
www.montague.com.au/trade-services
support.office@montague.com.au

Top-Qual Calthorpe Orchard
Batman Hwy & Valley Rd, Sidmouth
03 6394 7273

Orchard
15 Spring Hill Rd, Sidmouth
03 6394 7790
michaeljlees@bigpond.com

Leaning Church Vineyard
76 Brooks Rd, Lalla TAS
03 6395 4447
www.leaningchurch.com.au

Harvest information Service
1800 062 332
www.harvesttrail.gov.au

Brook Eden Vineyard
167 Adams Rd, Lebrina TAS
03 6395 6244
www.brookeden.com.au
mail@brookeden.com.au

Pipers Brook Vineyard
1216 Pipers Brook Rd, Pipers Brook
03 6382 7555
www.kreglingerwineestates.com/cellar-door
info@kreglingerwineestates.com

Dalrymple Vineyard
1337 Pipers Brook Rd, Pipers Brook
03 6382 7229
www.dalrymplevineyards.com.au
info@dalrymplevineyards.com.au

Delamere Vineyards
4238 Bridport Rd, Pipers Brook
03 6382 7190
www.delamerevineyards.com.au
info@delamerevineyards.com.au

Tamar Ridge Cellar Door
1A Waldhorn Dr, Rosevears
03 6330 1800
www.tamarridge.com.au/
info@tamarridge.com.au

FARM ADDRESSES AND CONTACTS | TASMANIA

DELORAINE

Christmas Hills Raspberry Farm (raspberries)
14 km north of Deloraine.
Bass Hwy, Elizabeth Town TAS
📞 03 6362 2740
✉ info@raspberryfarmcafe.com
Apply directly :
www.fruit-pickers-tasmania.com.au
www.raspberryfarmcafe.com
f tasberries

DEVONPORT

Sassafras Orchards
(20 km south of Devonport)
143 Native Plains Rd, Sassafras
📞 03 64 26 73 73
✉ sassafrasfarms@bigpond.com

Ayers G P & M W Pty Ltd
21 Pilgrims Rd, Spreyton TAS
📞 03 6427 3022

Spreyton Fresh
289 Tarleton Rd, Tarleton
📞 03 6427 2125
www.spreytonfresh.com.au
✉ jobs@spreytonfresh.com.au

Youngs Vegie Shed
317 Bass Hwy, Camdale
📞 03 6431 6087
www.youngsvegieshed.com
f Youngs Vegie Shed - Camdale

Ghost Rock Vineyard
1055 Port Sorell Rd, Northdown
📞 03 6428 4005
www.ghostrock.com.au
✉ sierra@ghostrock.com.au
f Ghost Rock Wines & Cellar Door

Lake Barrington Vineyard
1136 W Kentish Rd, West Kentish
📞 03 6491 1249
www.lakebarringtonestate.com.au
✉ info@lakebarringtonvineyard.com.au
f Lake Barrington Vineyard

SWANSEA

Milton Vineyard
14635 Tasman Hwy, Swansea
📞 03 6257 8298
www.miltonvineyard.com.au
✉ wine@miltonvineyard.com.au
f Milton Vineyard

Spring Vale Vineyard
130 Springvale Rd, Cranbrook
📞 03 6257 8208
www.springvalewines.com
✉ barry@springvalewines.com

FARM ADDRESSES AND CONTACTS | TASMANIA

HOBART

Granton Berry Farm
(28 km south of Hobart)
23 Eric Crt, Granton TAS 7030
📞 03 62 75 06 87

Wolfe Bros. Smallfruits
(14 km south of Hobart)
98 Wolfes Rd, Neika TAS 7054
📞 03 62 39 63 10
f Wolfe-Bros-Smallfruits

Fruit Growers Tasmania
262 Argyle St, Hobart TAS 7000
📞 03 6169 2059
www.fruitgrowerstas.org.au
Michael Tarbath
✉ admin@fruitgrowerstas.org.au
f FruitGrowersTasmania

Nierinna Blueberries
371 Nierinna Rd, Margate TAS
📞 03 62 67 25 81
f Nierinna-Blueberries

Wolfes Berry Farm
98 Wolfes Rd, Neika
📞 03 6239 6310
www.facebook.com/Wolfesberry

> **Harvest information Service**
> 📞 1800 062 332
> www.harvesttrail.gov.au

Sorell Fruit Farm
(strawberries, apricots, apples, etc)
174 Pawleena Rd, Sorell TAS
📞 03 6265 3100
✉ sorellfruitfarm@gmail.com
f SorellFruitFarm
www.sorellfruitfarm.com

Pegasus Sprouts
48b Browns Rd, Kingston
📞 03 6229 7090
www.sproutstas.com.au
✉ pegasus@sproutstas.com.au
f Pegasus-Sprouts

Westerway Raspberry Farm
1488 Gordon River Rd, Westerway
📞 0447 010 701
www.lanoma.com.au
To apply, fill in the forms on the website and send them to
✉ WesterwayJobs@hotmail.com

Meadowbank Estate
📞 0481 147 397
www.meadowbank.com.au
✉ peter@meadowbank.com.au
f Meadowbank - Tasmania

Derwent Estate Vineyard
329 Lyell Hwy, Granton
📞 03 6263 5802
www.derwentestate.com.au
✉ wine@derwentestate.com.au

FARM ADDRESSES AND CONTACTS | TASMANIA

Stefano Lubiana Wines
60 Rowbottoms Rd, Granton
03 6263 7457
www.slw.com.au
f Stefano Lubiana Wines & Osteria

RICHMOND

The Ragged Tier Cherry Garden
(cherries)
42 km east of Richmond.
166 Woolleys Rd, Kellevie TAS
03 62 53 51 14

J W Kirkwood Pty Ltd
(8 km north of Richmond)
«Ticehurst» Brown Mountain Rd,
Campania TAS 7026
03 62 60 44 63

Cape Bernier Vineyard
230 Bream Creek Rd, Bream Creek
03 6253 5443
www.capebernier.com.au
info@capebernier.com.au

Frogmore Creek Winery
20 Denholms Rd, Cambridge
03 6274 5844
www.frogmorecreek.com.au
cambridge@frogmorecreek.com.au

Pooley Wines
1431 Richmond Rd, Richmond
03 6260 2895
www.pooleywines.com.au
To apply, please fill in the form directly on the website.
f Pooley Wines

Craigow Vineyard
528 Richmond Rd, Cambridge
0418 126 027
www.craigow.com.au
info@craigow.com.au
f Craigow Vineyard

BRUNY ISLAND

Bruny Island Berry Farm
(berries)
Adventure Bay Rd, Adventure Bay
0434 760 325
brunyberries@bigpond.com

Harvest Information Service
1800 062 332
www.harvesttrail.gov.au

ACCOMMODATION | TASMANIA

Where to stay ➡ Check if you can stay at the farm !

HOBART

The Nook Backpackers
Dorm : From AUD $25/night
251 Liverpool St, Hobart
📞 03 6135 4044
www.thenookbackpackers.com
✉ info@thenookbackpackers.com

Narrara Backpackers Hobart
Dorm : From AUD $30/night
Twin room from AUD $79/night
88 Goulburn St, Hobart T
📞 03 6234 8801
www.narrarabackpackers.com
✉ info@narrarabackpackers.com

Hobart Central YHA
Dorm : From AUD $29/night
9 Argyle St, Hobart
📞 03 6231 2660
www.yha.com.au
✉ hobartcentral@yha.com.au

Montacute Boutique Bunkhouse
Dorm : From AUD $47/night.
1 Stowell Ave, Battery Point
📞 03 6212 0474
www.montacute.com.au
✉ hello@montacute.com.au

CYGNET / HUONVILLE

Base Camp Tasmania
From AU$18/night for a campsite.
959 Glenfern Rd, Glenfern
📞 03 6261 4971

> **How to get there?**
> 54 km south of Hobart
> 🚌 From AUD $11 (1h 08min)
> 🚗 (46 min)

LAUNCESTON

Pod Inn
Single room from AUD $47/night.
17-19 Wellington St, Launceston
📞 0475 555 549
www.podinn.com.au
✉ booking@podinn.com.au

Launceston Backpackers
Dorm : From AUD $25/night
Twin from AUD $65/night.
103 Canning St, Launceston
📞 03 6334 2327
www.launcestonbackpackers.com.au
✉ bookings@launcestonbackpackers.com.au

Book your bus ticket directly :
www.tasredline.com.au

ACCOMMODATION | TASMANIA

Launceston Holiday Park
711 W Tamar Hwy, Legana
📞 03 6330 1714
www.launcestonholidaypark.com.au
✉ launceston@islandcabins.com.au
From AUD $30/night for a campsite.

> **How to get there**
> 200 km north of Hobart
> 🚌 From AUD $44 (2.5h)
> 🚗 (2h 15min)

DELORAINE

Deloraine Hotel
Emu Bay Road, Deloraine
📞 03 6362 2022
From AUD $47 night for a single room.
www.delorainehotel.com.au
✉ info@delorainehotel.com.au

Deloraine Apex Caravan Park
51 W Parade, Deloraine
📞 03 6362 2673

> **How to get there**
> 232 km north of Hobart
> 🚌 From AUD $45 (4 hrs)
> 🚗 2h 34min

DEVONPORT

The Formby Hotel/Alexander Hotels and Backpackers
82 Formby Rd, Devonport
📞 03 6424 1601
Dorm : From AUD $35/night.
www.goodstone.com.au/the_formby
✉ formby@goodstone.com.au

Mersey Bluff Caravan Park
41 Bluff Rd, Devonport
📞 03 6424 8655
www.merseybluffcaravanpark.com.au
✉ bookings@mbcp.net.au

> **How to get there**
> 282 km north of Hobart
> 🚌 From AUD $71,60 (4h 45min)
> 🚗 3h 06min

SWANSEA

Swansea Holiday Park
2 Bridge St, Swansea
📞 03 6257 8148
www.swansea-holiday.com.au
From AUD $35/night for a campsite.

> **How to get there**
> 134 km from Hobart
> 🚌 From AUD $45 (2h 05min)
> 🚗 1h 46min

FRUIT PICKING SEASONS | VICTORIA

BRUNY

Neck Reserve Camping Area
3003 Bruny Island Main Rd, South Bruny

> **How to get there ?**
> 83 km south of Hobart
> 🚗 + ⛴ (1h 45 min)

Cloudy Corner campground
South Bruny TAS
📞 0439 106 147

The Pines Campsite
Cloudy Bay Rd, South Bruny

Captain Cook Holiday Park
786 Adventure Bay Rd, Adventure Bay
📞 03 6293 1128

VICTORIA

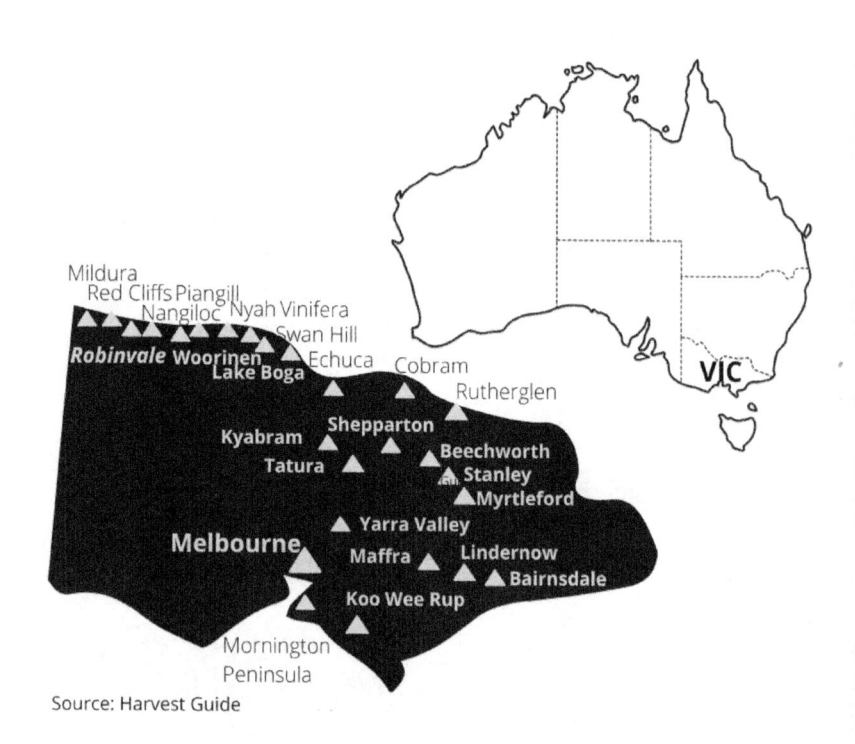

Source: Harvest Guide

374

FRUIT PICKING SEASONS | VICTORIA

Where to go, depending on the season

In Bairnsdale / Lindenow, high demand October through March for vegetables (average demand the rest of the year).

In Beechworth, high demand November and December for cherries. Average demand March through May for apples; February through April and June through August for grapes, and in March and April for hazelnuts.

In Cobram, high demand January through April for apples and pears (average demand in May); **November and December** for cherries; **January through April** for stone fruits (average demand in May and December).
Average demand throughout the year for lemons and vegetables.

In Echuca, high demand in February and March for tomatoes (average demand in January and April).

In Koo Wee Rup, high demand from September through December for asparagus.

In Maffra, average demand October through April for vegetables.

In Mildura, high demand June through August for lemons (average demand September through January and in May); **February through April, and June through August** for grapes (average demand in May and September); and **October and November** for vegetables (average demand December through February and May through September).

In Myrtleford, high demand in March and April for hops. Average demand for apples January through April; in March and April for hazelnuts; and in February, March and June through August for grapes.

375

FRUIT PICKING SEASONS | VICTORIA

In the Mornington Peninsula, high demand in December and January for cherries (average demand in November), and **November through April** for raspberries.
Average demand from March through November for apples, December through March for berries; and February through April for grapes.

In Nangiloc, high demand June through August, and November and December for lemons (average demand in January, May, September and October); **February through April and June through August** for grapes (average demand in January, May and September), and **October and November** for vegetables (average demand December through February and May through September).

In Nyah, high demand June through August and November and December for lemons (average demand in January, May, September and October); **February through April and June through August** for grapes (average demand in January, May and September); and **December through February** for stone fruits (average demand May through September and November).
Average demand for vegetables May through February.

In Robinvale, high demand January through April, and June through August for grapes; April, May and September for pistachios and almonds (average demand in March and June).
Average demand for vegetables May through February.

In Rutherglen, high demand in November and December for cherries. Average demand for apples March through May; and February through April; and June through August for grapes.

In Warragul, average demand year-round for tomatoes, and in February for apples.

376

FRUIT PICKING SEASONS | VICTORIA

In Shepparton, high demand in February and March for stone fruits (average demand in January); **in February and March** for apples and pears (average demand in January, April and May); **February and March** for tomatoes (average demand in January and April). Average demand in November and December for cherries, and January through March for vegetables.

In Swan Hill, high demand in June, July and from October through December (average demand in January, May, August and September), **from February through April and June through August** for grapes; **November through February** for stone fruits (average demand May through July and October); and **April and May** for pistachios and almonds (average demand in March and June).
Average demand for vegetables May through February.

In the Yarra Valley, high demand February through May for apples and pears.

High demand			Average demand									
	Jan.	Feb.	Mar.	April	May	June	July	Aug.	Sept.	Oct.	Nov.	Dec.
Bairnsdale / Lindenow												
Beechworth												
Cobram												
Echuca												
Koo Wee Rup												
Maffra												
Mildura												
Mornington Peninsula												
Myrtleford												
Nangiloc												
Nyah												
Robinvale												
Rutherglen												
Shepparton												
Swan Hill												
Warragul												
Yarra Valley												

FARM ADDRESSES AND CONTACTS | VICTORIA

Farm addresses and contacts

YARRA VALLEY

Yarra Valley Hillbilly Farms
Cnr Parker & Monbulk Silvan
Roads, Silvan VIC 3795
03 97 37 95 39
hillbilly.farms@live.com

Byrnes Hillndale Orchards
(apples)
120 Quayle Rd, Wandin North VIC
03 5964 4549

Cherryhill Orchards (cherries)
474 Queens Road, Wandin
East, Victoria 3139
03 59 64 42 35
jobs@cherryhill.com.au
www.cherryhill.com.au
For picking, contact Mali Hang at
1300 934 866
mali.hang@chandleragribusiness.com.au

Fresco Fresh (raspberries)
35 km east of Yarra Valley.
300 Station Rd, Wesburn VIC 3799
03 5967 2222
www.frescofresh.com.au
frescofresh.info@gmail.com
f frescofreshstrawberries

Chappies (cherries, raspberries, blackberries, etc.)
21 - 23 Parker Rd, Silvan VIC
03 97 37 95 34
enquiries@upick.com.au
www.upick.com.au
f chappiesupick

Blue Hills Berries & Cherries
27 Parker Rd, Silvan
03 9737 9400
http://upickberries.com.au
info@upickberries.com.au
f Blue Hills Berries and Cherries

Seville Hill Orchard
8 Paynes Rd, Seville
03 5964 3284
www.sevillehill.com.au
f Seville Hill Wines
info@sevillehill.com.au

Rieschieck Orchards
(apples)
13 Medhurst Rd, Gruyere
03 5964 9369

Maroondah Orchards
715 Maroondah Hwy, Coldstream
03 9739 1041

Berry Plant Suppliers
25 Phillips Rd, Toolangi
03 5962 9316

FARM ADDRESSES AND CONTACTS | VICTORIA

Jay Berries - U Pick
140 Wandin Creek Rd, Wandin
03 5964 4451
www.jayberries.com.au
 f Jay Berries
 ✉ info@jayberries.com.au

Johns Orchards Farm Work
Cambus Rd, Yering
03 9739 1570

Kookaberry Strawberry Farm
25 Lewis Rd, Wandin
0415 768 222
www.kookaberry.com.au
 f Kookaberry Berry Farm

Perry Certified Strawberry Runner Growers
1826 Healesville-Kinglake Rd, Toolangi
03 5962 9429

Brooklyn Orchards Pty Ltd
Apples and pears
525 Tarrango Road, Gladysdale
03 59 66 63 27
 ✉ jaquijohn@bigpond.com

Napoleone M V & Co Pty Ltd
Lemons, plums, tropical fruits
Rouget Rd, Wandin North
03 59 64 45 96
www.redrichfruits.com.au

Wandin Vale Orchards
Lot 56 Charteris Rd, Wandin East
04 18 38 01 12

S R Shaholli
Apples and pears
New Dookie Rd, Shepparton
03 58 21 26 59

> **Harvest Information Service**
> 1800 062 332
> www.harvesttrail.gov.au

SHEPPARTON

Erinhaven Orchard
Cnr Maneroo & Nathalia Rds, Bunbartha
03 58 26 94 66

D P & H L Stephens
(17 km north of Shepparton)
Nathalia Rd, Bunbartha VIC 3634
03 58 26 95 05

N M & B J Barolli
apples and pears
165 Hosie Rd, Shepparton East
03 58 29 24 22

Rockington Orchard
(86 km east of Shepparton)
Lot 1 Greta West Rd, Glenrowan
04 57 66 23 51

FARM ADDRESSES AND CONTACTS | VICTORIA

R P & M A Puckey (apples and pears) – 37 km west of Shepparton
«Summerlands»
Palmer Rd, Kyabram VIC 3620
📞 03 58 52 11 62

Farmwell Tomatoes Pty Ltd
Tomatoes
301 Harston Rd, Harston
📞 03 58 54 83 65

Harvest Labour Assistance
MADEC Australia
Suite 1 & 4, 461
Wyndham Street Shepparton
📞 03 5829 3600

Bisogni F (lemons)
Torgannah Rd 3644 Cobram
📞 03 58 72 11 13

Fruitworks (tomatoes)
📞 0358 215 688
Cnr Corio & Stewart Sts, Shepparton
f fruitworksshepparton

Diretto Orchards Pty Ltd
Benalla-tocumwal Rd, Yarroweyah
📞 03 58 73 23 71

Smith & Sons
«Passchendaele» Orchard Warby Range Rd, Glenrowan VIC 3675
📞 03 57 66 23 35

Rullo Orchards Pty Ltd
470 Old Dookie Rd, Shepparton East
📞 03 58 29 24 44

Hamilton P H & Son
Ardmona Rd, Ardmona VIC 3629
📞 04 09 93 75 24

Seeka Australia Pty Ltd.
4765 Barmah-Shepparton Rd, Bunbartha
📞 03 5826 9636

S T & R Varapodi
Cnr Turnbull & Lenne Rds, Ardmona
📞 03 58 29 00 83

Planet Produce
625 Midland Hwy, Shepparton East
📞 03 58 29 22 41

Nashi Haven
McPhersons Rd, Bunbartha VIC
📞 04 58 26 94 36

FARM ADDRESSES AND CONTACTS | VICTORIA

Besim & Sons (apples, pears)
106 Thompsons La, Kyabram
📞 03 58 52 14 84

J & N Nicosia (apples)
Catona Crs, Cobram VIC
📞 04 58 72 16 83

J V Orchards
383 Campbell Rd, Cobram
📞 03 58 72 22 87
f JV-Orchards

Scenic Drive Strawberries
(strawberries)
Torgannah Rd, Koonoomoo VIC
📞 04 58 71 12 63

H. V McNab & Son
pears, peaches, apples
145 Ardmona Rd, Ardmona
📞 03 58 29 00 16
✉ mail@mcnab.com.au
www.mcnab.com.au
Please apply on the website.

Ardmona Orchards Pty Ltd
325 Cornish Rd, Ardmona
📞 03 58 29 02 83

Pickworth Orchards
282 Ferguson Rd, Tatura
📞 03 58 24 25 32

Boris Fruit Shed (tomatoes)
Benalla Rd, Shepparton East VIC
📞 03 58 29 24 88
f BorisFruitShed

Gibbs K J
Invergordon VIC 3636
📞 03 58 65 53 05

Finer Fruit (tomatoes)
35 Vaughan St, Shepparton VIC 3
📞 03 58 31 13 78
f finerfruitshepparton
✉ inerfruitshepparton
@gmail.com

OzPac Australia Pty Ltd
(12 km from Shepparton)
540 Turnbull Rd, Ardmona VIC
📞 03 5820 7600
✉ gregd@ozp.com.au
f Ozpac-Australia-Pty-LTD

Crosbie Orchards
(apples, pears)
300 Macisaac Rd, Ardmona VIC
📞 03 58 29 03 52

Belstack Strawberry Farm
80 Bennetts Rd, Kialla West VIC
📞 03 5823 1324
www.belstackstrawberryfarm.com

FARM ADDRESSES AND CONTACTS | VICTORIA

Tranquil Hills Orchards
(lemons)
70 Wyatt Rd 3644 Cobram East
📞 04 29 17 96 39

ACN Orchards (apples)
Nathalia Rd, Bunbartha VIC
📞 03 58 26 94 37
f ACN Orchards

Jefsand park Lucerne
55 Ebbott Rd, Shepparton East
📞 0418 551 212
www.jefsand-park-lucerne.business.site

Red River Rural (breeder)
37 McGill St, Shepparton
📞 01300 068 067
www.redriverrural.com.au
✉ admin@redriverrural.com.au

Shepp East Fruit Packers
Lot 662 Midland Hwy, Shepparton East
📞 03 5829 2541

Masalki Pty Ltd (orchard)
255 Verney Rd, Grahamvale
📞 03 5821 1637

ARANA INTERNATIONAL
(wine wholesaler)
13 Banks Pl, Shepparton
📞 0401 501 919

Parris G M & Sons (apples)
New Dookie Rd, Shepparton VIC
📞 03 58 21 2185

Super Fresh Australia
(apples, pears)
610 Channel Road, Shepparton
📞 0424 883 767
✉ superfresh@westnet.com.au
www.super-fresh.com.au

Sunny Ridge Strawberry Farm
244 Shands Rd, Main Ridge VIC
📞 03 59 89 45 00
www.sunnyridge.com.au
✉ info@sunnyridge.com.au

P & A Vigliaturo Orchards
540 Simson Rd, Ardmona
📞 03 58 29 01 63

Murray River Produce
Murray Valley Hwy, Cobram VIC
📞 03 58 72 12 52

Greenwood L M & J E
«Greenwood Orchards» Main Rd, Merrigum VIC 3618
📞 03 58 55 23 41

D MacHeda
Healy Rd, Yarroweyah VIC 3644
📞 03 58 72 23 75

FARM ADDRESSES AND CONTACTS | VICTORIA

Plunkett Orchards
(pears, apples, apricots, peaches, nectarines)
255 Mcisaac Rd Ardmona, VIC
📞 03 58 29 00 15
www.plunkettorchards.com.au
Apply directly on the page
www.employment.plunkettorchards.com.au

Poulos Orchards (apples)
Doyles Rd, Shepparton VIC
📞 03 58 31 30 89
f Poulos-Orchards

Kutrolli Z & J (apples)
Mc Phee Rd, Shepparton
📞 03 58 21 23 51

Al Badry (apples)
1 Twisden Ct, Shepparton VIC
📞 03 58 22 07 20

Silverstein M & R (berries)
131 Prentice Rd, Shepparton East
📞 03 58 29 23 07

Boosey Fruit Pty (apples)
Chapel Rd, Cobram VIC 3644
📞 03 58 73 53 90

Gattuso G (apples)
Cobram VIC 3644
📞 03 58 72 11 70

Turnbull Bros Orchards Pty Ltd
Apples, pears, cherries
65 Turnbull Lane, Ardmona
📞 03 58 29 00 02
✉ admin@turnbullbrothers.com.au
www.turnbullbrothers.com.au

SPC Factory Sales
197-205 Corio St, Shepparton
📞 03 5821 7033
www.spcfactorysales.com.au
✉ info@spcafactorysales.com.au

LAKE BOGA/ SWAN HILL/ NYAH

Butler Orchards Pty Ltd
(12 km from Swan Hill)
Athorn Rd, Woorinen VIC 3589
📞 03 50 37 62 38

Harvest Labour Assistance
MADEC Australia
183-188 Beveridge Street
Swan Hill
📞 1800 062 332
✉ swanhill@madec.edu.au

Narrung Orchards
1 Murray Valley Hwy, Narrung VIC
📞 03 50 38 82 52
f Narrung-Orchards

FARM ADDRESSES AND CONTACTS | VICTORIA

W J Barbour
Nyah VIC 3594
03 50 30 25 25

Winter G J
Scown Rd, Tresco West VIC
03 50 37 21 78

Riverbend Orchard
3655 Murray Valley Hwy,
Wood Wood
03 50 30 53 85

Chislett Farms
833 Kenley Rd, Kenley
03 5038 8238
www.chislettfarms.com.au

B P Duffy
67 McAlpines Rd, Nyah VIC
03 50 30 23 67

AROUND MELBOURNE

Bon View Orchards Pty Ltd
Apples and pears
Browns Rd, Officer
03 59 43 23 56

Brimbank Orchards Pty Ltd
(13 km west of Melbourne)
280 Sunshine Rd, Sunshine VIC
03 93 11 81 17
f Brimbank-Orchards

Taranaki Farm
(70 km north of Melbourne)
5 Falloons Rd, Woodend VIC
0409 980 438
www.taranakifarm.com.au
shop@taranakifarm.com.au

Sunny Creek Fruit Berry Farm
(130 km east of Melbourne)
69 Tudor Rd, Trafalgar West VIC
03 56 34 75 26

Tuckerberry Hill (berries)
97 km south of Melbourne
31 Becks Rd, Drysdale VIC 3222
03 52 51 34 68
www.tuckerberry.com.au
f TuckerberryHill
tuckerberry@bigpond.com

Dinny Goonan Wines (grapes)
880 Winchelsea-Deans
Marsh Rd, Winchelsea South
03 5288 7100
www.dinnygoonan.com.au

Statewide Fruit Picking
21 Baynton Crs, Roxburgh Park
04 22 80 39 88
f Statewide Fruit Picking

Hand Picked Fruit & Veggies
181 Reynolds Rd, Doncaster East
03 98 42 31 11

FARM ADDRESSES AND CONTACTS | VICTORIA

Brimbank Orchards Pty Ltd
280 Sunshine Rd, Sunshine
03 93 11 81 17

The Big Berry
925 Gembrook-Launching Pl Rd,
Hoddles Creek
03 5967 4413
www.thebigberry.com.au
  The Big Berry

Aumann Family Orchard
(apples and pears)
246 Tindals Rd, Warrandyte
03 98 44 34 64
contact@aumannsproduce.com.au
www.aumannsproduce.com.au

Warrandyte Berry Farm
(34 km east of Melbourne)
raspberries, blackberries.
449-451 Ringwood-Warrandyte Rd,
Warrandyte South
0409 411 402
  warrandyteberryfarm
warrandyteberryfarm@gmail.com

Chaplin's Orchard
(123 km north of Melbourne)
Chaplins Rd, Harcourt
03 54 74 22 64
  Chaplin Orchards

Nippy's Fruit Juices Pty Ltd
Oranges
Essendon North VIC 3041
03 93 38 49 69
www.nippys.com.au

Just Picked Berries & Fruit
80 Old Plenty Rd, Yan Yean
04 12 63 65 35
info@justpicked.net.au
www.justpicked.net.au

ECHUCA

Bolitho L J (apples)
Bolitho Rd, Kyabram VIC 3620
03 58 52 11 37

MILDURA / RED CLIFFS / NANGILOC

B R&C L McGinniskin
Loop Rd, Nichols Point VIC
03 50 23 08 63

J Surace
Cowra Ave, Irymple VIC 3498
04 17 390 613

Lloyd Owen & Janice
Benetook Ave, Mildura VIC
03 50 23 34 67

FARM ADDRESSES AND CONTACTS | VICTORIA

Cavallo L
Newton Ave, Red Cliffs VIC
📞 03 50 24 21 78

Koola Grove (berries)
Iraak Rd, Nangiloc VIC
📞 03 50 29 16 89

Currans Family Wines (grapes)
(10 km from Mildura)
3391 San Mateo Ave, Koorlong
📞 03 50 25 71 54

Mammone V
Belar Ave, Irymple VIC
📞 03 50 24 56 38

F S Thatcher
Red Cliffs VIC 3496
📞 03 50 24 14 12

Harvest Labour Assistance
MADEC Australia
Cnr 10th Street and Deakin
Avenue Mildura
📞 1800 062 332
✉ harvest@madec.edu.au

Dichiera C & M
Blk 504, Red Cliffs
📞 03 50 24 16 34

Westridge Farm
Kulkyne Way, Iraak VIC 3494
📞 03 50 29 15 54

F Radman
Red Cliffs VIC 3496
📞 03 50 24 15 80

P M Dichiera
Calder Hwy, Merbein
📞 03 50 25 26 28

D J & K G McManus
Red Cliffs VIC 3496
📞 03 50 24 12 47

Deakin Estate
1596 Kulkyne Way, Iraak
📞 03 9682 5000
www.deakinestate.com.au
✉ deakin@wingara.com.au

Frank Sos
Colignan VIC 3494
📞 04 27 10 54 40

R P Barich
Merbein South VIC
📞 03 50 25 64 70

Castles Crossing Orchards
(lemons)
Castles Crossing Rd, Nangiloc
📞 03 50 29 14 56

FARM ADDRESSES AND CONTACTS | VICTORIA

P Brizzi
Azolia St, Red Cliffs VIC 3496
03 50 24 16 66

R J Treen
Birdwoodton VIC 3505
03 50 25 62 12

Panagiotaros A & A
Cowra Ave, Mildura VIC
03 50 23 15 64

Cavallo L
Red Cliffs
03 50 24 21 78

Cavallaro F D & P
Etiwanda Ave, Koorlong VIC
03 50 25 72 58

Strubelj F & D
Benetook Ave, Mildura VIC
04 50 22 21 22

Tall Poppy Wines
140 A Lime Ave, Mildura
03 5023 5218
www.tallpoppywines.com
f Tall Poppy Wines

Harvest Information Service
1800 062 332
www.harvesttrail.gov.au

STANLEY / BEECHWORTH

G A Primerano
1700 River Rd, Whorouly VIC
03 57 27 12 13

Nightingale Bros
(apples and pears)
708 Morses Creek Rd, Wandiligong
03 5750 1595
www.nightingalebros.com.au
admin@nightingalebros.com.au
(season from February through May)

J Christesen
Buckland Rd, Beechworth VIC
03 57 28 17 48

Bright Berry Farms (apples)
(40 km south of Stanley)
Great Alpine Rd, Eurobin
03 57 56 25 23
f Dessert-Shop/Bright-Berry-Farms

Sinclair Orchards Pty Ltd
(apples)
Beechworth Rd, Stanley VIC
03 57 28 65 01
sinclairapples@bigpond.com

FARM ADDRESSES AND CONTACTS | VICTORIA

High Grove (apples)
Mt Stanley Rd, Stanley VIC 3747
📞 03 57 28 65 26
www.higrove.com.au
✉ info@higrove.com.au

R J Tully (apples)
30 Tully Rd, Beechworth
📞 03 5728 1392

Rosewhite Kiwifruit Orchard
(apples)
RMB 2785 Rosewhite Rd,
Myrtleford
📞 03 57 53 52 55

Rockington Orchard
(53 km west of Beechworth)
Lot 1 Greta West Rd, Glenrowan
📞 03 57 66 23 51

Blue Ox Blueberries (berries)
77 Smith St, Oxley VIC 3678
📞 03 5727 3397
f Blue-Ox-Berry-Farm

Hilton H
Main Rd, Stanley VIC 3747
📞 03 5728 6584

MAFFRA

Gippsland Greenhouse Produce
(eggplant, tomatoes)
105 km from Maffra.
Highway, Yarragon Victoria 3823
📞 04 27 186 288
✉ info@gippslandgreenhouse.com.au
f Gippsland-Greenhouse-Produce

WARRAGUL

Newman's Berries
(raspberries, blueberries, blackberries)
21- 27 School Rd, Erica VIC
📞 0400 392 550

ROBINVALE

A Natale
Hocking Rd, Robinvale VIC
📞 03 5026 3978
f Natale-Farms

O'Brien P W & P M
Blk 96c, Robinvale VIC
📞 03 50 26 14 86

Brigante Bros
Robinvale South VIC 3549
📞 03 5026 4080
f Brigante-Bros

FARM ADDRESSES AND CONTACTS | VICTORIA

Zara C
Lake Powell, Bannerton
03 50 26 93 50

Olam Orchards Australia
(almonds)
2 Perrin St, Robinvale
03 50 26 33 44

A H & E J Conner
Murray Valley Hwy,
Boundary Bend
03 50 26 82 24

Zappia R
Newbriatan Rd, Robinvale VIC
03 50 26 31 29

Harvest Labour Assistance
MADEC Australia
68 -72 Herbert Street
Robinvale
1800 062 332
robinvale@madec.edu.au

Robinvale Organic Wines
243 Robinvale-Sea Lake Rd,
Robinvale
03 5026 3955
www.organicwines.com.au
info@organicwines.com.au

Bogicevic Michael (vegetables)
0350 260 228
Murray Valley Hwy, Wemen

Olivegrove Trading Company
0350 263 814
Tol Tol Rd, Robinvale VIC
www.robinvaleestate.com.au
oil@robinvaleestate.com.au

MORNINGTON PENINSULA

Drum Drum Blueberry Farm
28 Davos St Main Ridge
03 59 89 62 08
www.drumdrumfarm.com.au
drumdrumfarm@gmail.com

Mock Red Hill (apples)
1103 Mornington-Flinders Rd,
Red Hill VIC 3937
03 59 89 22 42
www.mockredhill.com.au
enquiries@mockredhill.com.au

Berrydale Farm (grapes)
21 km from the Mornington Peninsula.
125 Victoria Rd, Pearcedale VIC
03 59 78 62 16
f Berrydale-Farm

Flinders Farm (tomatoes)
2071 Boneo Rd Flinders VIC
03 59 89 00 47
ffarm@cdi.com.au

389

FARM ADDRESSES AND CONTACTS | VICTORIA

Atlanta Fruit Sales Pty Ltd
(apples)
1194 Stumpy Gully Road
Moorooduc
📞 03 59 78 83 74
✉ atlanta@surf.net.au
www.yvfruits.com.au

Staples R & A
(apples and pears)
144 Roberts Rd, Main Ridge
📞 03 59 89 62 55
www.staplesapples.com.au
✉ staples@staplesapples.com.au

Tamarillo Fruit Farm
100 Barcus Rd,
Main Ridge VIC 3928
📞 03 95 92 80 75

Red Hill Cherry Farm
69 Prossors Ln, Red Hill
📞 03 5989 2237
www.redhill-cherryfarm.com.au
f trevorholmes@pac.com.au

LAHARUM

Grampians Olive Co. (Toscana)
376 Olive Plantation Road
LAHARUM
📞 03 53 83 82 99
✉ info@grampiansoliveco.com.au
www.grampiansoliveco.com.au

BAIRNSDALE

FruitFarm Johnsonville
(apples, cherries, nectarines,
peaches, pears, plums)
17 km east of Bairnsdale.
54 Bumberrah Rd, Johnsonville
📞 03 5156 4549

BALLARAT

Buninyong Blueberry Farm
7189 Midland Hwy, Buninyong
📞 04 09 31 67 24
✉ ernie@
buninyongblueberries.com.au
www.buninyongblueberries.com.au
f Buninyong Blueberry Farm

Glenlyon Nutty Fruit Farm
18 Spring St, Glenlyon
📞 03 53 48 75 42

ACCOMMODATION | VICTORIA

BENDIGO

McLean Bros Glencoe Orchards
Apples and pears
Danns Rd, Harcourt VIC
📞 03 54 74 26 58

> **Harvest Information Service**
> 📞 1800 062 332
> www.harvesttrail.gov.au

KOO WEE RUP

Santo & Maria Giardina
3 Bickerton La, Mirboo North
📞 03 56 64 83 52

SMOKO

Gunnadoo Berries
Smoko Via, Bright VIC 3741
📞 03 57 59 25 07
f Gunnadoo Berries

Where to stay

➡️ **Check if the farm can host you !**

MELBOURNE

Selina - Melbourne Central
250 Flinders St, Melbourne
📞 +61 422 716 090
https://www.selina.com/australia/melbourne-cbd/
Dorm: From AU$D 38/night.

Melbourne Central YHA
562 Flinders St, Melbourne
📞 03 9621 2523
www.yha.com.au
✉ melbcentral@yha.com.au
Dorm: From AUD $36/night.

Flinders Backpackers
35 Elizabeth St, Melbourne
📞 03 9620 5100
www.flindersbackpackers.com.au
✉ info@flindersbp.com.au
Dorm: From AUD $26/night.
Twin from AUD $80/night.

Space Hotel
380 Russell St, Melbourne
📞 03 9662 3888
www.spacehotel.com.au
✉ stay@spacehotel.com.au
Dorm: From AUD $38/night.

ACCOMMODATION | VICTORIA

YARRA VALLEY

Enclave at Healesville Holiday Park
322 Don Rd, Badger Creek
📞 03 5962 4398
From AUD 38/night for a campsite.
www.enclavelifestylevillage.com.au
✉ info@enclavelv.com.au

BIG4 Yarra Valley Park Lane Holiday Park
419 Don Rd, Healesville
📞 03 5962 4328
www.parklaneholidayparks.com.au
From AUD $60/night for a campsite.

> **How to get there**
> **64 km east of Melbourne**
> 🚌 From AUD $9 (3 hrs)
> 🚗 1h

To find the nearest campsite, download the app
WIKICAMPS
www.wikicamps.com.au

> It is recommended to have your own transportation in the Shepparton area and the Yarra Valley.

SHEPPARTON

Victoria Lake Holiday Park
536 Wyndham St, Shepparton
📞 03 5821 5431
From AUD $28/night for a campsite.
www.viclakeholidaypark.com.au
✉ info@viclakeholidaypark.com.au

Strayleaves Caravan Park
Cnr Old Dookie Road & Mitchell St, Shepparton
📞 03 5821 1232
www.strayleavescaravanpark.com.au
✉ info@strayleavescaravanpark.com.au
From AUD $34/night for a campsite for a van, AUD $20/person for a tent.

BIG4 Shepparton Park Lane Holiday Park
7835 Goulburn Valley Hwy, Kialla
📞 03 5823 1576
www.parklaneholidayparks.com.au
From AU$43/night for a campsite.

392

ACCOMMODATION | VICTORIA

Moira Park Camp Ground
7 Moira Dr, Kialla West VIC

> **How to get there**
> 190 km north of Melbourne
> 🚆 From AUD $23 (2h 35min)
> 🚗 2 hrs

MILDURA

Apex RiverBeach Holiday Park
435 Cureton Ave, Mildura
📞 03 5023 6879
From AUD $33/night/campsite.
www.apexriverbeach.com.au
✉ holiday@apexriverbeach.com.au

BIG4 Golden River Holiday
199/205 Flora Ave, Mildura
📞 03 5021 2299
www.goldenriverholidaypark.com.au
From 39 AUD $/night for the campsite.

BIG4 Mildura Getaway - Holiday Park Mildura
478 Deakin Ave, Mildura
📞 03 5023 0486
www.big4.com.au/caravan-parks
From AU$39/night for a campsite.

Waterview Caravan Park
199 Ranfurly Way, Mildura
📞 0427 955 886

The Palms Caravan Park
7 Cureton Ave, Mildura
📞 03 5023 1774
www.thepalmscaravanpark.com.au
✉ palmscp@bigpond.net.au
From AUD $26/night for a campsite.

Calder Tourist Park
775 Fifteenth St, Mildura
📞 03 5023 1310
www.caldercp.com.au
✉ bookings@caldercp.com.au
From AUD $32,50/night for a campsite.

> **How to get there**
> 542 km north of Melbourne
> 🚌 From AUD $66 (8.5h)
> 🚗 5h 46min

MORNINGTON PENINSULA

Capel Sound Foreshore
Point Nepean Road, Foreshore Office, Capel Sound
📞 03 5986 4382
www.capelsoundforeshore.com.au
From AUD $29/night for a campsite.

ACCOMMODATION | VICTORIA

Whitecliffs To Camerons Bight
Rye VIC 3941
📞 03 5985 3288
www.whitecliffs.com.au
✉ admin@whitecliffs.com.au

Balnarring Beach Foreshore
154 Balnarring Beach Rd, Balnarring Beach
📞 03 5983 5582
www.balnarring.net
✉ balnarringforeshore@bigpond.com
From AUD $35/night for a campsite.

Point Leo Foreshore Camping
Point Leo Rd, Point Leo
📞 03 5989 8333
www.pointleo.com/camping-information-2
✉ info@pointleo.com

How to get there
76 km south of Melbourne
🚌 From AUD $22 (2h 50min)
🚗 1h

ROBINVALE

Robinvale Riverside Park
25 McLennan Dr, Robinvale
📞 03 5026 4646
www.robinvaleaccommodation.com.au
✉ info@robinvaleriverside.com.au
From AUD $25/night for a campsite.

Riverfront Caravan Park
27 Murray Terrace, Euston
📞 03 5026 1543

How to get there
468 km north of Melbourne
🚌 From AUD $56 (7h 30min)
🚗 5h 30min

BAIRNSDALE

Lake King Waterfront Caravan Park
67 Bay Rd, Eagle Point
📞 03 5156 6387
www.lakekingwaterfront.com.au
✉ lkwcaravanpark@gmail.com
From AUD $30/night for a campsite.

Nicholson River Holiday Park
915 Princes Hwy, Nicholson
📞 03 5156 8348
www.nicholsonriver.com.au
✉ info@nicholsonriver.com.au
From AUD $34/night for a campsite.

How to get there
283 km east of Melbourne
🚌 From AUD $30 (3h 50min)
🚗 3h 12min

FRUIT PICKING SEASONS | WESTERN AUSTRALIA

WESTERN AUSTRALIA

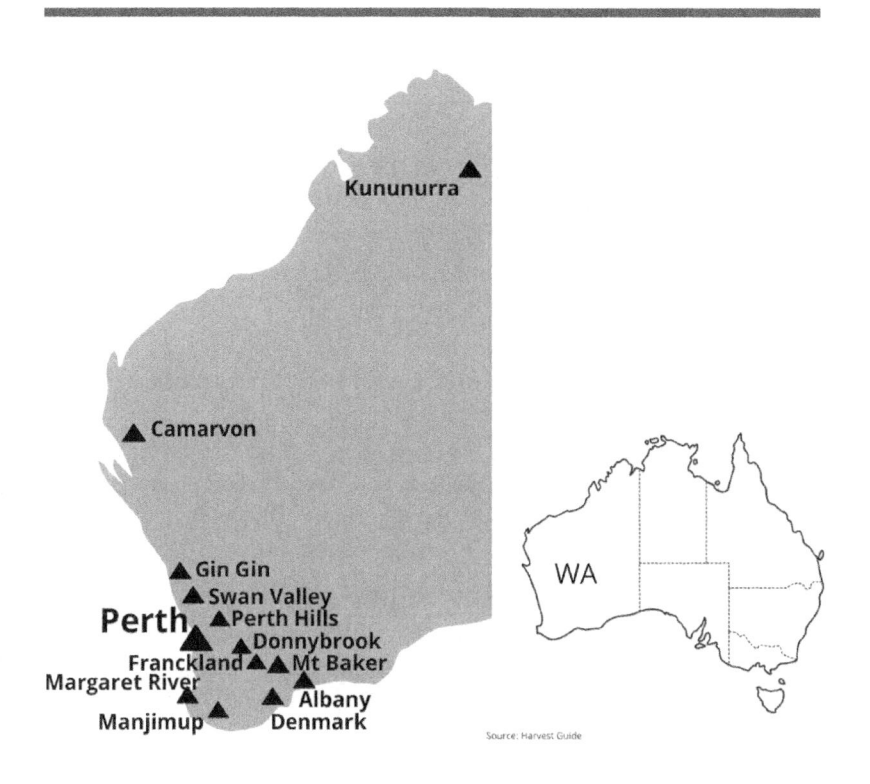

Where to go, depending on the season

In Albany, high demand November through February for strawberries (average demand March through May and in October).
Average demand May through August for olives; April and May, and June through September for grapes.

In Busselton, high demand September and October for avocados (average demand in August, November and December); average demand May through January for potatoes; and February through April, then June through August for grapes.

FRUIT PICKING SEASONS | WESTERN AUSTRALIA

In Carnarvon, high demand May through December for tomatoes; **January through March** for melons (average demand in April); **January and February** for mangoes (average demand in March, May and October); and **June and July, then October through December** for grapes and vegetables (average demand in May, August and September).
Average year-round demand for bananas.

In Denmark, average demand for berries December through March; and for grapes February through April, then from June through September.

In Donnybrook, high demand December through March for stone fruits (average demand in November).
Average demand for apples and pears year-round except January and October; for grapes February through April and June and September; and for tomatoes February through April.

In Frankland, high demand in July and August for grapes (average demand February through April, June and September). Average demand May through August for olives.

In Gingin, average demand year-round for lemons and vegetables; January and February, and June through August for grapes; July through September for olives; and November through January for stone fruits.

In Kununurra, strong demand for mangoes in October and November (average demand in December); **July through October** for melons/pumkin (average demand in May, June and November); average demand in April for lemons; and April through July for tree plantations.

FRUIT PICKING SEASONS | WESTERN AUSTRALIA

In Manjimup, high demand March and April for apples and pears (average demand February and May); **December** for stone fruits (average demand January and February); and **December through March** for vegetables.
Average demand for potatoes October through June; and for avocados December through February.

In Margaret River, high demand February through April for the harvesting of grapes (average demand June through August).

In Moora, high demand in October and November for lemons. Average demand from November through February for stone fruits.

In Mount Barker, strong demand November through February for strawberries (average demand March through May, and October); and **July and August** for grapes (average demand in March, April, June and September).
Average demand between November and January for cherries.

In Perth Hills, average demand November through April, and June through August for apples and pears.
Average demand October through March for stone fruits.

In the Swan Valley, strong demand July through August for the harvesting of grapes (average demand in January, February, June and September).
Average demand year-round for lemons and vegetables; for olives July through September; and for stone fruits November and December.

FARM ADDRESSES AND CONTACTS | WA

	Jan.	Feb.	Mar.	April	May	June	July	Aug.	Sept.	Oct.	Nov.	Dec.
Albany												
Busselton												
Carnarvon												
Denmark												
Donnybrook												
Frankland												
Gingin												
Kununurra												
Manjimup												
Margaret River												
Moora												
Mount Barker												
Perth Hills												
Swan Valley												

High demand / Average demand

Farm addresses and contacts

AROUND PERTH

Farm Fresh
(salads, cucumbers)
U4/ 27 Jacquard Way, Port Kennedy
08 95 24 55 08
sales@hcfarmfresh.com.au
www.hcfarmfresh.com.au

Stoneville Blueberry Farm
(Stone fruits)
240 Blue Wren Pl, Stoneville
08 92 95 07 67

Avowest Avocados
85 Carabooda Rd, Carabooda
08 94 07 51 00

Citrees Nursery (lemons)
12B Lakefarm Ret, Ballajura
08 92 48 60 03

Della-Pona E
Mundaring Weir Rd, Kalamunda
08 92 93 13 27

Berry Sweet Strawberry Farm
(strawberries)
Bullsbrook WA 6084
08 95 71 10 77
f Berry-Sweet-Strawberry-Farm
admin@berrysweet.com.au

Illawarra Orchard Pty Ltd
(apples, pears)
233 Illawarra Rd, Karragullen
08 93 97 60 94

FARM ADDRESSES AND CONTACTS | WA

Agrifresh Pty Ltd
(lemons, stone fruits)
Unit 12/ 41 Catalano Cct,
Canning Vale
08 94 55 45 38
www.agrifresh.com.au
job@agrifresh.com.au

Canning Orchard Pty Ltd
Brookton Hwy Cnr Gardiner Rd,
Karragullen
08 93 97 59 19

Leotta Nominees Pty Ltd
(Leotta's Fresh Stone Fruit)
741 Canning Rd, Carmel WA
0408 904 950
www.facebook.com/Leottas
leotnom@bigpond.com

Gullone D
Union Rd, Carmel WA 6076
08 92 93 52 18

Hills Market Garden Nominees
Lot 6 Canning Mills Rd, Kelmscott
08 93 90 57 54

Yanchep Springs (blackberries)
Lot 2818 Wanneroo Rd,
Wilbinga WA 6041
08 95 75 76 65

C W & J E Brockway
Llanelly Organic
Orchard Brockway Rd, Roleystone
08 93 97 56 33

Golden Grove Citrus Orchad
1378 Chittering Road
Lower Chittering 6084
08 95 71 80 74
info@goldengroveorchard.com
www.goldengroveorchard.com.au

Kato's 3000 Grapes
3000 W Swan Rd, Caversham WA
0431 596 489
Kato's at 3000

Choice Strawberrys
Shed, Carabooda WA 6033
08 95 61 8335

Edgecombe Bros Ltd (grapes)
Lot 1715 Gnangara Rd, Ellenbrook
08 92 96 43 07
info@edgecombebrothers.com.au
www.edgecombebrothers.com.au

Fawcett Orchards (lemons)
Scarp Rd, Serpentine WA 6125
08 95 25 23 15
Fawcett-Orchards

Harvest Information Service
1800 062 332
www.harvesttrail.gov.au

FARM ADDRESSES AND CONTACTS | WA

High Vale Orchard Pty Ltd
(apples)
35 Merrivale Rd, Pickering Brook
08 92 93 82 17
bookings@corecider.com
www.highvale.com

Willow Springs Orchard Pty
408, Albany Hwy, Bedfordale WA
08 93 99 51 15
www.wso-orchard.com.au
tony123wso@gmail.com
f Willow Springs Orchard Farm

Raeburn Orchards
Nectarines, peaches, cherries
95 Raeburn Rd, Roleystone
08 93 97 53 25
www.raeburnorchards.com
enquiries@raeburnorchards.com
f Raeburn Orchards

Gregorovich D & N
Patterson Rd, Pickering Brook
0892 93 83 01

KUNUNURRA

Ceres Farm
512 Packsaddle Rd, Kununurra
08 9168 1613
www.ceresfarm.com.au

Harvest Labour Assistance
08 9168 1500

Parker Poynt Plantation
(mangoes)
479 Jabiru Rd, Kununurra
0891 691 388

Cummings Brothers
0891 681 400
Research Station Rd, Kununurra

Bluey's Outback Farm
0891 682 177
blueysoutbackfarm
@bigpond.com
www.blueysoutbackfarm.com.au

Bardena Farms
0409 691 505
384 Packsaddle Rd KUNUNURRA

Barradale Farm
0891 691 386
barradale@wn.com.au

BUSSELTON/ DONNYBROOK

Glendalough Orchards
(Apples)
0897 311 273
38 Irishtown Rd, Donnybrook

Fruit Barn (Tomatoes)
0897 311 198
7 South Western Hwy, Donnybrook
f www.facebook.com/Fruitbarn
sales@thefruitbarn.com.au

400

FARM ADDRESSES AND CONTACTS | WA

Anstey Orchards
Goodwood Rd, Capel WA
08 97 31 71 01
f Anstey Orchards

Karintha Orchards Pty Ltd
(apples, pears)
South West Hwy, Kirup WA
08 97 31 01 06
karinthaorchards@bigpond.com
www.karinthaorchards.com.au

Harvey Citrus Pty Ltd (lemons)
RMB 4026 Fifth St, Harvey WA
08 97 29 38 61
www.harveycitrus.com.au
harveycitrus@icloud.com

Hazel Grove Orchard
(apples)
RMB 317 Tweed Rd, Bridgetown
08 97 61 19 21
f Hazel Grove Orchard

Atherton's Orchard Pty Ltd
(apples, pears)
Preston Rd, Lowden WA
08 97 32 12 37

Martella B & Sons
«Santa Rita», Kirup WA
08 97 31 62 76

Tassone Orchards Pty Ltd
Grimwade Rd, Kirup WA 6251
04 28 97 50 21

Hawter Bros
Hawterville Rd, Mullalyup
08 97 64 10 69
f Hawter Bros

Sunvalley Orchards
(apples, pears)
RMB 629, Donnybrook WA
08 97 31 11 74

Terace G & Sons (apples)
South Western Hwy, Donnybrook
08 97 31 1159

Jones LA
709 Charlies Creek Rd, Donnybrook
08 97 31 15 12

Barton Jones Wines
39 Upper Capel Rd, Donnybrook
0409 831 926
www.bartonjoneswines.com.au
info@bartonjoneswines.com.au

Perivale Orchards Pty Ltd
The Upper Capel Rd, Donnybrook
08 97 31 63 21
f Perivale Farm

FARM ADDRESSES AND CONTACTS | WA

Delfino G
RMB 624 Boyupbrook Rd, Donnybrook
08 97 31 11 69

Swanto Orchard
0897 311 021
297 South Western Hwy, Donnybrook

SWAN VALLEY

Stoneville Blueberry Farm (Stone fruits)
0892 950 767
240 Blue Wren Pl, Stoneville

Grape Growers Association Of W.A. (grapes)
0892 964 993
PO Box 179, Herne Hill WA

Kafarela's
706-712 Great Northern Hwy, Herne Hill
08 9296 0970

Sittella
100 Barrett St, Herne Hill WA
08 9296 2600
www.sittella.com.au
info@sittella.com.au

Windy Creek Estate
27 Stock Rd, Herne Hill WA
08 9296 1057
www.windycreekestate.com.au

Jarrah Ridge Wines
651 Great Northern Hwy, Herne Hill
08 9296 6337
www.jarrahridge.com

Talijancich Wines
26 Hyem Rd, Herne Hill WA
08 9296 4289
www.taliwine.com.au
admin@taliwine.com.au

Valley Wines
352 Lennard St, Herne Hill WA
08 9296 1147
www.valleywines.net.au

Olive Tech International (Olives)
0417 984 470
PO Box 3098, Broadway WA

MARGARET RIVER

Xanadu Wines
316 Boodjidup Rd, Margaret River
08 9758 9500
www.xanaduwines.com

FARM ADDRESSES AND CONTACTS | WA

Redgate Wines
659 Boodjidup Rd, Margaret River WA
📞 08 9757 6488
www.redgatewines.com.au
✉ info@redgatewines.com.au

Voyager Estate
41 Stevens Rd, Margaret River
📞 08 9757 6354
www.voyagerestate.com.au
✉ wineroom@voyagerestate.com.au

CARNARVON

Sweeter Bananas
1945 N W Coastal Hwy, North Plantations WA
📞 08 9941 9100
www.sweeterbanana.com

Gascoyne Gold Pty Ltd
424 N River Rd, North Plantations WA
📞 08 9941 8209
f Gascoyne Gold Pty Ltd

Bumbak & Son
📞 0899 418 006
f Bumbak & Sons

Harvest Information Service
📞 1800 062 332
www.harvesttrail.gov.au

ALBANY

Montgomery's Hill Wines
📞 08 9844 3715
Hassell Hwy, Kalgan WA
www.montgomeryshill.com.au
✉ winesales@montgomeryshill.com.au

Bunn Vineyard & Winery
📞 08 9842 6266
www.bunnwine.com.au
✉ admin@bunnwine.com.au

Wignall's Wines
📞 0898 412 848
448 Chester Pass Rd, Albany
www.wignallswines.com.au
✉ info@wignallswines.com.au

Genovese Olive Co
📞 0418 932 824
Chesterpass Rd, Albany WA

Eden Gate Blueberry Farm (blueberries)
Eden Rd, Youngs Siding WA
📞 08 98 45 20 03
✉ info@edengate.com.au
www.edengate.com.au

ATC Work Smart
5 Barker Road Albany WA
📞 08 6819 5300
www.atcworksmart.com.au

ACCOMMODATION | WESTERN AUSTRALIA

Willow Creek Strawberries Pty Ltd (strawberries)
984 Dempster Rd, Albany WA
📞 08 98 46 43 00
✉ job@agrifresh.com.au
www.agrifresh.com.au/home

Handasyde N M (strawberries)
Lot 2 Greatrex St, Lower King
📞 08 98 44 34 19
✉ neil@handasydestrawberries.com.au
www.handasydestrawberries.com.au

DWELLINGUP
(100 km south of Perth)

Oro Farms (apples, pears)
Oro Rd, Dwellingup WA
📞 08 95 38 10 15

Giumelli Steven
Polybrook Rd, Dwellingup WA
📞 08 95 38 10 67

Where to stay

➡ **Check if the farm can host you !**

PERTH

Ocean Beach Backpackers
1 Eric St, Cottesloe WA
📞 08 9384 5111
www.oceanbeachbackpackers.com.au
✉ backpackers@obh.com.au
Dormitory from AUD $24/night.
Twin room from AUD $81/night.

Hostel G Perth
80 Stirling St, Perth WA
📞 0402 067 099
www.hostelgperth.com
✉ reservations@hostelgperth.com
Dormitory from AUD $29/night.

Koalas Perth City Backpackers Hostel
286 Hay Street East Perth
📞 0417 260 398
www.koalasperth.com
Dormitory from AUD $17/night.
Twin room from AUD $47/night.

Spinners Hostel
342 Newcastle St, Perth
📞 08 9328 9468
www.spinnershostel.com.au
✉ admin@spinnershostel.com.au
Dormitory from AUD $28/night.

ACCOMMODATION | WESTERN AUSTRALIA

The Emperors Crown Hostel
85 Stirling St, Perth WA
📞 08 9227 1400
www.emperorscrown.com.au
✉ manager@emperorscrown.com.au
Dormitory from AUD $18/night.
Twin room from AUD $62/night.

The Witch's Hat
148 Palmerston St, Perth
📞 08 9228 4228
www.witchs-hat.com
✉ manager@witchs-hat.com
Dormitory from AUD $26/night.

Haus Accommodation
42 Francis Street, Northbridge
📞 08 9228 8170
Dormitory from AUD $23/night.
Family room (3 persons) from AUD $59/night.

The Shiralee
107 Brisbane Street, 6003 Perth
📞 08 9227 7448
Dormitory from AUD $22/night.
Twin room from AUD $58/night

Perth City YHA
300 Wellington St, Perth
📞 08 9287 3333
www.yha.com.au
✉ perthcity@yha.com.au
Dormitory from AUD $27/night.

KUNUNURRA

Kona Lakeside Caravan Park
Lakeview Dr, Kununurra

Discovery Parks - Lake Kununurra
Lakeview Dr, Kununurra WA
📞 08 9168 1031
www.discoveryholidayparks.com.au

Hidden Valley Caravan Park
110 Weaber Plain Rd, Kununurra
📞 08 9168 1790
www.hiddenvalleytouristpark.com
✉ nhvtp@westnet.com.au
Prices on request.

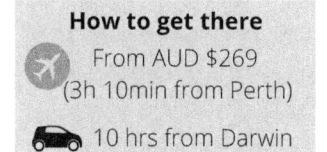

> **How to get there**
> ✈ From AUD $269 (3h 10min from Perth)
> 🚗 10 hrs from Darwin

BUSSELTON / DONNYBROOK

Dunsborough Beachouse YHA
201-205 Geographe Bay Road, 6281 Dunsborough
📞 08 9755 3107
Dormitory from AUD $38/night.

ACCOMMODATION | WESTERN AUSTRALIA

Dunsborough Inn Backpackers
50 Dunn Bay Road, 6281
Dunsborough
📞 08 9756 7277
www.dunsboroughinn.com.au
✉ bookings@dunsboroughinn.com.au
Quadruple room from
AUD $37/night.

> **How to get there**
> 223 km south of Perth
> 🚌 From AUD $63 (3h 45min)
> 🚗 2h 18min

SWAN VALLEY

Swan Valley Rest Cottage29
Toodyay Rd, Middle Swan
From AUD $72/night the three-bedroom apartment.

Discovery Parks - Lake Kununurra
Lakeview Dr, Kununurra WA
📞 08 9168 1031
www.discoveryholidayparks.com.au

Discovery Parks - Swan Valley
91 Benara Rd, Caversham
📞 08 9279 6700
www.discoveryholidayparks.com.au
From 32 AUD $/night the campsite.

> **How to get there**
> 14 km northeast of Perth
> 🚌 From AUD $9 (45 min)
> 🚗 22 min

MARGARET RIVER

Margaret River Backpackers YHA
66 Townview Terrace, 6285
📞 08 9757 9572
Margaret River Town
Dorm : from AUD $32/night.

Margaret River Tourist Park
44 Station Rd, Margaret River
📞 08 9757 2180
www.summerstar.com.au
✉ info@margaretrivertouristpark.com.au
Dorm : from AUD $32/night.

RAC Margaret River Nature Park
Bramley National Park, Carters Rd, Margaret River
📞 08 9758 8227
www.parksandresorts.rac.com.au
From AU$50/night for a campsite.

> **How to get there**
> 270 km south of Perth
> 🚌 From AUD $77 (4h 30min)
> 🚗 3 hrs

406

ACCOMMODATION | WESTERN AUSTRALIA

To book your bus ticket :
www.southwestcoachlines.com.au
www.integritycoachlines.com.au

CARNARVON

Coral Coast Tourist Park
108 Robinson St, Carnarvon
08 9941 1438
www.coralcoasttouristpark.com.au
info@coralcoastpark.com
From AUD $39/night for a campsite.

Carnarvon Caravan Park
477 Robinson St, Carnarvon
08 9941 8101
www.carnarvonpark.com.au
bookings@carnarvonpark.com.au

Outback Oasis Caravan Park
49 Wise St, Carnarvon
08 9941 1439
www.outbackoasis-caravanpark.com
outbackoasis@westnet.com.au
From AUD $25/night for a campsite.

How to get there
900 km south of Perth
From AUD $170 (12h 30min)
9h 40min

ALBANY

Acclaim Albany Holiday Park
550 Albany Hwy, Albany
08 9841 7800

Albany Gardens Holiday Resort
22 Wellington St, Albany
08 9841 4616
www.albanygardens.com.au
info@albanygardens.com.au
From AUD $53/night for a campsite.

BIG4 Emu Beach Holiday Park
8 Medcalf Parade, Albany
08 9844 1147
www.big4emubeach.com.au
From AUD $32/night for a campsite.

How to get there
415 km south of Perth
4h 45min

To find the nearest campsite, download the app
WIKICAMPS
www.wikicamps.com.au

Notes

Notes

Notes

Notes

Notes

Notes

This guide was updated in November 2022.

If you notice that one of the businesses mentioned in this guide has closed, or if you have any additional comments, please send us and email at contact@helpstage.com